EXPLORING TRUTH COMMISSION RECOMMENDATIONS IN A COMPARATIVE PERSPECTIVE

SERIES ON TRANSITIONAL JUSTICE

The Series on *Transitional Justice* offers a platform for high-quality research within the rapidly growing field of transitional justice. The research is, of necessity inter-disciplinary in nature, drawing from disciplines such as law, political science, history, sociology, criminology, anthropology and psychology, as well as from various specialised fields of study such as human rights, victimology and peace studies. Furthermore, the research is international in outlook, drawing on the knowledge and experience of academics and other specialists in many different regions of the world.

The series is aimed at a variety of audiences who are either working or interested in fields such as crime and justice; human rights; humanitarian law and human security; conflict resolution and peace building. These audiences include academics, researchers, students, policy makers, practitioners, non-governmental organisations and the media.

All books published within the series are subject to a double-blind peer review by recognised authorities in the field.

The General Editors of the Series are:
- Prof. Stephan Parmentier (Catholic University of Leuven, Belgium)
- Prof. Jeremy Sarkin (NOVA University of Lisbon, Portugal)
- Dr. Mina Rauschenbach (Université de Lausanne and University of Leuven)

The general editors receive support from an Advisory Board, consisting of internationally renowned academics and practitioners.

Published titles within this Series:

11. Ilse Derluyn, Cindy Mels, Stephan Parmentier and Wouter Vandenhole (eds.), *Re-Member. Rehabilitation, Reintegration and Reconciliation of War-Affected Children* (2012), 97894-000-0027-4
12. Anne-Marie de Brouwer, Charlotte Ku, Renée Römkens and Larissa van den Herik (eds.), *Sexual Violence as an International Crime: Interdisciplinary Approaches* (2012), 978-1-78068-002-6
13. Estelle Zinsstag and Martha Albertson Fineman (eds.), *Feminist Perspectives on Transitional Justice: From International and Criminal to Alternative Forms of Justice* (2013), 978-1-78068-142-9
14. Josep M. Tamarit Sumalla, *Historical Memory and Criminal Justice in Spain. A Case of Late Transitional Justice* (2013), 978-1-78068-143-6
15. Catherine Jenkins (ed.), Max du Plessis (ed.), *Law, Nation building and Transformation The South African experience in perspective* (2014), 978-1-78068-184-9
16. Susanne Buckley-Zistel and Stefanie Schäfer (eds.), *Memorials in Times of Transition* (2014), 978-1-78068-211-2
17. Nico Wouters (ed.), *Transitional Justice and Memory in Europe (1945–2013)* (2014), 978-1-78068-214-3
18. Agata Fijalkowski and Raluca Grosescu (eds.), *Transitional Criminal Justice in Post-Dictatorial and Post-Conflict Societies* (2015), 978-1-78068-260-0
19. S. Elizabeth Bird and Fraser M. Ottanelli (eds.), *The Performance of Memory as Transitional Justice* (2014), 978-1-78068-262-4
20. Bo Viktor Nylund, *Child Soldiers and Transitional Justice* (2016), 978-1-78068-394-2
21. Peter Malcontent (ed.), *Facing the Past: Amending Historical Injustices through Instruments of Transitional Justice* (2016), 978-1-78068-403-1
22. Francesca Capone, *Reparations for Child Victims of Armed Conflict: State of the Field and Current Challenges* (2017), 978-1-78068-438-3
23. Cheryl S. White, *Bridging Divides in Transitional Justice: The Extraordinary Chambers in the Courts of Cambodia* (2017), 978-1-78068-440-6
24. Jeremy Sarkin (ed.), *The Global Impact and Legacy of Truth Commissions* (2019), 978-1-78068-794-0
25. Camila de Gamboa Tapias and Bert van Roermund (eds.), *Just Memories: Remembrance and Restoration in the Aftermath of Political Violence* (2020), 978-1-78068-908-1
26. Grazyna Baranowska, *Rights of Families of Disappeared Persons* (2021), 978-1-83970-137-5

For previous volumes in the series, please visit http://tj.intersentia.com

EXPLORING TRUTH COMMISSION RECOMMENDATIONS IN A COMPARATIVE PERSPECTIVE

Beyond Words Vol. I

Elin SKAAR
Eric WIEBELHAUS-BRAHM
Jemima GARCÍA-GODOS

INTERSENTIA

Cambridge – Antwerp – Chicago

Intersentia Ltd
8 Wellington Mews
Wellington Street | Cambridge
CB1 1HW | United Kingdom
Tel: +44 1223 736 170
Email: mail@intersentia.co.uk
www.intersentia.com | www.intersentia.co.uk

Distribution for the UK and
Rest of the World (incl. Eastern Europe)
NBN International
1 Deltic Avenue, Rooksley
Milton Keynes MK13 8LD
United Kingdom
Tel: +44 1752 202 301 | Fax: +44 1752 202 331
Email: orders@nbninternational.com

Distribution for Europe
Lefebvre Sarrut Belgium NV
Hoogstraat 139/6
1000 Brussels
Belgium
Tel: +32 (0)800 39 067
Email: mail@intersentia.be

Distribution for the USA and Canada
Independent Publishers Group
Order Department
814 North Franklin Street
Chicago, IL 60610
USA
Tel: +1 800 888 4741 (toll free) | Fax: +1 312 337 5985
Email: orders@ipgbook.com

Exploring Truth Commission Recommendations in a Comparative Perspective: Beyond Words Vol. I
© Elin Skaar, Eric Wiebelhaus-Brahm and Jemima García-Godos 2022

Artwork on cover: Author Jan Jordaan, title 'Hurt', medium Linocut, 1999. From the Universal Declaration of Human Rights – International Print Portfolio, Article 5, published by Art for Humanity, South Africa, 1999.

ISBN 978-1-83970-178-8
D/2022/7849/18
NUR 828

British Library Cataloguing in Publication Data. A catalogue record for this book is available from the British Library.

PREFACE

The ambitions of those who establish truth commissions, and those who serve on them, are reflected in the names of these commissions. They often flag the term "truth" in various combinations with justice, reconciliation, clarification, never again (*Nunca Más*) – even friendship. How can truth commissions possibly contribute to all these ambitious aims? It is an underlying, but seldom explicit assumption, that many of these aspirations can only be fulfilled if the recommendations made by truth commissions also are implemented. The transformative potential of truth commissions arguably lies most directly in the body of recommendations put forward in their report. Commission recommendations usually include reforms in the legal, political and social fields, and reparations of various kinds. The list is often extensive. Yet, this in itself raises questions about expectations and the possibility of implementation. That is what this book is about: the implementation of truth commission recommendations.

Over the past four decades, although estimates vary, over fifty countries have established truth commissions to investigate patterns of gross human rights violations committed by repressive regimes and/or in the context of armed conflict. More than a third of these commissions have been in Latin America, making it a leading region in this search for truth. Constructing shared memories of the past, many believe, is crucial for healing divided societies after violent conflict and repression. Apart from documenting abuses, most truth commissions make recommendations to governments. The assumption is that these recommendations, if implemented well, will help individuals and societies heal, and aid societies in the transition from violence to peace, democracy, and reconciliation. We hope this book helps generate more realistic expectations, particularly on the part of victims and affected communities.

This book is the first of two volumes which jointly provide the first systematic study of the formulation and implementation of the recommendations of thirteen Latin American truth commissions in eleven countries (Argentina, Chile, Brazil, Ecuador, El Salvador, Guatemala, Haiti, Panama, Paraguay, Peru, and Uruguay), covering a period of 35 years (1983-2017). Coming out of a research project based at the Chr. Michelsen Institute (CMI), Bergen, Norway, and funded by the Research Council of Norway (2015-2017), the two *Beyond Words* volumes are the first ever to provide a systematic comparative analysis of the entire universe of recommendations made by all formal (i.e., state sponsored) truth commissions in a geographical region. Importantly, our analysis includes little known, under-researched cases like the truth commissions of Ecuador, Haiti, Panama, and Paraguay.

In this co-written book (Vol. I), we highlight variation in truth commission recommendations across Latin America. We trace the implementation of recommendations through interviews, legal documents and other primary sources, as well as secondary sources from academics and activists. We provide insights about how the internal dynamics of truth commissions as well as the political, social, and economic context in which they operate influence how recommendations are formulated. We also explore how the nature of the recommendations themselves as well as how the political, social, and economic environments shape which recommendations are implemented. The conclusion considers the findings' relevance to the crafting of future truth commission recommendations and reflects upon how the formulation and implementation of these recommendations shapes the impact of truth commissions on societies emerging from periods of violence and repression. We offer several important innovations for scholars and practitioners concerned with transitional justice in general and with truth commissions in particular.

Beyond Words Vol. II is a unique collection of studies of 11 Latin American countries covering all 13 formal truth commissions established in this region that submitted their final reports between 1984 and 2014. Based on original qualitative data and a common analytical framework, the main focus of each of the Volume's eleven country chapters is threefold: (i) to provide a brief background to the truth commission(s); (ii) to provide a detailed account of the formulation of the truth commissions' recommendations; and (iii) to analyse the implementation record of the recommendations, taking into account the actors and factors that have aided – or obstructed – implementation.

The two volumes can be read in tandem, but each volume stands on its own. The reader of both volumes will notice significant cross-over in the introductory chapters of the volumes. This is intentional on our part, in order to provide a common conceptual platform for two different outputs. For the benefit of those who do not have access to Vol. II, we provide a short synopsis of the implementation record of the eleven country cases in Chapter 5 of this book.

The core project team consists of Elin Skaar (Chr. Michelsen Institute, Bergen, Norway), Eric Wiebelhaus-Brahm (University of Arkansas at Little Rock), and Jemima García-Godos (University of Oslo). The data that forms the basis for our analysis was collected by three institutional partners in Latin America (Centro de Estudios Legales y Sociales (CELS, Argentina); Instituto de Democracia y Derechos Humanos de la Pontificia Universidad Católica del Perú (IDEHPUCP, Peru), and Facultad Latinoamericana de Ciencias Sociales (FLACSO, Guatemala); a research team based at Universidad de Salamanca in Spain; and a number of individual researchers and research assistants. As far as we know, this is the first attempt to systematically collect information on a critical part of a truth commission's legacy, namely the recommendations outlined in a report to the government once the truth commission has concluded its investigations into human rights violations. We have done this exhaustively rather than selectively. This volume analyses all recommendations made by all official truth commissions in Latin America that have ever successfully concluded their investigations by producing a final report.

Many people have made this project possible. First and foremost, we would like to thank the following researchers and research assistants for collecting and analysing data comprising the qualitative data base on which this volume draws: Héctor Centeno-Martín, Federico Ghelfi, Hugo Goeury, Tania Gómez, Martha Gutiérrez-Salazar, Sol Hourcade, Eduardo Hurtado, Elena Martínez-Barahona, Luz Palmás Zaldua, Marcela Perelman, Félix Reátegui, Sonia Rubio-Padilla, Augusto Rosas, Adriana Rudling, Luis Raúl Salvadó, Elena San José, Salvador Sánchez, Lisa-Marie Måseidvåg Selvik, and Diego Uchuypoma. We also want to highlight the very valuable contributions of our excellent project reference group, who have been actively involved since the project idea was first conceived: Stener Ekern, Joanna Quinn, Catalina Smulovitz, Astri Suhrke, Patricia Tappatá Valdez, Hugo van der Merwe, and the late José Zalaquett, who regrettably passed away before this project was completed. Dr Zalaquett served on the Truth and Reconciliation Commission in Chile, one of the first truth commissions in Latin America (indeed in the world). He was thus one of the early pioneers among commissioners, who laid the groundwork for how truth commissions could and should operate. A seasoned jurist with first-hand experience of both dictatorship crimes and truth commission work, we were very lucky to have José "Pepe" Zalaquett as part of our team.

We would further like to heartily thank all those who have provided insightful comments on various chapter drafts in this volume presented in a number of different fora, including various Rights & Gender cluster meetings at CMI (2016-2019); the European Consortium for Political Research (ECPR) conference in Prague (7-10 September 2016); the project authors' workshop in Pisac, Peru (November 2016); the ECPR conference in Oslo (6-9 September 2017); at the final 'Beyond Words' project workshop at Solstrand (15–17 September 2017); the Latin American Studies Association Congress in Barcelona (23–26 May 2018); and at the Democracy seminar at the University of Bergen (6 June 2018). We thank all those present at these different events who provided constructive and thoughtful comments. We are particularly grateful to Astri Suhrke and Onur Bakiner for constructive comments on the original project idea and on earlier drafts. Finally, we warmly thank Lisa-Marie Selvik for invaluable assistance with data summaries and preparation of various tables and figures; Marianne Tøraasen for cleaning up the data after a new round of recoding the data; Linn Liljeros for helping us revise tables and figures in accordance with the recoded data; and Dylan Wright for assisting with additional data coding.

We are grateful to Jeremy Sarkin and Stephen Parmentier, who enthusiastically welcomed the possibility of publishing the two *Beyond Words* volumes with Intersentia when we floated the idea to them during a conference on truth commissions organised in Lisbon in February 2018. Their support has been very important to us. Mina Rauschenbach in the Intersentia editorial team has patiently waited for drafts of the manuscript and expertly handled the long process that goes into converting a book manuscript into a publication. We are also indebted to the blind reviewers who provided encouraging and useful suggestions for tightening and finalising the text. A warm thank you to Ahmed Hegazi and Ella Brice-Jeffreys at Intersentia for editing the manuscript and steering the process towards submission.

Behind every CMI project and publication, there is an internal administrative support team who provide invaluable input. A big thank you to Steinar Hegre, Ingvild Hestad, Lars Ivar Høberg, Chris Jakob, Reidunn Ljones, Aksel Mjeldheim, Bjørn-Ivar Nilsen, Guri Stegali, Robert Sjursen, and Hong Kim Tran.

Any errors in this volume are, as always, the chief responsibility of the authors.

Elin Skaar, Eric Wiebelhaus-Brahm,
and Jemima García-Godos
Bergen, Little Rock, Oslo
February 2022

CONTENTS

LIST OF ACRONYMS AND ABBREVIATIONS

APDH	*Asamblea Permanente por los Derechos Humanos* (The Permanent Assembly for Human Rights, Argentina)
CEDHU	Ecumenical Human Rights Commission (Ecuador)
CEH	*Comisión para el Esclarecimiento Histórico de Guatemala* (Commission for Historical Clarification, Guatemala)
CELS	*Centro de Estudios Legales y Sociales* (Center for Legal and Social Studies, Argentina)
CEMDP	*Comissão Especial de Mortos e Desaparecidos Políticos* (Special Commission on Deaths and Political Disappearances, Brazil)
CIDH	*Comisión Inter-Americana de Derechos Humanos* (Inter-American Commission on Human Rights)
CMAN	*Comisión Multi-Sectorial de Alto Nivel* (High Level Multisectoral Commission, Peru)
CNRR	*Corporación Nacional de Reparación y Reconciliación* (National Corporation for Reparation and Reconciliation, Chile)
CNV	*Comissão Nacional da Verdade* (National Truth Commission, Brazil)
CNVJ	*Commission Nationale de Vérité et de Justice* (National Truth and Justice Commission, Haiti)
CNVR	*Comisión Nacional de Verdad y Reconciliación* (National Commission for Truth and Reconciliation, Chile)
CODEHUPY	*Coordinadora de Derechos Humanos del Paraguay* (Coordinating body for Human Rights in Paraguay, Paraguay)
COMIPAZ/ComiPaz	*Comisión para la Paz* (Commission for Peace, Uruguay)
Comisión Rettig/ Rettig Commission	*Comisión Nacional de Verdad y Reconciliación* (National Commission for Truth and Reconciliation, Chile)

Comisión Valech/ Valech Commission	*Comisión Nacional sobre Prisión Politica y Tortura* (National Commission on Political Imprisonment and Torture, Chile)
CONADEP	*Comisión Nacional sobre la Desaparición de Personas* (National Commission on the Disappeared, Argentina)
CVES	*Comisión de la Verdad para El Salvador* (Commission on the Truth for El Salvador, El Salvador)
CVJ	*Comisión de Verdad y Justicia* (Truth and Justice Commission, Paraguay)
CVR	*Comisión de la Verdad y Reconciliación* (Truth and Reconciliation Commission, Peru)
DGVJ	*Dirección General de Verdad, Justicia y Reparación* (Paraguay)
ESMA	*Escuela de Mecánica de la Armada* (Naval Academy, Argentina)
FAFG	*Fundación de Antropología Forense de Guatemala* (Forensic Anthropology Foundation of Guatemala, Guatemala)
FAMIDESA	*Asociación de Madres y Familiares de Uruguayos Detenidos Desaparecidos* (Association of Mothers and Families of Uruguayans Detained and Disappeared, Uruguay)
FARC	*Fuerzas Armadas Revolucionarias de Colombia – Ejército del Pueblo* (Revolutionary Armed Forces of Colombia – People's Army, Colombia)
FASIC	*Fundación de Ayuda Social de las Iglesias Cristianas* (Chile)
FLACSO	*Facultad Latinoamericana de Ciencias Sociales* (Latin American Faculty of Social Sciences, Guatemala)
FMLN	*Frente Farabundo Martí para la Liberación Nacional* (Farabundo Martí Front for National Liberation, El Salvador)
IACHR	Inter-American Commission on Human Rights (*Comisión Inter-Americana de Derechos Humanos*)
IACtHR	Inter-American Court of Human Rights
ICC	International Criminal Court
ICTJ	International Center for Transitional Justice

IDEHPUCP	*Instituto de Democracia y Derechos Humanos de la Pontificia Universidad Católica del Perú* (Institute of Democracy and Human Rights at the Pontificial Catholic University of Peru, Peru)
INDI	National Institute of Indigenous People (Paraguay)
LGBTQ	Lesbian, Gay, Bisexual, Transgender, and Queer
MEDH	*Movimiento Ecuménico por los Derechos Humanos* (Ecumenical Movement for Human Rights, Argentina)
NGO	non-governmental organization
NIHR	National Institute of Human Rights
NPA	National Plan of Action
PNR	*Programa Nacional de Reparación* (National Reparations Program, Guatemala)
PTC	Panama Truth Commission (*Comisión de la Verdad de Panamá*)
REMHI	*Recuperación de la Memoria Histórica de Guatemala* (Recovery of Historical Memory Project, Guatemala)
SELADEH	*Secretariado Latinoamericano de Derechos Humanos* (Latin American Secretariat of Human Rights)
SERPAJ	*Servicio Paz y Justicia* (Peace and Justice Service)
SGBV	sexual and gender-based violence
TC	Truth Commission
TCR	Truth Commission Recommendation
TOC	Table of Contents
TRC	Truth and Reconciliation Commission
UCR	*Unión Cívica Radical* (Radical Civic Union, Argentina)
UN	United Nations
UNGA	United Nations General Assembly
UNOHCHR	United Nations Office for the High Commissioner of Human Rights
URNG	*Unión Revolucionaria Nacional Guatemalteca* (Guatemala's National Revolutionary Union, Guatemala)

LIST OF TABLES AND FIGURES

TABLES

FIGURES

CHAPTER 1

EXPLORING RECOMMENDATIONS

Every people has the inalienable right to know the truth about past events concerning perpetration of heinous crimes and about the circumstances and reasons that led, through massive or systematic violations, to the perpetration of those crimes.[1]

– Diane Orientlicher (UN Independent Expert)

In recent decades, dozens of countries have established official truth commissions to investigate patterns of gross human rights violations committed by repressive regimes and/or in the context of armed conflict. Approximately a third of these commissions have been in Latin America, making it a leading region in this search for truth. Constructing shared memories of the past, many believe, is crucial to healing divided societies after violent conflict and repression. Apart from documenting abuses, most truth commissions make recommendations to governments, typically outlining further measures to address past abuses and/or to prevent such abuses from happening again. It is generally assumed that these recommendations, if implemented well, will prompt further measures to address past abuses such as compensating surviving victims and their families for past suffering, and promote the types of reforms that may aid societies in the transition from violence to peace, democracy, and reconciliation.

A significant comparative literature on truth commissions notwithstanding,[2] to date, there is no systematic cross-national study of the formulation and implementation of truth commission recommendations. Hence, we know little about whether and under what conditions recommendations are more or less likely to be implemented. This knowledge gap has been increasingly recognized (United Nations General Assembly 2013). As the first

---

[1]   "Updated Set of Principles for the protection and promotion of human rights through action to combat impunity". 2005 report by independent expert Diane Orientlicher. Cited in Salmón (2006, 341), see also footnote 19, p. 331.

[2]   See, for example, Bakiner 2014, 2016; Brahm 2007, 2009; Chapman 2009; Dancy, Kim, and Wiebelhaus-Brahm 2010; Freeman 2006; Freeman and Hayner 2003; Hayner 1994; Hayner 2011; Olsen, Payne, and Reiter 2010a; Skaar, García-Godos, and Collins 2016; Wiebelhaus-Brahm 2010a, 2010b.

United Nations (UN) Special Rapporteur on the promotion of truth, justice, reparation, and guarantees of non-recurrence, Pablo de Greiff, warned shortly after taking office in 2012, truth commissions around the world would "face various challenges which can lead to the non-implementation of recommendations. Among these challenges are overly broad mandates, flawed choices of commissioners, and insufficient and unreliable funding streams" (United Nations Office for the High Commissioner of Human Rights 2013).

In this book, we analyze the recommendations of 13 Latin American truth commissions established by 11 countries since 1983. Specifically, we address two main research issues: (i) What kinds of recommendations have Latin American truth commissions made, and why?; and (ii) How, when, and by whom have the recommendations been implemented? Through a comparative approach, we uncover the factors that shape the recommendations produced by truth commissions. Furthermore, our comparative framework enables us to examine patterns of implementation across time and space to identify characteristics of recommendations and contextual factors that shape the likelihood of implementation. In the conclusion, we also speculate on the short- and long-term impacts of these recommendations on the societies in which they are implemented.

Thus, one contribution is to compare the circumstances under which recommendations are formulated. Recommendations are the product of bureaucratic processes within commissions, which are in turn embedded in particular political, economic, and social contexts. We explore how these factors shape the nature of the recommendations that are produced. As we will show, there is enormous variety in the size of truth commission final reports and the level of detail provided therein – ranging from a few pages to multiple, thick volumes. Likewise, there is considerable variation in the amount of space devoted to recommendations in those reports. Over time, recommendations have tended to become increasingly numerous, spanning from individual victim reparations to complex structural and institutional reform. In the pages to come, we explore the factors that shape the recommendations sections of these final reports.

Second, we examine the implementation record of these recommendations in a comparative framework. Specifically, we examine the circumstances under which recommendations are more or less likely to be implemented. Again, context matters. Factors such as political will, civil society, available resources, and unforeseen events such as natural disasters and economic crises influence the probability that governments will implement truth commission recommendations. Our comparative approach also reveals that the nature of the recommendations themselves shapes whether and how they are implemented.

The diversity of our 13 truth commission cases creates a laboratory for examining how the type, range, and complexity of truth commission recommendations influence their implementation record. While recognizing that implementation is also determined by broader contextual factors, we focus on the triangular relationship between the processes that shape the formulation of truth commission recommendations, the nature of these recommendations, and the degree of implementation.

Third, we are interested in how these recommendations shape post-conflict/post-authoritarian societies. We argue that the nature of the recommendations themselves can influence how much of an effect they produce. Although we are not principally concerned with the *impact* of truth commissions in this book, we do take the position that implementation of their recommendations influences some of the short-term as well as long-term impact of truth commissions. Ultimately, if we have a better sense of what types of recommendations are more likely to be implemented, commissioners may be able to craft their reports to increase the probability of their having a more substantial impact. Thus, this project has policy implications in relation to the design of truth commissions by providing empirical information about what kinds of recommendations are more (or less) likely to be implemented in different socio-political contexts.

In this introductory chapter, we first discuss the definitional problems in the study of truth commissions and our method of case selection. Next, we review the existing literature on the impact of truth commissions on societies emerging from periods of conflict and repression. We argue that this literature has often failed to carefully trace a causal connection between truth commissions and the myriad of outcomes often attributed to them. Although truth commission processes that are very public may have a significant effect on society, the commission's final report, of which the recommendations are a critical part, is the most concrete legacy of these temporary bodies. Hence, we argue that recommendations are an important link in making many causal arguments about the impact of truth commissions. Yet, this link has rarely been considered explicitly. From there, we discuss the nature of truth commission reports, in which they present their recommendations. Finally, we provide an overview of our study and the plan for the book.

1. TRUTH COMMISSION DEFINITIONS AND CASE SELECTION

One of the challenges of studying truth commissions comparatively is determining the "universe" of cases. Like many other comparative studies, we adopt Priscilla Hayner's (2011, 11) seminal definition of a truth commission. A truth commission is

> (1) focused on past, rather than ongoing, events; (2) investigates a pattern of events that took place over a period of time; (3) engages directly and broadly with the affected population, gathering information on their experiences; (4) is a temporary body, with the aim of concluding with a final report; and (5) is officially authorized or empowered by the state under review.

This is a more restrictive definition than Hayner's (1994, 600) earlier conception of truth commissions as "bodies set up to investigate a past history of violations of human rights in a particular country – which can include violations by the military or other government forces or by armed opposition forces." It is, however, similar to Mark Freeman's (2006, 18) definition of a truth commission as

> an *ad hoc*, autonomous, and victim-centered commission of inquiry set up in and authorized by a state for the primary purposes of (1) investigating and reporting on the principal causes and consequences of broad and relatively recent patterns of severe violence or repression that occurred in the state during determinate periods of abusive rule or conflict, and (2) making recommendations for their redress and future prevention.

Even though Hayner's definition is widely accepted, for a variety of reasons, cross-national studies vary significantly in the cases they include (Brahm 2009; Stewart and Wiebelhaus-Brahm 2017).

Ambiguity surrounding key elements of the truth commission definition has led studies to define their samples in a variety of ways. Here, we highlight some Latin American bodies that have occasionally been defined as truth commissions, but which we exclude. First, Hayner (2011) is not always consistent in the application of her own definition. In the second edition of her book, she is much clearer in distinguishing official, government-instigated commissions from unofficial, non-state-based investigations compared to the first edition. Investigations by non-governmental organizations (NGOs) are actually somewhat common in Latin America, as is evidenced variously by the Archbishop of São Paulo and the World Council of Churches' *Brasil: Nunca Mais* project, Servicio Paz y Justicia's *Uruguay: Nunca Más*, and the Human Rights Office of the Archbishop of Guatemala's *Recuperación de la Memoria Histórica* project. While these are valuable contributions to addressing past injustice, we confine ourselves to examining only state-sponsored truth commissions because, unlike NGO-based investigations, such sponsorship entails an obligation on the part of the state to implement the recommendations. Moreover, to reduce ambiguity in the meaning of "pattern of events", we restrict ourselves to truth commissions that investigate a certain political era, defined here as a particular regime's time in power or the length of a civil war. This leads us to exclude bodies such as the Honduran Truth and Reconciliation Commission that investigated events surrounding the 2009 coup. These considerations leave us with the 16 truth commissions in 13 Latin American countries outlined in Table 1.1.

Table 1.1. Latin American Truth Commissions (in chronological order)

Country	Name of Commission	Years of operation	Recommendations?
Bolivia	National Commission for Investigation for Forced Disappearances (*Comisión Nacional de Investigación de Desaparecidos Forzados*)	1982–84	No report completed.
Argentina	National Commission on the Disappeared (*Comisión Nacional sobre la Desaparición de Personas (CONADEP)*)	1983–84	Yes.
Uruguay	Investigative Commission on the Situation of Disappeared People and its Causes (*Comisión Investigadora Parlamentaria Sobre Situación de Personas Desaparecidas y Hechos que la Motivaron*)	1985	Yes.
Chile	National Commission for Truth and Reconciliation (*Comisión Nacional de Verdad y Reconciliación (Rettig)*)	1990–91	Yes.
El Salvador	Commission on the Truth for El Salvador (*Comisión de la Verdad para El Salvador (CVES)*)	1992–93	Yes.
Haiti	National Truth and Justice Commission (*Commission nationale de vérité et de justice (CNVJ)*)	1994–96	Yes.
Ecuador	Truth and Justice Commission	1996–97	No report completed.
Guatemala	Commission for Historical Clarification (*Comisión para el Esclarecimiento Histórico de Guatemala*)	1997–99	Yes.
Uruguay	Commission for Peace (*Comisión para la Paz (COMIPAZ)*)	2000–02	Yes.
Panama	Panama Truth Commission (*Comisión de la Verdad*)	2001–02	Yes.
Peru	Truth and Reconciliation Commission (*Comisión de la Verdad y Reconciliación (CVR)*)	2001–03	Yes.
Chile	National Commission on Political Imprisonment and Torture (*Comisión Nacional sobre Prisión Política y Tortura (Valech)*)	2003–05[3]	Yes.

(continued)

---

[3]   The first Valech report in Chile was published on November 29, 2004 and detailed the results of a six-month investigation. A revised version was released on June 1, 2005. The commission was reopened in February 2010 for 18 months, adding more cases. For more details on the Valech report, see Collins (2016); Collins (2017); Ferrara (2014).

Table 1.1 *continued*

Country	Name of Commission	Years of operation	Recommendations?
Paraguay	Truth and Justice Commission (*Comisión de Verdad y Justicia (CVJ)*)	2004–08	Yes.
Ecuador	Truth Commission (*Comisión de la Verdad*)	2008–10	Yes.
Brazil	National Truth Commission (*Comissão Nacional da Verdade (CNV)*)	2012–14	Yes.
Bolivia	Truth Commission (*Comisión de la Verdad*)	2017–2021	Yes.*
Colombia	Commission for the Clarification of Truth, Coexistence, and Non-Repetition (*Comisión para el Esclarecimiento de la Verdad, la Convivencia y la No Repetición*)	2018–Present	No, still underway.

Sources: Compiled by authors from Hayner (2011); monthly bulletins from the International Center for Transitional Justice (at http://ictj.org/); and reports published by United States Institute of Peace Digital Truth Commission Digital Collection (at http://www.usip.org/publications/truth-commission-digital-collection).

Note: The truth commissions are listed in chronological order according to the year they were established. Truth commissions marked in **bold** published a final report with recommendations and, thus, are included in our study. See Appendixes I and II.

Note *: The Bolivian Truth Commission was ongoing at the time of this research, and delivered its report in 2021. It is therefore not included in our study.

Because our study is interested in the implementation of recommendations, we exclude truth commission cases in which the commission has not produced a final report. In such situations, there are no recommendations to study. In Table 1.1, note that four cases are not in bold. Two truth commissions, Bolivia's National Commission for Investigation of Forced Disappearances and Ecuador's Truth Commission to Impede Impunity, ended before the final report was concluded. In addition, Bolivia's Truth Commission and the truth commission included in the government-FARC peace accord in Colombia,[4] Commission for the Clarification of Truth, Coexistence, and Non-Repetition, were just getting underway as our data collection ended. As such, they had not produced recommendations in time for our analysis. As a result, these four cases are not further addressed in the book.

Thus, the country cases listed in bold in Table 1.1 provide an exhaustive list of official state-sponsored truth commissions in Latin America that have produced recommendations. In total, we have 13 commissions in 11 countries in the study.

---

[4]   The 2016 peace agreement signed between the Colombian government and the *Fuerzas Armadas Revolucionarias de Colombia - Ejército del Pueblo* (Revolutionary Armed Forces of Colombia - People's Army).

2. WHAT DO WE KNOW ABOUT TRUTH COMMISSIONS AND THEIR RECOMMENDATIONS?

Since the 1980s, truth commissions have become important mechanisms through which past human rights abuses committed during repressive regimes or periods of armed conflict are confronted. Latin American countries in particular have been at the forefront of establishing formal "truth and justice" mechanisms after military dictatorships or civil war (Sikkink and Walling 2007; Skaar, García-Godos, and Collins 2016; Sikkink 2011). As such, Latin American truth commissions have served as models for truth commissions established in other parts of the world, including the more famous South African Truth and Reconciliation Commission (TRC) that was modelled on Chile's National Commission on Truth and Reconciliation (better known as the Rettig Commission after its chairperson, Raúl Rettig).

Almost from the start of global truth commission experimentation, debates have waged over their effects. The best-intentioned of truth commissions seek to provide neutral, authoritative histories of periods of mass human rights violations. The most common, explicit goals of truth commissions have included clarifying and acknowledging past abuses, meeting the needs of victims, contributing to justice and accountability, delineating institutional responsibility for past abuses, promoting reform, reducing tensions over the past, and ultimately promoting reconciliation (Hayner 2011). Yet, their relative weakness, in that they are temporary and are unable to compel the state to respond to the investigation, has left them wanting in the eyes of many. In the 1990s, there was much ambivalence about truth commissions. They were viewed as a compromise solution between prosecution and amnesia or formal amnesty (Skaar 1999). For some, they appeared to be cost-free measures performed under the pretence of reconciliation, but really provided political cover for amnesties or other compromises with perpetrators (Mamdani 2002). Still, in general, for better or worse, truth commissions have been perceived as relatively successful in fomenting national debate and creating new national myths (Grandin 2005; Wilson 2001). This, in turn, has led other states to emulate early adopters in the hope of achieving the same perceived objectives (Daly 2008; Kritz 2009).

By the millennium, in the wake of the perceived success of the South African TRC, truth commissions became widely viewed as important, if not essential, forms of transitional justice (Daly 2008; Dancy, Kim, and Wiebelhaus-Brahm 2010). In fact, international law and transnational activists increasingly support what some have called a "truth commission norm" (Wiebelhaus-Brahm 2011; Hirsch 2014). Scholars now often argue that truth commissions are uniquely suited to advancing several post-conflict/post-authoritarian goals. According to this logic, truth commissions can, among other things, promote peace by retributively "naming names" of perpetrators (Popkin and Roht-Arriaza 1995); collect evidence for later prosecutions (Stahn 2001); heal victims and allay their need for revenge (Hayner 2011); limit the range of permissible lies open to political entrepreneurs and recommend reforms that deter future abuses (Ignatieff 1996); and promote reconciliation between former opponents (South African Truth and Reconciliation Commission, and Tutu 1998). Overall, truth commission advocates contend that the best truth commissions can serve as a salve for a fractured society emerging from an abusive period by helping to promote the rule of law and by providing victims with information and official recognition. As an indication of their broad acceptance as a valuable transitional justice tool in their own right, by the early 2000s, Tristan Anne Borer (2006) identified 26 different explicitly stated goals or expectations for truth-finding initiatives, including acknowledgment, coexistence, promoting a human rights culture, justice, *nunca mas* (never again), reconciliation, and promoting the rule of law – to mention but a few. As truth commissions are implemented in a growing variety of contexts, interest in their legacy and impact endures (Sarkin 2019).

Not everyone is enamoured with truth commissions, however.[5] While they may not be as potentially destabilizing as trials, sceptics often attack positive claims made about truth commissions. In particular, the empirical evidence for claims about the reputedly transformative psycho-social and intergroup benefits of truth-telling is limited (Mendeloff 2009). The criticism typically takes one of two forms. First, some have highlighted the limited empirical evidence to support the claims that truth commissions have the benefits that supporters claim (Mendeloff 2004). Second, any impacts attributed to truth commissions may actually be the result of other factors, such as amnesties, which frequently accompany them (Snyder and Vinjamuri 2003/04). More troubling, truth commission revelations may even fuel renewed anger and accentuate intergroup divisions.

What empirical evidence is there regarding the actual achievements (and risks) of truth commissions? To be sure, there is plenty of wishful thinking as to what kind of benefits truth commissions may provide. The quantitative turn in transitional justice research was a response to an overreliance upon anecdotes and impressionistic conclusions in the early qualitative studies. However, these broader, cross-national studies have reached inconsistent

---

[5]   There also are a series of negative claims made by truth commission sceptics. For an overview of positive as well as negative claims regarding truth commission impact, see Skaar, Malca, and Eide (2015), chapter 2.

findings with respect to the effects of truth commissions on a variety of dependent variables – many of which feature among Borer's 26 goals. The work of scholars like Kim and Sikkink (2010) supports the claim that truth commissions promote human rights, whereas other scholars (Wiebelhaus-Brahm 2010b; Olsen, Payne, and Reiter 2010.) find that, to the contrary, human rights worsen in the wake of truth commissions. Olsen, Payne, and Reiter (2010) and Olsen et al. (2010) find that truth commissions are more likely to have a positive outcome if balanced by amnesties. Furthermore, cross-national research does not find a consistent relationship between truth commissions and democracy (Wiebelhaus-Brahm 2010b). More generally, a host of methodological challenges have bedevilled quantitative studies of transitional justice impact (Stewart and Wiebelhaus-Brahm 2017; Thoms, Ron, and Paris 2010).

One challenge with this research is that it often does not adequately take account of qualitative differences in truth commissions. Truth commissions certainly vary considerably in terms of how they were constructed and the powers and resources granted to them, among other things. Yet, truth commissions are usually treated as dummy variables, either present or absent, paying no heed to the quality of the commissions. Some commissions have been fraught processes that were made to fail: the result of cynical politics on the part of state officials. One tactic leaders have used is to establish a commission to signal to the international community that something is being done to address human rights abuses (Grodsky 2008). Uganda's President Museveni, for example, created a commission to investigate his predecessors. Then, he starved it of resources and left it to languish in relative obscurity until the political winds had blown over (Quinn 2004). Even the most exemplary commissions have limited powers and may have insufficient resources. More recent cross-national research that does take account of qualitative differences finds that the impact of truth commissions on accountability for past human rights violations has been positive over time in nine Latin American countries, all of which are included in this study. In an analysis capturing the development in truth-finding in the Latin American region over a time period of more than three decades, Skaar et al. (2016) find a clear movement from impunity to accountability in the area of truth-finding for all nine countries, although there is substantial variation among the different countries due to the particular qualities of each truth commission.[6] The authors point out that while rare, backsliding occurred in some countries, particularly where "official indifference to or denial of truth commission reports has negated the acknowledgement function of state-backed recovery" (Skaar, Collins, and García-Godos 2016, 284).

---

[6]   See Figure 12.2 (Chapter 12, page 284) for a visual presentation of the truth dimension of accountability over time for nine Latin American countries.

James Gibson (2005, 344) writes that the "success of truth commissions depends upon their ability to establish and maintain legitimacy with ordinary citizens." Truth commissions often generate high expectations. In places like South Africa, failure to deliver on some of the more ambitious aims of the TRC fuelled widespread criticism among the citizenry (Backer 2010). While truth commissions generate mixed expectations, the most effective at garnering legitimacy are likely those that produce a final report that sets an agenda for further measures to address the past and to instigate reforms.

To sum up, the establishment of truth commissions in countries around the world has often generated broad expectations among academics, activists, policymakers, victims, and mass publics that they will lead to a variety of peace and justice-related outcomes – objectives that typically are cited to justify their creation. Yet, the actual evidence for their effects, positive or negative, is relatively limited. In general, insufficient attention has been paid to the causal processes through which truth commissions may have an effect.

Truth commissions generally serve several functions, through which they theoretically might contribute to the effects often attributed to them. Truth commissions may play a *ceremonial function* in that the investigation and the giving of testimony affect victims, perpetrators, and bystanders. The process of uncovering information creates a form of theatre. Commissions may have more of an effect on society if they conduct public hearings and/or more purposefully engage with the media and civil society. Acts and ceremonies also frame the introduction of reports and findings to the public.

Truth commissions also serve a *reporting function* (Mendeloff 2004). Precisely how and on what a commission reports depends upon the truth commission's mandate and the judgement of commissioners. It may vary from the systematic recollection of facts and data to the historical interpretation of events and processes. The report forms the basis of a *transformative function* that potentially makes similar abuses less likely in the future.

The *transformative potential* of truth commissions arguably lies most directly in the body of recommendations put forward in their final reports. Truth commission recommendations usually include proposals to reform legal, security, political, and social institutions. They also frequently recommend reparations of various kinds and other sorts of measures to further address past violations. The list of recommendations is often extensive. The tendency over time has been towards longer lists of recommendations; more recent truth commissions have tended to produce more recommendations.

This in itself raises questions about expectations and the feasibility of implementation. In general, there are many obstacles to implementing truth commission recommendations. Governments may have other priorities. Powerful interests who are threatened by the recommendations may create roadblocks. According to the Office of the United Nations High Commissioner for Human Rights (2006, 31),

> Successfully implementing commissions' recommendations has been a major challenge, even in instances where there has been a legal obligation on the part of the Government to act. Even where there is sufficient political will, there may not be sufficient institutional capacity or funds to undertake the recommended measures.

There is significant pessimism about the implementation of truth commission recommendations. Hayner (2011, 193), for example, concludes that "[n]o one has yet analysed how many of the thousands of recommendations by truth commissions have been implemented, but it is clear that implementation generally remains weak". Upon the tenth anniversary of the Peruvian CVR, a generally highly regarded truth commission, a report from the International Center for Transitional Justice (ICTJ) found that the implementation record had been abysmal (Correa 2013). In general, though, implementation has attracted comparatively little attention. This project provides rich data with which to evaluate these claims.

Moreover, the relationship between the nature of recommendations and the prospects for their implementation has largely been neglected in the existing scholarly literature. Many qualitative studies of truth commissions make little reference to either (Amstutz 2005; Chapman 2009). Even recent qualitative work that focuses explicitly on the impact of truth commissions, such as Ferrara's (2014) detailed analysis of Chile's Rettig Commission, gives recommendations rather short shrift. As for the large-N studies that attempt to evaluate the impact of truth commissions and other transitional justice mechanisms on outcomes such as peace, democracy, and human rights (Wiebelhaus-Brahm 2010b; Olsen, Payne, and Reiter 2010; Sikkink 2011), they largely fail to take account of qualitative differences in truth commissions, such as type of recommendation and degree of implementation. Only recently has the Transitional Justice Research Collaborative collected data on the recommendations of truth commissions.[7] However, the database consists only of categories of recommendations derived from truth commission reports and does not contain any information on their implementation.

Yet, there is a small and growing amount of literature that is concerned with what happens after truth commissions launch their reports. Concentrating on Latin America, there is a handful of studies that have tried to assess the importance of truth commission recommendations. Already in the mid-1990s, Mark Ensalaco

---

[7]   https://www.transitionaljusticedata.com/.

(1994b, 666), in his analysis of what were then recent truth commissions in Chile and El Salvador, wrote that,

> The most important contributions of these most recent truth commissions, given the manner in which they were constituted, derived from their advisory function. The commissions' recommendations concerning the adaptation of the political constitutions and legal statutes to reflect international human rights standards, and institutional reforms of the judiciaries and militaries, consisted of the legal and institutional prerequisites of societies that are truly protective and promotive of human rights.[8]

Mike Kaye (1997) provides a more thorough assessment of the implementation record of the recommendations made by two investigative commissions in Central America: the Salvadoran Commission on the Truth and the Honduran National Commissioner for the Protection of Human Rights' investigation of disappearances. He provides an evaluation of these commissions' contributions to justice, reconciliation, and democratization. Although Kaye's analysis was carried out very soon after the two final reports were released, he provides some indication of the implementation status of recommendations. For instance, he points out that some military officials were removed from positions of authority in El Salvador due to their involvement in human rights violations (Kaye 1997, 704). However, most recommendations had failed to be implemented at the time of writing. Interestingly, Kaye (1997, 707) notes that

> While the [Salvadoran] Truth Commission and the [Honduran] Valladares Report were very similar in terms of their reconciliation measures and their support for criminal prosecutions, the level of implementation was far higher in Honduras than in El Salvador.

In the years after, a few other studies have given some examination to recommendations and their implementation. Following up on Kaye's analysis, for example, Margaret Popkin (2000) provides a more extensive overview of the implementation record of the Salvadoran truth commission's recommendations in the approximately first five years following the release of the commission's report. Shifting focus to Peru, Lisa J. Laplante and Kimberley Theidon (2007) analyse the implementation record of the Peruvian truth commission recommendations, specifically recommendations made on reparations to victims, exemplified by the government's "Plan of Reparations 2005–2006" approved by executive decree in 2005. They find that, at least initially, the government was unwilling to allocate the resources necessary to implement the reparations plan. On the subject of likelihood of implementation of

---

[8]   Note, however, that given the short time span between the issuing of the two truth commission reports and the publication of Ensalaco's article, the positive evaluation must have been based on the text of the truth commission reports rather than on an actual analysis of their implementation record.

recommendations, in his analysis of Chile's Rettig Commission and the Salvadoran Commission on the Truth, Eric Wiebelhaus-Brahm (2010b) finds that recommendations are more likely to be implemented when party politics are more competitive and when civil society is more robust. While they are all useful building blocks, these earlier studies did not look at recommendation implementation systematically, and most assessments occurred quite soon after the commissions completed their work.

With the passage of time, scholars of transitional justice have the benefit of operating within a larger time frame for analysing and assessing implementation. In her detailed analysis of the legacies of Chile's Rettig Commission, Anita Ferrara (2014) makes a strong argument for why it is important to employ a long-term perspective when one tries to understand the larger contributions of truth commissions. She shows how the Rettig Commission was the precursor for reparation programs, more truth-finding initiatives, memorialization projects, and criminal prosecution for human rights violations. In his dissertation work, Carlos Fernandez Torné analyses truth commissions in Nepal and Sri Lanka. He argues that truth commissions should be understood as processes that generate vertical accountability relationships between the state and civil society and horizontal accountability relationships within the state. According to (Torné 2017, i), "These accountability relationships take place prior to the establishment of a [truth commission], during their work and as a result of the recommendations compiled in the final report". Although not comprehensive in their approach, both of these studies are more rigorous attempts to connect truth commission recommendations to their broader, long-term impact.

The most comprehensive and systematic exploration of the impact of truth commission recommendations' implementation to date is the work of Onur Bakiner (2014, 2016). Distinguishing direct and indirect impact, he assesses existing theoretical explanations in light of empirical evidence drawn from 15 truth commissions from around the world. He argues that direct impact may take place through the implementation of recommendations, and indirect impact, through civil society mobilization for change. He concludes that often the impact of truth commissions comes long after the commission itself has ceased to exist, casting doubt on the findings of many earlier studies. In line with Ferrara's (2014) findings, he further argues that,

> Truth commissions' positive judicial impact (i.e., human rights accountability) tends to appear several years after the end of the process, in great part as a result of broader changes in politicians' and judges' attitudes on human rights trials. Negative judicial impact (i.e., impunity) favors only a small subsection of perpetrators, while the overall climate of impunity is likely caused by factors other than truth commissions' amnesty procedures (Bakiner 2016, 113).

He concludes that truth commissions *do* promote political and judicial change, albeit modestly, especially when human rights and victims' groups pressure governments for policy implementation (Bakiner 2014). These effects are often through recommendations, in that

> truth commissions' recommendations are incorporated into policy in some countries because politicians take the initiative to implement them, whereas in other cases implementation takes place despite the reluctance, or even hostility, of the political leadership, as a result of continuous civil society mobilization (Bakiner 2014, 14).

These conclusions suggest that recommendations can play a catalytic role. They outline causal mechanisms through which recommendations may cement commissions' legacies. Bakiner's (2016) distinction between direct and indirect impact of truth commissions is helpful for us in understanding the role that recommendations play in assessing the legacy of truth commissions. At the conceptual level, however, it is necessary to differentiate the "implementation" of specific recommendations from the "impact" of the truth commission that issued them. Implementation is understood here as both a process (the implementation process) and specific events (implementing events) that result in some policy, legal, or procedural change. To paraphrase Eric Brahm's (2007) distinction between truth commission success and impact, recommendations may be implemented without substantially affecting the behaviours and attitudes of individual actors. As implementation is often the product of long, not necessarily successful struggles, accurately assessing their implementation record requires the painstakingly collection of finely tuned data, encompassing long periods of time. Existing studies, however, do not pay sufficient attention to timing, context, or the nature of the recommendations themselves. Rectifying this is precisely the strategy taken by this project.

Indeed, the volume rightly indicates early on that issues of causality are a major challenge when looking at recommendations. Implementing recommendations may change behaviours or attitudes, but causal pathways may be long and circuitous, as implementation itself triggers other actions that ultimately have some sort of impact.

3. A BRIEF BACKGROUND TO TRUTH COMMISSION REPORTS

Truth commission recommendations are obviously context-specific. The reports that we analyze in this book were written at different points in world history. More specifically, they were issued in response to a variety of different national conflicts, situated in very different national, sub-regional, and international political and legal contexts. Nevertheless, it makes sense to look for potential commonalities across the reports.

There are many different ways of grouping the reports, each emphasizing a different dimension that we think might matter in terms of truth commission recommendations' implementation. First, we may group the reports in accordance with the *type of conflict* they address: military (bureaucratic) authoritarianism (as in Argentina, Chile, Uruguay, Brazil, Paraguay, Panama and Haiti), internal armed conflict (El Salvador, Guatemala), or a mixture of the two (Peru). Our expectations are that recommendations addressed to the state only (as in military dictatorships) may be of a qualitatively different character than those truth commission recommendations made to redress violations committed by various armed (state and non-state) groups. Moreover, we know that human rights violations committed during internal armed conflict tend to be more severe in type and scale than violations committed during periods of military authoritarianism.[9] This may require different types of recommendations.[10]

Second, we may group the reports according to *when they were written*. Some truth commissions operated soon after transitions to democratic rule or to peace (i.e. during the first electoral cycle following the transition). These we call *transitional commissions* (as in Argentina, the Rettig Commission in Chile, Uruguay's Investigative Commission on the Situation of Disappeared People and its Causes, Guatemala's Commission for Historical Clarification, and those in El Salvador, and Peru). Other commissions, by contrast, were established several years or even decades after the restoration of democratic rule – so-called *post-transitional commissions* (Panama, Paraguay, Ecuador, and Brazil, along with the second truth commissions in Chile and Uruguay).[11] All of these post-transitional commissions released their final reports after the turn of the millennium. They (plus the transitional commission in Peru, which launched its report in 2003) constitute the "late" commissions in terms of world time (see below). Timing matters for several reasons. As time goes by, human rights issues may become less contentious, especially recommendations that touch on the area of criminal prosecution. Perpetrators retire, pass away, or may lose their political influence in the long run. With the passing of time, it also is possible that reparatory measures have been instigated by the government. When such a policy is set in motion independently of a truth commission, there will be no need for a subsequent commission to recommend such a measure.

---

9   For an overview of the main types of violations committed in the countries that issued the reports under analysis here, see Table 1.3 in Skaar, García-Godos, and Collins (2016, 17–18).

10 However, it should be noted that previous comparative work has found no systematic differences between groups of countries/conflicts in terms of how truth-finding efforts affected the issue of accountability. See Skaar, García-Godos, and Collins (2016).

11 'Post-transitional' is a concept used by various transitional justice scholars to denote the period following the initial transitional period. Skaar (2011) defines this as the first five years (or first electoral period) after political transition, whereas Collins (2010) takes a broader approach.

Third, there is what we call the *world-time factor*.[12] Latin American truth commissions have spanned three decades from the first report issued by Argentina's CONADEP in 1983 until Brazil's National Truth Commission (CNV) concluded its report in 2014. Over time, the global legal and normative context relevant to dealing with severe human rights violations has changed dramatically. Importantly, more recent truth commissions have earlier commissions as role models, hence potentially leading to a copycat effect. There also is a growing epistemic community propagating a "truth commission norm" (Hirsch 2014).

Fourth, we could group the reports according to *who has written them*. Most commissions have drawn their commissioners exclusively from the ranks of citizens of the country. Other commissions, by contrast, were run by foreigners. In Latin America, this has occurred in cases where the UN was involved in ending the conflict and setting up the truth commission, as in the cases of El Salvador and Guatemala. Finally, still other commissions, including that of Haiti, have had a mix of nationals residing in the country and in the diaspora. National ownership of truth commission recommendations may become an issue once the reports have been concluded and submitted to the government and the implementation process starts. We hypothesize that the implementation of truth commission recommendations will get a boost where nationals have sat on the commission, at least in part because commissioners may remain a lobbying force for implementation long after the recommendations have been delivered.

Finally, we categorize countries based upon their national *income*. Latin American countries' economic fortunes have often fluctuated dramatically, buffeted by debt crises and changes in global commodity prices, among other things. Because it would be highly complex to measure economic conditions pertaining when action was taken on each individual recommendation and there is not an obvious comparative measure for those recommendations for which no action was taken, we focus on the country's income in the year in which the report is published. A report issued in the midst of poor economic circumstances seems less likely to gain attention. Poorer countries also may lack the capacity to act upon recommendations and may direct the limited resources available toward broader economic development goals rather than targeting past abuses.

All of these are factors that may shape the content of truth commission reports, and hence also their recommendations. These things also may influence the likelihood that at least some types of recommendations are implemented. Table 1.2 provides a synthesis of the factors discussed above.

---

[12] For a discussion of the "world-time" concept and its implications for transitional justice, see Skaar and Wiebelhaus-Brahm (2013b).

Table 1.2. Key characteristics of Latin American countries with truth commission reports

Report (year released)	CONFLICT		REPORT TIMING		WORLD TIME			COMMISSION MEMBERS		WORLD BANK INCOME GROUP*		
	Post-authoritarian	Post-conflict	Transitional	Post-transitional	Cold War	Post-Cold War	Post-Rome Statute/South AfricaTRC	Nationals only	Foreign or mix	Low	Lower Middle	Upper Middle
Argentina (1984)	X		X		X			X				X
Uruguay (1985)	X		X		X			X				X
Chile (1991)	X		X			X		X			X	
El Salvador (1993)		X	X			X			X		X	
Haiti (1996)	X		X			X			X	X		
Guatemala (1999)		X	X			X			X		X	
Panama (2002)	X			X		X	X	X				X
Uruguay (2003)	X			X		X	X	X				X
Peru (2003)		X	X			X	X	X			X	
Chile (2004)	X			X		X	X	X				X
Paraguay (2008)	X			X		X	X	X			X	
Ecuador (2010)	X			X		X	X	X				X
Brazil (2014)	X			X		X	X	X				X

* Category taken from year in which the report was released. World Bank data goes back only to 1987, so Argentina and Uruguay (1985) are categorized as of 1987. For more on the World Bank's categorization, see https://datahelpdesk.worldbank.org/knowledgebase/articles/378834-how-does-the-world-bank-classify-countries.

As Table 1.2 shows, our cases provide variation along several dimensions. First, 10 of our truth commissions occurred in post-authoritarian contexts, whereas two are post-conflict (El Salvador and Guatemala) or a mix of the two (Peru). Second, just over half of the truth commissions were set up immediately or soon after the transition to democracy and/or peace, i.e., within five years of the end of the transition.[13] There are six post-conflict truth commissions in our sample (Panama, Paraguay, and Ecuador, along with the second truth commissions in Chile, the second commission in Uruguay, and the truth commission in Brazil). Third, in terms of world time, the majority of the commissions were established in the 1980s, 1990s and early 2000s. Two commissions, Argentina's and Uruguay's (1985) occurred during the Cold War. Four commissions occurred during the 1990s, a time when many argue human rights were at their peak global influence. The other seven truth commissions occurred in the 2000s, in the aftermath of the South African TRC and the signing of the Rome Statute on the International Criminal Court. All but one of these latter commissions were post-transitional. Only three commissions occurred after the UN issued its Basic Principle Guidelines in 2005 (Paraguay, Ecuador, and Brazil).

Fourth, most truth commissions have had only nationals as commissioners. The three exceptions in our sample are the two truth commissions set up as part of UN-sponsored peace processes in El Salvador and Guatemala. In these cases, commissioners were invited from abroad to provide an aura of neutrality in the midst of very tense political settings. By contrast, Haiti's truth commission had a mix of nationals living in Haiti and Haitians from the diaspora. Finally, we distinguish countries based on their national income in the year in which the final reports were issued. We use the World Bank's income groupings: low, lower-middle, upper-middle, and high.[14] Only one of our cases, Haiti, falls in the low-income category. Five others, Chile (1991), El Salvador, Guatemala, Peru, and Paraguay were ranked lower-middle income when the truth commission reports were released. The remaining seven truth commission reports were published when their respective countries were classified as upper-middle income by the World Bank.

In the book, we seek to uncover the extent to which this variation in Latin American countries' experiences has affected the formulation and implementation of truth commission recommendations.

---

[13]   We use five years as a cut-off point because this is a common electoral cycle in many countries and thus captures the electoral period of the first government in place after transition (Skaar 2011).

[14]   For more information on how the income group thresholds are determined, see https://datahelpdesk.worldbank.org/knowledgebase/articles/378833-how-are-the-income-group-thresholds-determined.

4. AN OVERVIEW OF METHODOLOGY

As we further describe in Chapter 2, our study is unprecedented in its breadth. For the 13 truth commissions that have issued reports, we have: (i) collected and systematized information on truth commission recommendations into a qualitative database; (ii) identified factors that influence how recommendations are formulated by truth commissions as they craft their reports; and (iii) collected data on which of these recommendations have actually been implemented. From there, we (iv) develop theory-based explanations for the variation in implementation across countries, over time, and by type of recommendation. Where possible, relevant information for this study was obtained from secondary sources. However, interviews with commissioners, activists, and leaders of victims' groups were conducted in all 11 countries in order to construct a thick narrative of the formulation and implementation processes. We worked with research teams based in three different Latin American countries plus Spain: Centro de Estudios Legales y Sociales – CELS (Argentina), El Instituto de Democracia y Derechos Humanos de la Pontificia Universidad Católica del Perú – IDEHPUCP, Facultad Latinoamericana de Ciencias Sociales – FLACSO (Guatemala), and Universidad de Salamanca (Spain), as well as several individual researchers to collect this primary and secondary data. Here, we briefly comment on these four phases of the project.

4.1. THE FOUR PHASES OF THE PROJECT

1. Cataloging and Categorizing Truth Commission Recommendations Into a Qualitative Database

We have assembled a comprehensive list of all recommendations from each of the 13 truth commissions in the study. From there, we created categories to identify characteristics of recommendations that might influence the probability of their implementation. For example, the Office of the UN High Commissioner for Human Rights (2006, 29) argues that, "The more specific and realistic a commission can be in these recommendations, the more likely they will be implemented." Although this makes intuitive sense, there is little empirical evidence to support this contention. In our project, recommendations contained in all reports produced by Latin American truth commissions were catalogued and coded on the basis of several dimensions, including whether they were: universal (e.g., judicial reform, which affects all people in the country) versus targeted (measures affecting specific groups of people); collective versus individual (such as victims' reparations); those that would influence the structure of institutions versus those that would not;

and whether the language of the recommendations is general versus specific. The two truth commission reports with some of the most comprehensive lists of recommendations (Guatemala and Peru) were used as the basis for developing the typology. Since the Latin American reports, with few exceptions, are in Spanish, we have created a multilingual database in which recommendation data can be found in English as well as in the language in which the final report was originally published. We frequently refer to the recommendations throughout this book. Please note that unless formal English translations of the recommendations of a report exist, all translations of recommendations into English in this book are made either by the data collection team responsible for the country case in question, or by the authors of this book. The data collected was organized and systematized in an Excel-database, which was then analysed by the research teams manually. This process is elaborated in more detail in Chapters 2 and 3.

2. Analyzing the Formulation of Truth Commission Recommendations

The implementation of truth commission recommendations is our central interest. However, we also need to know something about the context in which those recommendations were formulated to understand their nature. We examine the multiple interests and ideas that shape the formulation and inclusion (or exclusion) of truth commission recommendations. Personalities within the commission are often important. As such, the composition of the truth commission team, both commissioners and staff, must be considered. Recommendations also are formulated within the confines of the commission's mandate and the broader legal framework in which the truth commission operates. In addition, the formulation of recommendations must be seen in light of other transitional justice and reform activity in the country that might make some recommendations redundant and others too sensitive. For example, if a reparations program has been established prior to the commission's final report, there may be no need for such a recommendation. Finally, truth commissions formulate their recommendations in the context of political debates among (domestic and international) actors involved in the truth commission process. Commissions face real or imagined pressures to craft recommendations in line with important interests.

3. Analyzing the Implementation of Truth Commission Recommendations

From there, we investigate which recommendations have been implemented, and the factors that shaped the process and degree of implementation. Implementation is likely to be influenced by several factors, including public awareness of the recommendations, the legitimacy of the commission, the relative power of pro- and anti-truth commission and reform elements, and international factors. The balance of forces between the "drivers of justice" and "the spoilers of justice" has rightly been stressed in the literature on transitional justice mechanisms in general, and is highly relevant to contextual explanations of implementation or lack thereof (Skaar and Wiebelhaus-Brahm 2013; Sriram 2013). A key issue is *who* will be affected by the recommendations and what power they have to promote or obstruct implementation. Finally, the international community may play a role in pressing for implementation, although the international community often seems increasingly unwilling to take on this role (Hayner 2011). In some cases, external actors appear as "spoilers of justice" (Sriram 2013).

The *nature* of the recommendations themselves also matters. More specific recommendations might be more likely to be implemented if they are easier and more straightforward to carry out. Conversely, broad, general recommendations may require consent or further action from multiple institutions, such as the executive, parliament, judiciary, and/or other national and/or local authorities. It may not be obvious which state agent is responsible for the implementation of a particular recommendation. The role of sub-national authorities also is a little-explored, but potentially significant factor.

The diversity in Latin American experiences with regard to *timing* is both a challenge and a blessing. To take account of the potential influence of world-historical time, we divide our cases into three groups according to the time of truth commission establishment: (i) early cases (1980s); (ii) middle-tier cases (1990s); and (iii) late cases (2000s and 2010s). The time dimension allows us to explore factors that may influence the shape and form of truth commission recommendations, such as shifting norms, changes in domestic institutions, and changes in the regional institutional framework for human rights.

4. Developing a Theory of Truth Commission Recommendations

The data collected will provide the basis for identifying general patterns of how different types of truth commission recommendations have been implemented over time. These patterns, in turn, will enable us to formulate more generally applicable principles regarding the formulation and implementation of truth commission recommendations. For instance, some *types of truth commission recommendations* are probably more (or less) likely to be implemented in certain contexts. It is probably easier for governments to implement specific, concrete recommendations (such as economic compensation to victims and their families, pension schemes, etc.) which do not threaten entrenched interests than to undertake larger structural changes involving many state agents and large investments over time (such as judicial and police reform). Another working hypothesis looks to the concept of *political will*, but links it to the literature on the balance of power between forces in transitional justice situations as a principal explanation for the degree of implementation (Zalaquett 1992). A third hypothesis is rooted in the *concept of norm diffusion*: implementation of certain recommendations in more recent truth commissions may be more likely because previous truth commissions in the region have pursued such measures and/or they are promoted by influential regional and global actors as just and desirable (Sikkink 2011). Implementation may prove more likely when they connect to regional or international norms.

4.2. CASE SELECTION

Our focus on Latin American cases has several benefits. First, most truth commissions in the region occurred quite some time ago. This allows us to explore the timing of recommendations and their implementation. It is possible that the more time that has passed, the more likely it is that we may observe implementation. This is particularly true for complex recommendations that require the involvement of many different actors and/or a lot of resources. By contrast, we might expect a flurry of implementation activity immediately following the truth commission as public (and sometimes international) attention is focused on the truth commission and its findings. With time, other policy issues may then overshadow the recommendations and activists may splinter as they pursue diverse agendas. As a result, we might expect a slowing of implementation activity over time. A second benefit is that these truth commissions operated over a broad span of time. Since some of the oldest truth commissions in the world are found in Latin America, established in the early 1980s, significant time has passed in which to trace the implementation record of these early truth commission recommendations. For truth commissions established in the 1990s and the 2000s, the length of time during which implementation could have taken place is naturally shorter. More recent truth commissions have functioned in a global environment in which transnational activists, intergovernmental organizations like the UN, and states promote truth commissions and other forms of transitional justice. The resulting variation enables us to explore how world-historical time matters. Third, focusing on one region enables us to hold cultural and historical factors constant to a limited extent. To be sure, each of the 11 countries we examine has experienced its own unique political and socio-economic development; yet, there are likely greater commonalities across Latin American societies with respect to attitudes towards human rights, government's relationship with the people, how to address injustice, and the like, than if we had randomly selected truth commission cases from around the world. There is clear evidence that countries have learned from previous truth commissions across the region. Thus, overall, Latin America presents a natural laboratory in which to explore the implementation of truth commission recommendations.

5. PLAN FOR THE BOOK

In the coming pages, we explore the fate of truth commission recommendations in Latin America. Chapter 2 takes a deeper look at the project's methodology. The project is unprecedented in its scope: we examine 13 truth commissions in 11 Latin American countries. The chapter describes how our research team conducted interviews with truth commission staff, politicians, and activists to gain insights into the processes through which commissions crafted their recommendations. We explore how the passage of time and interviewees' desire to protect their legacy create challenges for data analysis. We also collect primary and secondary sources, supplemented with interview data, to trace the implementation of those recommendations. We explain how we constructed our database to facilitate cross-case comparison. In addition, we discuss how we address questions of causality.

Chapter 3 provides a broad comparative overview of the types of truth commission recommendations produced by Latin American truth commissions. We develop a typology of recommendations and a code for various characteristics of recommendations. Through this, we can identify patterns in recommendation design across cases. In addition, we can identify how truth commission recommendations have changed over time.

Chapter 4 examines the dynamics of recommendation formulation. We discuss the strategic calculations of commissioners and staff as they craft their recommendations, by recreating internal debates. We trace how the domestic and international environment influences the design of recommendations. Finally, we consider how evolving international truth commission norms and the growing influence of the UN and transnational activists, among others, have shaped recommendations.

Chapter 5 takes stock of the implementation record of the 13 individual truth commissions analysed in this volume. We do so on a country-by-country basis, providing short stories from each of the 11 Latin American countries. The main story told by examining these historical experiences of implementation is that the implementation record for Latin American truth commission recommendations is far more impressive than first anticipated.

Chapter 6 carries out a comparative analysis of the implementation record of truth commission recommendations around Latin America. We explore what types of recommendations are more or less likely to be implemented. In addition, we examine the timing of implementation. We consider how a range of domestic and international actors attempt to advance or prevent implementation to serve their own interests. Finally, we address the challenges and possibilities that democratic practices pose for the implementation of truth commission recommendations.

Chapter 7 reflects upon the theoretical and policy implications of the project. We examine how the implementation, or lack thereof, of truth commission recommendations relates to debates about the impact of truth commissions. From there, we outline the policy implications of our research. First, we highlight some pitfalls to avoid when crafting recommendations. Next, we explain how commissioners and staff might design their recommendations to increase the likelihood of their implementation.

CHAPTER 2

RESEARCHING RECOMMENDATIONS

Words are but the signs of ideas.

– Samuel Johnson, lexicographer (1709–84)

A truth commission recommendation is, in essence, a constellation of words that proposes an action that implies change. Behind each recommendation there is an idea – which we must assume that commissioners had in mind when issuing precisely this recommendation, formulated just so. Yet, it is not always straightforward to know what a recommendation is, or how it is meant to bring about the desired change. Presumably, that has to do with how and by whom the recommendation is implemented. Coming to grips with what a truth commission recommendation fundamentally is, is the task ahead.

This chapter provides a detailed discussion of the project's methodology. We describe our methodological choices in depth. We explain how we constructed our database to facilitate cross-case comparison. Further, we discuss how we address questions of causality. On the surface, exploring truth commission recommendations seems like a relatively straightforward task: one must consult those who were involved in the formulation of recommendations; assemble a checklist of the recommendations which are outlined in truth commissions' final reports; and check off the ones for which relevant action was taken. As with all research projects, the systematic study of truth commission recommendations has involved several methodological choices, some of them expected, others unexpected. Nevertheless, collecting systematic data on the hundreds of recommendations produced by 13 truth commissions, some dating back as far as 1984, across 11 countries, is a challenging endeavour.

As outlined in the previous chapter, we have two major interests in examining truth commission recommendations. First, we focus on the formulation of the recommendations themselves. We seek to understand why commissioners ended up with the particular set of recommendations they did and not others. In talking with commission staff and others who were involved in the process, we are cognizant of how the passage of time and interviewees' desire to protect their legacy can create challenges for data analysis, among other things. Second, we focus on the implementation of the recommendations. We collect data on which of these recommendations have actually been implemented, taking into account nuances of the degree of implementation. Finally, we examine how the characteristics of recommendations as well as contextual factors shape the likelihood that particular types of recommendations get implemented.

To capture information on formulation and implementation, we developed a qualitative database with all recommendations on a country-by-country basis in which we identify, catalogue and typologize the recommendations that have appeared in the commissions' final reports. Distinguishing recommendations is less straightforward than one might assume. For example, while in one truth commission report a single recommendation may contain one specific activity, another report may address a similar issue through a complex set of multiple sub-recommendations. This is a record-keeping challenge in terms of how we address complicated, multi-pronged recommendations in the database.

Organizationally, this chapter follows the road map suggested by our research questions. We start with considerations regarding the design of the database, as this required decisions concerning the object of study, operationalization, definitions, and typologies. This is followed by separate discussions of methodological challenges arising from data collection on the formulation and implementation processes. As the project aims to develop theoretical tools to understand the effects of truth commission recommendations, we devote a section to the issue of determining causal relationships between a recommendation and actual implementation. We round off the chapter with a summary and discussion of the implications of our methodological choices for the study of truth commission recommendations.

1. CONSTRUCTING A DATABASE FOR CROSS-COUNTRY COMPARISON

The construction of a database covering detailed information from 13 different truth commission reports, collected and systematized to facilitate cross-country comparison, has been a team effort. The data was collected and fed into the database by four teams based in four different countries, three Latin American and one European: CELS in Argentina, working on Argentina, Brazil, Chile, and Uruguay; IDEHPUCP in Peru, working on Ecuador, Paraguay, and Peru; FLACSO in Guatemala, initially working on Guatemala; and Universidad de Salamanca in Spain, also working on Guatemala as well as El Salvador. The work on Haiti and Panama was conducted by independent researchers. The data collection teams consisted of a mix of senior and junior scholars with an interdisciplinary background spanning Political Science, Human Geography, Law, Sociology, and History. The teams were given the same instructions for data collection and recording, using a codebook developed by the project core team as a guide.

The four teams plus individual researchers jointly had the language skills (Spanish, Portuguese, French, and English) required to collect, enter, and analyse the data. Our research teams conducted interviews with truth commission staff, politicians, and activists to gain insights into the processes through which commissions have crafted their recommendations. We supplement our interview data with secondary sources to trace the implementation of those recommendations. A final output of the data collection and analysis is the production of 11 country reports by the research teams, presenting in narrative form the process of formulation and implementation of truth commission recommendations in each country (Skaar, Wiebelhaus-Brahm, and García-Godos (eds.) 2022).

The first stage of the data collection process began with the design of a qualitative database of truth commission recommendations. Our goal was to catalogue all recommendations explicitly presented by each truth commission, in either a specific section or a chapter devoted to recommendations, in their respective final reports. Eleven of the commission reports are in Spanish, reflecting the fact that most Latin American countries have Spanish as their official language. Brazil's commission report is in Portuguese and the Haitian truth commission report is in French. Although several countries, such as Guatemala, El Salvador, Ecuador and Peru, have large indigenous populations, it is worth noting that, to date, no truth commission report has been issued in any indigenous language. Peru, however, does have a short version of the report in Quechua. Using the original truth commission reports, our research teams recorded all recommendations verbatim in the original language (Spanish, Portuguese, or French). Further, there are references to the specific page(s) in the relevant final report on which the recommendation was found. Each recommendation was later classified according to categories discussed in Chapter 3.

Once we identified the corpus of recommendations (see Chapter 3 for details), the teams went on to collect detailed data on the formulation and implementation of specific truth commission recommendations. All research teams relied on a combination of primary and secondary sources. On-site fieldwork was carried out in all 11 Latin American countries that have had truth commissions fitting our definition. For data on *recommendation formulation*, we attempted to interview as many former commissioners and staff as possible in order to gain insights into the debates that shaped the inclusion (or exclusion) of particular recommendations in the truth commission report. We also spoke with victims and activists who were engaged in the truth commission process. This was supplemented by media accounts at the time, memoirs of those involved, and other secondary sources. Questions to be answered included: What was the origin of specific recommendations? Why was a particular recommendation included in the final report? Why were other recommendations excluded?

For data on *recommendation implementation*, we rely on a wide range of written sources (government documents, newspaper reports, etc.) together with interviews conducted with a wide variety of relevant informants in government agencies and ministries, institutions charged with following up on truth commissions' work, human rights organizations, legal scholars and others. We sought information on the following questions: Was a particular truth commission recommendation implemented or not? If yes, who or what was responsible for implementing it? Were there any actors actively supporting implementation? Were any actors blocking the implementation of a given truth commission recommendation? What, if any, structural factors proved to be beneficial to or obstacles to implementation? This data was entered into the database by the respective research teams. The database contains summary data on formulation and implementation, while country studies provide a richer, narrative analysis of the fate of each truth commission's recommendations (Skaar, Wiebelhaus-Brahm, and García-Godos (eds.) 2022).

We implemented several measures to better ensure the uniformity of data across all 11 countries, despite the sprawling nature of the project. First, researchers were selected for their knowledge of the cases, existing contacts in the country, and their relevant language expertise. Second, we constructed a codebook to guide researchers as they collected data on the 13 different truth commissions. Then, in-field training was carried out with most data collectors; those who joined the project team later were trained by existing team members. We also held a mid-project meeting in Pisac, Peru, to get feedback from researchers on the methodology and to make adjustments where necessary.

2. DEFINING AND COUNTING RECOMMENDATIONS

The universe of truth commission recommendations obviously depends on how we define a truth commission recommendation, and on how we count them. We have, to the best of our knowledge, never come across a working definition of a truth commission recommendation. When the word "recommendation" is mentioned in the scholarly literature on transitional justice generally and truth commissions specifically, it is largely left undefined – i.e., it is left to the reader to provide meaning. This includes core works on truth commissions, such as Bakiner (2016), Ferrara (2014), Freeman (2006), and Hayner (2011). Even scholarly articles that deal directly with truth commission reports and recommendations – of which there are only a handful – refrain from defining the concept (Paulson and Bellino 2017, Torné 2015). In short, "recommendation" is not a term of art in the literature on truth commissions. To make any meaningful comparative analysis, however, we need to know what we are comparing.

For the purposes of this book, we define a truth commission recommendation as

> any measure suggested by a truth commission that calls upon the state to take action that addresses past human rights violations and/or is designed to promote non-repetition.

We limit our analysis to the truth commission recommendations mentioned in the section of a truth commission report called "*Recommendaciones*" (in Spanish), or the equivalent. This strategy avoids having to pore over the many thousands of pages of truth commission report material in the search of recommendations that may be "hidden" in other parts of the text. Although certain truth commission recommendations may inadvertently escape our attention through this method, we are assured of capturing the measures that *commissions themselves* have judged to be most consequential. They would not have buried important recommendations elsewhere in the report where readers might not identify them.

2.1. DISTINGUISHING A TRUTH COMMISSION RECOMMENDATION

It can be hard to nail down a truth commission recommendation. This is partly because truth commission reports vary greatly in terms of how they formulate and present their recommendations. A careful reading of all the truth commission reports in our study shows that truth commissions formulate and delimit their recommendations in a number of different ways. Going from the simple to the more complex, a truth commission recommendation may be brief and with a single aim. The third recommendation given by the Panamanian truth commission is an excellent example: "To create a Special Prosecutor to investigate the human rights violations and crimes against humanity".[16] As simple as that. On the more complex side of the spectrum, we find recommendations such as the recommendation (number 42) in the El Salvador report:

> The Commission feels it would be useful if this report and its conclusions and recommendations and progress towards national reconciliation were analyzed not only by the Salvadorian people as a whole but also by a special forum comprising the most representative sectors of society which, in addition to the above-mentioned objectives, should strive to monitor strict compliance with the recommendations. It is not for the Commission to indicate how such a forum should be established.

---

[16] 'Que se cree una Fiscalía Especial para investigar las violaciones a los derechos humanos y delitos de la humanidad' (*Informe Final de la Comisión de la Verdad. "La verdad os hará libres"*, 2002).

However, a National Commission for the Consolidation of Peace (COPAZ) was established under the peace agreements as "a mechanism for the monitoring of and the participation of civilian society in the process of change resulting from the negotiations". It therefore seems appropriate that the task referred to by the Commission should be entrusted primarily to COPAZ. However, given the scope the importance of the subject-matter dealt with in this report, the Commission would like to suggest to COPAZ that, to this end, it consider expanding its membership so that sectors of civilian society that are not directly represented in COPAZ can participate in this analysis. Moreover, COPAZ is the body entrusted by the agreements with preparing preliminary legislative drafts related to the peace process. In this sphere, it has a crucial role to play in the implementation of the recommendations in the present report that call for legal reforms.[17]

Getting at exactly what the last recommendation in the El Salvador report wants the government to do requires careful interpretation. A single truth commission recommendation, as delineated in the report, does not always recommend just one thing. A recommendation may be split into two or more identifiable parts, like in the following example taken from Chile's Rettig Commission final report. One of the sections of the report is dedicated to "Recommendations for restoring the good name of people and making symbolic reparation", in order to "keep alive the memory of what happened so that it may never happen again". To achieve this aim, its second recommendation in this section lists "Some suggestions for restoring the good name of people and making symbolic reparation", which (specifically) include:

- setting up a commemorative monument that would list all the victims of human rights abuses from both sides;
- building a public park in memory of those who lost their lives, to serve as a place of commemoration and a lesson, as well as a place for recreation and for bolstering a life-affirming culture.
- giving the recently created "National Human Rights Day" the importance it deserves so that each December 10 will be observed throughout the country with public observances and ceremonies in the schools and other gestures aimed at symbolic reparation;
- organizing campaigns, cultural celebrations, and the like, so that we may continue to move toward creating a climate of national reconciliation.[18]

Each of the *sub-recommendations* (marked by asterisks) are specific suggestions of actions that may serve as symbolic reparations (i.e., commemorative

---

[17] Comisión de la Verdad para El Salvador (CVES). *De la locura a la esperanza. La guerra de 12 años en El Salvador*, rec. No. 42. Translation by El Salvador research team.

[18] *Informe de la Comisión Nacional de Verdad y Reconciliación* (Informe Rettig), English version *Report of the Chilean National Commission on Truth and Reconciliation*, Part 4, Chapter 1, Section B, para. 2 at p. 1059.

monument, memory park, "National Human Rights Day", campaigns and cultural celebrations). More generally, sub-recommendations are typically an operationalization or specification of the overall truth commission recommendation.[19] Governments could take action on one or more of these items without necessarily implementing all four. We thus find it useful to distinguish between main recommendations and sub-recommendations, which together constitute the universe of truth commission recommendations.

(i) **Main recommendations** refer to identifiable and implementable recommendations (in the datasets that provide the foundation for the analysis in this book, each of these recommendations has its own identification number). These are the recommendations delineated by the commissions themselves.

(ii) **Sub-recommendations** refer to concrete items into which some recommendations are broken down. Sub-recommendations are actionable items within an explicitly articulated recommendation.

Sometimes, main recommendations contain only one recommendation; in other instances, as in the example above, two or more sub-recommendations may be embedded within a single main recommendation. Our goal is to isolate *individually* actionable items. This requires careful reading of the text in truth commission reports. For the purposes of studying patterns of implementation, as we explain in more depth below, we focus on the sub-recommendation level.

Sometimes it is difficult to locate a recommendation when it is "hidden" in an extended block of text, with no indication of where the recommendation actually starts or stops. We then have to decipher the text to locate the recommendation. Here is a recommendation made by Chile's Rettig Commission to illustrate:

> Our recommendations in this regard are directed to the Ministry of Education so that it may study the possibility of devising a program of reparation. The starting point for the program should be a diagnosis of the problem and should involve the participation of those who have suffered, human rights organizations, professional associations, the National Teachers Association, and other relevant bodies. Among the measures we regard as most interesting we suggest the following:
>
> –   A portion of scholarships for higher education should be reserved for the children of human rights victims who are ready for such studies.

---

[19] Some truth commission reports explicitly code sub-recommendations by using either separate numbers or letters (i.e., 1(i), 1(ii), 1(iii), etc., or 1a, 1b, 1c, 1d).

- Study should be given to the possibility of cancelling debts that the children, spouses, or other immediate relatives of such victims have incurred with the state or universities, provided the proper authority approves.
- Young people and adults who did not complete their studies and do not have a trade should be regarded as having a right to enrol in certain institutes and centers for technical training.
- Similar opportunities and incentives should be provided for surviving spouses or partners, or other immediate family members, should they request it.
- We urge that educational measures be organized in the framework of our recommendations for social reparation so that they may make it as easy as possible for people to acquire a profession or trade, complete their training, or retrain for that purpose. We also urge that the government assume the costs within certain limits and time frames, once the scope of the demand has been assessed. Finally, we urge that the aim must always be to reincorporate the relatives of human rights victims into society and that the stigma and risks of isolation that might derive from granting special aid be avoided.[20]

From this text, we may extract a concrete truth commission recommendation, namely that *the Ministry of Education devise a program of reparations*. The rest are suggestions for concrete reparations and how the programme should be organized. For the purposes of assessing implementation, there are four distinct things that the Ministry is being asked to do: consult stakeholders on how to address educational dimensions of reparations; establish a scholarship program; eliminate student debt; and give priority access to educational opportunities to victims. This brings us to the next challenge: how do we delimit different recommended actions so that we can count the number of recommendations?

2.2. THE "COUNTING PROBLEM"

How does one count the number of recommendations? In this context, it is not true that all roads lead to Rome. How we define a truth commission recommendation will obviously directly influence how many recommendations we count. In this project, we have concluded that Latin American truth commissions jointly have made around 1000 recommendations in their final reports. In this and the next section we will try to explain how we arrived at this number. This number is not arbitrary, but rather the fruit of a series of conscious

---

20 *Informe de la Comisión Nacional de Verdad y Reconciliación* (Informe Rettig), English version *Report of the Chilean National Commission on Truth and Reconciliation*, Part 4, chapter 1, section D, para. 4(b), at pp. 1070–1071.

choices. In the end, we chose to focus on individually actionable items. Different choices would have revealed different numbers.

The numbering styles and the varying levels of detail with which truth commission recommendations are formulated in the reports give rise to what we may call the "counting problem". In various ways, this challenge exists for all of truth commission reports. Counting is clearly easier where recommendations are kept brief and are clearly numbered. They become increasingly difficult to distinguish as recommendations become longer, more complex, and more detailed. It is important to note that the degree of difficulty in counting recommendations does not necessarily coincide with the amount of ink devoted to recommendations. Some truth commission reports have only a few, very concrete, recommendations, such as the 1985 Uruguayan truth commission and Argentina's CONADEP. Even here, though, there are different ways of counting their recommendations. By contrast, other truth commission reports, such as that of Ecuador, have a long list of truth commission recommendations, yet they are easy to count because they are listed one by one and consecutively numbered; each of these truth commission recommendations contains a single, clear recommendation and no sub-recommendations.

In fact, there seems to have been a learning process over time. Some of the early truth commission reports – notably Chile's first report *Informe Rettig* – were rather muddled in the way they presented their recommendations. By contrast, later reports, such as those from Ecuador and Brazil, communicate their recommendations in a more stringent way, thus leaving less guess-work for the reader – or for implementing agents.

Let us start with the simplest scenario. Counting is easy in the cases where the commissioners have actually numbered the recommendations one by one, *and each number contains only one identifiable and implementable action item*. The only truth commission reports in our sample that present their recommendations in such a straightforward way are the reports of Panama (11 recommendations), El Salvador (43 recommendations), and Ecuador (155 recommendations). Here is one example. Nicely and clearly stated in the report's final section conveniently labelled "Conclusions and Recommendations", the Ecuadorian truth commission's second recommendation was to

> Call on those responsible for the violation of human rights so they can, voluntarily, accept their responsibility for the committed violations, provide the information they have available so cases can be solved, and apologize publicly to the victims.[21]

---

[21]   *Informe de la Comisión de la Verdad Ecuador 2010: Sin verdad no hay justicia*, p. 405. Translation from the Spanish original to English by Ecuador research team members.

The remaining 10 reports, by contrast, communicate, group and detail their recommendations in a myriad of different ways. This makes it more challenging to "count" the exact number of recommendations than it may at first appear. There are two principal ordering schema to be addressed: (i) the numbering procedures used by the truth commission reports themselves, and (ii) the commissioners' level of detailed instructions regarding each truth commission recommendation. We have tried to solve these challenges by distinguishing sub-recommendations of actionable items, as discussed in the previous section.

One complication emerges when a truth commission report itself uses numerals and/or letters to identify its truth commission recommendations. However, the way it does so may undercount the things the state is actually being asked to do. The two earliest truth commission reports, which incidentally have the shortest sections on recommendations in our sample, illustrate this point. The parliamentary commission in Uruguay that submitted its report in 1985 recommended the following:

1. Forward background documentation presented by the Parliamentary Investigative Commission [for Disappeared Persons], for all purposes, to the Supreme Court and the Executive Branch.
2. Extend for a period of 90 days the deadline agreed for the above-mentioned Commission, by Resolution of 9 April 1985.[22]

Since the truth commission recommendations are numbered 1 and 2, we may automatically assume that there are indeed two recommendations. However, a closer reading of the text reveals that the first recommendation actually *recommends two separate actions*: (i) submission of its report to the Supreme Court, and (ii) submission of the report to the government. For the purposes of assessing implementation, we treat this as effectively two recommendations because one action could be taken without the other.

Moving to Uruguay's neighbour Argentina, where CONADEP issued its report in 1984, recommendations were confined to the final page of the report. Yet, this single page presents multiple counting options. Since the "counting problem" we encounter for the Argentina truth commission is typical of many other reports – and would presumably apply to truth commission reports in other regions of the world too, we discuss this in some detail here.

---

[22] *Informe Final de la Comisión Investigadora Parlamentaria Sobre Situación de Personas Desaparecidas y Hechos que la Motivaron*, 1985: 8. Translation from the Spanish original to English by CELS research team members.

In their entirety, the recommendations put forward by CONADEP read as follows:

The facts presented to this Commission in the depositions and testimonies speak for themselves. They lead us to recommend to the various State authorities certain measures which will help to ensure that this curtailment of human rights is never repeated in Argentina. The aim of these recommendations is also to press for a judicial investigation into the facts denounced to us. We therefore recommend:

a)   That the body which replaces this Commission speeds up the procedures involved in bringing before the courts the documents collected during our investigation.

b)   That the courts process with the utmost urgency the investigation and verification of the depositions received by this Commission.

c)   That the appropriate laws be passed to provide the children and/or relatives of the disappeared with economic assistance, study grants, social security and employment and, at the same time, to authorize measures considered necessary to alleviate the many and varied family and social problems caused by the disappearances.

d)   That laws be passed which:

   1.   Declare forced abduction a crime against humanity.

   2.   Support the recognition of and adhesion to national and international human rights organizations.

   3.   Make the teaching of the defence and diffusion of human rights obligatory in state educational establishments, whether they be civilian, military or police.

   4.   Strengthen and provide ample support for the measures which the courts need to investigate human rights violations.

   5.   Repeal any repressive legislation still in force.[23]

In essence, CONADEP advised that the evidence it had gathered should be turned over to the courts, and that the courts should act on this information i.e., as the first truth commission in the region, CONADEP made a case for criminal prosecution of human rights perpetrators. Moreover, the commission recommended reparations for those who had family members who were disappeared (a central feature of state repression in Argentina in the 1970s and 1980s). Finally, CONADEP recommended legal reforms in several mentioned fields that were designed to prevent future human rights violations. The substance of the recommendations is clear.

---

[23]   *Informe de la Comisión Nacional Sobre la Desaparición de Personas*, 1986: 446. There is an official English translation of the CONADEP report (1986): www.desaparecidos.org/ nuncamas/web/english/library/nevagain/nevagain_001.htm.

However, if we want to *count* these recommendations, there are several possible options. Paragraph c), in particular, presents several alternatives. Reparations could be counted as one recommendation. Alternatively, this recommendation could be treated as two sub-recommendations:

(i) that the appropriate laws be passed to provide the children and/or relatives of the disappeared with economic assistance, study grants, social security and employment and, at the same time,
(ii) to authorize measures considered necessary to alleviate the many and varied family and social problems caused by the disappearances.

A third possibility would be to break the recommendation down into six parts. Essentially, laws could be passed to provide the children and/or relatives of the disappeared separately with (i) economic assistance, (ii) study grants, (iii) social security, and (iv) employment. At the same time, the state could (v) authorize measures considered necessary to alleviate the many and varied family problems and (vi) social problems caused by the disappearances. Theoretically, government action could proceed at different speeds for each of these measures. Some could be fully implemented, while simultaneously others could be completely ignored.

Finally, paragraph d), strictly speaking, only demands that laws be passed. The details for which laws should be passed is found under paragraphs d) 1–5. In other words, CONADEP itself explicitly breaks out the recommendation labelled d) into five separate sub-recommendations.

Thus, these examples from the very earliest truth commission report in Latin America with one of the briefest sets of recommendations reveals the complexity of counting recommendations – and, later, of assessing implementation. Should we count CONADEP as delivering four, six, eight, nine, or thirteen distinct recommendations? All are viable answers.

In the study, we have chosen to focus on the *substance* of the recommendations rather than slavishly adopting the numbering schemes of the commissions themselves. In the case of CONADEP, we have opted to count its recommendations quoted above as follows:

a)= 1 recommendation
b)= 1 recommendation
c)= 1 recommendation containing 6 sub-recommendations
d)= 5 recommendations

This gives us a total of eight recommendations and six sub-recommendations, or a total of 13 (7 + 6 = 13) distinct measures that the Argentine government considered acting upon.[24] We approach other commissions' recommendations in the same manner.

We took several steps to ensure data consistency across all truth commission reports. First, we provided the research teams with a codebook and written instructions. In addition, we provided training on this issue at the project's Pisac meeting. Finally, we had another team member independently review the recommendations and count them to ensure inter-coder reliability.

3. FORMULATION

The extent of existing research on the 13 truth commissions included in this study varies considerably. Most of the existing research on Latin American truth commissions focuses on Chile's Rettig Commission (Collins 2016; Ferrara 2014; Skaar 1994), and the commissions in El Salvador (Barahona 2016; Ensalaco 1994b; Kaye 1997; Martínez-Barahona et al. 2021; Popkin and Roht-Arriaza 1995), Guatemala (Chapman and Randall 2001; Corntassel and Holder 2008; Crosby 2011; García-Godos and Salvadó 2016; Martín 2021; Popkin and Roht-Arriaza 1995; Quinn 2003), and Peru (Falcón 2005; Garcia-Godos 2008; García-Godos and Reátegui 2016; Gianella Malca 2015; Laplante and Theidon 2010; Laplante and Theidon 2007). Quite a few comparative studies have also been done on two or more of the truth commissions established in the "Southern Cone" (Argentina, Brazil, Chile, Paraguay and Uruguay), often as part of a larger analysis of national transitional justice processes (De Brito 1992; Roniger 1999). In fact, more often than not, the studies of truth commissions form part of a broader analysis of how a particular country has addressed past human rights violations. Other truth commissions have attracted comparatively little attention. Even for the four more widely studied commissions, with the exception of research cited in Chapter 1, relatively little attention has been paid to the implementation of recommendations or the long-term effects of the commissions more generally. Thus, although a full study of the workings of each of these truth commissions would be a valuable contribution, such an enterprise is outside the scope of this study. Nonetheless, we need to know

---

[24]   Note that the main recommendations, "That laws be passed which ..." (in paras. c and d), is just a general introduction to the sub-recommendations and, therefore, has no substantive meaning of its own. As a result, we count only the sub-recommendations as actionable items here. Note also that the CELS team coding of the Argentine data interpreted the recommendations as containing four main and seven sub-recommendations, with a total of nine actionable items (see Table 3.3. in the next chapter). For the purpose of the aggregate data used in this volume, we follow CELS.

something about the context in which recommendations were formulated to understand their nature. While we provide more detail on individual cases elsewhere (Skaar, Wiebelhaus-Brahm, and García-Godos (eds.) 2022) and in Chapter 5 of this volume, in this volume we focus principally on patterns across cases (Chapters 3 and 6).

We thus examine the multiple interests and ideas that shaped the formulation and inclusion (or exclusion) of truth commission recommendations, as well as the particular socio-political and legal contexts in which they were formulated. To start with, the composition of the truth commission, namely commissioners and staff, must be considered. Individual personalities, experience, knowledge, and social networks, among other things, often play an important role in commissions' interpretation of their mandates and in the crafting of final reports. The same factors may be significant for recommendations, which also are formulated within the confines of a truth commission mandate and the broader legal framework in which the truth commission operates. In addition, the formulation of recommendations must be seen in light of other contemporaneous transitional justice and reform activity in the country that might make some recommendations redundant and others too sensitive. For example, if a reparations program has been established prior to the commission's final report – as was the case in Brazil – there may be no need for such a recommendation. Finally, truth commissions formulate their recommendations in the context of political debates among (domestic and international) actors involved in the truth commission process. Commissions face real or imagined pressures to craft recommendations in line with important interests.

The context surrounding the workings of truth commission is relatively well documented in various studies on Latin American truth commissions,[25] providing a good starting point for our research. In an attempt to recreate the circumstances surrounding the formulation of recommendations themselves, our teams interviewed commissioners and relevant actors directly involved or closely monitoring the work of the respective commissions. As will be discussed in Chapter 4, the task of formulating recommendations was given differing degrees of importance in the working plans and agendas of the commissions. In the cases of Paraguay and Ecuador, for example, the commissions' senior staffers were in charge of the recommendations, showing a strong focus on future implementation, while the commissioners focused much more on truth-finding (Reátegui, with Uchuypoma, and Hurtado 2022; Reátegui, Gómez, and Hurtado 2022). The Salvadoran Commission on the Truth, by contrast, wrote its report in New York City, where the foreign commissioners had fled in fear for their safety (Martínez-Barahona et al. 2022).

---

[25] See, among others, Collins (2010); Skaar, García-Godos, and Collins (2016); Wiebelhaus-Brahm (2010a, b).

In collecting primary data about the formulation of truth commission recommendations, we asked our informants about several things. First, we wanted to identify the people and other actors involved in the formulation of the recommendations. Second, we sought a clearer picture of how the drafting process took place. Specifically, we explored the extent to which crafting recommendations was a deliberative process. We asked at what stage of the process truth commissions started to discuss recommendations. Further, we explored how commissioners and staff envisioned the role of truth commission recommendations, both at the time and with the benefit of hindsight. Often, writing final reports, including recommendations, is outsourced and/or rushed to meet deadlines imposed by the commission's mandate. As such, in our interviews, we worked to recreate the role of outside consultants and domestic civil society groups in the formulation process, as well as the role of UN agencies, international organizations, and transnational activists. Relatedly, we also asked whether specific examples from other countries were studied to provide a blueprint. To the extent possible, our goal was to reconstruct the domestic and international context in which commissions devised a set of measures to further address the past and promote progressive change.

The presence of a specific section in truth commission reports entitled "Recommendations" is in itself a good indicator that commissioners attached at least some degree of importance to these measures. The language used, however, in the formulation of specific recommendations is not always clear or indicative of the importance placed on the recommendation. Moreover, language may not provide a clear indication of the authors' intentions. The specific language used in the recommendations can go in the direction of an order or a directive. In that sense, formulation of truth commission recommendations can be analogized to a legal formulation of a "mandatory" directive. The operational relevance for us is how to interpret specific textual formulations when they *do not* have clear "mandatory" directives. We have taken this into account in our own definition of truth commission recommendations.

While all truth commissions focus on truth and victims, some of them are particularly interested in addressing the deep-rooted causes of armed conflict, as was true of the Guatemalan and Peruvian commissions. This orientation influences the kind of recommendations that are likely to be made. There is a difference between recommendations related to the fact-finding functions of truth commissions and those recommendations arising out of the historical interpretation of the past. Our teams have found that some recommendations are so broad and structural in nature, that they can be seen rather as a vision for the future than an implementable directive, as in the case of El Salvador. Thus, it could be that certain recommendations are not intended to be implemented, but rather function like political statements. While there may be a symbolic ambition to such recommendations, their content and formulation might make them "unimplementable".

In the interview situation, one challenge is the issue of memory and how people remember. Recollecting discussions and processes that took place decades ago is obviously difficult, let alone identifying how specific ideas and mechanisms to be included as recommendations were born and developed. As observed by our teams, recommendations themselves are perceived differently depending upon whether and how the government has acted upon them. Accordingly, it might be easier for respondents to identify and remember those recommendations that have been implemented, or at least generated substantial debate, rather than those that passed into oblivion. The opposite can also apply: that some important recommendations (for example, initiating processes of criminal accountability) ignored by a given government take center stage in the memory of commissioners, while other less important recommendations that have been implemented escape from memory. It also is the case that interviewees' recollections may consciously or unconsciously seek to frame their role in as flattering a light as possible. This is a common feature of interview data, particularly when seeking to reconstruct events that happened years, if not decades, in the past. As we illustrate elsewhere (Skaar, Wiebelhaus-Brahm, and García-Godos (eds.) 2022), there was variation in the amount of detail about the formulation process that we were able to uncover. We have sought to deal with these challenges by interviewing as many people as possible.

4. IMPLEMENTATION

Collecting data about the actual implementation of truth commission recommendations presented a number of challenges for our research teams. A first issue relates to the definition of a truth commission recommendation and the presence of sub-recommendations, as discussed above. The complexity of the task of determining if implementation took place, therefore, depends in part on the number of (sub-)recommendations: the higher the number, the more that needs to be tracked down. While breaking down more complex recommendations into implementable action items multiplies the work, as we argued earlier, such an approach provides the most accurate assessment of the extent to which truth commission recommendations have in fact been acted upon.

Our teams discovered that frequently we were not the first to monitor the implementation of truth commission recommendations. Whenever an agency or government institution had already been mandated to follow up on the implementation of recommendations, for example, it was easier to gather information on implementation. Such is the case of Brazil, for instance, where recommendations include a series of institutions to monitor and follow-up on implementation. Follow-up bodies have become a staple of truth commission recommendations precisely for their expected role in the implementation process.[26]

Similarly, the creation of government agencies designed to protect human rights may contribute to the implementation of recommendations. Monitoring and follow-up mandates concerning truth commission recommendations can be found in a diverse array of institutions, such as Ombudsman's offices, national human rights offices, ministerial councils, and reparations programs. In the particular case of reparations programs, such bodies directly monitor and implement recommendations involving victim reparations. In all cases, though, institutions take time to be established and to reach operational levels. More generally, there are differences between those institutions that are set up specifically to supervise truth commission recommendation implementation and government bodies with a more general human rights mandate, as will be discussed in Chapter 5. The supervision bodies are typically small, often temporary, and narrowly mandated to follow-up on the truth commission's recommendations and evaluate their implementation. Though these follow-up bodies vary substantially in form, structure, mandate and permanence, they all share the common goal of making sure that the recommendations of the truth commission are implemented. Sometimes these follow-up institutions are established to focus on only one kind of recommendation, typically on reparations (where national reparations programmes are established). The second form follow-up can take is to task permanent bodies with protecting and promoting human rights more generally, such as Chile's Human Rights Secretariat or Ecuador's National Observatory of Human Rights Violations.

In the previous sections, we mentioned the formulation of recommendations oriented towards more structural societal changes. Our teams observed that this type of recommendation is less likely to be implemented. Among other things, such an undertaking would require the redistribution of wealth and challenging economic elites who typically hold political power as well. For instance, land reform would require complex decisions about whether land should be redistributed, what land should be included, how beneficiaries should be determined, and how existing landowners should be compensated, if at all. These types of recommendations obviously fall far beyond the capabilities

---

[26] Given the years of political turmoil that followed the end of Brazil's truth commission, for example, follow-up bodies can potentially function as a safeguard with regard to future truth commission recommendation implementation. There are now several "toolboxes" or "toolkits" available to truth commissions that were not there for the earlier commissions to use, such as the UN truth commission toolkit document (United Nations, 2010) and the ICTJ's guide on truth commissions (International Center for Transitional Justice, 2013).

(legal and political) of a centralized monitoring agency. Delicate negotiations and political compromise would be necessary. Design and implementation would encompass multiple government agencies, likely across different levels of government. The same type of complexity may apply to certain institutional reforms. In other words, monitoring agencies may not be able to effectively deal with recommendations that require more substantial political will. A more general lesson is that reforms that are deemed to be more technical in nature are less likely to be controversial, whereas politicized issues are more difficult. It can be difficult to predict what recommendations will be more politically contentious, however.

To collect data on implementation, our teams interviewed relevant actors in specialized government agencies. In addition, we consulted with human rights organizations, victims' organizations and other civil society groups with an interest in addressing histories of human rights violations. The emphasis has been placed both on the implementation process and on the identification of implementing events. By implementing events, we refer to some action that moves the recommendation closer to being fully realized. Examples of such events might be the introduction of legislation, the drafting of regulations, or the issuance of executive orders, for example. The process of implementing recommendations may require several steps to come to fruition. Rather than treating recommendations as either implemented or not, our data shows *any* progress toward implementation, even if it was ultimately not fully implemented. To facilitate comparative analysis, we operate with three stages or degrees of implementation: (i) full implementation; (ii) partial implementation, which indicates some action was taken toward implementing the recommendation, but progress remains short of what is envisioned in the final report; and (iii) no implementation, in which we find no evidence of any action being taken to implement. In this way, we provide details on the number of veto points facing each recommendation. Note also that implementation is not necessarily a linear process; there may be advances and setbacks over time. This means that the time period during which data has been collected provides a snapshot of implementation at a given point in history, rather than a fixed verdict on the implementation rate for a particular truth commission recommendation. The data enables researchers to make choices about tracing historical action on each recommendation.

For some recommendations, it proved very difficult to find any information at all. It may have to do with how well-known the truth commission and its report are. It may have to do with the level of knowledge in various ministries and (potential) implementing agencies on the content of recommendations. It may also have to do with the passage of time. Things may have happened in the wake of a truth commission that effectively implemented the recommendation, without implementing agencies knowing that implementation (for instance of an institutional reform) was causally linked to the recommendation. While the recommendation may or may not have been the initial impetus, long battles over implementation may obscure the original spark for change. Where we were unable to find evidence of implementing events or to verify that no action was taken, we have coded them as "no information". Although we treat this category as the same as no implementation in the analysis to follow, we code it separately in the database so other researchers can make their own choices, and perhaps it may prompt future research.

Nonetheless, the amount of information gathered exceeded our expectations. The richness and complexity of the data collected about truth commission recommendation implementation necessitates a narrative form and analysis to be fully described and interpreted. The actual data coding has been carried out in three (or more) stages. First, the individual researcher or research team working on a particular truth commission report collected and coded the rate of implementation to the best of their ability. To ensure that coding was systematic across all cases, the core project team next went through all the datasets and recoded the data to ensure that how we assessed "high" or "partial" or "no" implementation was consistent across cases. Finally, the core research team coded each recommendation according to a list of 10 substantial areas of interest that will be discussed in greater detail in the next chapter. Although Chapter 5 provides a brief summary of this material, the country studies provide more elaborate treatment (Skaar, Wiebelhaus-Brahm, and García-Godos (eds.) 2022).

One challenge in examining the implementation of truth commission recommendations relates to determining causality. In other words, we seek to establish a causal connection between a societal, legal, and/or institutional change and a specific truth commission recommendation. For example, if a process of judicial reform has taken place in a given country and such a process was recommended by the truth commission, what evidence do we require in order to conclude that the reform took place in response to a specific truth commission recommendation? In many instances, truth commissions are not the only actors pressing for various reforms. Proposals may have been circulating in policy circles prior to the commission as well. In countries like El Salvador and Haiti where UN missions were present, they were pressing for many of the same reforms that the respective truth commissions called for in their final reports (Selvik 2021). Where civil society is robust, organizations also may have long been demanding the same types of changes put forward in commission recommendations. Thus, the counterfactual presents itself: had the truth commission not been created, or had it not put forward specific recommendations, might the reforms have happened anyway?

Ultimately, this concern is less significant than it might appear. Truth commissions have long been recognized as relatively weak institutions. They are temporary bodies with limited ability to compel cooperation from governments or any other actor during or after their operations. A whole range of contextual factors shape the likelihood of recommendations being implemented. Among other things, the interests of domestic and international stakeholders, the world-historical time period in which these debates are being waged, and the country's level of development will likely determine whether particular recommendations will be acted upon. We are not suggesting that truth commissions on their own are typically sufficient to bring about dramatic change. Rather, in some instances, truth commission recommendations may serve as catalysts for change by putting new issues on the agenda. At other times, those recommendations may lend added weight to persistent demands. To use statistical language, by instigating or sustaining attention on demands for change, truth commissions may interact with other factors to promote change. In Chapter 5 and in the project's country studies (Skaar, Wiebelhaus-Brahm, and García-Godos (eds.) 2022), we explore these causal relationships in greater depth.

5. SUMMARY AND IMPLICATIONS OF THIS METHODOLOGICAL APPROACH

This chapter has provided a summary of the methodological approach we have taken in this project. Through a combination of field research and archival studies, supplemented by secondary sources, our team has concluded a truth commission study that is unprecedented in scale. We have produced a rich cache of data on the formulation and implementation of truth commission recommendations that will be a boon for transitional justice, human rights, and peacebuilding practitioners and scholars. In the next four chapters, we examine the patterns revealed by the 13 truth commissions' recommendations. In Chapter 3, we examine the tremendous variety of recommendations that have been produced by Latin American truth commissions. In Chapter 4, we examine in greater depth the factors that have shaped the formulation of recommendations across these cases. In Chapter 5, we provide short case studies of implementation for each of the 13 truth commissions analysed in this volume. In Chapter 6, we explore the recommendation characteristics and contextual factors that appear to influence the likelihood of implementation.

CHAPTER 3

COUNTING AND CLASSIFYING RECOMMENDATIONS

The color of truth is grey.

– Andre Gide, author, Nobel laureate (1869–1951)

Physically, the final reports of the 13 Latin American truth commissions that we analyze in this book are very different. When you pick up a copy of the Argentine CONADEP report issued in 1984, you hold in your hand a single volume soft-cover book, slightly smaller than the size of an A4 sheet, weighing about half a kilo. The *Nunca Más* report is still available in bookstores in Buenos Aires and across the country, and it has appeared in numerous editions over the past 30 years – including a full English translation of the entire text. By contrast, the much more recent Peruvian commission's report is a behemoth, counting nine full volumes and thousands of pages. In part because of its size, the report is only available online – and only in Spanish. Some truth commission reports, such as those issued by the commissions in Panama and Uruguay, are difficult to find physically or digitally, either within the country or internationally.

This chapter takes stock of the 13 reports with one overall question in mind: What is the nature of truth commission recommendations in Latin America? We provide a descriptive overview and analysis of the roughly 1000 recommendations made by 13 truth commissions spread across 11 Latin American countries that finalised their reports in a time-period spanning almost three decades (1984–2014). Where commissions issued more than one report, such as interim reports or abridged versions, we focus only on the full, final report. For readers interested in more details, Appendix 2 contains the full names of the truth commissions and their final reports, both in their original language and in English translation, where such exist.

These final reports constitute an impressive variety of documents in terms of length, content, and detail. Yet, they have one thing in common: all the reports seek to influence debate about both the past and the future. They attempt to shape views of the past by constructing a historical narrative of a period of the country's past in which widespread human rights violations occurred. The commissions used their investigative powers to assemble evidence and testimony that served as the basis for their descriptions of that period. The commissions also crafted recommendations in the hope these would remake society in multiple, positive ways.

As explained in Chapter 2, we define a truth commission recommendation as:

> any measure suggested by a truth commission that calls upon the state to take action that addresses past human rights violations and/or is designed to promote non-repetition.

This chapter focuses on the reports' recommendations, i.e. measures that the various commissions hope will be implemented by the state after they conclude their work and hand over their final reports to the government.

The primary aim of this chapter is to provide an overview of all the recommendations made by formal truth commissions in Latin America to date and map the substantive types of recommendations the various truth commissions have made. This is a necessary step before turning to *why* they have crafted them in the way they have, which we consider in the next chapter, and then evaluating their implementation (the subject matter of Chapters 5 and 6). Our working assumption (as outlined in Chapter 1) is that the type and complexity of a truth commission recommendation may be one of the many factors that determine the likelihood of its implementation – and hence also its potential impact.

The chapter starts with a descriptive analysis of the reports of the 13 truth commission reports in Latin America. Based on qualitative analyses of the data collected by our research team, the recommendations are then mapped according to an eight-fold categorization of the substantive content of the recommendations: institutional reform, legal reform, constitutional reform, criminal prosecutions, reparations, non-repetition measures, follow-up measures, and other measures. This mapping permits us to identify major trends in recommendations across reports and country contexts, tracing similarities as well as differences, and to undertake comparative analysis across cases as well as across time.

Two temporal dimensions are of particular interest. First, we explore whether there are differences in recommendations made by truth commissions that were some of the region's earliest experiments versus those that have occurred more recently. In other words, is there a temporal dimension to recommendations? Second, are there differences between those truth commissions that carried out their investigations and issued their reports soon after their country's transition to democracy and/or peace – such as Argentina's CONADEP or Chile's Rettig Commission – and those that issued their reports several decades after the transition to democratic rule, such as Brazil? In short, we explore whether there are systematic differences between transitional and post-transitional commissions. Beyond the temporal dimensions, we also want to know whether there are substantive differences between the recommendations made by truth commissions established after military dictatorships, on the one hand, and truth commissions established after internal armed conflict on the other.

This chapter is organized as follows: The next section provides a descriptive account of the 13 Latin American truth commission reports. Based on a content analysis of these reports, we then identify a list of seven substantive categories of recommendation that can be used for comparative analysis, plus an eighth residual 'other' category. We then move to the recommendations themselves. Section 3 provides a descriptive overview of all the recommendations in the 13 reports, and these are analyzed in more detail in section 4. Section 5 outlines the coding system we have used for recommendations in this project, whereas, in section 6, we comment on the importance of different dimensions or characteristics of recommendations, such as whether they address events in the past or whether they point to the future. The concluding section (section 7) proposes a system for coding the recommendations and offers some tentative conclusions.

1. THE NATURE OF TRUTH COMMISSION REPORTS

Truth commission reports are historical documents and should be interpreted as such. It is, therefore, important to note at the outset that the 13 truth commission reports discussed here were written in response to a variety of different national conflicts, and at different points in what we elsewhere call "world time" (Skaar and Wiebelhaus-Brahm 2013b). As a result, each commission is situated in a distinct national, sub-regional, and international social, political, economic, and legal context. These multi-dimensional contexts, spanning three decades, differ across cases. Whereas most Latin American truth commissions operated in post-military rule contexts, the El Salvadoran, Guatemalan, and Peruvian commissions carried out their work after the end of internal armed conflict. About half of the commissions were set up immediately or soon after the transition to democracy and/or peace (Argentina, the first commissions in Uruguay and Chile, El Salvador, Haiti, Guatemala, and Peru), while the other half were established at least one electoral cycle after transition to democratic rule had occurred (Panama, Paraguay, Ecuador, the second truth commissions in Chile and Uruguay, and Brazil).[27]

---

[27] We use Skaar's (2011) definition of post-transitional justice – originally used narrowly for "prosecution of the military for gross human rights violations *at least one electoral cycle after the transition*" (Skaar 2011b, 29) (emphasis added). Cath Collins also uses the term 'post-transitional justice', but in a more comprehensive way, with no defined cut-off point between transitional and post-transitional justice. Rather, Collins introduces a set of characteristics that distinguish transitional from post-transitional justice (Collins 2010, 22). Both scholars focus mainly on prosecutions in these early works on post-transitional justice. By contrast, in this book, we use "post-transitional" to denote the period in which the search for accountability for past human rights violations continues – beyond the initial transition period.

Levels of international involvement in running truth commissions also vary considerably. Only two commissions in our study, El Salvador and Guatemala, invited commissioners from abroad to provide an aura of neutrality in the midst of very tense political settings. Both were set up as part of UN-sponsored peace processes. The others had only their own nationals as commission members. Haiti's truth commission is unique in having a mix of nationals living in Haiti and Haitians from the diaspora. International influence also may have been exerted in more subtle ways, such as through the provision of funding for commissions and through diplomatic and normative rhetorical pressure.

Just as the contexts for the establishment of the 13 commissions vary across time and space, so, as noted earlier, do the physical aspects of their final reports. There is considerable variation with respect to length, language, the proportion of the report devoted to recommendations, structure, themes covered, and the actual number of recommendations. We provide this descriptive information below so that readers unfamiliar with one or more of these reports may gain a clearer understanding of the basis of our analysis.

1.1. LENGTH

Report length varies tremendously across the region. At one extreme, the entire parliamentary commission in Uruguay's report is only four pages long. By contrast, the Peruvian truth commission report encompasses eight huge volumes spanning thousands of pages. At least physically speaking, these are very different documents to compare.

1.2. LANGUAGE

Eleven of the commission reports are in Spanish, reflecting the fact that most Latin American countries have Spanish as their official language. Brazil's truth commission report is in Portuguese and the Haitian truth commission report is in French. It is worth noting that, although several countries such as Guatemala, El Salvador, and Ecuador have large indigenous populations, to date, no truth commission report has been issued in any indigenous language. Even though the name of the Paraguayan truth commission report, *Informe Final. Anive haguâ oiko*, suggests it is more attune to minority sensibilities, it too is written in Spanish. This overall trend is deeply troubling, for it means that some of the most vulnerable victims, many of whom do not read or speak the dominant language, do not have access to the reports or their findings.

English-language versions exist for some, but not all, of the reports. Of the English translations that exist, some are complete, whereas others are only sections of reports. Some translations are official, others unofficially produced by academics or members of civil society (see Appendix I). In our dataset, all recommendations made in the 13 truth commission reports have been entered in their original language, using the exact wording that is used in the report. English translations are provided for each recommendation, so that the data is bilingual and accessible to a larger audience.[28]

1.3. THE RECOMMENDATIONS SECTION

Most truth commission reports have an easily identifiable section labelled 'Recommendations' (*'Recomendaciones'* in Spanish), which usually – but not always – appears near or at the end of the report. Just as the reports vary greatly in length, they also differ widely with regard to the number of pages allocated to recommendations. As Table 3.1 illustrates, there is no clear relationship between the length of the overall report and the space allocated to recommendations.

Table 3.1. 13 Latin American truth commissions' final reports – an overview

Truth commission	Year of final report	Name of report	Length of report (pp)	Number of pages allocated to recommendations	% of report pages allocated to recommendations
Argentina (CONADEP)	1984	*Informe de la Comisión Nacional sobre la Desaparición de Personas*	420	1	0.3
Uruguay (Parliamentary Commission)	1985	*Informe Final de la Comisión Investigadora Parlamentaria Sobre Situación de Personas Desaparecidas y Hechos que la Motivaron*	4	1	5.0
Chile (Rettig)	1991	*Informe de la Comisión Nacional de Verdad y Reconciliación (Informe Rettig)*	1303	48	3.7
El Salvador (CVES)	1993	*De la locura a la esperanca. La guerra de 12 años en El Salvador*	198	13	6.8
Haiti (CNVJ)	1996	*Si m pa rele: 29 September 1991–14 Octobre 1994*	242	46	19.0

(continued)

---

[28] Official English translations of truth commission reports have been used where such exist. Where not, our research teams have carried out the English translations. Datasets for individual truth commissions are available from the authors upon request. The data sets will also be made available at https://www.cmi.no/data/beyondwords.

Table 3.1 *continued*

Truth commission	Year of final report	Name of report	Length of report (pp)	Number of pages allocated to recommendations	% of report pages allocated to recommendations
Guatemala (CEH)	1999	*Guatemala: Memoria del Silencio*	4383	26	0.6
Panama (PTC)	2002	*Informe Final de la Comisión de la Verdad. "la verdad os hará libres"*	633	1	1.2
Uruguay (Peace Commission)	2003	*Informe Final de la Comisión para la Paz*	85	7	8.2
Peru (CVR)	2003	*Informe Final de la Comisión de la Verdad y Reconciliación*	3371 + 492	189	5.0
Chile (Valech I)	2004	*Informe de la Comisión Nacional sobre Prisión Politica y Tortura (Informe Valech)*	635	18	2.8
Paraguay (CVJ)	2008	*Informe Final. Anive haguá oiko*	113	21	18.6
Ecuador	2010	*Informe de la Comisión de la Verdad Ecuador 2010: Sin verdad no hay justicia*	462	23	5.0
Brazil (CNV)	2014	*Relatório da Comissão Nacional da Verdade*	3388	11	0.3

Source: 13 truth commission reports plus country datasets prepared for this project. See Appendix I for full names of reports.

Note: The information is chronologically ordered, according to when the final reports were issued.

As Table 3.1 shows, the sheer size of the reports varies from the Uruguayan Parliamentary Commission's mere four pages to approximately 4000 pages in the cases of Guatemala, Peru and Brazil (Table 3.1, column 4). The number of pages allocated specifically to recommendations also varies dramatically, from a single page in each of Argentina's CONADEP, Uruguay's Parliamentary Commission, and Panama's truth commission to the almost 200 pages devoted to recommendations by the Peruvian CVR 2003 (Table 3.1, column 5). The amount of space allotted to recommendations in the remaining reports falls somewhere in between these two extremes.

The number of pages allotted to recommendations is a first indication of how extensive they are in some cases. However, the number of pages with recommendations does not necessarily reflect the relative weight given to recommendations in each, as this depends on the length of the report too. The proportion of the total number of pages in the report allocated to recommendations varies from under one per cent (for Argentina, Guatemala, and Brazil) to close to 20 per cent (Haiti and Paraguay) (Table 3.1, column 6). Interestingly, the percentage of pages devoted to recommendations seems to be inversely proportional to the total length of the report. Two of the most extensive reports (Guatemala and Brazil) have relatively speaking the shortest sections on recommendations, whereas two of the shortest reports in terms of page length (Haiti and Paraguay) have the highest percentage of pages devoted to recommendations. Although beyond the focus of this study, this suggests that commissions placed very different levels of emphasis on the construction of historical narratives and the presentation of evidence and testimony.

1.4. HOW TRUTH COMMISSIONS STRUCTURE AND PRESENT THEIR RECOMMENDATIONS

When picking up a truth commission report – regardless of size and length – a good place to start to gain a quick overview of the report's foci is to consult the table of contents (TOC). Towards the end of the TOC, there is usually a section called "Conclusions and Recommendations", or simply "Recommendations". A close reading of how recommendations sections are treated in the TOC of each of the reports reveals a range of issues that the commissioners want the respective governments to address once their work is concluded.

In Table 3.2, we have included the themes explicitly listed in the TOCs of the English translations of all the final reports in the study. This list of around 30 issues describes objectives that should, ideally, be achieved *after* a truth commission has concluded its work. Although there are overlapping concerns with the well-known list of impacts that truth commissions aspire to achieve assembled in the literature by Tristan Anne Borer (2006) and others,[29] there are some important differences. Whereas the aspirations listed in mandates allude to aims or objectives that truth commission wishes to achieve (i.e. healing, justice, national unity, peace, etc.), the recommendations rather flag concrete actions (i.e. administrative reparations, constitutional

---

29 Professed aims, drawn from truth commission mandates, from the widely cited article by Tristan Anne Borer (2006) and a range of other sources, make an impressive list of objectives, including (in alphabetical order) accountability, acknowledgment, amnesty, apology, coexistence, confession, dignity, forgiveness, healing, human rights culture, justice, mental health, mercy, national unity, *nunca más* or "never again", peace, political impact, (non-prosecutorial) punishment, reconciliation, reconstruction, remorse, reparations, repentance, responsibility, restoration, retribution, rule of law, and, finally, truth (Skaar 2018, 6).

reforms, legal reform, forensic anthropological investigations, sexual violence against women etc. (see details in Table 3.2.). One factor accounting for the differences may be that, whereas Borer draws her list of truth commission goals from their mandates, our list draws on final report TOCs for the section on recommendations. Thus, while Borer highlights the priorities of policy-makers who designed the commissions, our data reflect the assessments of commissioners and staff after weighing the evidence.

Table 3.2. Areas highlighted by truth commissions in their sections on recommendations

• administrative reparations	• mechanisms for follow-up of TC recommendations
• compensation	
• eradication of structural causes directly linked to the acts examined	• national plan for forensic anthropological investigations
• follow-up commission	• non-repetition
• follow-up measures to ensure implementation of recommendations	• other recommendations
	• peace promotion
• general recommendations	• preservation of memory
• guarantees of non-repetition	• prevention of future violations
• human rights observation	• recommendations directly related to findings of report
• institutional measures	
• institutional reform	• rehabilitation
• institutional reform to prevent future violations	• reparations
• judicial reform	• restitution
• law reform	• satisfaction
• legal and constitutional reforms	• sexual violence against women
• legal reform, measures aimed at national reconciliation	• specific recommendations

Note: We retained different wording of similar issues to provide a snapshot of the main headings of TOCs as they appear in the reports. Exact duplicates, however, are excluded.

Though most truth commission reports flag important themes in their TOCs, the reports differ widely as to how they further group, define, and specify their recommendations (see Appendix II for details). Some reports present their main issues in a very general way; other reports provide a lot of detailed information on each topic that they flag. We find it helpful to think of the recommendations' section of a truth commission report as a tree with branches. Some trees have only a trunk and a few strong branches, while other trees branch out into minute little twigs. The Panama report, for instance, has one thick trunk. It simply lists its recommendations individually, like numbers on a string, without any obvious organizing principle. One report, Uruguay's 2003 Peace Commission report, merely divides its recommendations into "general" and "specific", with no reference to substantive content. By contrast, the Chilean Rettig report more resembles a huge sprawling tree with many thick branches and numerous thinner ones. It divides its section on recommendations into three different chapters (*capítulos*), each covering a particular theme: (i) recommendations for reparations; (ii) prevention of human rights violations; and (iii) other recommendations. The Chile Valech report, too, is very detailed. Although the Valech report is the only report in our sample that focuses its recommendations on principally one theme (reparations), its TOC provides the most detail on what kind of reparations it recommends. "Reparations" is broken down into symbolic, legal and administrative, and social welfare-related issues, each of which is further broken down into even more refined categories. Social welfare-related issues, for example, are further refined into recommendations regarding, social, health, education, housing, and other. In sum, some reports use multi-level headings to group their recommendations, others not. All this is listed in the TOC.[30]

The variation in complexity among the TOCs of the different reports reflects, of course, the fact that each report is written in a unique environment, responding to specific human rights violations, and making specific recommendations to a government that is operating within a specific national, sub-regional, and international context. This complexity has implications for how we identify and count recommendations, as well as for how we assess their level of implementation. Regardless of organizational principles, it is important to stress that page layout is obviously less important than the substance of the recommendations themselves. Obviously, we need to go beyond the TOCs and dig further into the text in the recommendations' section to find out what the truth commission is actually advising the government to do once the work of the commission has been concluded and the report handed over to the government. This is the focus of the next section.

2. THE UNIVERSE OF TRUTH COMMISSION RECOMMENDATIONS IN LATIN AMERICA

The richness in detail and variety in structure of the recommendations is interesting in and of itself, since we may see it as a statement by the commissioners of what they perceive as most important to communicate to the government. However, this diversity presents significant methodological challenges for comparative analysis. Therefore, as described in greater depth in Chapter 2, we distinguish main recommendations (henceforth TCRs) and sub-recommendations (henceforth sub-TCRs) in the report text. As we explained,

---

[30]   The reports present their levels of recommendations in several different ways, using numbers (Roman, Arabic), letters (capital letters and small letters), bullet points, and/or plain text. Similarly, sub-recommendations are frequently denoted by a series indication, such as a, b, c; i, ii, iii; etc. To locate the actual recommendations and sub-recommendations, as we discuss in Chapter 2, we have gone beyond the notations used by the commissions and examined each actionable item on an individual basis.

we depart from the structure of presentation of recommendations adopted in the reports in favour of establishing a system whereby we identify and record each individual actionable item contained in the recommendation sections of the reports.

We begin by exploring how recommendations are presented in the individual truth commission reports. Specifically, we test whether the more main recommendations and sub-recommendations a report outlines, the more detailed instructions the truth commission offers to the government. This may have implications for the implementation of recommendations, which is the subject of Chapters 5 and 6 of this book. Through careful content analysis of all the recommendations listed in each report, we have identified all main recommendations and sub-recommendations produced by the 13 truth commissions. In total, the methodology outlined in Chapter 2 yielded a dataset of almost 1000 recommendations.[31] Table 3.3 provides the most comprehensive effort at systematizing and counting the recommendations of state-sponsored truth commissions in Latin America over three decades of truth commission practice.

Table 3.3. Main recommendations and sub-recommendations made by 13 Latin American truth commissions (1984–2014)

Truth commission report	Number of main recommendations	Number of sub-recommendations	Total recommendations (= actionable items)
Uruguay Parliamentary Commission 1985	2	0	2
Argentina CONADEP 1984	4	7	9
Uruguay Peace Commission 2003	8	2	10
Panama 2002	11	0	11
Chile Valech I 2004	28	14	42
El Salvador 1993	43	0	43
Brazil CNV 2014	29	14	43
Peru CVR 2003	82	0	82
Guatemala 1999	84	0	84
Chile Rettig 1991	48	62	110
Ecuador 2010	155	1	156

(continued)

---

[31]   Four country expert teams and a number of individual researchers and research assistants recorded all the recommendations in datasets, one for each truth commission. The core team then cleaned up the data to make the entries comparable across datasets and country cases. Exactly how we performed the coding and counting is elaborated in Chapter 2.

Table 3.3 *continued*

Truth commission report	Number of main recommendations	Number of sub-recommendations	Total recommendations (= actionable items)
Haiti CNVJ 1996	75	91	166
Paraguay 2008	177	25	202
Total:	746	216	960

Sources: All original truth commission reports. See Appendix II for details on sources and Appendix IV for summary tables.

Note: Truth commissions are listed from fewest to greatest total number of recommendations.

Our first observation is that *the total number of recommendations varies tremendously from report to report.* At one extreme are the two recommendations for Uruguay's Parliamentary Commission. At the other extreme is the collection of 202 recommendations from Paraguay's commission. Truth commissions seem to fall into three distinct groups based upon the number of recommendations. First, Paraguay, Haiti, Chile Rettig, and Ecuador clearly stand out with more than 100 recommendations each. Second, Peru and Guatemala form a middle group with between 50 and 100 recommendations each. Finally, the remaining truth commissions (Argentina, both Uruguayan commissions, El Salvador, Panama, Chile Valech, and Brazil) issued fewer than 50 recommendations each.

There also is enormous variation in terms of whether reports have sub-recommendations or not. Several commissions have none, whereas Haiti tops the list with 91 sub-recommendations. In addition, Brazil's commission and the two Chilean ones stand out for the number of sub-recommendations relative to main recommendations. We did not find evidence of a conscious strategy in how recommendations are laid out, or that commissions learned from each other. Rather, presentation appears to be the result of authors' professional background and stylistic proclivities. There also does not appear to be a relationship between the number of sub-recommendations and the likelihood of implementation. Densely written recommendations do not appear to jeopardize their effectiveness.

If we organize this data chronologically, as in Figures 3.1 and 3.2 below, the patterns suggest several hypotheses. Specifically, there are no clear patterns in terms of the (total) number of recommendations, although there are some signs that time, political regime and national economy may be relevant. In general, the number of recommendations has increased with more recent commissions, suggesting an expansion of expectations about what state responses to atrocities are appropriate. Human rights and transitional justice norms have expanded with time. Arguably, a truth commission norm has emerged, supported by a growing consensus that they fulfil certain human rights obligations under international law (Hirsch 2007; Hirsch 2014; Wiebelhaus-Brahm 2011). Information and communication technologies and a growing network of transnational expertise facilitate the spread of knowledge about earlier commissions. In addition, although again there are exceptions, commissions that followed civil war tend to produce more recommendations than post-authoritarian commissions. Civil wars tend to engulf more of society and are more likely to generate significant reconstruction needs, so there may be more topics to cover. Civil wars also are more likely to draw in external actors, who may promote a whole range of reforms that commissioners may tap into.

Finally, it appears that commissions in poorer countries produce more recommendations. With the exception of Chile, the wealthier countries of the Southern Cone and Panama had fewer recommendations. Several factors may explain this. One explanation may relate to the strength of civil society. Past research finds that wealthier societies tend to have more robust civil societies (Kamstra et al. 2016). When civil society is weaker, commissioners may decide that they need to take advantage of their platform to highlight a broader range of policy needs. Second, this finding may be related to ethnic diversity. Earlier research finds that ethnic diversity hampers economic development under authoritarian regimes (Collier 2000). The comparative lack of ethnic diversity in wealthier countries in the region may have eliminated the need for specific recommendations targeting indigenous peoples and other minorities. Third, research has also shown that countries with greater ethnic diversity tend to be more violent (Thorp, Caumartin, and Gray Molina 2006). Since minorities in Latin America historically have suffered economic and political marginalization in addition to being targets of violence, commissioners in countries with high ethnic diversity may have seen the report as a unique opportunity to draw attention to these issues. The countries in our sample with the highest ethnic diversity (Guatemala, Ecuador and Peru) all had truth commissions that gave a relatively high number of recommendations.[32] Overall, though, there are not consistent patterns across cases, and there is an insufficient number of cases to explore whether these differences are statistically significant.

Not all truth commission reports present their recommendations in a complex, multi-level format. In fact, five of the truth commission reports use main recommendations only. As mentioned, the *number of sub-recommendations too varies*, from none (Uruguay's Parliamentary Commission, El Salvador, Guatemala, and Panama) to 91 (Haiti). This is reflected in Figure 3.1, where main recommendations are recorded in blue and sub-recommendations are in red. The height of each column shows the total number of recommendations made by each truth commission report, which are listed chronologically according to the year in which they were published. When considering the total number of recommendations, they seem to form two "waves" rather than any form of linear development.

---

[32] For an overview of the percentage of indigenous people as a total of the population, see Thorp, Caumartin, and Gray Molina (2006), 454.

Figure 3.1. Latin American truth commissions' main recommendations
and sub-recommendations (1984–2014)

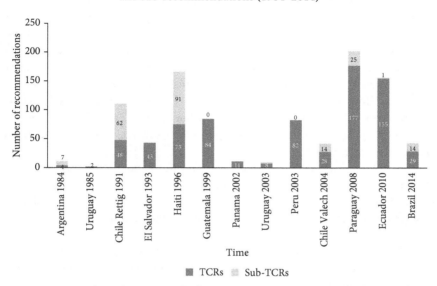

Source: Recommendations' sections of all Latin American truth commission reports. See Appendix IV for details.

However, there seems to be no clear pattern across time, levels of wealth, or the nature of violations in terms of the complexity with which truth commission reports present recommendations. Two commissions stand out in terms of a penchant for differentiating between main and sub-recommendations as an organising principle: Chile Rettig (1991) and Haiti (1996). Two later commissions, Chile Valech (2004) and Brazil (2014), also differentiate between main and sub-recommendations, but to a much lesser extent. Paraguay (2008) too has some sub-recommendations, but, in light of the large number of recommendations, they are proportionally few. We have found no obvious explanation for why these five, and no other truth commission reports, have structured their recommendations in this way. Interviews with commissioners and staff did not reveal any insights. The fact that two of the three reports with the most complex structures are grouped together timewise is most likely a result of chance. In other ways, these three commissions vary significantly across many dimensions, lending further support for the notion that commissions are not mimicking each other. Paraguay and Ecuador may be exceptions; both structured their reports in similar ways, based upon UN guidelines. In the end, the choice of how to organize recommendations may simply reflect the stylistic preferences of the lead authors of the recommendations' sections of the final reports.

In sum, since distinguishing between main and sub-recommendations is basically a reflection of how truth commission reports present recommendations, these distinctions do not necessarily have bearing on the contents or importance of the recommendations. The same actionable items can be presented in multiple ways. We are able only to speculate about the reasons behind commissions' stylistic choices in presenting their recommendations. What one truth commission lists as a main recommendation another may list as a sub-recommendation. In some cases, sub-recommendations may clarify what the main recommendation means. This clearly matters for counting purposes. However, having concluded that the overall number of specific measures a truth commission calls for is what matters most, in much of our subsequent analysis, we do not distinguish between main recommendations and sub-recommendations.

What do we see when we focus on specific actionable items, what we henceforth call simply recommendations. Figure 3.2 below provides a visual impression of the *total* number of recommendations over time. In exploring recommendations, we distinguish the following time periods:

(i) 1980s–1990s: The transition period, in which many countries in Latin America attempted transitions from either military dictatorship or armed civilian conflict to democratic rule;

(ii) 2000–2004: A period characterized by a markedly increased global focus on human rights and transitional justice; and

(iii) 2005–2014: A period characterized by the rise of populism and democratic backlash.

Figure 3.2. Trends in Latin American truth commission recommendations (1984–2014)

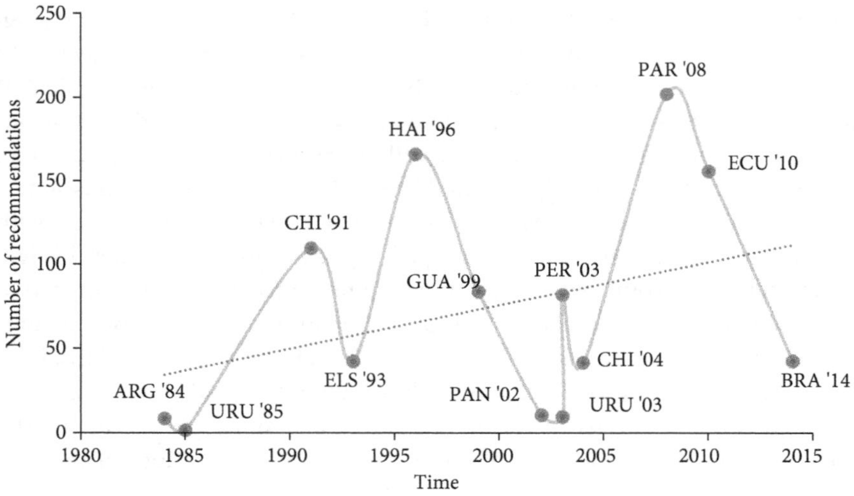

Source: See Table 3.3 above

The data in Figure 3.2 suggest three observations. First, truth commissions themselves are not evenly spread out across time. Most twentieth-century truth commissions were created as part of the so-called Third Wave of Democratization.[33] There also is a distinct clustering of truth commissions around the millennium. Whereas there were only seven truth commissions established during the first 14 years (1984-1999) of the study, four occurred in five years (2000–2004) during the middle period. Then, only three commissions were created during the last 10 years of our data (2005–14). These trends arguably coincide with the gradual spread of a truth-seeking norm (Hirsch 2014, 2007), as there was a gradual expansion of truth commissions in the region. In the twenty-first century, truth commissions have become increasingly separated from transitional contexts (Wiebelhaus-Brahm 2019). This is evident in Latin America where several post-transitional truth commissions have existed.[34]

Second, in line with our expectations, there seems to have been a general increase over time in the overall number of recommendations made in truth commission reports – as indicated by the dashed trend line in Figure 3.2 above. Later truth commissions (i.e., those established after 2000) observed that earlier commissions often proved to be important catalysts for mobilization around justice and human rights issues in their respective countries. Recognizing this opportunity, truth commissions have increasingly used their reports to set the agenda regarding dealing with the past and promoting non-repetition of abuses. Nonetheless, the number of truth commission recommendations did not increase over time in a linear fashion. Rather, the numbers of recommendations in these three periods fall into distinct patterns. There was a steady increase during the first period, topped by Haiti in 1996. Then follows a relatively low number of truth commission recommendations during the middle period (2000–05). A steady decrease from the peak with Paraguay 2008 to the trough of Brazil in 2014 brings the number of recommendations back to roughly the starting point of Argentina in 1984. While on average there is a slow upward trend, *there are only small differences between early and later commissions* in terms of the number of truth commission recommendations they produce.

---

[33]   This is Samuel Huntington's term, used about the wave of democratization that swept the world after the Berlin Wall fell in 1989 (Huntington 1991). The tides have turned, as there is now a distinct ongoing anti-democracy wave affecting all regions of the world (Diamond 2020). This may have negative consequences for transitional justice measures more generally and for the implementation of truth commission recommendations specifically. We see this particularly in Brazil when considering the fate of the 2014 recommendations under the populist government of Jair Bolsonaro since 2019. See more in Chapter 5.

[34]   We note that truth commissions have recently been established in Bolivia (more than three decades after the end of military rule) and in Colombia; the latter as part of a wider transitional justice process linked to the peace agreement. See, for example, Acosta (2017) and Fabra-Zamora et al. (2021).

We also want to know whether there are any systematic differences between truth commissions set up after periods of military authoritarianism versus after periods of internal armed conflict. Two of the three commissions in our sample that were established at the end of internal armed conflict – Guatemala (1999) and Peru (2003) – have numbers of recommendations that fall into the mid-range (defined as between 50–100 recommendations). The third post-armed conflict commission, El Salvador (1993) with 43 recommendations, falls into the high end of the low-number category group (50 recommendations or fewer). Therefore, there seems to be a relationship between the nature of past abuses and the number of recommendations, though our sample is too small to make a definite statement.

Finally, we asked whether there are any systematic differences between so-called transitional and post-transitional commissions in terms of the number of recommendations. We hypothesized that post-transitional commissions would issue fewer recommendations than transitional commissions because, as time passes, some of the transitional justice issues pressing at the time of transition may already have been resolved or are perceived by the truth commission as less urgent. It turns out that there is little empirical support for this in the Latin American context. As documented in Chapter 1, the 13 truth commissions we analyze fall into two groups of roughly equal size. Seven commissions were set up immediately or soon after transitions to democracy and/or peace (i.e., during the first electoral cycle following the transition), whereas we consider the remaining six to be post-transitional commissions. Post-transitional commissions are found in Brazil, Ecuador, Panama, and Paraguay, along with the second truth commissions in Chile and Uruguay. All six post-transitional commissions released their final reports after the turn of the millennium. They (plus the transitional commission in Peru, which released its report in 2003) constitute "late" commissions in terms of world time.

Apart from this commonality, though, the commissions vary tremendously in terms of the number of recommendations that they made to their respective governments. Paraguay and Ecuador are among the top-three of all the truth commissions analyzed in this book with regard to their high number of recommendations. By contrast, Panama is at the very low end. There are probably country-specific reasons for this huge variation. For instance, there was a lack of genuine democratization after the transition in Paraguay as the right-wing Colorado Party remained in power after long-time dictator Alfredo Stroessner was overthrown in a military coup in 1989. It was only after the change in political leadership in 2008 that the truth commission was finally established as the first transitional justice mechanism in the country. Similarly, the truth commission in Ecuador was established two decades after the main violations had taken place in the 1980s, and the truth commission was perceived by many as a cure-all remedy for the country's past (Reátegui and Hurtado 2022).[35] Panama's transition, too, lacked a perfectly clean break with the past. The limited ambitions of the truth commission (reflected in the low number of recommendations) suggest scepticism on the part of commissioners about what they expected would result from their efforts (Rudling 2022).

In fact, the recommendation numbers may reflect levels of confidence that commissioners have in the prospects of implementation. However, the relationship may be an inverted U rather than linear, in which relatively small and large numbers of recommendations may happen where there is low confidence of implementation. Small numbers may be driven by a feeling of "why waste one's time on an extensive list of recommendations when the prospects for implementation are bleak?". At the same time, high numbers may reflect commissioners' feelings that the recommendations represent their one shot to put issues on the agenda. Even if they are not likely to be acted upon, such an opportunity to inject these ideas into the policy discussion may not come along again.

In the cases of Chile and Uruguay, the relatively low number of recommendations may be explained by the fact that they were both follow-up commissions to earlier commissions. Chile Valech addressed only the issue of torture, which had been left out of the mandate of the earlier Rettig Commission. Hence, it is reasonable to expect the range and number of recommendations to be smaller, as many recommendations had already been made by the first truth commission in 1991. In a way, the reverse was true for Uruguay. The first Uruguayan state-sponsored truth commission, the Parliamentary Commission, focused narrowly on the issue of the detained-disappeared and made only two recommendations. Uruguay's second commission, by contrast, had a wider mandate, though it too focused its recommendations relatively narrowly.

The most interesting case here is Brazil's CNV, which, after a thorough investigation into years of human rights violations three decades after they had taken place, decided to make a very limited list of recommendations to the government upon concluding its work. This may be explained by the fact that the CNV also was, for all practical purposes, a follow-up commission building upon earlier truth-finding bodies and reports (Mezarobba 2016, Torelly 2018). Moreover, extensive reparation programs were in place long before the CNV issued its recommendations. Hence, some of the issues normally advocated by truth commissions in their recommendations had already been addressed by previous governments.

---

[35] There is very little literature on the Ecuadorian truth commission. A focus on victims can be found in Reyes et al. (2018).

To sum up:

- First, on average, *late truth commissions tend to have higher numbers of recommendations than early truth commissions.* The relationship is not linear, though, but has the shape of two distinct "waves".
- Second, *the numbers of recommendations made by post-internal armed conflict commissions tends to be in the middle range* (i.e., not very few, but not very many either).
- Third, *there is no distinguishable difference between transitional and post-transitional truth commissions in terms of the number of recommendations that they make.*

This may be because there is a big overlap between "late" truth commissions and post-transitional commissions, as both types were most frequently established after the turn of the millennium.

The descriptive data in this section draws a picture of many different truth commission scenarios. Some commissioners have chosen to put a lot of effort into making many, or long and detailed recommendations. Others have kept the recommendations section short and succinct. Interesting as these different approaches to recommendations may be, we must stress that the *number* of recommendations may not necessarily be what matters most. In general, we should be careful not to draw any conclusions from the number of recommendations regarding the *substantive importance*, as the number of truth commission recommendations tells only part of the story. In the next section, therefore, we move on to the content of these recommendations, which is the focus of the remainder of the chapter.

3. DEVELOPING CATEGORIES OF TRUTH COMMISSION RECOMMENDATIONS

At the outset of this chapter, we posed three key questions: (i) Are there systematic differences between early and later commissions in terms of what kind of recommendations they produce? (ii) Are there systematic differences between the recommendations made by transitional and post-transitional commissions? (iii) Do the recommendations made by post-military dictatorship commissions and those made by commissions addressing violations committed during internal armed conflict differ substantially?

To facilitate comparative analysis, we developed a set of eight categories, including "other", that allow us to systematically analyze the roughly 1000 recommendations articulated in the 13 truth commission reports. We have arrived at these eight categories in a two-step process of (1) analyzing the themes flagged by the reports themselves in their table of contents, and (2) close reading of all individual recommendations made by all commissions. We begin by examining the categories that truth commission reports themselves delineate.

3.1. STEP ONE: THE TABLE OF CONTENTS

Our first selection criterion is the frequency with which categories of recommendations are mentioned in the 13 reports. We have used the TOCs for the reports' sections on recommendations to identify the main themes *as identified by the commissions themselves*.[36] The five themes that are most common (i.e., mentioned in three or more reports) are listed in Table 3.4, whereas thematic issues flagged by only one or two reports are assembled in Table 3.5.[37] In both tables, we list the theme words exactly as they are presented in the English translation of each of the TOCs. This is why the same words may occur more than once. The number of entries in the column "Theme as referenced in report" in Table 3.5 corresponds to the number in the next column.

Table 3.4. **Frequently mentioned recommendation themes in truth commission reports' TOCs**

Theme as referenced in report	Number of reports mentioning theme	Our category name
Reparations/administrative reparations	6	**Reparations**
Follow-up commission/mechanisms for follow-up of truth commission recommendations/follow-up measures to ensure implementation of recommendations	5	**Follow-up mechanisms**
Law reform/legal reform	3	**Legal reform**
Institutional reform to prevent future violations/institutional reform (to strengthen democratic process)/ institutional reform/institutional measures	3	**Institutional reform**
Non-repetition/guarantees of non-repetition/prevention of future violations	3	**Non-repetition measures**

Source: TOCs of 13 truth commission reports.

Thus, looking at the themes mentioned in three or more of the truth commission reports, five clear concerns stand out: reparations, follow-up measures, legal reform, institutional reform, and non-repetition measures.

---

[36] See section 3 in this chapter and Appendix II for more details on the themes revealed in reports' tables of contents.

[37] Note that one truth commission report – the first Uruguayan report from 1985 – simply divides its recommendations into "specific recommendations" and "general recommendations".

Table 3.5. Less frequently mentioned recommendations themes

Themes mentioned in two reports	Themes mentioned in one report
– compensation – human rights observation – preservation of memory/satisfaction – restitution – rehabilitation	– eradication of structural causes directly linked to the acts examined – judicial reform – measures aimed at national reconciliation – national plan for forensic anthropological investigations – peace promotion – recommendations directly related to findings of report – other recommendations – sexual violence against women

Source: TOCs of 13 reports.

There are overlaps in the content of themes listed in Tables 3.4 and 3.5, which means that commissions may use different words to denote the same thing or may operate with different levels of specification. For the most part, the themes in Table 3.5 are more specific sub-categories of those mentioned in Table 3.4. Four of the five themes mentioned in two truth commission reports (preservation of memory/satisfaction, restitution, compensation, rehabilitation) are, in fact, central components of reparations and/or measures of non-repetition. Judicial reform may be considered part of institutional reform. That Truth commission reports operate with different key words while referring to the same thing is confirmed in step two of this analysis.

3.2.   STEP TWO: THE RECOMMENDATIONS THEMSELVES

To ensure that no important categories of recommendations in the reports have been overlooked, we have supplemented the list of themes drawn from the tables of contents with a substantive reading of each of the 960 recommendations. In our substantive reading of the recommendations, we kept in mind various questions.[38] Is the recommendation victim-centered? Is it aimed at institutions, laws or constitutions? Are there any common themes not captured by commissions' own categorization explored in step one?

Two general themes stand out that were not specifically delineated by commissions themselves in their reports. One is *criminal accountability* for perpetrators of human rights abuses. Since a truth commission has no prosecutorial power, but may nevertheless recommend judicial action in the

---

[38]   We particularly focused on the three reports that either list strings of recommendations (Panama and Ecuador) or that divide recommendations into "general" and "specific" (Uruguay) in search for additional themes.

field of human rights abuse, we explore the frequency with which commissions recommend criminal prosecution of the perpetrators of human rights violations. The second is *constitutional reform*. We decided, for analytical purposes, to distinguish legal reform from constitutional reform because the approval procedures for the two are markedly different in most countries. Numerous other issues are mentioned in the various reports, but do not form sufficiently large groups to warrant separate categories for the purposes of comparative analysis.

Recommendations that do not fit into any of the main categories have been placed in an "other measures" category.[39] This brings the total number of recommendation categories to eight.

(1) **Institutional reform**: reform of the courts, the police, the military, public prosecutors, and/or other state institutions; may include measures to improve civilian oversight and public accountability, to introduce new training programs, and the like; may seek the creation of new institutions, such as a human rights ombudsperson;[40]

(2) **Legal reform**: creation of new laws or revision of existing laws; *Habeas corpus* laws and other measures designed to curb the state's ability to detain individuals arbitrarily and indefinitely are prominent examples;

(3) **Constitutional reform**: constitutional amendments;

(4) **Criminal prosecution**: prosecution of individuals responsible for past crimes, through truth commissions either having established implicit or explicit evidentiary criteria and, based upon them, having identified individuals they have concluded are responsible in their final report; or turning over evidence to the state and urging public prosecutors to use it as the foundation for building criminal cases;

(5) **Reparations**: reparations for victims in one or more forms, including compensation, restitution, rehabilitation, and satisfaction; may be material and/or symbolic measures; may target individuals, groups, and/or communities as intended beneficiaries;

(6) **Non-repetition measures**: reduction of probability that the types of human rights violations that occurred in the past will recur in the future; may include educational reform and other measures designed to promote awareness and understanding of other groups in society;

---

[39] For information on the questions that worked as guidelines for the coders, see excerpts from the codebook in Appendix III.

[40] For a comprehensive discussion of institutional reform recommendations made by seven truth commissions from different regions of the world (Chile, Guatemala, Kenya, Peru, Sierra Leone, South Africa, and Timor Leste), see Mayer-Rieckh and Varney (2019). The report organizes these recommendations into six groups: security sector; vetting; legal and constitutional reforms; measures related to human rights; judicial reforms; and other institutional reforms. Our definition of institutional reform is more specific than theirs.

(7) **Follow-up measures**: creation of bodies to carry on commission work; may monitor or coordinate the implementation of truth commission recommendations; may further address past human rights violations such as by extending investigations or managing reparations programs; and

(8) **Other measures**: addressing past human rights abuses by means not covered by the other categories articulated above.

Importantly, the seven substantive categories are not intended to be exhaustive or mutually exclusive. Particularly, there may be blurred borders between constitutional, legal and administrative reforms; between legal reforms and non-repetition; and between reparations and non-repetition measures, to cite just three possibilities. Our primary goal here is to provide a descriptive overview of some of the ways in which the content of recommendations can be categorized. Any one given recommendation may fit several recommendation categories. This, in our opinion, reflects the true complexity of the recommendations. We shall return to this point in more detail later in this chapter. But first, a note of clarification of the potential overlap between reparations and non-repetition measures.

3.3. CLARIFYING THE LINK BETWEEN REPARATIONS AND MEASURES OF NON-REPETITION

All but one of the truth commission reports we have analyzed has issued recommendations regarding reparations, making the importance of reparations in post-dictatorship/post-conflict Latin America unquestionable.[41] This aligns with global as well as regional law and practice. In this particular category of recommendations, victims are in focus. Victims' rights encompass the right to truth, the right to justice, and the right to reparations. These rights have been the subject of UN treaties and rulings from the Inter-American Court of Human Rights. According to the United Nations *Basic Principles and Guidelines*, there are five central components to reparations:[42]

> "*Restitution* should, whenever possible, restore the victim to the original situation before the gross violations of international human rights law or serious violations of international humanitarian law occurred". This includes, for example, the return of lost property, civic status, or jobs.

---

[41] See Garcia-Godos (2008); de Greiff (2006a), and the chapters on Argentina, Chile, Brazil, El Salvador and Haiti in Skaar, Wiebelhaus-Brahm, and García-Godos (eds.) (2022).

[42] UN General Assembly Resolution (2005). See: http://www.un.org/ga/search/view_doc.asp?symbol=A/%20RES/60/147. For the concrete examples of measures used under each point we draw on Arthur (2016, 292).

"*Compensation* should be provided for any economically assessable damage, as appropriate and proportional to the gravity of the violation and the circumstances of each case, resulting from gross violations of international human rights law and serious violations of international humanitarian law". Measures include, for example, cash payments or pensions provided to victims for the harm they suffered, costs to cover legal assistance and medical services etc.

"*Rehabilitation* should include medical and psychological care as well as legal and social services".

"*Satisfaction* should include, where applicable, any or all of the following:
(a) Effective measures aimed at the cessation of continuing violations;
(b) Verification of the facts and full and public disclosure of the truth to the extent that such disclosure does not cause further harm or threaten the safety and interests of the victim, the victim's relatives, witnesses, or persons who have intervened to assist the victim or prevent the occurrence of further violations;
(c) The search for the whereabouts of the disappeared, for the identities of the children abducted, and for the bodies of those killed, and assistance in the recovery, identification and reburial of the bodies in accordance with the expressed or presumed wish of the victims, or the cultural practices of the families and communities;
(d) An official declaration or a judicial decision restoring the dignity, the reputation and the rights of the victim and of persons closely connected with the victim;
(e) Public apology, including acknowledgement of the facts and acceptance of responsibility;
(f) Judicial and administrative sanctions against persons liable for the violations;
(g) Commemorations and tributes to the victims;
(h) Inclusion of an accurate account of the violations that occurred in international human rights law and international humanitarian law training and in educational material at all levels."
Measures could be, for example, the offering of public apologies and full disclosure of the facts about state-led abuse.

"*Guarantees of non-repetition* should include, where applicable, any or all of the following measures, which will also contribute to prevention:
(a) Ensuring effective civilian control of military and security forces;
(b) Ensuring that all civilian and military proceedings abide by international standards of due process, fairness and impartiality;
(c) Strengthening the independence of the judiciary;
(d) Protecting persons in the legal, medical and health-care professions, the media and other related professions, and human rights defenders;

(e) Providing, on a priority and continued basis, human rights and international humanitarian law education to all sectors of society and training for law enforcement officials as well as military and security forces;

(f) Promoting the observance of codes of conduct and ethical norms, in particular international standards, by public servants, including law enforcement, correctional, media, medical, psychological, social service and military personnel, as well as by economic enterprises;

(g) Promoting mechanisms for preventing and monitoring social conflicts and their resolution;

(h) Reviewing and reforming laws contributing to or allowing gross violations of international human rights law and serious violations of international humanitarian law".

Measures include, for example, reforms of abusive state institutions to ensure such crimes do not recur.

In the UN framework then, guarantees of non-repetition are considered part and parcel of reparations. Moreover, this section is the most detailed of the five components. We chose to distinguish non-repetition as a separate thematic category of recommendations, distinct from other types of reparations, because we find it allows us to distinguish measures aimed at addressing past harms to individuals or collectives (essentially backward-looking measures) from those aimed at the reform of laws and state institutions (essentially forward-looking). We therefore use the term "reparations" to refer to backward-looking measures, while "guarantees of non-repetition" refers to forward-looking measures in the remainder of the book. According to prominent legal scholar and transitional justice expert Naomi Roht-Arriaza (2016, 9), guarantees of non-repetition serve an explicitly preventative purpose. Their meaning and content have changed across time, but they may include demobilization and dissolution of armed groups as well as vetting and institutional reforms focused on the security and justice sectors, among other things. According to Onur Bakiner,[43] almost all truth commissions recommend something along these lines, but the broad nature of these recommendations makes assessment very difficult. Guarantees of non-repetition can include legislation; education; the creation of new institutions (like the Ombudsman's office) or the reform/ elimination of existing institutions (especially repressive institutions); rule-of-law reform; security-sector reform; and the cultivation of a culture of human rights observance/tolerance/social justice. Because they are forward-looking, most of these measures are likely to also have been recommended by other domestic and international actors. As such, domestic and international

---

[43] Personal communication.

pressure and the recommendations themselves may be mutually reinforcing, thereby increasing the chances of change.

4. WHAT HAVE LATIN AMERICAN TRUTH COMMISSIONS RECOMMENDED?

Table 3.6 below provides an overview of recommendations in each of the eight categories developed in the previous section by commission.

Table 3.6. Distribution of main categories of truth commission recommendations

Truth commission recommendation categories	Truth commission report has at least one recommendation belonging to this category	Recommendation in this category NOT mentioned in report
Institutional reform	Argentina 1984, Brazil 2014, Chile Rettig 1991, Chile Valech I 2004, Ecuador 2010, El Salvador 1993, Guatemala 1999, Haiti 1996, Panama 2002, Paraguay 2008, Peru 2003, Uruguay 2003	Uruguay 1985
Legal reform	Argentina 1984, Brazil 2014, Chile Rettig 1991, Chile Valech I 2004, Ecuador 2010, El Salvador 1993, Guatemala 1999, Haiti 1996, Panama 2002, Paraguay 2008, Peru 2003, Uruguay 2003	Uruguay 1985
Constitutional reform	Brazil 2014, Chile Rettig 1991, Chile Valech I 2004, Ecuador 2010, El Salvador 1993, Haiti 1996, Paraguay 2008, Peru 2003	Argentina 1984 Guatemala 1999 Panama 2002 Uruguay 1985 Uruguay 2003
Criminal prosecutions	Argentina 1984, Brazil 2014, Chile Rettig 1991, Ecuador 2010, Guatemala 1999, Haiti 1996, Panama 2002, Paraguay 2008, Peru 2003	Chile Valech I El Salvador 1993 Uruguay 1985 Uruguay 2003
Reparations	Argentina 1984, Brazil 2014, Chile Rettig 1991, Chile Valech I 2004, Ecuador 2010, El Salvador 1993, Guatemala 1999, Haiti 1996, Panama 2002, Paraguay 2008, Peru 2003, Uruguay 2003	Uruguay 1985
Measures for guarantees of non-repetition	Argentina 1984, Brazil 2014, Chile Rettig 1991, Chile Valech I 2004, Ecuador 2010, El Salvador 1993, Guatemala 1999, Haiti 1996, Panama 2002, Paraguay 2008, Peru 2003, Uruguay 2003	Uruguay 1985

(continued)

Table 3.6 *continued*

Truth commission recommendation categories	Truth commission report has at least one recommendation belonging to this category	Recommendation in this category NOT mentioned in report
Follow-up measures	Argentina 1984, Brazil 2014, Chile Valech I 2004, Ecuador 2010, El Salvador 1993, Guatemala 1999, Haiti 1996, Panama 2002, Paraguay 2008, Peru 2003, Uruguay 2003	Chile Rettig 1991 Uruguay 1985
Other	Chile Valech I 2004, Ecuador 2010, El Salvador 1993, Haiti 1996, Panama 2002, Paraguay 2008, Peru 2003, Uruguay 1985, Uruguay 2003	Argentina 1984 Brazil 2014 Chile Rettig 1991 Guatemala 1999

Table 3.7 presents our findings in a slightly different way by taking into account the number of recommendations in each category i.e., how many recommendations each commission made (second column), the number of thematic areas covered by the recommendations (third column), and the thematic areas *not* covered (last column).

Table 3.7. Number and thematic foci of recommendations

Truth Commission	Total number of recommendations	Thematic areas covered	Thematic area NOT covered by recommendations
Uruguay 1985	2	1	Institutional reform, legal reform, constitutional reform, criminal prosecutions, reparations, non-repetition measures, follow-up measures
Argentina (CONADEP) 1984	9	6	Constitutional reform, other
Chile Rettig 1991	110	6	Follow-up measures, other
Uruguay Peace Comm. 2003	10	6	Constitutional reform, criminal prosecutions
Panama 2002	11	7	Constitutional reform
Chile Valech I 2004	42	7	Criminal prosecutions
Brazil CNV 2014	43	7	Other
El Salvador 1993	43	7	Criminal prosecutions
Peru CVR 2003	82	8	
Guatemala 1999	84	6	Constitutional reform, other
Ecuador 2010	156	8	
Haiti CNVJ 1996	166	8	
Paraguay 2008	202	8	
Total number of recommendations:	960		

(continued)

Table 3.7 *continued*

Sources: Original truth commission reports for all commissions. See also Appendix IV for summary tables in which the number of truth commission recommendations are calculated.

Note: Truth commissions are ordered according to the number of recommendations they have given, from low to high.

The two tables suggest some important conclusions.

(i) Most truth commission reports have made recommendations in most of our categories

The most interesting finding is that, regardless of how many recommendations they craft, *Latin American truth commissions have generally opted for a wide range of recommendations*, spread across several categories. In fact, the overwhelming majority of truth commission reports include all or almost all recommendation categories. Even commissions that made few recommendations spread them across many different thematic areas. The only significant exception is the first state-sponsored truth commission in Uruguay, which, in its four-page report *Informe Final de la Comisión Investigadora Parlamentaria Sobre Situación de Personas Desaparecidas y Hechos que la Motivaron* (1985), focused its recommendations in line with its very narrow mandate. As such, it recommended only two things: that its report be submitted to the Supreme Court of Justice; and that it be submitted to the executive. Because of its very specific mandate, brief report, and abbreviated set of recommendations, this report is substantially different from the other truth commission reports in our analysis.[44] Nevertheless, we decided in favour of inclusion as we wanted to know if this commission was an important predecessor of the later Peace Commission of 2003. Since its report was so thin and its recommendations so narrow, it does not figure prominently in our analysis.

(ii) Almost all truth commission reports recommend reform of the state apparatus and the legal system

All but one truth commission (Uruguay 1985) issued recommendations pertaining to institutional reform or legal reform. This in line with findings from other regions of the world. As stated by Mayer-Rieckh and Varney (2019, 19),

> Truth commissions tend to focus on institutions and groups in the security sector that allowed, facilitated, promoted or committed violations. Such institutions generally

---

[44] Note that some scholars do not consider the Uruguayan *Comisión Investigadora Parlamentaria Sobre la Situación de Personas Desaparecidas y Hechos que la Motivaron* a 'true' truth commission.

include the armed forces, the police, intelligence services, penitentiary services as well as parastatal and non-state armed groups.

These measures are a central focus of efforts to promote non-repetition. Note that there were wide-spread judicial and legal reforms in most Latin American countries and the Caribbean in the 1990s and early 2000s, heavily supported by the World Bank and the Inter-American Development Bank (Biebesheimer 2000; Dakolias 1996; Domingo 1999; Rowat, Malik, and Dakolias 1995; Shihata 1995). Truth commissions' concern with reform of state institutions should be viewed against this backdrop. While truth commissions recommended institutional and legal reform with improved human rights protection as an explicit aim, judicial reform in the region was undertaken for a host of other reasons too, such as to facilitate foreign direct investment and enhance economic development (Lora 1997) and to enhance the power of an incumbent president – judicial reform as a so-called insurance policy (Finkel 2008). Importantly, increased human rights protection may be the (unintended) consequence of judicial and legal reform even in the cases where there are factors other than human rights concerns motivating the reforms (Skaar 2011b). In the end, some reforms of the state apparatus and the legal systems may be traced back to truth commission recommendations, others not.

(iii) Almost all truth commission reports recommend reparations

All but one truth commission (Uruguay 1985) recommended reparations to victims. This was not unexpected since many of the truth commissions in the Latin American region were established by the state in response to demands from victims' organizations, claiming "truth" and "justice". We should also not forget the development of global norms of reparations during this period (de Greiff 2006b, de Greiff 2006c, 2008) and the importance of the Inter-American Court of Human Rights (IACtHR) in promoting regional norms of reparations through its many rulings involving several of the countries in our analysis. Reparations recommended by the IACtHR included victims' right to truth, the abolition of amnesty laws (because these laws precluded prosecution of perpetrators of human rights abuses and hence provided obstacles to victims' right to justice), and the right to reparations.[45]

---

45   For specific Court rulings, see for example, IACtHR (10 September, 1996) and IACtHR (2011). For a more general discussion of the role of the Inter-American Court and Commission with respect to transitional justice and victims' rights, see Salazar and Antkowiak (2007) and in particular Cassel (2007) and Dulitzky (2007). See also Pasqualucci (2013) and Sandoval (2008).

(iv) Almost all truth commission reports have recommended non-repetition measures

All but one truth commission (Uruguay 1985) recommended some form of non-repetition measure. This is supported by the broader literature that finds that many Latin American truth commissions made a call for "*nunca más*" (Brody and Gonzáles 1997; Crenzel 2012). At least some of this strong focus on *nunca más* – or "never again" – should be viewed in the light of civil society organizations demanding truth, justice and never again. There was a strong NGO movement, particularly in some of the Southern Cone countries (Chile, Argentina, and Uruguay), that had non-repetition on its agenda, exhorting strong pressure on the governments during and after their transitions to democracy (Barahona de Brito 1997; Roniger 1999; Skaar 1994).

(v) Few truth commission reports have proposed constitutional reform

Constitutional reform is the category in which the fewest truth commissions have made recommendations. Eight truth commission reports included recommendations advocating constitutional reforms (Chile Rettig, El Salvador, Haiti, Guatemala, Peru, Chile Valech, Ecuador, and Brazil), while the remaining five (Argentina, Uruguay 1985, Uruguay 2003, Panama, and Paraguay) did not. Why? Constitutional reform (along with judicial reform) was widespread in Latin America in the 1980s and 1990s (Harris and Roa-García 2013; Nino 1989; Nino 1992; Sabsay 1998; Van Cott 2002). Many countries used transitions from military dictatorship to democratic rule or from internal armed conflict to peace to revise their constitutions; so-called constitutional moments. The work of truth commissions and their emphasis on constitutional reform (or not) should be seen against this backdrop. Latin American truth commissions were usually the product of political compromises in which military-era constitutions were kept in place. One hypothesis for this finding is that commissions that did include constitutional reform may have calculated that their recommendations would provide additional ammunition for domestic and international advocates pressuring governments to dismantle anti-democratic features of the political system. By contrast, the commissions that avoided advocating constitutional reform may have done so because they were pessimistic about the possibility of success or feared the military would use it as a pretext to return to power. Argentina and Uruguay 1985 may exemplify this logic best. The first truth commission in Chile, the Rettig Commission, also carried out its work in a context where several presidential attempts at amending the Pinochet-designed constitution had failed (Ensalaco 1994a; Montes and Vial 2005). The other three commissions that were silent on constitutional reform were post-transitional cases, so constitutional issues might have been dealt with already or they may have concluded that the impetus for such reforms would be harder to instigate outside of transitional contexts.

(vi) Some truth commissions call for criminal prosecutions

Some, but far from all, truth commissions recommended criminal prosecution of alleged perpetrators of human rights abuses. Criminal prosecution of those responsible for human rights violations has been one of the most contentious issues in transitions from authoritarian rule and/or internal armed conflict to democratic rule in Latin America (Huyse 1995; Leebaw 2008; Lessa et al. 2014; Malamud-Goti 1991; Méndez 1997; Nino 1991; Pion-Berlin 1994; Skaar 1999). Since most Latin American truth commissions were accompanied by amnesty laws, passed either before the commissions were set up or soon thereafter, the legal room for prosecution of alleged perpetrators of human rights breaches was typically limited. In fact, only Paraguay did not have (and still does not have) an amnesty law – mainly because the Stroessner government enjoyed significant support even after he left power, thereby making prosecutions politically unlikely (Collins 2016b).

For the other 12 truth commissions, commissioners had to weigh how to respond to existing amnesty laws. While nine commissions recommended criminal prosecutions (Argentina 1984, Brazil 2014, Chile Rettig 1991, Ecuador 2010, Guatemala 1999, Haiti 1996, Panama 2002, Paraguay 2008, Peru 2003), four others (Chile Valech I, El Salvador 1993, Uruguay 1985, and Uruguay 2003) did not. Of those in which such recommendations were absent, the presence of amnesty laws at the time when the commission reports were released may provide a partial explanation for their reluctance to pronounce on criminal prosecution. However, given the fact that many other commissions made the opposite choice in similar circumstances, other factors must be responsible for this reluctance. In the Chilean case, creative legal strategies were already slowly eroding the amnesty and some prosecutions had begun by the time the Valech Commission issued its report, so, in that case, commissioners may have reasoned that such a recommendation was unnecessary. In El Salvador, the largely foreign-run commission knew it would face a hostile reception from the government and legislature. In Uruguay, referenda had demonstrated public support for existing amnesties (Lessa and Fried 2011; Skaar 2011a).

Note that we define criminal prosecutions narrowly. In particular, we look for recommendations making specific calls for the prosecution of individuals for past crimes. If we had broadened the category to include all suggested measures that might in some way make prosecutions more likely, the picture may have been different. A broader classification of criminal prosecution could potentially have included anything ranging from our narrow definition of an explicit order to prosecute (as Argentina's CONADEP and Panama's commission did, for example)[46] to suggestions of criminal justice reform that may, in turn, increase the likelihood for criminal prosecutions for past human rights violations. Of the commissions that did not explicitly mention criminal prosecution, one must differentiate between the commissions that simply refrained from mentioning criminal prosecution and those with a mandate that explicitly forbade such a recommendation. For instance, the Guatemalan commission was not allowed to name names and did not include names of alleged perpetrators or a call for prosecution in its report.[47]

(vii) Truth commissions generally recommend follow-up measures

All truth commissions but two (Uruguay 1985 and Chile Rettig 1991) recommended follow-up measures in their final reports. We have defined follow-up measures narrowly to include only the establishment of so-called follow-up bodies to oversee the implementation of recommendations. In fact, many truth commissions called on the state to set up such bodies. For instance, the last recommendation made by the Panamanian truth commission was "To create a follow-up body to lend continuity to all the material investigated, the declassified documents, the DNA evidence, as well as the remains recovered, which were produced by the investigations of the Panamanian Truth Commission". In theory, the presence of such follow-up bodies puts continued pressure on the state to act upon other recommendations, which are measures designed to further address the past and prevent violations in the future.

Sometimes, the devil is in the details. Although Chile Rettig did not directly include a call for a follow-up body among its 48 recommendations, it recommended that specific measures be taken to compensate the relatives of the victims. As a result, the legislature enacted Law No. 19.123, published in the Official Daily on February 8, 1992, to create the National Corporation for Reparation and Reconciliation (*Corporación Nacional de Reparación y Reconciliación* (CNRR)), a temporary, decentralized state organ under the Ministry of the Interior with a two-year mandate to provide compensation to victims' families and to develop programs to foster a "culture of respect for human rights" in Chile (Edelstein 1994). According to Collins (2016a, 128), the CNRR was a successor body designed to complete assessment of still-pending individual cases, locate the disappeared, and administer

---

[46]   Argentina's CONADEP urged that "b) That the courts process with the utmost urgency the investigation and verification of the depositions received by this Commission". In a similar vein, the Panama truth commission report recommended that the government "reopen those cases of human rights violations which occurred during the period under investigation, where the investigations of the Truth Commission have contributed new elements of conviction."

[47]   See http://www.usip.org/publications/truth-commission-guatemala.

reparations.[48] In practical terms, then, although not directly recommended by Chile Rettig, the CNRR was set up in its wake and was for all practical purposes a follow-up body in line with the follow-up bodies recommended by other truth commissions in our study.[49] Thus, aside from the unusual 1985 Uruguayan Parliamentary Commission, follow-up bodies are almost universal in Latin America.

(viii) The "other" category

Striking a balance between a typology that is nuanced enough to sufficiently cover the major differences between various types of recommendations while at the same time not over-simplifying complex realities is a challenge. Though few in actual numbers, some recommendations did not fit into any of our seven substantive categories. These we have collected in an "other" category. A more refined dataset or one developed for other regions may find recommendations dealing with such things as purges/vetting and education to be more plentiful and, hence, find such categorizations more useful.

Vetting is a common global transitional justice practice (Bates, Cinar, and Nalepa 2020). Like with prosecution and reparation, truth commissions sometimes recommend vetting processes. In Latin America, though, vetting has been an important issue only in the Salvadoran truth commission report, so we do not include this as a separate category here.[50] If analyzing truth commission reports in Eastern Europe or Africa, for example, vetting might be a useful category.

The same applies to education. In the 13 truth commission reports we examined, "education" refers to a wide range of activities. Most often, it refers to various forms of human rights education for different sectors of society. Sometimes, the focus is on technical training of government officials such as judges, police, and the military, where the aim is to ensure a better knowledge of human rights as a step to prevent recurrence of violent acts. For instance, the Peruvian truth commission recommended "a sustained training program for judges, prosecutors and lawyers in human rights, humanitarian law and democratic culture". In other instances, education refers to improved

---

[48]   In 1996, the CNRR added almost 900 names, giving a cumulative total of 3,195 recognized victims of death and disappearance at that time. The final fate and whereabouts of 1,183 of the 3,195 remained unknown upon the CNRR's conclusion (Collins 2016a, 128).

[49]   Due to strict coding procedures, we have not recorded this as a follow-up body in our dataset.

[50]   On the subject of vetting in the Latin American context, see also Bakiner (2016, 89). On vetting and lustration, see Chapter 6, section 3.4 of this book.

human rights knowledge among educators and school children. Still other recommendations call for free education for children of victims of state abuse, which is a form of reparation and might be linked to fostering a right to education in general. Thus, recommendations mentioning education target a wide variety of actors and, depending upon their focus, may be tied to other categories such as legal or institutional reform, or to reparations. Therefore, we have decided not to include it as a separate category in our analysis, but rather to code recommendations referring to education according to the goal that fostering or facilitating (human rights) education was meant to promote.

5. TOWARD A CODING SYSTEM

Since our recommendation categories are not exhaustive or mutually exclusive, a given recommendation may fit multiple categories. We may think of this as a Venn diagram, where the overlapping sections mark overlapping categories. An example from Brazil's truth commission illustrates this point nicely. The second recommendation listed in the commission's report calls for the

> Establishment, on the part of competent bodies, of *legal responsibility – criminal, civil and administrative* – held by public officials in the gross human rights violations committed during the period under CNV investigation, removing for said authorities the applicability of amnesty provisions set forth in the articles of Law No. 6683 of August 28, 1979, as well as other constitutional and legal provisions (emphasis added).

Thus, this recommendation falls at the intersection of three different categories (institutional reform, legal reform, and criminal prosecution), as illustrated in Figure 3.3 below.

Figure 3.3. Illustrating overlapping categories in recommendations: the example of Brazil

Recommendations vary considerably in their complexity. Some are short and specific. Others are complex, tying together disparate goals in a single recommendation. Had we repeated this exercise for all recommendations in the dataset, Venn diagrams with two or three circles would not be uncommon. Even four or, in rare cases, five circles are not unheard of. In short, many recommendations are formulated in such a way that they contain multiple objectives. The more complex the recommendation, the higher the likelihood that it fits within two or more categories.

The Salvadoran and Panamanian truth commissions provide opposing extremes. In the case of the Salvadoran report, one third of its 43 recommendations fall into only one category. About half (22 out of 43) fall into two categories, and six recommendations fit three categories. The recommendations made by the Panama commission, by contrast, are easier to classify. Seven out of 11 clearly fall into one category only. Two more recommendations fit into two categories and the two last recommendations may be classified into three and four categories respectively. By way of example, the latter two are:

(i) To improve juridically the law that organizes the National Police so as to ensure that the control and development of the National Police and any other organization dedicated to public security stays in the hands of civilian authorities [fitting the institutional, legal, and non-repetition categories].

(ii) To create a Special Prosecutor to investigate the human rights violations and crimes against humanity [fitting the institutional, criminal, non-repetition, and follow-up categories].

Table 3.8 below shows, for each truth commission, how many of the recommendations we have coded as pertaining to each of the eight main categories listed above. In total, we have recorded 1537 category entries across the total number of 960 recommendations. This means that, on average, each recommendation contains elements belonging to roughly two categories.

To make it easier for the reader to appreciate commissioners' priorities, we provide the proportion of recommendations classified in each category in Table 3.9 below. To use the Argentinian truth commission report as an example, 78% of the nine recommendations made by CONADEP had an element of institutional reform, 89% had an element of legal reform, 33% had to do with criminal prosecution, 22% with reparations, 56% with non-repetition and 11% with follow-up. Note that the percentages do not add up to 100% because many of the recommendations fall into two or more categories.

Table 3.8. The number of recommendations made by Latin American truth commissions by category

	ARG 1	BRA 2	CHI 3 (Rettig)	CHI 4 (Valech)	ECU 5	ELS 6	GUA 7	HAI 8	PAN 9	PAR 10	PER 11	URU 12 (1985)	URU 13 (2003)	Total number TRCs by category
Total Truth Commission Recommendationss														
Total number of TCRs	9	43	110	42	156	43	84	166	11	202	82	2	10	960
TCRs by type														
Institutional	7	18	51	8	47	23	27	93	2	58	53	0	2	389
Legal	8	11	39	7	39	12	22	31	2	62	13	0	4	250
Constitutional	0	2	7	1	1	2	0	3	0	8	6	0	0	30
Criminal	3	2	2	0	9	0	2	11	2	15	4	0	0	50
Reparations	2	10	18	16	33	5	38	12	3	62	23	0	1	223
Non-repetition	5	25	90	22	114	26	36	26	5	106	40	0	6	501
Follow-up	1	2	0	5	4	7	3	16	2	16	6	0	2	64
Other	0	0	0	1	4	2	0	4	2	9	4	2	2	30
Total number of coded TCR entries	26	70	207	60	251	77	128	196	18	336	149	2	17	1537

Source: Data collected in connection with Beyond Words project. Details for each truth commission are found in Appendix IV.

Table 3.9. Percentages of recommendations by category from Latin American transitional and post-transitional truth commissions

| | Percentage of Recommendations by Category | | | | | | | | | | | | |
| | Transitional Commissions | | | | | | | | Post-Transitional Commissions | | | | |
	ARG	URU' 85	CHI (Rettig)	ELS	HAI	GUA	PER	PAN	URU' 03	CHI (Valech)	PAR	ECU	BRA
Total number of recommendations	9	2	110	43	166	84	82	11	10	42	202	156	43
Percentage by Category													
Institutional	78	0	46	54	56	32	65	18	20	19	29	30	42
Legal	89	0	36	28	19	26	16	18	40	17	31	25	26
Constitutional	0	0	6	5	2	0	7	0	0	2	4	1	5
Criminal	33	0	2	0	7	2	5	18	0	0	7	6	5
Reparations	22	0	16	12	7	45	28	27	10	38	31	21	23
Non-repetition	56	0	82	61	16	43	49	46	60	52	53	73	58
Follow-up	11	0	0	16	10	4	7	18	20	12	8	3	5
Other	0	100	0	5	2	0	5	18	20	2	5	3	0

Note: Commissions are grouped based upon whether they are transitional or post-transitional. Within each of these two groups, the truth commissions are listed chronologically according when they released their final reports.

When interpreting this data, we exclude the first truth commission in Uruguay because it made only two recommendations, neither of which fit into any of the seven main categories used in our analysis; both of its recommendations are classified as "other". If we look at the proportion of recommendations that fit different categories for the remaining 12 truth commissions, some patterns emerge.

First, in general, institutional reform appears to have a stronger emphasis for commissions established in the immediate aftermath of political transitions compared to post-transitional contexts. The percentage of recommendations that fit this category tends to be much higher in transitional contexts.[51] This likely represents a perception among commissioners that the fluidity of transitional situations opens greater possibility for institutional change. This strong focus on institutional change should also be seen in the context of the wave of judicial reform sweeping across Latin America in the 1990s, supported by external actors, such as the World Bank and the Inter-American Bank (Biebesheimer 2000; Buscaglia 1995). This was an era of (re)establishing democratic institutions after prolonged periods of military authoritarianism or civil war (Domingo and Sieder 2001; Frühling 1998), and truth commissions were part of this larger regional scenario. This also coincides with the frequent call to make recommendations for judicial reform which the observers of truth commissions have repeatedly noted (Hayner 2001; Minow 1998).

Second, legal reform seems to be less prominent in post-conflict contexts. Perhaps this reflects the fact that authoritarian regimes are more likely to have used law and order institutions to infringe upon human rights, whereas a larger proportion of violations in civil wars will likely result from combat.

Third, there does not appear to be a pattern in terms of constitutional reform recommendations. While commissions varied in terms of the number of recommendations mentioning constitutional reform, there is not much variation in terms of the proportion of recommendations that call for such a change. Overall, only a small number of recommendations are focused on constitutional reform, suggesting that commissioners deemed it unlikely they would be acted upon, either because of the political climate or the difficulty of amendment procedures.

Fourth, most commissions called for governments to take further steps to hold those responsible for past human rights violations criminally accountable. To be sure, who should be targeted and how suspects should be identified varied considerably. However, commissions display broad consensus on the importance of holding individuals accountable. Of the commissions

---

[51] For transitional truth commissions, the percentages of recommendations for institutional reform vary between 32–78%; most are 50% or more. For post-transitional truth commissions, all are under 50% and some as low as 20%.

not explicitly calling for criminal prosecutions, one made no specific recommendations at all (Uruguay 1985) and another recommended vetting of top military officials as a milder form of sanction (El Salvador). The two other commissions not specifically recommending criminal trials were post-transitional and perhaps judged that evidence and other procedural obstacles might prove insurmountable (Uruguay 2003), or considered it unnecessary since trials for dictatorship crimes were already taking place in national courts (Chile Valech).

Fifth, again with the exception of Uruguay's 1985 commission, all Latin American truth commissions have called for some form of reparation for victims. While reparations are common recommendations, they appear to be a stronger focus for more recent commissions. Almost all truth commissions established in the twenty-first century devote at least 25 per cent of their recommendations to reparations. This coincides with the shift to a more victim-centered rhetoric in international law and transitional justice practice (De Feyter et al. 2005; de Greiff 2006b; García-Godos 2013 and 2016; Michel and Sikkink 2013; Office of the UN High Commissioner for Human Rights; Pena and Carayon 2013; Salazar and Antkowiak 2007; Sandoval-Villaba 2009; Sveaass 2013; United Nations General Assembly 2005).

Sixth, with two exceptions (Uruguay 1985 and Haiti), truth commissions devoted almost half or more of their recommendations to non-repetition measures. Some truth commissions, like Chile Rettig and Ecuador, have non-repetition elements in three quarters or more of all recommendations. This strongly suggests that Latin American truth commissions have been distinctly forward-looking in terms of recommendations. There is significant variation among truth commissions in terms of the percentage of recommendations that are coded as Non-repetition, though. It seems like countries in Central America tend to have less of a focus on these kind of measures. This may possibly be due to relatively weak civil society, greater poverty, and fewer links to transnational activists who might push for such measures.

Finally, almost universally, Latin American truth commissions recognized that further official state stewardship would be necessary to better ensure the implementation of their recommendations. At least implicitly, they concluded that civil society would not be sufficient. Rather, commissions typically found it important to call for an official follow-up body to guide and monitor implementation.

Summing up these findings across all Latin American truth commission reports, the three largest categories of truth commission recommendations are non-repetition measures (33 per cent), followed by institutional reform (26 per cent) and legal reform (16 per cent). Reparations make up around 15 per cent of the total number, while other categories each constitute 5 per cent or less. The distributional data are in Table 3.10 below.

Table 3.10. Category of truth commission recommendations (TCRs)
as percentage of all recommendations

Recommendation category	Total number of recommendations by category	Percentage of total recommendations	Systemic vs. non-systemic
Non-repetition	501	33	systemic
Institutional	389	25	systemic
Legal	250	16	systemic
Reparations	223	15	non-systemic
Follow-up	64	4	non-systemic
Criminal	50	3	non-systemic
Constitutional	30	2	systemic
Other	30	2	non-systemic
Total number of TCRs for all reports	1537	100%	

Source: See also Table 3.8 above.

The finding that reparations only make up around 15 per cent of the total number of recommendations made by Latin American truth commissions is somewhat unexpected. Given that truth commissions are set up as a response to human rights violations suffered by individuals, one might have expected a far greater focus on reparatory measures – especially in truth commissions that have reconciliation as an explicit aim. Moreover, Latin America is a region in which human rights activists and victims are comparatively well organized (Collins 2010; Sikkink 1993; Skaar 1994). More in line with expectations, constitutional reform, follow-up measures, and calls for criminal prosecution of perpetrators of human rights abuses each constitute less than five per cent of the total share of truth commission recommendations. Finally, the "other" category lumps together the recommendations that do not fit any of the other seven categories, but account for barely two per cent of the total share of truth commission recommendations. In Chapter 5, we take up the question of whether some truth commission recommendation categories are more likely to be implemented than others.

Lastly, we distinguish between *systemic* and *non-systemic* recommendations. We define *systemic* narrowly to mean recommendations the aim of which is to reform existing state institutions, laws, or constitutions – i.e., to strengthen democratic structures and legal frameworks and thereby contribute to non-repetition of human rights violations. We also include here the introduction of new permanent state institutions and the passage of new laws. In other words, this type of recommendation introduces substantial change to the political system. As such, we exclude from systemic recommendations the setting up of follow-up bodies, for example, which, while they may lead to systematic change, do not represent it on their own.

Non-systemic recommendations, by contrast, refer to measures aimed at individuals or collectives, or the creation of non-permanent structures. Table 3.10 outlines how we have defined each of our recommendation categories in this dichotomy. The distribution emerges more clearly in the pie chart in Figure 3.4.

Figure 3.4. Distribution of recommendation categories across 13 Latin American truth commission reports

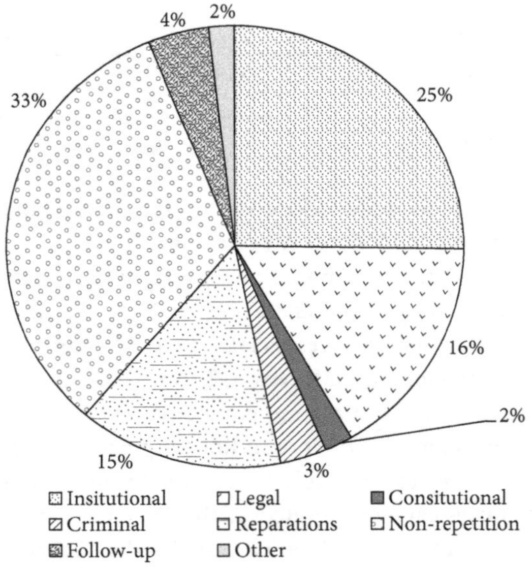

Note: Percentages reflect findings in Table 3.10 above. Percentages are calculated based on the detailed findings provided in Table 3.8.

If we define legal reform, institutional reform, constitutional reform, and non-repetition measures as "systemic", collapse the three categories into one, and group the remaining categories (reparations, criminal prosecution, follow-up, and other) as "non-systemic", we get a rather skewed distribution between systemic and non-systemic recommendations as clearly visualized in Figure 3.5 below.

Figure 3.5. Systemic versus non-systemic recommendations across 13 Latin American truth commissions

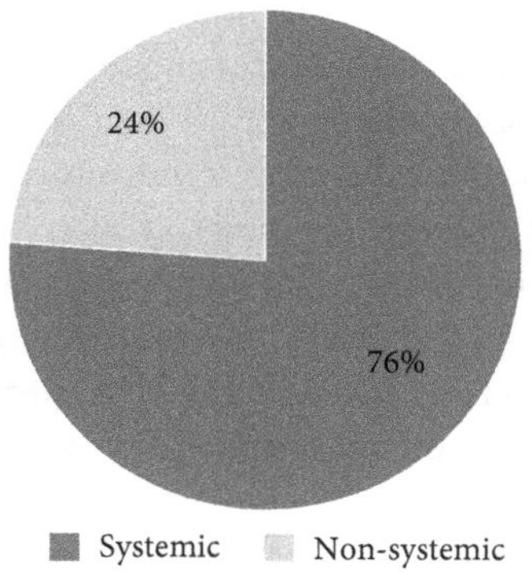

Note: Percentages are based on Table 3.10 above.

A final important – and unexpected – finding from our analysis is that *more than three quarters of all recommendations made by state-sponsored truth commissions in Latin America aim at systemic change.* Only reparations are clearly non-systemic. This means that recommendations, broadly understood, have prevention of future human rights violations – *nunca más* – as a central goal.

6.   RECOMMENDATION CHARACTERISTICS

We have hypothesized in this book that it is not only the type of recommendation that matters for implementation. The way a recommendation is phrased may also contribute to the likelihood of implementation. Further coding is therefore necessary to address this question. To do this, we introduce three additional typologies, jointly intended to capture different descriptive characteristics of recommendations, across the eight main categories introduced above:

(i)   *general versus specific* (in terms of what the government is being asked to do);
(ii)   *targeted* (measures affecting specific groups of people) *versus universal* (measures which affect all people in the country e.g., judicial reform); and
(iii) *backward-looking versus forward-looking* (i.e., does the recommendation address the past or does it seek to prevent future human rights violations).

We use this coding to explore patterns of implementation in Chapter 6.

6.1. GENERAL VERSUS SPECIFIC

A recommendation may be phrased in quite general terms or involve detailed instructions to the government on how it should be implemented. Here is an example of a general recommendation from the Chile Rettig report: "We must accordingly strive to assure that the effort to introduce respect for human rights into our culture can function over the long run."

Very often, a general formulation raises many questions and many potential ways of interpreting (and implementing) the recommendation. For instance, how should the government define and implement "respect for human rights" into Chilean culture? How would officials and civil society judge whether they have achieved the commission's goals? The vagueness of general recommendations makes this difficult.

Interpretation, and possibly implementation, becomes easier if the commission gives specific instructions. The distinction becomes clearer when we consider an example of a specific recommendation. Consider the following from the Brazilian report: "Acknowledgment, by the Armed Forces, of their institutional responsibility for grave human rights violations during the military dictatorship (1964 to 1985)." While such a symbolic measure may take verbal, written, and/or ceremonial form, what is being asked and of whom it is being asked are clearly stated in the recommendation.

We also find this general versus specific dichotomy when two different commissions' recommendations essentially recommend the same thing, but with very different degrees of specificity. Here is how the Haitian truth commission report has phrased its recommendation on reparation – in quite general terms:

> The creation of a special commission on reparations of damage caused to victims of the de facto regime that emerged from the coup of September 29 1991, *to meet legal, moral and material obligations described* [in this report] (emphasis added).

Contrast this with the detailed instructions to the government provided by the Paraguayan truth commission with respect to setting up a follow-up body to oversee the implementation of the recommendations:

> Create a National Human Rights Secretary, attached to the Presidency of the Republic, which will among other have the following purposes:

> (i) Elaborate a National Plan of Action of human rights, with the participation of the different state and governmental agencies and organizations of civil society. Once elaborated, the execution will be coordinated with the offices that work on the subject.

(ii)   Drive the implementation and monitor the recommendations presented by the Justice and Truth Commission, Paraguay (CVJ) (*Comisión de Verdad y Justicia* in Spanish).

(iii) Increase and refine constantly the records of victims and offenders of human rights violations.

(iv)   Continue the task of search and identification of the forcibly disappeared and unofficially executed, initiated by the CVJ.

(v)   Intervene as procedural subject in the disputes promoted by the CVJ in courts, in favor of dictatorship's victims.

(vi)   Be part, with active procedural legitimation, to intervene as representatives of victims of human rights violations in the proceedings of all nature which initiate before a court of the Republic, as under the jurisdiction of international law.

(vii) Hold all the files and material resources of the CVJ and increase the documentary collection of the CVJ's files.

(viii) Coordinate the integral reparation program of medical and psychosocial assistance to the people who were victims of human rights violations.

(ix)   Design with base in the present recommendations, a program of collective reparations for the communities which were affected by the collective attacks and suffered communal destruction.

(x)   Organize, when necessary, other programs of integral reparation for the victims of human rights violations addressed by the CVJ report, as it is the case of Paraguayan political exiles.

(xi)   Create mechanisms of participation and consultation with the civil society's organizations and the victims' movement, for the full compliance of its functions.

(xii) Make concerted efforts to ensure that women and minority groups participate in the public consultations aimed to elaborate, apply and evaluate the reparation programs.

We hypothesize that it is easier for a government to implement a specific recommendation than a general recommendation. In such circumstances, the commission has provided the state with a clear policy prescription and particular criteria by which civil society and the international community can hold it accountable. By contrast, the government can claim that general recommendations are not making particular demands on the state and can thus more easily ignore them. Alternatively, they can enact what some might consider to be half-measures and claim to have satisfied the commission's recommendation.

There are at least two circumstances in which this expectation might not hold true. First, if the level of detail in the recommendation is so high and there are so many things the government has been asked to do that the task may be perceived by the state as too overwhelming. Second, specific recommendations may be impractical. For example, a commission may recommend a very specific set of reparations measures. However, if the recommended measures are so generous as to cause serious budget trade-offs, it may be a political non-starter.

6.2. TARGETED VERSUS UNIVERSAL

Some recommendations target either specific individuals or groups as the beneficiary of a recommendation. This is typical for many reparations measures, for instance. By contrast, other types of recommendations may potentially benefit all citizens of a country and are, therefore, universal in character.

Here is an example of a targeted recommendation from the Guatemala report:

> That the Government promote extraordinary legislative measures that, in the case of adoptions carried out without the knowledge or against the will of the natural parents, adopted persons, or their relatives, may seek review of such a decision. Such a review should be carried out taking into account the opinion of who at the time was adopted and in such a way as to promote between adoptive families and the natural cordial relations to avoid further trauma in the adopted person.

And here is an example of a recommendation of universal character, also from the Guatemalan commission:

> That, to this end, the Government, in coordination with the organizations of Guatemalan civil society, particularly with indigenous and human rights organizations, promote a massive campaign of dissemination of the report in accordance with the social, cultural and linguistic diversity of Guatemala.

We hypothesize that recommendations targeting an identifiable group of people are easier to implement than wide-ranging measures. Universal measures may be more difficult to implement for several reasons. First, they are likely to require many stages to achieve complete implementation. Second, they are likely to involve a broader range of organized interests, some of which will oppose implementation. Third, because of their scope, they are likely to be more expensive to implement.

By contrast, an alternative hypothesis may be that *targeted recommendations would be harder to implement because beneficiaries of targeted measures are likely to be the poor and marginalized who lack the political power to pressure for implementation.*

6.3. BACKWARD-LOOKING VERSUS FORWARD-LOOKING

Recommendations also vary in terms of whether they are primarily focused on the past or the future.[52] Backward-looking recommendations try to

---

[52]   For a conceptual discussion of the differences between backward- and forward-looking measures, see Van de Poel (2011).

amend a past wrong. For example, reparations are measures delivered to address victims' past suffering. The prosecution of alleged perpetrators of human rights violations also addresses past crimes. By contrast, forward-looking recommendations seek to nurture future changes, to promote the Latin American mantra of *nunca más*. Typically, institutional, legal, and constitutional reforms are measures explicitly aimed at bringing about conditions that better ensure the non-repetition of human rights violations. Here are two more examples from the Guatemalan report that exemplify a backward-looking and forward-looking recommendation respectively:

> That the President of the Republic, in the use of its constitutional prerogatives, establish a commission which, under its authority and immediate supervision, examine the conduct of the officers of the Army and of the officers of the various State security forces and bodies in active duty during the period of the armed confrontation, with the objective to examine the adequacy of the actions of the officers in the exercise of their duties in that time to respect for the minimum standards set by the international instruments of human rights and international humanitarian law. [backward-looking]

> That the CEH's Report be studied as part of the Guatemalan Army's educational curriculum. [forward-looking]

Some recommendations may contain a combination of backward-looking and forward-looking elements. This is not surprising in light of the fact that addressing past violations is often connected with promoting a brighter future. Yet another example from the Guatemalan truth commission illustrates this type of recommendation:

> [That] the former commander of the Guatemalan National Revolutionary Unity, with the primary purpose of restoring dignity to the victims, asks for forgiveness in a public and solemn manner before society as a whole, before the victims, their families, and their communities, and acknowledges the responsibility of the former guerrillas for the acts of violence connected with the confrontation that have caused the Guatemalan population to suffer.

In these instances, we have coded appropriately.

We hypothesize that backward-looking recommendations will be more difficult to implement. Our logic is based on two factors. First, backward-looking measures are more likely to have a dramatic effect on those who remain powerful. This is most clearly so with criminal prosecution, but the provision of other forms of justice for past crimes is an acknowledgement of a wrong and may be perceived as a precursor to criminal accountability in the future. Second, forward-looking measures are more likely to connect to economic development priorities like the rule of law and good governance that are likely to attract attention from international donors.

In sum, we propose that it is not only the categories of recommendation that matter for implementation, but also these different characteristics. There may, of course, be interactions between these different kinds of variables.

7. CONCLUSION

This chapter has made some interesting findings. Some are methodological, others more substantive.

7.1. METHODOLOGICAL CONTRIBUTIONS

In this chapter, we have explained how we have constructed a database consisting of all recommendations issued by all formal Latin American truth commissions in a period spanning three decades (1984–2014). This is, to the best of our knowledge, the first attempt at providing an exhaustive overview of all recommendations issued by all truth commissions in an entire region across time. Previous scholarly work on recommendations has been scarce, and, where such exists, it mainly focuses on only one or two types of recommendations, or on a small number of truth commission cases. In terms of scope, then, this is by far the most thorough effort to date to explore recommendations and their importance. Methodologically, we have proposed a two-step procedure to identify the recommendations. Based upon a survey of the themes flagged in the TOCs of all 13 truth commission reports, supplemented by a detailed reading of all truth commission recommendations for all reports, we have identified seven main categories of recommendations plus one "other" category, leaving us with eight categories of recommendations: institutional reform, legal reform, constitutional reform, criminal prosecution, reparations, non-repetition measures, follow-up measures, and other measures. Our substantive categorization encompasses the vast majority of recommendations issued across the 13 commissions; only 30 recommendations fall into the "other" category. We use this tool for both individual case and cross-country analyses.

Our methodological approach is based on a bottom-up approach, taking what truth commission reports themselves flag as their most important contributions in the field of recommendations with a close reading of what they actually tell governments to do. This approach has resulted in a set of seven substantive categories that are not mutually exclusive. In particular, there are blurry borders between measures of non-repetition and reparations – but also between measures of non-repetition on the one hand and institutional, legal or constitutional reform on the other. Critics may have wished to see "cleaner" categories. Yet, we believe that forcing our recommendations into the straightjacket of one category only would not do justice to the complexity of the vast majority of recommendations. Moreover, it could result in misleading findings regarding which recommendations are more or less "implementable". Other researchers can take this data and adapt the coding scheme to their particular research question.

7.2. SUBSTANTIVE FINDINGS

Latin American truth commission reports show impressive variation in terms of the size/length of their reports, the space they have allotted to recommendations in their final reports, and in the themes covered by the recommendations.

Report length varies from the skinny four-page report issued by Uruguay's Parliamentary Commission in the early 1980s to the impressive multi-volume, several thousand-page report issued by the Peruvian CVR almost two decades later. The number of recommendations made by the reports varies considerably too: from two in the case of the first Uruguayan truth commission to 202 for the Paraguayan commission – i.e., one hundred times as many. Despite this enormous variation, except for Uruguay's first commission, the other 12 truth commissions generally have been concerned with a common set of central issues, as captured by our seven substantive categories. Nonetheless, with the exception of the Ecuadorian and Paraguayan truth commissions, which both were clearly inspired by the UN Guidelines, every commission seems to have invented its own unique template in the way it structured its recommendations.

Focusing first on the commonalities, if we look across all 13 reports, more than three quarters of all recommendations are so-called systemic; that is they are aimed at reforming state institutions, constitutions and legal frameworks to strengthen democratic institutions and practices. This is one of our most important findings. Much of the transitional justice literature is very focussed on victims' right to truth, justice and reparations. Yet only a relatively small proportion of truth commission recommendations are actually concerned with victims' needs. They seem to be more geared toward the future; to securing stronger institutions, devising better laws and legal frameworks, and promoting human rights education. Hence, there seems to be a strong interest in preventing similar violations in the future. This clear forward-looking aspect of truth commissions was not something we anticipated when we started this project.

In this chapter, we posed the questions whether there is systematic variation in recommendations across different contexts: temporal (early/late and transitional/post-transitional) and the nature of the transition (post-military dictatorship and post-internal armed conflict). We find that older commissions had more abbreviated sections on recommendations than more recent commissions.

Furthermore, there are differences in recommendations depending upon whether the commission was established right after the transition or at some later point in time. The post-transition commissions include two that were follow-up commissions to earlier truth commissions and, hence, had relatively narrow mandates. Chile Valech focused on torture and prisoners only; the second commission in Uruguay was concerned with collecting supplementary information to that gathered by parliamentary commissions and by the civil society-led project SERPAJ (*Servicio Paz y Justicia*). Similarly, although Brazil's CNV was the country's first official truth commission, it built upon earlier truth-finding bodies and reports (Mezarobba 2016). By the time the truth commission was established, the government had already enacted extensive reparations programs. Hence, reparations did not figure prominently in the CNV's final report. This is in contrast to the Chilean Valech Commission's exclusive focus on reparations. In some ways, the nature of past human rights violations shapes recommendations too. Recommendations produced by post-authoritarian truth commissions differ in some respects from those that emerge in post-civil war contexts, to address the different forms that violations took. Legal reform is more likely to be a priority in the former context, for example.

In sum, this chapter has provided some important tools for comprehensively examining the extent and types of recommendations made by Latin American truth commissions, focusing on differences and similarities. Yet, several questions remain. In the next chapter, we consider recommendation formulation to get some purchase on why recommendations took the forms that we have seen. Then, we proceed to examine whether these characteristics are related to the likelihood of their implementation.

CHAPTER 4

FORMULATING RECOMMENDATIONS

A poor idea well written is more likely to be accepted than a good idea poorly written.

– Isaac Asimov, scientist and writer (1920–1992)

Why do truth commissions give the recommendations that they do? This is not merely a rhetorical question. Truth commission reports are written documents. We can thus think of them as pure text. We can also think of them as policy documents. As we know, the dual aim of a truth commission is to document a specified set of human rights violations committed over a particular period of time, frequently by identifying alleged perpetrators (often institutions responsible such as the military, state agents, paramilitaries, etc.), and to provide recommendations to the government for follow-up action after the commission's work has been completed. The information documented by truth commissions is more often than not very contentious. One should not expect their recommendations to be any less controversial.

The aim of this chapter is to explore the processes through which the sets of recommendations presented in the final versions of truth commission reports are formulated. By the formulation process, we refer to all of the actions that contribute to the development of the recommendations presented by truth commissions. This begins with the identification of ideas to be included and the needs to be met, followed by the design and methods to be applied. Then, commissions deliberate and select the measures to be included. Finally, the recommendations are drafted. Formulation does not happen in a vacuum. To varying degrees, recommendations are shaped by drafters' interactions (or lack thereof) with actors outside the commission.

In this chapter, we analyze recommendations both as textual and contextual items. Why are recommendations formulated the way they are? Who decided what is to be recommended and on what grounds? Do recommendations express realistic goals or revolutionary dreams? Whether we read recommendations as concrete suggestions for action to be taken by the governments to which the truth commission reports are handed, or as expressions of hope for a better future, there is a normative element present in the formulation process of all recommendations. The *raison d'être* of recommendations is to suggest alternative ways of doing things in order to achieve various forms of justice and ultimately promote *nunca más*, never again. This normative agenda turns truth commission recommendations into highly contested matters. While commissioners might identify certain measures as necessary to address the past and to guarantee non-repetition, they might face resistance from certain groups in society. Recommendations may threaten the status of powerful actors. Other groups may fear that recommendations will not go far enough to transform society. As such, a broad array of actors are likely to try to shape the recommendations presented by the truth commission.

Thus, an analysis of the processes through which truth commission recommendations are formulated needs to take into account both the normative nature of the recommendations, as well as the contentious character of the measures being recommended. With this awareness in mind, this chapter draws upon the experiences of the 13 Latin American truth commissions to discuss the dynamics at work in the process of formulating truth commission recommendations. We start with a brief discussion of the phases involved in the formulation process. Next, we provide an in-depth discussion of the various factors influencing the design, deliberation and formulation of truth commission recommendations. We differentiate between internal factors, referring to the dynamics *within* a truth commission and among its members, and contextual factors, referring to the ways in which social actors *outside* the truth commission seek to shape the contents of the final report. An overview of the Latin American experience shows a combination of participatory consultation practices to collect inputs for the recommendations, with a more technical-internal approach at the deliberation and drafting stages, where a number of factors are at play.

1. THE PROCESS OF FORMULATING TRUTH COMMISSION RECOMMENDATIONS

Truth commission reports are written documents that are the product of often extensive investigation and internal debates as much as the result of strategic calculations on the management of real and anticipated external pressures from government and powerful actors in society. Understanding the formulation of truth commission recommendations implies identifying the various tasks or phases that the process involves. While the UN and transnational activists like the ICTJ advocate processes that are transparent and inclusive, we find no evidence of a specific blueprint for how the formulation of recommendations should take place. Nonetheless, it is possible to outline the tasks typically involved based on the Latin American experience and insights from the policy-making literature.

Sketching an outline of an ideal-type formulation process helps us to understand the process in a systematic way. Although not all truth commissions share these features, the formulation process usually involves five phases. First, often the set-up of the commission itself can shape the recommendations ultimately produced. Second, at the start of their work and throughout the commission's life, commissioners and staff make strategic choices to complete the work ahead, which will shape their final conclusions. Third, and often toward the end of the commission's life, there is sometimes an explicit input-gathering phase in which proposals for recommendations are collected from stakeholders. Fourth, there is a deliberation phase, in which potential recommendations are the subject of debate and scrutiny. Lastly, the final versions of recommendations are drafted. We discuss each of these phases in more detail below.

1.1. THE PHASES OF FORMULATION

The mandate of the truth commission plays a key role in the set-up of the commission, and, in it, recommendations that may be months or years away are already being shaped. Mandates typically outline commissions' structures, powers, and expected outcomes. If the truth commission is mandated to provide recommendations, this particular task would have to be included in the commission's work plan. Among other things, this would imply allocating resources (such as technical capacities and funding) for formulation and establishing responsibilities internally in order to get the work done. If the mandate does not explicitly call for such an output, commissions need not allocate resources and effort for recommendations. Even in such circumstances, though, commissioners recognize the opportunity to set the agenda and frequently take it upon themselves to present recommendations in their final reports.

The next phase involves the *how* and *when* of truth commission recommendations' design. That is, commissions identify a strategy for coming up with their recommendations. For example, commissions need to decide whether formulation will be done internally, through assigning specific commissioners and/or staff members, or whether to outsource the responsibility to a consultant. They need to decide how participatory a process it will be; whether actors outside the commission will be invited to present proposals or participate in dialogue about the final report. The strategy chosen implies different requirements in terms of the planning of activities, the time-scale in which they occur, and the scope of the endeavour. While it seems common-sensical to choose a strategy for dealing with recommendations as early as possible, experience shows that commissions tend to devote little attention to recommendations until the proverbial last minute. Why is this so?

One likely reason behind the later engagement with recommendations is the desire for them to be informed by the commission's findings. In order to recommend appropriate measures, the systematic patterns of past abuse and its causes ought to be identified first before determining how best to deal with the past and to prevent the recurrence of past violations. While this sounds logical, waiting until the data have been analyzed is probably not feasible if the goal is to make formulation a participatory process. With limited budgets, commission staff may not be sufficient to engage in such forward thinking. It will simply take more time to collect and synthesize input from stakeholders before finalizing the report, while simultaneously collecting evidence and testimony to produce a definitive history of the period under investigation. Rapidly approaching deadlines may make such a strategy infeasible. In general, time and resource constraints often make formulation less deliberative and consultative than would be normatively desirable.

The process of gathering input and identifying specific recommendations is a third phase. The way in which this happens largely will depend upon the strategy adopted earlier in the commission's work. Is it a participatory process? Are suggestions collected from a varied pool of social actors, such as human rights organizations, political parties, victims' groups, and other interests? By contrast, individuals within the commission may be assigned the task of assembling a draft list, based upon the findings in the report. Whether solicited or not, individuals who give testimony to truth commissions may offer their thoughts on what should be done next. A combination of both situations also is possible. The number of recommendations identified at this stage can be large or small and differs from case to case.

A fourth phase in the formulation process is the deliberation over the ideas that have been collected. It is at this stage that specific recommendations will be subject to scrutiny and debate within the commission – and possibly also discussed with external actors. The scope of the deliberation process will be determined by the strategy chosen by the commission concerning recommendations, but not entirely so. Civil society actors and other interests might nonetheless have a say, whether invited or not. They may put public pressure on the commission, or lobby politicians and international partners to intervene on their behalf to better ensure that their views are heard.

The format, scope, and length of the deliberation phase will be determined by the mandate and commissioners' strategic choices. Commissions may hold private meetings with stakeholders to get input or ask individual victims as part of their testimony. Commissioners may consult with international experts and study the experiences of other truth commissions. They might organize public events, seminars, and other types of outreach activities to get feedback from the public. Civil society organizations may organize such events themselves if they feel commissions have been insufficiently receptive to their input. The scope of deliberation also differs. Sometimes, engagement is fairly superficial; elsewhere, consultation is in-depth. Deliberation may be on a general level or organized to deal with specific themes in turn. Commissions may issue public calls for participation or invite specific groups to provide input. Finally, the length of time for which commissions engage in deliberation also varies considerably, as it balances time and resource constraints.

The fifth and final phase of the formulation process is the actual drafting of the recommendations to be included in the final report. The drafting of the actual text may already have begun during the deliberation phase, given that debate will be on the basis of different proposals presented mostly in written form. It is at this stage that commissions finalize their recommendations. They make final determinations of what proposals to include and engage in wordsmithing to get the language they desire before the manuscript goes to print.

As mentioned earlier, we expect overlaps between the different phases. It is important to bear in mind that, although the ideal type presented above helps us systematize the formulation process, there is nothing fixed about the span of time in which the full process – that is, all the tasks involved – will be carried out. Ideally, the process could run through the entire period of the mandate of a truth commission. In practice, this is seldom the case, and the work with recommendations is often allocated far less time than other commission activities.[53]

1.2.   ACCESSING DATA ON THE FORMULATION PROCESS

For in-depth knowledge of which items make it into the recommendations section of a truth commission report and, furthermore, how they were formulated, we rely upon several types of data. In some instances, we had access to first-hand accounts from commissioners and staff who were involved in selecting and writing the recommendations. Because individual perceptions and recollections vary, we sought as many voices as possible for each truth commission. In practice, several obstacles presented themselves. Particularly for those truth commissions that took place further in the past, many of the commissioners had passed away. The survivors were often frail or inaccessible. Few published memoirs exist, and we were unable to gain access to individuals' diaries and other papers. In the best-case scenario, we actually got to meet and talk to commissioners and staff who were part of the formulation process. However, respondents could not always remember these details, or they remembered partially or incorrectly. In other instances, interviewees shared only selected parts of their knowledge regarding the formulation process that lay behind every single recommendation.

---

[53]   See, for example, Bakiner (2016), Chapman and Ball (2001), Ferrara (2014), Hayner (2011), and Popkin (2000).

As a result of these realities restricting access to primary sources, we have also relied on secondary sources when analysing the formulation of truth commission recommendations. First and foremost, we have drawn on in-depth studies of the 13 truth commissions included in our analysis, prepared by country experts who have been part of the research project on which this book is based (Skaar, Wiebelhaus-Brahm, and García-Godos (eds.) 2022) Among other things, the researchers were explicitly tasked with gathering data on the formulation process. They used a wide range of secondary sources to better understand the context from which recommendations emerged. We have also tried to gather systematic information on the internal workings of the commissions. For each commission: Who actually wrote the recommendations? Was one person, or a sub-committee responsible? How was the work organized? There is significant variation.

2. FACTORS AFFECTING THE FORMULATION OF TRUTH COMMISSION RECOMMENDATIONS

Once we have outlined the different phases of the formulation process, we can now proceed with a key question for this chapter: What factors are at play in the formulation of truth commission recommendations? Based on our empirical material (Skaar, Wiebelhaus-Brahm, and García-Godos (eds.) 2022), we find it useful to differentiate between internal factors – those referring to the inner workings *within* a truth commission and the dynamics among its members – and contextual factors – referring to the involvement of social actors *outside* the truth commission.

The internal factors – those originating within the commission itself, its organization and dynamics – can influence all stages of the formulation process, basically because the formulation process happens within the commission, albeit in interaction with external actors and factors. Numerous aspects of a truth commission can be observed here, but we propose focusing on three internal factors: the organizational aspects of the commission; the composition of the commission; and the findings of the reports. By organizational aspects, we consider elements such as the commission's mandate, the strategic design, structure of the work and its dynamics, and how the recommendations fit in the overall work of the commission. This includes deliberation over specific recommendations; that is, the internal discussion within the commission about particular measures. The composition of the commission involves the commissioners themselves and, based upon their backgrounds, the constituencies or perspectives that they bring to the commission. The findings of the report are the result of the investigative mandate of the commission and are arguably the most determinative factor in shaping the recommendations.

Identifying what happened and the causes behind violations constitutes (or at least should constitute) the basis for the formulation of recommendations.

Similarly, a number of contextual factors can be observed. We propose highlighting two: the specific socio-political context surrounding the commission, including pressure from different stakeholders; and world time and the diffusion of norms and models regarding human rights and accountability globally. The national, socio-political context in which the commission carries on its work can affect the formulation of recommendations, particularly in terms of agenda-setting, and pressure from different stakeholders and interest groups, near or far, in positions of power or from the grassroots. "World time" refers to the world history in which commissions and their reports occur, particularly the normative standards promoted by the international community (Skaar and Wiebelhaus-Brahm 2013b).

In the remainder of this chapter, we discuss the impact that internal and external factors have in the process of formulation of truth commission recommendations, providing examples from our empirical material.

2.1. ORGANIZATIONAL FACTORS: MANDATE, WORK STRATEGY, AND DYNAMICS

Some truth commission mandates state that the commissioners should make recommendations, whereas others do not. Some may even specify what kind of recommendations the government expects. This guidance may shape the commission long before the formulation process starts: commissioners may shape their investigations, public engagement, and other activities in order to satisfy the demands set by the mandate. However, it is not obvious that commissioners wholly stick to the mandate given them. To find this out, we need to analyze the recommendations empirically, in light of the mandates.

Of the 13 truth commissions in our study, only the mandate of the Argentine commission failed to mention the delivery of recommendations. For other commissions, the charge to produce recommendations took different forms. For example, Chile's Rettig Commission (1991) had a mandate to formulate recommendations on reparations and legal and administrative measures for non-repetition. In Guatemala, the mandate of the *Comisión de Esclarecimiento Histórico* (1999) included "the formulation of recommendations to promote peace and national reconciliation", in particular, measures to preserve the memory of victims, to promote a human rights culture, and to strengthen the democratic process. In Peru, the mandate of the *Comisión de la Verdad y Reconciliación* (CVR, 2003) clearly requested the development of reparation measures for victims of human rights violations, as well as recommendations for institutional, legal, and educational reforms and guarantees of non-repetition. Furthermore, the mandate requested a follow-up mechanism to ensure the implementation of recommendations.

The organization, planning, and structure of the work carried out by the commissions varies among countries. However, the inclusion of recommendations in a commission's mandate is indicative of the commission's need to design and plan how recommendations are going to be worked with. Brazil provides an interesting example of a participatory design that took advantage of digital tools for the gathering of recommendation proposals and suggestions from the public. In August 2014, four months before the end of its mandate, the CNV made available on its official website an online form to send in suggestions about recommendations to be included in the final report. The form was open for roughly 20 days and 399 suggestions were received (Ghelfi et al. 2022). The CNV later reported that 307 of these were considered valid, although it could not provide information about the type of actors participating in the initiative. The development of this online tool did require planning on the part of the CNV. At the same time, with only four months left to complete its mandate, it is reasonable to consider that public participation was not the commission's primary tool to collect inputs for the recommendations.[54]

Truth commissions around the world vary tremendously in terms of size and staffing levels (Chapman and Ball 2001; Hayner 2011; Quinn 2003). Yet, Latin American cases look rather similar. For example, the number of commissioners is relatively homogenous. Although the number of commissioners in the 13 truth commissions studied here ranged from three in the case of El Salvador to 13 in the case of Peru, most commissions had either six (Uruguay Peace Commission, Haiti) or seven (Chile Valech, Brazil, Ecuador, Paraguay, Panama) members. Two commissions (Argentina's CONADEP and Uruguay's Parliamentary Commission 1985) had 11 members each.

Focusing only on the number of commissioners does not tell the whole story, though. Several of the truth commissions had secretariats to aid the commissioners. For instance, although El Salvador's commission formally numbered only three foreigners, a broader team ranged from 12 to 20 persons over the course of its operation; like the commissioners, most of the staff were foreigners due to the country's extreme polarization (Buergenthal 1994). According to one of the foreign consultants, the daily on-the-ground work was mainly done by this extended team, not by the three commissioners.[55]

---

[54] Information and communication technologies are changing many aspects of truth commission operations (Mezarobba and Cesar Jr 2016; Pelsinger 2010; Wiebelhaus-Brahm 2013). The fact that most Latin American truth commissions pre-date the widespread availability of such technology has limited their impact aside from in Brazil.

[55] Personal communication with Patricia Valdez, consultant to the Salvadoran commission.

In some cases, members of the secretariat were also considered commission members. Latin America's very first commission, Argentina's CONADEP, not only had a large commission consisting of 11 high-profile commissioners, it also had a secretariat of five additional well-known people who were each responsible for one substantive area of the commission's work (such as denouncements, procedures, documentation, administrative matters, judicial/legal matters). Several other truth commissions, too, divided the commissioners into teams responsible for different aspects of the truth commission's operations.[56] Through this, some form of division of labour was developed, which would include the selection and formulation of recommendations.

Overall, the Latin American experience shows that truth commissions tend to apply some form of open, participatory process to gather and identify recommendations, involving a great variety of sources and social actors, as well as existing sources (previous commissions, petitions, claims, documents, etc.) and specifically designed mechanisms. We can distinguish two ideal-type strategies for the formulation process of truth commission recommendations: open and closed processes.[57] In short, open processes involve stakeholders, and perhaps the general public in suggesting recommendations. By contrast, in closed processes, commissioners debate, develop, select, and formulate recommendations without (at least official) external input.

In an open process, a truth commission designs mechanisms for gathering recommendations from a number of sources. Effectively, it issues an open invitation to suggest recommendations to the commissioners. Examples of this include public hearings, calls for (written) proposals, or even consciously collecting or soliciting suggestions while taking victims' testimonies. In principle, such approaches are desirable because they empower citizens and model democratic policy formation. It also may better ensure that recommendations meet the needs of victims.

Such openness may have undesirable side-effects, however. After years of repression, at least some segments of society may not trust an official call for input. It also may reinforce existing power dynamics in society, in which better connected groups are given a voice, but not the marginalized. It also may distort the past. In some instances, formulating recommendations has become an opportunity to address all that has "gone wrong" in society and, hence, needs

---

[56] For details, see Appendix VI.
[57] Beyond the Latin American region, the extent to which stakeholders can and should be brought into the process of suggesting recommendations is a central concern to many more recent truth commissions. For instance, the Canadian Truth and Reconciliation Commission invited stakeholders into the process of identifying important recommendations. Stakeholders were also invited to help monitor the implementation process once the report was published. See Government of Canada (2019).

fixing, but may be very tangentially related to the past violations the commission was mandated to examine.

In closed processes, by contrast, commissioners select and formulate the recommendations largely in isolation, based upon their life experience and the knowledge they have accumulated from working on the commission. In doing so, like in open processes, they are guided and restricted by the commission's mandate. Moreover, the recommendations are shaped more decisively by their own biases and the findings of their investigation. Unfortunately, since these are closed processes, it is much harder to find data on the selection process.

A purely closed process runs counter to transitional justice and good governance norms. Guidance from the UN and transnational activists suggests that truth commissions can have powerful demonstration effects for burgeoning democracies by operating in an open and transparent fashion. A closed process robs the commission, and society, of the insights and lived experience of victims as measures to address the past and promote non-repetition are crafted. In fact, formal processes may side-line marginalized groups. Paul Gready and Simon Robins caution that "new" civil society, "an emergent, unpredictable and more diverse sector ... hostile to both mainstream formal politics and mainstream civil society", is often excluded from transitional justice processes (Gready and Robins 2017, 959). As Eric Wiebelhaus-Brahm (2021a) documents in the case of the Tunisian Truth and Dignity Commission, the voices of the marginalized – whether based upon age, gender, race, ethnicity, or socioeconomic class – may not be heard even if the process is open. Thus, closed processes may not necessarily do worse in meeting the needs of marginalized groups provided drafters are attuned to those needs.

Regardless of how open the process of identifying a set of potential recommendations is, once the commissioners have received all the proposals, they must finalize the list. They have to select from the pool of possible recommendations – possibly also being allowed to add their own ideas to what has been assembled through other means. Research conducted for this project shows that there is a level of openness and participation in the collection of suggestions from the different sectors of society as a base for the formulation of recommendations. Now, typically, the winnowing and wordsmithing begins in earnest.

More recent truth commissions tend to exhibit more open processes, likely driven in part by the development of norms of openness and participation in transitional justice, and governance more generally. Ecuador is a good example. Opting for a technical, in-house approach to the formulation of recommendations, the Ecuadorian commission took as its baseline existing recommendations presented in previous years by public agencies and NGOs working in the field of human rights. This basis was combined with suggestions collected through interviews with victims to develop a set of questions to guide workshops with victims in the cities of Guayaquil, Quito and Loja. The aim of the workshops was to explore what victims considered to be appropriate reparation, as well as to get feedback on some reparatory measures arising from the baseline of recommendations. The workshops' conclusions were then systematized in the form of a recommendations list which was presented, debated and revised at a meeting with thematic groups and representatives from state institutions. This was followed by a meeting with human rights NGOs, to collect their feedback and inputs. The strategy applied aimed to provide legitimacy to the formulation process of the truth commission recommendations in Ecuador (Reátegui et al. 2022).

The Paraguayan commission took a similar approach. The questionnaire used to collect victims' testimonies included a question concerning suggestions and recommendations that the individual victim would like to pose to the commission. Land restitution, memory initiatives, comprehensive reparations, the fight against impunity, and the search for the disappeared figured among the most prominent issues raised by respondents (Reátegui et al. 2022). The commission also approached human rights organizations to provide inputs to the recommendations via a questionnaire prepared for that purpose (Valencia 2011).

Even in early truth commission examples, though, the strength of civil society helped to ensure that the formulation of recommendations was not entirely closed. Argentina's CONADEP included a handful of recommendations that aimed to prevent, repair and eventually avoid the repetition of human rights violations. As argued by Hourcade et al. (2022a),

> The connections between CONADEP and the human rights movement are reflected in the formulation of the recommendations: most of CONADEP's recommendations had already been articulated by family members and activists during the dictatorship, as was reflected in IACHR's report following its *in loco* visit, and, as we have established, was used as a model by the commissioners.

In Chile, the Rettig Commission consulted victims as well as domestic and international human rights organizations. According to Lira and Loveman (2005), the commission surveyed 109 victims' organizations, human rights groups, universities and academic centers, political parties, and religious entities, and received more than seventy responses. Input from the *Vicaría de la Solidaridad* (Vicariate of Solidarity), which was the main documentation center for human rights violations in Chile, stands out.

Overall, of the commissions in our study, the task of formulating recommendations was given different degrees of importance relative to other responsibilities. In the cases of Paraguay and Ecuador, for example, the commissions' senior staffers were in charge of developing recommendations, while the commissioners focused much more on truth-finding (Reátegui, Gómez, and Hurtado 2022; Reátegui, with Uchuypoma, and Hurtado 2022). The Salvadoran Commission on the Truth, by contrast, approached the tasks of investigation and recommendation formulation sequentially. Ultimately, the commission wrote its report in New York City, where the foreign commissioners had fled in fear for their safety (Martínez-Barahona et al. 2022).

2.2. BACKGROUND OF COMMISSIONERS

The composition of the truth commission team, particularly the commissioners (but also senior staff) must be considered. As argued by Kimberly Lanegran (2015, 70), "as important as it is to establish a selection process designed to achieve the greatest possible legitimacy [for] the truth-seeking body, excellent plans are only as good as the work of people who implement them". Individual personalities, experience, knowledge, and social networks, among other things, often play an important role in commissions' interpretation of their mandates and in the crafting of final reports. The same factors may be significant for recommendations, which also are formulated within the confines of a truth commission mandate and the broader legal framework in which the commission operates. To make at least a preliminary sketch of the commissioners, we have collected data on their backgrounds using publicly available material such as truth commission reports, country case reports, and news reports.[58]

Looking across country experiences, there are some significant trends to be found among Latin American truth commission commissioners. First, all commissions have designated specific commissioners in charge of organizing and running the truth commission, including the writing of the final report and its recommendations. Second, the vast majority of commissioners are men. For instance, 14 out of 15 commissioners appointed to Argentina's CONADEP and 7 out of 8 commissioners in the Chile Rettig commission were men. Only one commission, Haiti's CNVJ, was headed by a woman. This is not so surprising when taking into account that the commissions operated in countries and in historic times where not many women had a prominent public voice. A third general observation is that an overwhelming majority of commissioners are legal scholars or legal practitioners. While interdisciplinarity and diversity are principles explicitly valued in truth commissions globally, this is not always without friction. In Haiti, the (female) head of the truth commission was a sociologist whereas the rest of

---

[58] For the 13 truth commissions studied in this book, data has been gathered on commission members such as their background, profession, discipline, institutional affiliation, and political affiliation. See Appendix VI.

the commission members were lawyers, a situation that led to both a clash between disciplinary approaches and personalities (Selvik 2022).

Commissioners in most Latin American truth commissions were citizens of the country that established the commission. However, there are some exceptions. Truth commissions were established in El Salvador and Guatemala as part of UN-brokered peace agreements ending their respective civil wars. In these cases, all commissioners were foreigners, appointed by the UN with the agreement of the respective national government, in order to ensure neutrality and legitimacy in a politically fragile context. This, however, left the truth commission without a domestic champion after the commission ended (Popkin 2000; Wiebelhaus-Brahm 2010).

While neutrality and legitimacy are important selection criteria in most commissions, individual merit, representativeness, and moral standing seem to be equally important. In Peru, the CVR was composed of 12 members from different sectors of society, including the armed forces, human rights organizations, religious congregations and academia. The moral standing of the appointed president of the CVR, philosophy professor and former rector of the Catholic University in Peru, Salomón Lerner, was impeccable (Reátegui and Uchuypoma 2022).[59] This composition gave the CVR the moral and political legitimacy it needed to conduct its work amid a political climate still recovering from the abrupt political transition of 2000. Nonetheless, years later, the CVR would be criticized for the assumed leftist orientation of some of its members (García-Godos and Reátegui 2016).

Individual commissioners can also play a key role in shaping the direction of specific commissions, and in the formulation of recommendations. In Argentina, according to Eduardo Crenzel, the recommendations chapter was drafted by commissioner and former Supreme Court judge Ricardo Colombres, based upon input from human rights organizations (Crenzel 2008). Several sources characterize Colombres as a committed participant in the commission's work, based on his political experience and commitment to human rights (Hourcade et al. 2022a). In Paraguay, the recommendations were elaborated by commissioners with expertise in specific fields. For example, Alberto Alderete (current head of the National Institute for Rural and Land Development, the government body in charge of land policy in Paraguay) was an expert on agrarian reform and usurped lands; Oscar Ayala (current coordinator at CODEHUPY[60]) and Julia Cabello contributed to the work on indigenous peoples, while Edwin Sokol worked on gender issues. Commissioners Carlos Beristain and Carlos Postillo had broad

---

[59] See also interview with Salomón Lerner Febres (Talavera and Salmón (2002)).
[60] CODEHUPY (*Coordinadora de Derechos Humanos del Paraguay*) is an umbrella organization/ coordinating body for human rights NGOs in Paraguay. See webpage at http://codehupy.org. py/quienes-somos/.

experience on the search for the disappeared, while legal expert Dionisio Gauto contributed to the area of historical memory (Reátegui, Gómez, and Hurtado 2022). Where commissioners possess diverse experience and expertise, this may be an effective strategy for crafting recommendations that address a diversity of policies and stakeholders.

2.3. TRUTH COMMISSION REPORT FINDINGS

The findings of a truth commission must be considered a determining factor in the formulation and content of truth commission recommendations.

Let us look at a few examples. In Argentina, CONADEP's estimate of the number of people disappeared by the time the report was released was 8,960. This motivated the commission to identify as a first recommendation the transfer of all the documentation gathered by the commission on disappearance cases to the judicial authorities, to initiate investigation.

While all truth commissions focus on truth and victims, some of them are particularly interested in addressing the root causes of conflict. Of the Latin American commissions, Guatemala and Peru stand out in this regard. This orientation influences the kind of recommendations that are likely to be made. There is a difference between recommendations related to the fact-finding functions of commissions and those recommendations arising out of the historical interpretation of the past. Some recommendations are so broad and structural in nature that they might be better seen as a vision for the future rather than as an implementable policy directive. In Guatemala, the commission characterized the systematic victimization of the Mayan indigenous peoples as genocide, thus laying the foundation for a whole set of recommendations calling for recognition, participation, inclusion and non-discrimination of the Mayan population. In Peru, where 75 per cent of the victims came from an indigenous peasant background, the final report and its recommendations put great emphasis on institutional and educational reform to combat racial and ethnic discrimination.

In Chile, the Valech report focused on arbitrary detention and torture, documenting the systematic use of torture against people unlawfully detained. The recommendations elaborately focused, therefore, on different forms of reparation in support of victims, as well as on a number of institutional measures to secure human rights and guarantees of non-repetition. While in Paraguay, the comprehensive issue of arbitrary land expropriations documented by the commission led to a focus on land restitution in the set of recommendations.

While the findings of a truth commission might be highly relevant and important, recommendations will also be shaped by how the truth commission is temporally situated relative to other transitional justice mechanisms and reform processes that may have preceded it. When policy or institutional reform has been put in motion at an earlier stage, certain kinds of recommendations may be rendered superfluous if they have already been addressed through other means. We see this most clearly in the Brazilian case. There, 30 years went by between the atrocities committed by the government during the period 1946–1988 and the truth commission established by Dilma Rousseff's government in 2012. When the CNV issued its report in 2014, there were very few references to reparations to victims, mainly because extensive reparations programs had already been established and implemented (Ghelfi et al. 2022, Mezarobba 2016).

2.4. SOCIO-POLITICAL CONTEXT AROUND THE COMMISSION

Truth commissions do not operate in a vacuum. Their work is situated within specific national, regional, and global contexts. The socio-political context surrounding their work has an important role to play in shaping truth commission recommendations. As mentioned earlier, commissions (and commissioners) are often contested, and the explicit support, alliance or confrontation with different actors can shift the attention of the public in favour or against the commission's agenda.[61]

In Guatemala, the UN monitoring of the implementation of the peace accords set the framework for the work of the truth commission. Emerging from armed conflict in 1996, there were powerful forces at work in setting the record straight as to what happened during the conflict. Most importantly, a shadow report was elaborated by the Catholic Church (the Recovery of Historical Memory Project – REHMI report). The CEH's final report, *Memory of Silence,* was met with both the indifference of the incumbent government and the condemnation of the armed forces, which went so far as to publish an alternative report on civil war atrocities (Centeno-Martín 2022).

Commissioners are often exposed to various forms of indirect and direct pressure when they select and formulate their recommendations. Let us not forget that commissioners have been appointed by either presidents or legislatures. Therefore, although, as noted earlier, they do not necessarily do so, commissioners are expected to be loyal to the commission's mandate. Further, commissioners may be concerned with not "rocking the boat" too hard by making very controversial recommendations, which may overshadow other

---

[61] Note that contestation can also be internal to the commission. In Brazil, one of the commissioners resigned and another commissioner left informally during the first phase of the commission's work due to internal disagreements over what the overall political project of the truth commission should be (Torelly 2018, 204).

aspects of the report once it is published. Throughout the Latin American experiences, human rights organizations and victims' groups stand out as a pressure group with regards to truth commissions. They are often supportive and critical at the same time. Mayan organizations put forward their demands in Guatemala, while the Argentine Mothers of Plaza de Mayo would not let go the issue of the disappeared. In Peru, commissioner Sofía Macher, a representative of the human rights sector, contributed as a mediator of concerns from human rights organizations and victims' organizations.

In addition, as previously noted, the formulation of recommendations must be seen in light of other contemporaneous transitional justice and reform activity in the country that might make some recommendations redundant and others too sensitive. For example, if a reparations program has been established prior to the commission's final report, there may be no need for such a recommendation. This might be especially likely for post-transitional truth commissions. Truth commissions formulate their recommendations in the context of political debates among (domestic but also international) actors involved in the truth commission process. Commissions face real or imagined pressures to craft recommendations in line with important interests.

2.5. TRAVELLING OF NORMS AND MODELS

In many respects, each truth commission report is a product of its time. Time matters because it acts as a proxy for a host of contextual factors that form the regional and global historical and political backdrop against which the truth commission reports are written. It is in terms of what Skaar and Wiebelhaus-Brahm (2013b) call "world time", the global Zeitgeist in which the commission and report occur, that we need to understand the learning and travelling of norms and models. As we discuss in Chapter 6, greater global attention to the rights of indigenous peoples, women, and sexual minorities seems to have inspired some of the more recent commissions in our data (see also Wiebelhaus-Brahm and Wright 2021).

Research on a so-called truth commission norm indicates that truth commission architects and commissioners look to other examples for models (Hirsch 2007, 2014). It is feasible that there might also be a "learning" effect when it comes to recommendations. By the turn of the twenty-first century, truth commission reports were commonly available online, either singly or in collections such as that of the United States Institute of Peace. In the mid-2000s, the UN Rule of Law Toolkits outlined best practices for truth commissions and other transitional justice processes. Furthermore, external reports or documents, outside the truth commission sphere, dealing with the particular country's human rights issues, might have influenced the commissioners when they drafted the report and its recommendations. We have looked for similarities across reports to see if we can discern any "copy-cat" effect and consulted secondary literature on the subject. Temporal trends in formulation are further explored by Wiebelhaus-Brahm and Wright (2021).

The most obvious similarity across the 13 truth commission reports is the striking parallels between the final reports of the Paraguayan and Ecuadorean truth commissions. Finalized and published only two years apart, these two reports are very similar in structure. Paraguay's *Informe Final. Anive haguâ oiko* (2008) lists five categories of recommendations: (i) satisfaction, (ii) restitution, (iii) compensation, (iv) rehabilitation, and (v) non-repetition. Compare this to Ecuador's report *Informe de la Comisión de la Verdad Ecuador 2010: Sin Verdad no hay Justicia* published two years later (2010), which also divides its recommendations into the same categories, but adding one final category: (i) satisfaction, (ii) restitution, (iii) rehabilitation, (iv) compensation (*indemnización*), (v) guarantees of non-repetition, and (vi) administrative reparations. There has seemingly been a learning effect here. At least, it is quite clear that the two commissions have used the same model document to structure their recommendations. In fact, they both follow the structure and guidelines set up by the UN Basic Principles on the Right to Remedy and Reparations (2005), which sets international standards for accountability and victims' rights to truth, justice and reparation. The Basic Principles have been very influential in giving shape to victim reparation programs that followed, as is the case of several Latin American reparations programs established since the mid-2000s (García-Godos 2018).

Another important actor in promoting and shaping international standards across the region is the Inter-American System of Human Rights. This is true both in terms of legal doctrine and jurisprudence (Reátegui et al. 2022). The Inter-American system has been involved in a number of country-specific cases that have set precedents not only for the countries involved, but for the region and international human rights law in general (Basch et al. 2010; Cerna and Farer 1992; Engstrom 2018).

Norms also travel through groups of international experts and consultants, as well as through international NGOs. For example, in Peru, The International Center for Transitional Justice played an important role in the formulation process of the recommendations chapter, providing input in particular to the design of a reparations proposal (Reátegui and Uchuypoma 2022).

In terms of the content of recommendations, research on victim reparations programs shows that, over the past 20 years, there has been an expansion on the types of violations addressed by reparation programs, and, therefore, also in the forms of reparations established to address the needs of victims (García-Godos 2018). This expansion relates to the inclusion of types of violations and forms of reparations within the set of recommendations forwarded by truth commissions. For example, torture was included in the Valech report in Chile in contrast to the Rettig report. A focus on sexual and gender-based violence (SGBV) first appears in our data from the Haitian truth commission and led to the elaboration of specific recommendations to address these issues in the country.[62] Attention to SGBV is present in two more truth commission reports that followed: the commissions in Paraguay and Ecuador. The learning and travelling of norms involve, therefore, not only models about how to structure recommendations, but also their content: what is to be addressed.

3. CONCLUSION

In this chapter, we have explored various aspects related to the formulation of truth commission recommendations by considering formulation as a process itself. The advantage of this approach is that, rather than treating formulation as "drafting", we focus on mechanisms and dynamics affecting the formulation of recommendations. Collecting data about the formulation process turned out to be more challenging than first envisaged, likely due to the fact that it is those recommendations that were indeed implemented that best come to mind when asking commission staff and stakeholders involved, while those left on the cutting-room floor, so to speak, have been forgotten. Another reason for the paucity of formulation data is that the focus of truth commissions is typically on the findings, with recommendations being granted less attention, in both the memory of actors and in official records.

In an attempt to systematize the factors that are at play in the formulation of truth commission recommendations, we differentiated between internal and contextual factors influencing this process. Based on our empirical material, we have identified internal factors such as the organizational aspects of the commission, the composition of the commissions, the background of the commissioners, and the findings of the reports; and external factors such as the specific socio-political context around the commission, as well as world time and the diffusion of norms on human rights and accountability regionally and globally.

An overview of the Latin American experience shows a combination of participatory practices to collect inputs for the recommendations, with a more technical, internal approach at the deliberation and drafting stages. The issues included in recommendations are (not surprisingly) much in tune with commissions' mandates, but perhaps most importantly, they strongly reflect the findings of truth commissions' reports. Recommendations also reflect the world time in which they are formulated, with inputs also from international human rights standards and institutions; the implication of this being that newer sets of recommendations are likely to be more encompassing, addressing more victim

---

[62]   See also section 4 on new themes in truth commissions in Chapter 6 of this book.

groups and types of violations. The specific socio-political contexts in which recommendations are shaped, formulated, and deliberated are important for setting the agenda and understanding the pressure that different social actors can exert. Each country case would demand an ample study of these contexts, and we have only highlighted a few examples from a wide material.[63]

Finally, it is important to recognize that, given the focus of this project on the implementation of truth commissions, we can present only modest findings on the inner dynamics, controversies, and deliberations within specific commissions in general, let alone regarding the country-specific process of formulating recommendations. Nonetheless, we hope that this will contribute to raising interest for future research on the formulation of truth commission recommendations.

---

[63] See more details on country cases in the second volume of this series (Skaar, Wiebelhaus-Brahm, and García-Godos (eds.) 2022).

CHAPTER 5

CASE STUDIES OF IMPLEMENTATION

Uttering a word is like striking a note on the keyboard of the imagination.

– Ludwig Wittgenstein, philosopher (1889–1951)

What has happened to the roughly 1000 recommendations that Latin American truth commissions have made over the past four decades? Did they remain just words on paper, or have they been implemented? This is a highly relevant empirical question if one is concerned with the impact and relevance of truth commissions. This chapter zooms in on each of the 13 formal truth commissions established in Latin America between the mid-1980s and the mid-2010s to provide a flavour of the implementation record of their recommendations. Whereas most qualitative comparative work on truth commissions focuses on their establishment, mandates, and operations (Bakiner 2016; Hayner 1994; Hayner 2011; Wiebelhaus-Brahm 2010), we present 13 mini case studies of truth commissions, focusing specifically on their recommendations and the degree of implementation.

The final reports of these commissions have, as suggested earlier in this book, made a wide range of recommendations covering numerous substantive issues. In Chapter 3, we introduced seven substantive categories plus an "other" category to group and systematize the recommendations: Institutional reform, legal reform, constitutional reform, criminal prosecution, reparations, non-repetition measures, follow-up measures, and "other" measures. When coding the recommendations according to these categories, we ended up with 1512 coded recommendations, based on the fact that recommendations are sometimes crafted in complex ways such that one recommendation asks the state to do multiple things. Each of these coded recommendations is what we refer to as an *action item*. They are the units of analysis in this chapter.

The following analysis is based on three main types of source material: (1) data on implementation for each of the 13 truth commissions, specifically collected for the *Beyond Words* project, of which this volume forms a part;[64] (2) the country chapters written for each of the truth commission cases, using the data collected for this project, which appear in a companion volume

---

[64] See Appendix IV for the coded data on implementation for each truth commission.

(Skaar, Wiebelhaus-Brahm, and García-Godos (eds.) 2022); and (3) secondary sources. Note that the secondary literature is very uneven. There is quite a large scholarly literature on some of the truth commissions, namely Chile's Rettig Commission, Argentina's CONADEP, Guatemala's Commission for Historical Clarification and Peru's CNV,[65] though surprisingly few scholars have concerned themselves specifically with their recommendations. For other less well-known truth commissions, like those of Haiti, Panama, Ecuador, and Paraguay, there is much less literature – particularly in English.

Each of our mini case studies starts with quoting the first recommendation of one of the truth commission reports. We do this for two reasons. First, commissioners may place the most important recommendation first. Hence, the first recommendation sends a signal to the government of where its main priorities should lie in terms of implementation. Second, the first recommendations of the 13 truth commissions provide a snapshot of the contrast in content, style, length, and level of detail that the reports provide in their recommendations – which in turn, we argue, may have implications for the rate of implementation.

The case studies are structured according to three different regions: the Southern Cone, the Andes, and Central America and the Caribbean.[66] Just as there is some commonality among human rights violations across regions, transitional justice activism also has frequently been a cross-border endeavour (Lessa 2019; Roht-Arriaza 2005). Within each of the regions, we have ordered the case studies chronologically according to when the commission published its final report. In the two cases where a state has established more than one truth commission (Uruguay and Chile), we discuss the commissions jointly since the second truth commission frequently is premised on the first.

We start our analysis in the southernmost part of the Southern Cone, where the first formal truth commission was established while most of the countries on the continent were still ruled by military dictatorships or suffering internal armed conflict.

1. THE SOUTHERN CONE

Located in the southernmost part of South America, the Southern Cone consists of five countries. All five countries formed part of the so-called

---

[65]   Guatemala's Commission for Historical Clarification and Peru's Truth and Reconciliation Commission both feature among "The Five Strongest Truth Commissions" in Pricilla Hayner's widely cited book, *Unspeakable Truths* (Hayner 2011). Listed among her "Other Illustrative Truth Commissions" we find several Latin American truth commissions: those of Argentina, Chile Rettig, El Salvador, Haiti, Chile Valech, Paraguay, and Ecuador. Notably, neither of the two Uruguayan truth commissions is included here, nor that of Panama. Hayner's book was published before the Brazilian truth commission was established.

[66]   We here follow the same structure as the case studies presented in Skaar, Wiebelhaus-Brahm, and García-Godos (eds.) (2022).

Operation Condor network, which collaborated to hunt down and extinguish opposition connected with the political left; the so-called "red threat", in the 1970s and 1980s (McSherry 2012). This network of repression resulted in the deaths and disappearances of thousands of people in the sub-region. Decades later, the same countries that formally collaborated to kill their citizens are now collaborating to bring the perpetrators to justice (Lessa 2019). Truth commissions have played an important role in this development.

1.1. ARGENTINA (1984)

> The organism which replaces this Commission should accelerate the process of remitting the documents collected during the investigation ordered by the Executive Branch to the justice system.

The first recommendation of the commissioners serving on the Argentine truth commission, headed by novelist Ernesto Sábato, was to ensure that the material collected during the commission's investigation into human rights abuses be sent over to the courts so that legal procedures against those responsible could start. The commission had documented 8,961 cases of enforced disappearance and extra-judicial killings, carried out by a brutal military dictatorship comprising a series of military juntas operating between 1976 and 1983. The truth commission's bold first recommendation that the government prosecute should be seen against the backdrop of Raúl Alfonsín's presidential campaign, where justice was one of the chief promises made to the Argentine population (Garro 1993). The Argentine commissioners had no models to look to. As reflected in the title of a famous book, *Radical Evil on Trial*, by one of the president's closest advisors, Carlos Nino (1996), the commissioners were carrying out an experiment on how to deal with human rights abuses in the form of the written word. Alfonsín's government intended CONADEP to be a precursor to criminal prosecutions of the military junta that had ruled Argentina since 1976.

Argentina was the first country in Latin America, perhaps in the world, to have a formal truth commission that both completed its work and issued a report that was made public.[67] Established shortly after the military regime collapsed following its defeat in the Falklands war against Great Britain in the early 1980s, the Comisión Nacional sobre la Desaparición de Personas, commonly known as CONADEP, issued its famous *Nunca Más* report in 1984. The *Informe de la Comisión Nacional Sobre la Desaparición de Personas*

---

[67]   There is disagreement in the literature on which investigative bodies are truth commissions (Stewart and Wiebelhaus-Brahm 2017). Many point to the 1974 Commission of Inquiry into Disappearances in Uganda as the world's first truth commission. Its report is not publicly available, however (Winston 2020).

(the so-called CONADEP report) made only nine recommendations. Yet, these measures laid the ground for a human rights policy that was to become one of the most thorough settlements of dictatorship crimes in all of Latin America (Skaar, Collins, and García-Godos (eds.) 2016). Most of the recommendations advised institutional and legal reform. Specifically, CONADEP recommended that the Argentine government take measures to prevent atrocities from happening again by undertaking extensive legal reform and the adoption of international human rights law. The commission also advocated criminal prosecution of those responsible for human rights violations, and, further, that measures be taken to compensate the victims of abuse. Finally, CONADEP advised that a body be established to oversee the implementation of all the above measures.

We identified 26 implementable action items from the nine recommendations delineated in the CONADEP report (see Appendix IV). All of the recommendations have been highly implemented (Hourcade et al. 2022a). As such, CONADEP has one of the best implementation records on the continent. However, two important qualifications need to be made. First, the number of recommendations is very modest compared to those made by later truth commissions in Latin America. Second, one must recognize that it took over three decades to reach this point of full implementation. Different measures have been implemented at different times, involving a number of different governments of different ideologies. Most progress in human rights matters, directly linked to the recommendations of CONADEP, was made under the governments of Nestor and Christina Kirchner (2003–2007 and 2007–2015 respectively) (Roehrig 2009). Only in 2003, the amnesty laws of 1986 and 1987 were declared null and void – first by Parliament and then by the Supreme Court (Mezarobba 2016; Smulovitz 2012) – which opened up the possibility of criminal prosecution of perpetrators of human rights violations. Criminal prosecutions are still ongoing as of 2020, including massive court cases involving hundreds of defendants from the dictatorship era and thousands of witnesses; the so-called *Operación Condor* trials and the *Mega Causas* (Lessa 2019).

Nonetheless, with all of the implemented recommendations, questions of causality arise. The recommendations themselves were not enough to bring about change. At best, CONADEP was jointly responsible with other factors. Moreover, the truth commission probably was not necessary to bring about the reforms and trials outlined in the recommendations. Given national, regional, and global civil society mobilization around junta-era abuses, it is plausible that Argentina could have reached this point without the truth commission. What is indisputable is that the work of Argentina's truth commission and the implementation of its recommendations, together with all the other actions undertaken by successive Argentine governments to address past human rights violations, makes Argentina a regional leader in transitional justice (Balardini 2016).

1.2. URUGUAY (1985 AND 2003)

Uruguay (Parliamentary Commission, 1985)

Advises the House of Representatives to refer the proceedings to the Supreme Court of Justice.

Uruguay Comisión para la Paz (Commission for Peace, 2003)

The Commission advises maintaining a strictly administrative Follow-up Ministry tasked with performing follow-up and support of pending proceedings and processes (pending fingerprint comparisons and expert evaluations, correction of death certificates, exhumation of bodies buried in anonymous graves and possible repatriation of mortal remains).

In many ways, the first truth commission in Uruguay followed the example set by Argentina's CONADEP when it boldly, albeit indirectly, recommended criminal prosecution; a recommendation which was in practice ignored by the government in power at the time of the report's release as well as by subsequent governments. Almost two decades later, the second (formal) truth commission in Uruguay first recommended that a follow-up body be established. This priority was to make sure, or at least increase the chances, that the recommendations made by the commission would actually be implemented.

Argentina's closest neighbour, tiny and sparsely populated Uruguay, is possibly the country in Latin America that has had the most attempts at truth finding after it went through a democratic transition from military dictatorship in 1985. Interestingly, the number of truth-finding attempts has been inversely proportional to the severity of repression, as the death toll from dictatorship crimes in Uruguay is among the lowest in the region with only 123 politically-motivated assassinations and 192 cases of enforced disappearance. Note, though, that the human cost of repression in Uruguay was nevertheless high. Of a population of around 2.8 million at the time, as many as half a million may have fled the country and more than 60,000 persons were arrested and detained (Lessa and Skaar 2016, 78). This was reportedly the highest percentage of detainees *per capita* in the world (Sondrol 1992). As a result, Uruguayans have for decades been deeply divided over criminal accountability for military-era abuses. Until very recently, Uruguay's amnesty law (*Ley de Caducidad de la Pretensión Punitiva del Estado*), which was enacted by the first democratically-elected government in 1986, proved highly durable; referenda narrowly upheld amnesty on two separate occasions (Lessa and Skaar 2016; Skaar 2011b). In such an atmosphere, truth commissions were a way for activists to keep attention on the past. Criminal prosecution of alleged human rights perpetrators was not on the agenda of the executive or the courts, though civil society kept pushing for criminal accountability (Skaar 2011a).

Since the scope for action through the courts was limited, a lot of energy has gone into truth finding. By some counts, five separate commissions (official and unofficial) have delved into Uruguay's past. Here, we limit our discussion to the commission established by left-wing parliamentarians to investigate forced disappearances in 1985 and the truth commission established almost two decades later by then-President Jorge Batlle, which made its report public in 2003.[68] *Comisión Investigadora Parlamentaria Sobre (la) Situación de Personas Desaparecidas y Hechos que la Motivaron* (The Parliamentary Investigative Commission on the Situation of Disappeared Persons and Its Causes) was established by the Uruguayan Chamber of Representatives on April 9, 1985, to investigate the cases of disappeared persons of Uruguayan nationality during the military dictatorship (June 1973 to March 1985) and the reasons behind these crimes (Lessa 2013a). Possibly due to the controversy that this investigation stirred up (Parliament was deeply divided over whether such investigations should take place at all), the commission is largely unknown, both within Uruguay and outside the country. It received little attention during its operation and has largely been neglected in practical terms as well as by scholars ever since. Its report, with the rather cumbersome title *Informe Final de la Comisión Investigadora Parlamentaria Sobre Situación de Personas Desaparecidas y Hechos que la Motivaron* (1985), documented that disappearances had indeed taken place in Uruguay during the military dictatorship (1973–1985).[69] The commissioners, though, made only two simple suggestions right at the beginning of their brief report: that the commission hand over its report to the Supreme Court and to the Executive, and that these two actors take appropriate action in accordance with the findings of the investigative commission's work within the next 90 days. No further action was specified.[70]

---

[68] The three other truth commissions in Uruguay are: (i) The parliamentary commission *Comisión Investigadora de las Personas desaparecidas y Hechos que lo Motivaron* and the *Comisión Investigadora sobre Secuestro y Asesinato Perpetrados contra los ex legisladores Héctor Gutiérrez Ruiz y Zelmar Michelini* (Investigative Commission on the Kidnapping and Assassination of Representatives Zelmar Michelini and Héctor Gutiérrez-Ruiz), (ii) Investigative Commission Requested by Senator Juan Carlos Blanco in Relation to His Conduct in the Ministry of External Relation in the Case of Elena Quinteros, and (iii) the investigation by the regional NGO *Servicio Paz y Justicia* (SERPAJ), which concluded its work with the publication of its report *Uruguay: Nunca Más* in 1989. These do not fit our definition of truth commissions, and hence are not included in our analysis, because they either focus on specific events (the first two) or are not state-sanctioned (the third example).

[69] The original report was stored in the archives of the Uruguayan Parliament and is not publicly available. However, there is a modern reproduction made by the Uruguayan government in 2007, now available online in an edited five-volume collection. This 2007 publication by the Uruguayan government of the truth commission reports was reproduced as a part of implementing a recommendation from the 2003 *Comision para la Paz*. The five-volume publication is titled *Investigación Histórica sobre Detenidos Desaparecidos*, and the truth commission reports are reproduced in Vol IV. See: http://archivo.presidencia.gub.uy/_web/noticias/2007/06/2007060509.htm.

[70] Original text in Spanish: http://archivo.presidencia.gub.uy/_web/noticias/2007/06/tomo4.pdf.

The commission did indeed hand over the report both to the Supreme Court and to the Executive, so both recommendations were fully implemented. However, all action on past human rights abuses ended there – and stalled for many years to come. The report and its contents were never acted upon by then-President Julio María Sanguinetti of the Partido Colorado, which was sympathetic to the military, or by the Supreme Court, which also had been sympathetic to the military during the dictatorship period (Skaar 2011b). So, although the commission achieved a 100 per cent implementation rate, it had little, if any, observable impact on how the Uruguayan government has dealt with the legacy of human rights violations. The lesson we can draw from the first truth commission in Uruguay is thus that even strong implementation records do not automatically indicate significant impact.

The second formal truth commission in Uruguay, the *Comision para la Paz* established by President Jorge Batlle of the Colorado Party almost two decades later, was of a different character. The commission issued its final report in 2003, *Informe Final de la Comisión para la Paz*, which listed 10 recommendations in all, from which we have identified 17 implementable items. Most importantly, the commission advised the government to establish a follow-up commission (which the Government did the same day it received the final report), that the executive accept the conclusions of the report (which it did), and that the report of the commission be made public (which it was). The commission further advised that various laws be revised, that enforced disappearance be established as a separate crime, that international treaties on human rights be ratified, that educational programs on human rights be established, that Uruguay's history of repression be included in curricula in schools, that a body for the protection of human rights be established, and that reparations be made. All recommendations have been either "highly implemented" (76 per cent) or "partially implemented" (24 per cent). Thus, the *Informe Final de la Comisión para la Paz* has a relatively strong implementation record. It is worth noting that progress in non-repetition measures is most lacking. Interestingly, the commission made no recommendations pertaining to constitutional reform or criminal prosecution – most probably due to the strong presence of the amnesty law, *Ley de Caducidad*.

1.3. CHILE (1991 AND 2004)

Chile Rettig (1991)

> [That] the authorities see fit to provide the measures and resources necessary to implement cultural projects for the purpose of vindicating the memory of the victims both individually and collectively.

Chile Valech (2004)

> Elimination of the criminal records of the identified individuals [victims] subject to the Commission's ruling, and restitution of civil and political rights arising from accessory penalties handed down in proceedings on which the Commission has ruled.

The first recommendations made by the first and second truth commissions in Chile respectively send an important message: while the first commission investigated deaths due to extra-judicial execution or forced disappearances, the second truth commission focussed exclusively on torture – an issue not dealt with at all by the first commission. The first commission drew the attention of the government to reparations and victims' needs, specifically projects aimed at memorialization.[71] This, in essence, was meant to commemorate the dead; hence reparations for the families of the victims of political violence who had died, and for society writ large. The second commission focussed on restoring the rights of (surviving) victims whose rights had been violated during the dictatorship period.

Besides Argentina's CONADEP, another influential truth commission in the Southern Cone that has received a lot of scholarly attention is Chile's *Comisión Nacional de Verdad y Reconciliación*.[72] More widely known as the Rettig Commission after its head, Raúl Rettig, it was established by left-wing president Patricio Aylwin soon after Chile's formal return to democracy in 1990. In its final report, the Rettig Commission documented what is now common knowledge: that around 3,000 people had been killed or disappeared in Chile during General Augusto Pinochet's rule (1973–1989). The commissioners were ambitious, yet quite prudent, in their recommendations. In contrast to the truth commission reports in Argentina and Uruguay, the Rettig Commission issued 110 recommendations (in total, we coded 207 actionable items) (Hourcade et al. 2022b). The bulk of the recommendations were made in three areas: institutional reform, legal reform and – the largest category of all – non-repetition. In fact, 90 of the 110 recommendations had elements of non-repetition. This emphasis was, no doubt, a response to the state's obvious direct involvement in massive human rights violations during the period of

---

[71] The Chilean experience with memory projects, also followed by Argentina, Uruguay, and other countries, has resulted in a growing scholarly literature on memorialization and the politics of memory. Some of this work is directly connected to the work of truth commission, some not. See, for example, Atencio (2014); Bakiner (2016); Barahona de Brito, González-Enríquez, and al. (2001); Bickford (2000); Collins, Hite, and Joignant (2013); Crenzel (2012); de Brito, González-Enríquez, and Aguilar (2001); Jelin (2007); Jelin (2010); Kaiser (2002); Lessa (2013b); Lessa and Druliolle (2011); Saona (2014); Schneider (2011).

[72] For thorough accounts of the Rettig Commission and its work, see for example, Bakiner (2016); Barahona de Brito (1997); Ferrara (2014); Roniger (1999).

military authoritarianism. This had left many Chileans, who were proud of the country's long uninterrupted democratic history, in a state of shock. In addition to these three major areas of emphasis, the Rettig Commission also offered recommendations regarding constitutional reform, and some in the field of reparations. Criminal prosecution, probably perceived as politically impossible given the political and legal constraints at the time, was given short shrift. While the commission operated, the 1978 Amnesty Law was in place and Pinochet was still head of the Armed Forces and remained so until he stepped down and became a senator-for-life in 1998 (Garretón 1999).

Three decades have passed since the Rettig Commission's recommendations were made. The overall picture of implementation is very encouraging. We have empirical evidence that, since 1991, 160 of the 207 actionable items (that is, almost 80 per cent of all recommendations) have been either "highly" or "partially" implemented (Hourcade et al. 2022b).[73] About 60 per cent of the recommendations involving institutional reform and almost all of the recommended legal measures have been implemented. Albeit few in number, all recommendations that have to do with constitutional reform or criminal prosecution have also been implemented. The recommendations that have been partially implemented, but where further action is still needed, are in the areas of legal reform, reparations, and non-repetition measures.

Because the Rettig Commission focussed almost exclusively on executed and detained-disappeared individuals, there was strong pressure from Chilean civil society to establish a new commission to focus on political prisoners and survivors of torture, widespread problems during the Pinochet dictatorship. The second truth commission in Chile, *Comisión Nacional sobre Prisión Política y Tortura* (or Valech Commission after the head of the commission, Bishop Sergio Valech) therefore had political imprisonment and torture as its explicit mandate (Collins 2017). The Valech Commission's final report, *Informe de la Comisión Nacional sobre Prisión Política y Tortura*, issued in 2004, documented that 38,254 people had been imprisoned for political reasons and that most had been tortured. The commission also found an additional 30 people who had been disappeared or executed who had not been recorded by the Rettig Report.

Informe Valech issued 42 recommendations, most of which had to do with non-repetition (22) and reparations to victims (16). Institutional (8) and legal (7) reform were also on the agenda of the commissioners. The commissioners did not recommend that a follow-up body be established.

By the end of 2017, about half of the recommendations had been highly implemented, and another 28 per cent had been "partially implemented"

---

[73] Strikingly, no recommendation is positively recorded as *not* implemented, whereas information is missing or not available for a little less than a quarter (46) of the actionable items. Since it is quite possible that some of the recommendations recorded here as 'no information' have in fact been implemented, the total number of implemented recommendations in Chile is likely to be *higher* than what our analysis suggests.

(Hourcade et al. 2022b). This means that implementation is well on its way. Unlike many the respondents of other truth commissions analyzed here, the Chilean government seems to have been doing particularly well in the areas of reparations and guarantees of non-repetition.

1.4. BRAZIL (2014)

> Acknowledgment, by the Armed Forces, of their institutional responsibility for grave human rights violations during the military dictatorship (1964 to 1985).

The first thing the Brazilian truth commission demanded in its final report, handed over to then-President Dilma Rousseff in 2014, was that the Armed Forces own up to their crimes committed more than three decades earlier. Brazilians had been waiting a long time for this apology (Schneider 2014). Scholars, too, have asked whether the truth commission and the apology came too late (Schneider 2013).

At the time of writing, Brazil is the last country in Latin America to have successfully completed an official truth-finding process with the public launch of a truth commission report. The *Comissão Nacional da Verdade* (CNV) (National Truth Commission) was established in May 2012, almost three decades after the transition to democracy, to investigate atrocities committed during the military dictatorship (1964–1985).[74] Its core mandate was to clarify the circumstances of the disappearance of persons. The CNV was criticized for its narrow focus, which left out the most pervasive repressive method used by the dictatorship: imprisonment and torture. It was also critiqued for not focusing sufficiently on human rights violations perpetrated against indigenous peoples and peasants (Ghelfi et al. 2022). In its final report, *Relatório da Comissão Nacional da Verdade*, the commission documented a total of 434 cases of assassination and disappearance and disclosed the names of 377 perpetrators responsible for these crimes, including high-ranking military officials and junta members.

Despite its voluminous report of almost 4,500 pages, the truth commission made only 29 recommendations, most of which were aimed at rectifying persistent democratic deficiencies in the army, security sector, and prisons. Part of the explanation for this relatively short list of recommendations has to do with time. In the previous three decades, there had been several efforts at dealing with past human rights violations through other means than a formal, state-sanctioned truth commission. The first official acknowledgment of state responsibility for human rights violations preceded the CNV by almost 20 years.

---

[74] The CNV also looked into crimes committed before the dictatorship, effectively covering the period between 1946 and 1988 in its investigations.

Notably, the *Comissão Especial sobre Mortos e Desaparecidos Políticos* (Special Commission on Deaths and Political Disappearances) (CEMDP), established in 1995, itself laid the ground for an extensive reparations program (Mezarobba 2016).

In light of what had preceded it, the CNV paid little attention to reparations. Criminal justice and constitutional reform were also allocated little room in the report, though the commission did make an explicit call for criminal prosecution of perpetrators of human rights abuses. By contrast, institutional and legal measures make up almost half of the recommendations and non-repetition almost a quarter (Ghelfi et al. 2022). The CNV divided the recommendations into four main groups: institutional measures, constitutional and legal reforms, and follow-up measures.

Some of the CNV's recommendations are quite complex. Of the 29 recommendations explicitly delineated in the report, we identified 70 specific actionable measures that span all eight of the categories used in our study. At the time of writing, we found no evidence of action on more than half of the measures articulated in the report. Only 4 per cent of all recommendations had been highly implemented, while 34 per cent had been partially implemented.

Given the short time-frame for studying implementation (our data goes through 2016), it is difficult to read trends. On the one hand, it is encouraging that there was progress on implementing over a third of all recommendations, and that some had already been fully implemented. Most progress had been made in the field of truth and memory. A special feature of the Brazilian case is the establishment of multiple, smaller truth-finding initiatives. During and after the CNV's operations, about 90 truth commissions were created within very diverse sectors: unions, social movements, universities and legislative bodies (Ghelfi et al. 2022). A number of memory initiatives can be found at the local and state level. Among other types of implemented recommendations, we find the issuance of death certificates for disappeared persons; the establishment of *Sistema Nacional de Prevención y Combate a la Tortura* (National System for the Prevention and Combat of Torture) (Secretary of Human Rights, 2015); and the *Red Latinoamericana de Reparación Psíquica* (Latin American Network of Psychological Reparation), created in November 2015 within the existing structure of Testimony Clinics of the Ministry of Justice's Amnesty Commission. Recommendations recorded as partially implemented include four legislative acts that were presented to Parliament but (at the time of our research) not yet approved.

More generally, we find some progress has been made on all types of recommendations. In other words, there is no field in which the government has neglected to do anything at all. Nonetheless, despite this relatively positive picture of the early phase of implementation, there is reason to be pessimistic for the future. Since Dilma Roussef was impeached as President in 2016, corruption scandals and economic crisis have dominated Brazilian politics. Moreover, there has been a significant ideological shift to the right, which has weakened the climate of respect for human rights. The current president, Jair Bolsonaro, is openly pro-military, a fan of the dictatorship period, and speaks positively of the use of torture. We should accordingly not expect much political support for further implementation of the CNV's recommendations in the near term.[75]

1.5. PARAGUAY (2008)

Create a National Human Rights Secretary, attached to the Presidency of the Republic, which will among other things pursue the following purposes:

(i) Elaborate a National Plan of Action of human rights, with the participation of the different state and governmental agencies and organizations of civil society. Once elaborated, the execution will be coordinated with the offices that work on the subject.

(ii) Drive the implementation and monitor the recommendations presented by la Comisión de Verdad y Justicia (CVJ).

(iii) Increase and refine constantly the records of victims and offenders of human rights violations.

(iv) Continue the task of search and identification of the forcibly disappeared and unofficially executed, initiated by the CVJ.

(v) Intervene as procedural subject in the disputes promoted by the CVJ in courts, in favour of dictatorship's victims.

(vi) Be part, with active procedural legitimation, to intervene as representatives of victims of human rights violations in the proceedings of all nature which initiate before a court of the Republic, as under the jurisdiction of international law.

(vii) Hold all the files and material resources of the CVJ and increase the documentary collection of the CVJ's files.

(viii) Coordinate the integral reparation program of medical and psychosocial assistance to the people who were victims of human rights violations.

(ix) Design with base in the present recommendations, a program of collective reparations for the communities which were affected by the collective attacks and suffered communal destruction.

(x) Organize, when necessary, other programs of integral reparation for the victims of human rights violations addressed by the CVJ report, as it is the case of Paraguayan political exiles.

(xi) Create mechanisms of participation and consultation with the civil society's organizations and the victims' movement, for the full compliance of its functions.

(xii) Make concerted efforts to ensure that women and minority groups participate in the public consultations aimed to elaborate, apply and evaluate the reparation programs.

---

[75] For analyses of the human rights situation under the Bolsonaro regime, see for example Hunter and Power (2019) and Schneider (2020).

The first recommendation of Paraguay's Truth and Justice Commission (CVJ) report is the longest and most detailed "first" recommendation of all in our sample. In a way, this recommendation provides a mini summary of the central concerns documented in the report as a whole, which issued a whopping 202 recommendations to the Paraguayan state. Paraguay had waited a long time for its truth commission. There were many things to repair.

Unlike other Southern Cone countries, Paraguay can be characterized as a personalist dictatorship under Alfredo Stroessner, who was ousted in a military coup in 1989 after ruling Paraguay with an iron fist – and strong military backing – for over three decades. The Paraguayan Commission of Truth and Justice (*Comisión de Verdad y Justicia* – CVJ) was established in 2003 to investigate the crimes and abuses committed during Stroessner's regime (1954–1989) and after up until 2003. This post-transitional commission was the third official attempt at truth-finding. Two previous attempts had stalled: The first commission was created within the Public Ministry in 1993–1994, but it was never properly funded. Another attempt to establish a truth commission in 1996–1997 stalled in Congress (Reátegui, Gómez, and Hurtado 2022).[76] When finally successfully established, the CVJ had a broad mandate to investigate a wide range of crimes. In its final report, *Informe Final. Anive haguâ oiko*, the commission documented 58 arbitrary executions, 337 enforced disappearances, 19,862 cases of arbitrary detention, 18,772 cases of torture, and 3,470 victims of forced exile. The CVJ also documented the extensive violence suffered by peasant communities, many of which were indigenous, especially during the 1970s. Many of the violations had been detailed in the dictatorship-era police documents aptly named the Terror Archives, discovered in 1992.[77]

The commission's broad mandate and findings are reflected in its extensive list of 176 recommendations (articulating 336 distinct actionable items); it is the longest and most detailed list of recommendations made by any Latin American truth commission. The CVJ was mandated to recommend the adoption of measures to prevent the recurrence of human rights violations, to consolidate the democratic rule of law, and to foster a culture of peace and harmony among Paraguayans (Comisión de Verdad y Justicia 2008).

The CVJ organized its recommendations into five broad thematic areas, in line with the UN Guiding Principles: satisfaction, restitution, compensation, rehabilitation, and guarantees of non-repetition. In fact, about one-third of all its recommendations (106 out of 336) had elements of non-repetition. Substantively, the commission made recommendations in a broad range of policy areas targeting many different kinds of institutions and actors/beneficiaries: civil-military control, military justice, legal reform, judicial independence,

---

[76]   See also Pelli (2003).
[77]   See Collins (2016); González Vera (2002); Pa (2008).

land reform, access to archives, criminal prosecutions, interculturalism, exiles, indigenous people, journalists, education, labour rights, codes of conduct, witness protection, prison conditions, gender rights, international human rights treaties – to mention but a small selection of issues flagged by the CVJ. The report's strong focus on violations committed against indigenous people, and the large number of recommendations addressing indigenous people and their rights, is a special feature of this report.

Needless to say, the Paraguayan government has faced a daunting task in implementing such a large, diverse set of recommendations. Assessing the rate of implementation in all these different areas has also been a tall order. We were unable to find implementation data for more than 70 per cent of the recommendations, a sign of inaction. Nonetheless, given the size of the pool, we still have data for almost 100 measures, more than the total number of recommendations for most of the other cases in our study.

We see some interesting implementation patterns in the data for the Paraguay case. Of the 28 per cent of actionable items for which we have information, 39 per cent have been highly and 48 per cent partially implemented, whereas only 12 per cent had not been implemented at the time our data analysis was concluded.[78] In 2016, eight years following the release of the CVJ's final report, progress had been made in the implementation of institutional and legal reforms, and with respect to non-repetition measures – including in the field of human rights education. The picture is more mixed for reparations: nine measures have been highly or partially implemented, whereas six more have not been implemented.[79] Building on reparation efforts that were in place before the CVJ concluded its work, the commission pushed for expanding access to reparations to more groups of victims, like exiles and indigenous communities.[80] The reparations program was very ambitious; making up almost 20 per cent of all recommendations (62 out of 336). More progress has been made with respect to symbolic reparations than material reparations. Much effort has been made in the field of memorialization, such as the establishment of museums and preservation of historical sites.[81] Illegal appropriation of land and land tenure is still a big issue in Paraguay. Judges have been accused of supporting landowners in many such cases (Reátegui, Gómez, and Hurtado 2022). The reports made several recommendations with respect to criminal prosecutions. There has been some, but still very limited progress in these matters compared to neighbouring

---

[78]   The percentages as a total of all recommendations are 11 per cent highly implemented; 14 per cent partially implemented and only 3 per cent not implemented.

[79]   Note that information is lacking for 47 out of the total 62 reparations measures. See Appendix IV.

[80]   For a discussion of reparations more generally in the Paraguayan case, see Arellano (2014) and Collins (2016). For reparations to exiles, see Arellano (2012).

[81]   For an analysis of memorialization, see Roniger, Senkman, and Sánchez (2015).

countries, in spite of the fact that Paraguay has no amnesty law in place that would preclude prosecution of alleged human rights violators (Collins 2016).

2. THE ANDES[82]

Distinct from the Southern Cone, there was no repressive network along the lines of Operación Condor connecting the countries of the Andean region. Each country suffered a different kind of authoritarian regime, with different kinds of repression. To date, only two countries – Ecuador and Peru – have established truth commissions to document the violence and concluded the work with a final report.[83]

2.1. ECUADOR (2010)

> To offer victims and the Ecuadorian society a declaration in the name of the State, made by the President of the Republic accompanied by the Minister of Defense and Government, and by the Commanders of the Armed Forces and the Police; that recognizes the facts and accepts the responsibility of the State in the violation of human rights established in the Final Report of the Truth Commission, ask forgiveness for what happened and commit to prevent such regrettable events from happening again, as well as to promote their clarification and inquest when necessary.

The Ecuadorian truth commission report's first recommendation focused on the victims of repression. Specifically, it stressed the need for victims to receive an official apology from the state; not only from the executive, but also the military and police. Further, the apology should be accompanied by a promise that violations would never be repeated in the future. In this sense, the recommendation is both backward-looking and forward-looking. Overall, as signalled in its first recommendation, the report placed special emphasis on non-repetition measures.

Ecuador has a history that differs in important ways from the other countries analyzed in this study. A small Andean country, it did not suffer a military dictatorship; nor did it have a conflict that can be described as an internal armed conflict or civil war. Nevertheless, the Ecuadorian Truth Commission was

---

[82]   Geographically, the Andes (Andes mountain range) extend through the western part of South America spanning Colombia, Venezuela, Ecuador, Peru, Bolivia, Argentina, and Chile. For our purposes, we define Argentina and Chile as part of the Southern Cone rather than the Andes.

[83]   Bolivia established the National Commission for Investigation for Forced Disappearances in 1982, but the commission dissolved before completing its investigation and producing a final report. For more details, see Hayner (2010).

established in 2007 to investigate human rights violations committed between 1984 and 1988 under democratically elected León Febres-Cordero in his efforts to crush a guerrilla movement and repress social movements and human rights organizations.[84] The commission further investigated state repression and abuses committed under subsequent presidencies up to 2008, a period characterized by extreme political instability (Reátegui, with Uchuypoma, and Hurtado 2022).

Characterized by strong presidential support and active victims' participation, the Ecuadorian Truth Commission was tasked with investigating, clarifying and preventing impunity regarding violence and human rights violations. The Commission's voluminous final report, released in September 2010, provided information about 456 victims, including 365 victims of torture, 269 victims of illegal detention, and 68 victims of extrajudicial execution (Comisión de la Verdad 2010, 53). Although it is one of the least known truth commission reports in Latin America, *Informe de la Comisión de la Verdad Ecuador 2010: Sin verdad no hay justicia* issued an ambitious reform agenda with 156 recommendations (which we have coded as 251 actionable items) dealing with reparations, justice, and institutional reform. Like the Paraguayan CVJ, the Ecuador commission organized its recommendations into five broad thematic areas, in line with the UN Guiding Principles: satisfaction, restitution, compensation, rehabilitation, and guarantees of non-repetition. The report placed special emphasis on non-repetition measures: almost half (114 out of 251) of all recommendations were aimed at non-repetition.

We have data on implementation for around 100 recommendations (specifically, 173 out of 252 actionable items), that is two-thirds of all recommendations. In total, 16 per cent of all actionable items have been highly implemented, 37 per cent partially implemented and 15 per cent have not yet been implemented. Information is missing for 31 per cent of the recommended measures. Since our estimate of implementation is on the conservative side, it is fair to say that, given the relatively short time-span (10 years), Ecuador's implementation record is encouraging, with over half of all recommendations in the process of implementation (at the end of 2017).[85] The Ecuadorian government has made progress in human rights protection through a number of diverse measures. Although it is difficult to make a direct causal link to the recommendations made in the report, these measures substantially address the

---

[84]   An earlier commission, the Truth and Justice Commission, had been established a decade earlier, but disbanded in 1997 prior to successfully concluding its work. For more details, see Hayner (2010).

[85]   The implementation rate (based on available data only) is twice as high for Ecuador as for Paraguay, although Paraguay has had a longer time-span (two more years) than Ecuador in which to implement the truth commission's recommendations. Part of the explanation may, of course, simply be missing information: twice as much information on implementation is lacking in Paraguay compared to Ecuador. However, other explanations for these differences could also be political will, resources, etc. – an issue we will not address in this chapter.

problems highlighted by the truth commission (Reátegui, with Uchuypoma, and Hurtado 2022). These steps include a number of legal measures and the ratification of various international human rights treaties.

The government also has adopted measures to ensure reparations to victims, through a law on reparations adopted in 2013, through material and symbolic reparations, and through judicial sanctions.[86] The government has established a Reparations Program to ensure cooperation between the ministries involved in the implementation of reparations to victims related to healthcare, education, and employment. Government efforts at monetary compensation are in place, but, like most countries, there is a large gap between the expectation of victims and what the government can offer. Regarding the large category of non-recurrence measures, we observe the most progress in the field of human rights education. This is well underway for public employees and in the school system, though not yet for schoolteachers.

A new Constitution enacted in 2008 marked a new turn in how human rights are understood in Ecuador. According to Reátegui, with Uchuypoma, and Hurtado (2022),

> The Constitution incorporated the *"sumac kawsay"* concept (*buen vivir* in Spanish) from the Kichwa people and declared a new form of social coexistence based on the recognition of the cultural diversity in the country, the construction of a harmonic relationship with nature, and the search of a sustainable way of living. The National Development Plan formulated in 2017 adopted this approach and included it as its main guideline.

By contrast, although there have been attempts to reform the judiciary, and the government has successfully implemented a program to protect victims and witnesses from intimidation, progress in criminal prosecutions has been minimal.

In sum, there has been some progress on human rights protection through a diverse set of measures adopted by the Ecuadorian government, though many of these measures are not directly related to the Commission's recommendations. The process of implementing recommendations is far from over. Despite active participation of victims in the truth commission, the construction of a collective memory about the violent past has proved hard to achieve.

2.2. PERU (2003)

> Develop policies and standards for the indispensable collaboration between the National Police, municipalities and citizens.

---

[86] For a discussion of the judicialization of the cases documented by the Ecuadorian truth commission, see Parada Galarza (2020); Solís Chiribog (2019).

Interestingly, the Peruvian truth commission chose to highlight the importance of positive collaboration between the national police and its citizens. This may seem like an odd choice, but it reflects the commission's explicit focus on institutional reform and non-repetition measures.

When the regime of Alberto Fujimori started to crumble under a stream of corruption revelations at the turn of the millennium, there was a political opening for setting up a body to investigate the human rights violations committed over recent decades. The Peruvian Truth and Reconciliation Commission (*Comisión de la Verdad y Reconciliación*, CVR) conducted an investigation of the violence that had taken place in the country during the period 1980–2000. The CVR concluded that crimes against humanity had been committed by illegal armed organizations (the Shining Path and the Tupac Amaru Revolutionary Movement) and by state security forces. It also asserted that almost 70,000 people had been killed or disappeared during the conflict (Reátegui and Uchuypoma 2022). The Peruvian truth commission and its 2003 report are among the most comprehensive truth-finding exercises in Latin America. The *Informe Final de la Comisión de la Verdad y Reconciliación* (abbreviated version: *Hatun Willakuy*) issued 82 recommendations (which we have coded as 149 unique implementable items).

The Peruvian government has frequently been criticized for not sufficiently following up on these recommendations, particularly in the area of reparations (Laplante and Theidon 2007). Yet, our analysis reveals that 41 per cent of all recommendations have been highly implemented and another 47 per cent have been partially implemented. With almost complete information, this means that only 10 per cent of all recommendations remain unimplemented. We think it is fair to characterize this as an overall strong implementation record. In particular, the government has followed up on recommendations that have to do with institutional reform, legal change, and constitutional reform. About half of the 40 non-repetition measures have been highly implemented and another 13 partially implemented. The CVR called for immediate prosecutions. There have been advances and set-backs in the area of criminal prosecutions – including the world-famous trial of ex-president Fujimori himself (Burt 2009; Gamarra 2009). Although there was a severe setback in the area of criminal prosecutions with the presidential pardon of Fujimori in 2017 (Cornejo Chavez, Pérez-León-Acevedo, and García-Godos 2019), trials are still ongoing.

Some of the progress on criminal justice for victims of human rights violations is directly attributable to the work of the truth commission (Cueva 2004).[87]

---

[87] According to Holá et al., "Prosecutions in Peru followed the recommendation of the Truth and Reconciliation Commission which issued its final report in 2003. As of May 2017, according to Peruvian human rights groups, 'prosecutors had only achieved rulings in 78 cases related to abuses committed during the armed conflict [...], and only 17 convictions' Holá, Mulgrew, and van Wijk (2019).

However, Peru is lacking when it comes to implementing recommendations dealing with reparations.[88] Only 3 out of 23 such measures have been highly implemented, while 19 more have been partially implemented. The saga of the establishment of the *Lugar de la Memoria, la Tolerancia y la Inclusión Social* in Lima is illustrative of the sometimes long, tortuous implementation processes for some recommendations. It took three years from when the museum essentially was ready to open until its formal inauguration took place in December 2015 during the government of Ollanta Humala Tasso. This delay was because of drawn-out internal struggles over how to present the role of the Shining Path in the internal armed conflict. Likewise, all follow-up measures are either partially implemented (five out of six) or hardly at all (one out of six). Two issues that the Peruvian commission has been commended for addressing – also in its recommendation – are the rights of indigenous people and sexual violence against women.[89]

3. CENTRAL AMERICA AND THE CARIBBEAN

Moving further north, we get into Central America, a region ravaged by civil war for decades. Two countries, El Salvador and Guatemala, managed the transitions from internal armed conflict to peace in the mid-1990s, aided by the United Nations. The UN was also actively involved in setting up truth commissions as part of the peace settlements.[90] Likewise, Haiti also in the 1990s set up a truth commission in the midst of UN peace-building efforts, this time with help from Haitians living in exile in Canada. Unlike South America, the involvement of foreign commissioners on national truth commissions is typical for this region. The only country in our sample here that had a fully national truth commission was the little-known commission in Panama.

3.1. EL SALVADOR (1993)

The findings on the cases investigated by the Commission on the Truth and published in this report give the names of officers of the Salvadorian armed forces who are personally implicated in the perpetration or cover-up of serious acts of violence, or who did not fulfil their professional obligation to initiate or cooperate in the

---

[88]   On reparations generally in Peru, see Bunselmeyer (2020); Correa (2013); Garcia-Godos (2008); Gianella Malca (2015); Laplante and Theidon (2007); Pa (2008).

[89]   See, for example, Duggan, Bailey, and Guillerot (2008); Falcón (2005); Kravetz (2016); Rubio-Marín (2008). See also more on this in the next chapter in this book.

[90]   The UN involvement in the El Salvador peace negotiations was a global first and was to serve as a model for many other peace processes in which truth commissions were discussed – including Guatemala, Angola, and Mozambique.

investigation and punishment of such acts. [A] For those officers who are still serving in the armed forces, the Commission recommends that they be dismissed from their posts and discharged from the armed forces. [B] For those now in retirement or discharged, the Commission recommends application of the measure described in paragraph C below.

El Salvador's truth commission was the only commission in Latin America to explicitly name perpetrators of human rights violations in its final published report. It was also one of the very few truth commissions to advocate vetting[91] of state officials involved in human rights abuses. Even more, it flagged this in its very first recommendation. This rather atypical measure, at least for Latin America, can be attributed to heavy international involvement.[92]

The UN-negotiated transition from civil war to peace in El Salvador in the early 1990s included the establishment of a truth commission, *Comisión de la Verdad para El Salvador* (CVES) in 1991.[93] The commission was fully funded by international donors. The three commissioners were foreigners because no Salvadoran was deemed capable of carrying out a neutral investigation.[94] Ownership of the truth-finding process hence became an issue.

UN Secretary Boutros Boutros-Ghali launched the commission's final report, *De la locura a la esperanza. La guerra de 12 años en El Salvador*, on March 15th, 1993. Tasked with investigating "serious acts of violence" committed between 1980 and 1991, the report documented widespread atrocities committed against the civilian population in a civil war that cost around 75,000 lives. It investigated atrocities committed by state officials as well as violations committed by the guerrilla movement, the FMLN (*Frente Farabundo Martí para la Liberación Nacional;* Farabundo Martí Front for National Liberation).

The commission was also tasked with "recommending the legal, political or administrative measures" which arose from the investigation (Buergenthal 1994, 501). The CVES issued 43 recommendations, which were classified into four main groups. Group one contained nine recommendations designed to penalize and disqualify the persons who had committed and/or were accomplices in human rights violations. The second group consisted of 16 specific recommendations that sought to eliminate the structural causes which had set

---

91 According to Collins (2020a, 24), lustration may be understood as "cleaning up" the civil service and other public institutions while vetting may be understood as performing background checks to prevent "unsuitable" people being hired, promoted or elected.

92 For an account of why it did so, see an article written by one of the international commissioners, also former head of the Inter-American Court of Human Rights, Thomas Buergenthal (Buergenthal 1994).

93 For an account of the transition, see Baloyra-Herp (1995); Popkin (2000); Walter and Williams (1993); Pa (2008).

94 The CVES team included an additional 12–20 persons over the course of the investigation, all of them foreigners, due to the country's extreme polarization (Buergenthal 1996).

the stage for the violence. The third section, consisting of 38 recommendations, aimed to avoid the recurrence of violent acts by means of institutional reforms. Finally, the last group contained 12 recommendations, designed to provide reparations to the victims of the conflict (Martínez-Barahona et al. 2022). Of the 43 recommendations made (which contained 77 actionable items), the most items were aimed at non-repetition (26), institutional reform (23), and legal reform (12). The report placed little emphasis on reparations (5) or constitutional reform (2). Notably, despite naming names, a call for criminal prosecutions was explicitly omitted from the report. This included investigations into the brutal assassination of Archbishop Oscar Romero in 1987, which had received world-wide attention.[95]

We have to understand this truth commission report in the context of a highly politicized and fragile political context, where the work of the truth commission needs to be seen as part of the larger peace process. The Salvadoran government did not really support the commission. The government, the Armed Forces of El Salvador and the Judicial Branch all rejected the CVES report. Moreover, the government effectively guaranteed freedom from prosecution for civil war crimes through an amnesty law issued only five days after the final report was launched.[96] In many ways, then, truth became a substitute for justice (Popkin and Roht-Arriaza 1995). As detailed by Margaret Popkin (2000), the El Salvador transition to peace was a peace without justice. Years later, other scholars confirmed that the price for the Salvadorian transition, reflected in the truth commission's work and recommendations, was to abstain from justice (Martínez-Barahona et al. 2022).

Bearing in mind this complicated political context, the implementation record for the Salvadoran truth commission is not impressive, but not abysmal either. As a result of the United Nation's reporting mechanisms, it has been possible to obtain detailed information on the implementation of most of the recommendations (Martínez-Barahona et al. 2022). About half (12 out of 23) institutional measures, about two-thirds (8 out of 12) of legal measures, and more than two-thirds (18 out of 26) of non-repetition measures have been either highly or partially implemented. The creation of new institutions, for example, seems not to have met much political opposition. For instance, a National Judicial Council was set up to help judicial reform. Reforming existing institutions, by contrast, proved to be much more difficult. As mentioned initially, the report placed substantial emphasis on removing people from office who had been involved in repressive acts, whether they worked in the armed forces, the judiciary, the civil service, or the FMLN command. Contrary to the advice of

---

[95] For analysis of the importance of this particular murder case, see for example, Karl (1991); Peterson and Peterson (2008); Sobrino (2016); Pa (2008).

[96] El Salvador's Supreme Court many years later, on July 15, 2016, struck down the amnesty law in a historic ruling, thus opening up for the criminal prosecution of civil war crimes.

the truth commission, the government did not follow up on this. A proposed constitutional reform that would have changed the election procedures for Supreme Court judges did not go through either. This was a serious blow to the rule of law given the tremendous responsibility the judiciary had for allowing impunity for gross human rights violations. With an unreformed judiciary and a blanket amnesty in place, criminal prosecutions became almost impossible for many years (Collins 2010; Barahona 2016). In short, reforming existing institutions where power dynamics were at play seems to have been very difficult.

Commissioners were not in the country to champion the recommendations. Faced with security threats, they fled the country in the commission's last weeks to write the final report elsewhere. The Supreme Court in El Salvador, which was heavily criticized in the report for having done little to hinder or combat the rampant human rights violations taking place during the 12-year-long civil war, was totally opposed to implementing any of the several reforms targeted at the judiciary in general and the Supreme Court in particular.

Nonetheless, despite this infertile environment, 40 per cent of all recommendations have, in fact, been 'highly implemented', and another quarter of the recommendations 'partially implemented'. A third had seen no action as of the end of 2017. According to experts,

> Successive ARENA governments did little to drive implementation of the Truth Commission's recommendations, until political power changed hands in 2009 ... Since then, some progress has been made to implement the recommendations (especially those related to justice and reconciliation), for example, the recent declaration of the unconstitutionality of the Amnesty Law (Martínez-Barahona et al. 2022).

Thus, there is still some hope for more implementation.

3.2. GUATEMALA (1999)

> That the President of the Republic, on behalf of the State of Guatemala and with the primary purpose of restoring dignity to the victims, recognize to Guatemalan society as a whole, before the victims, their families, and their communities, the events described in this report, ask forgiveness for them and assume the responsibilities of the State for the violations of the human rights violations connected with the internal armed conflict, particularly for those committed by the army and the security forces of the State.

The first recommendation of the Guatemalan truth commission report focussed on the dignity of the victims. With the CEH concluding that 200,000 people were killed in the bloody civil war, many of whom were found dumped in mass graves, this focus is understandable.

Like in El Salvador, the Guatemala truth commission was created in 1994 as part of the peace process negotiated by the UN between the government and the revolutionary group *Unión Revolucionaria Nacional Guatemalteca* (URNG). The peace agreement signed in 1999 ended more than three decades of internal armed conflict (1960–1999). The *Comisión para el Esclarecimiento Histórico de Guatemala* (henceforth CEH) documented over 200,000 killed and disappeared, 626 massacres committed by state and paramilitary groups, as well as widespread extrajudicial executions, torture, and forced displacement in its 1999 final report, *Guatemala: Memoria del Silencio*. Most of the victims were indigenous Mayans; many were women and children.

The commissioners were tasked with identifying the individual as well as structural causes of the violence. They made recommendations regarding truth, justice, and reparations. In total, the CEH's final report outlines 84 recommendations (which we have classified as 128 actionable items), emphasizing non-repetition (36), institutional reform (27), and legal reform (22). Importantly, the largest share of recommendations was given to victims in terms of reparations (38 measures in total). Only two recommendations dealt with criminal prosecutions. Constitutional reform was not even mentioned.

In substantive terms, the recommendations were divided into three main groups. The first group, comprising six recommendations, was concerned with honouring the memory of victims by obliging the government to ask for pardon on behalf of the state and the URNG, constructing memory sites, and recognizing the multiculturalism of Guatemalan communities. The second group, comprising 24 reparations measures, included the establishment of a National Reparations Program (*Programa Nacional de Reparación*, PNR), the search for detained-disappeared people (with a special focus on kidnapped and forcibly adopted children), and a policy of reparations. The third group, made up of 13 recommendations, aimed to foster a culture of respect for human rights through various measures such as the dissemination and teaching of the findings of the final report, education on culture of peace, observance of human rights through the adoption of international human rights mechanisms, the diffusion of international humanitarian law, protection of human rights defenders, and administrative procedures to screen bureaucrats responsible for human rights violations during the armed conflict (Martínez-Barahona et al. 2018).

More than two decades after the CEH issued its final report, over 60 per cent of all the recommendations remain unimplemented. Implementation is low across the board. Of the recommendations that have been implemented, measures toward non-repetition seem to be most successful (one-third, 12 out of 36, highly implemented), followed by institutional reform measures (11 out of 27 measures have been highly or partially implemented). Less than a quarter of proposed legal reforms (5 out of 22) have been implemented. Reparations to victims have been largely ignored (only one-third implemented). Even the recommendation to establish a follow-up body to oversee the implementation of all recommendations has been ignored by successive Guatemalan governments.

Nevertheless, the Guatemala truth commission succeeded in helping to place the topic of sexual violence against women on the international agenda.[97] It is also one of the few truth commissions in Latin America that have investigated violations committed against indigenous people and made recommendations to address these wrongs.[98] Interestingly, although Guatemala's Commission for Historical Clarification features among "The Five Strongest Truth Commissions" in Hayner's (2011) well-known comparative work, our data indicate that Guatemala is the country with the lowest implementation rate of all the cases included in our study.

3.3. HAITI (1996)

> The creation of a special commission on reparations of damage caused to victims of the de facto regime that emerged from the coup of September 29 1991, to meet legal, moral and material obligations described [in this report].

Victims' reparations seem to have been at the forefront of the minds of the commissioners of the Haitian truth commission when they wrote their extensive list of 166 recommendations.

The Haitian National Truth and Justice Commission (*Commission Nationale de Vérité et de Justice*, CNVJ) sought to uncover the truth about human rights abuses committed during the military regime in power between 1991–1994, end impunity, and reform the justice system in Haiti. Haiti is the only case in Latin America where a diaspora has been actively engaged in establishing a truth commission. According to Joanna Quinn (2019, 1830),

> Thin sympathetic engagement is a basic, cognitive understanding of the needs of the other. It played an important role in how elites from the Montreal Haitian diaspora were able to influence an NGO in their adopted country, Canada, the International Centre for Human Rights and Democratic Development, to work with the diaspora to secure a truth commission in Haiti.

According to Selvik (2021),

> The CNVJ's 1996 final report entitled "*Si m pa rele*" listed a comprehensive body of recommendations including reparations, institutional and administrative reform,

---

97   On the topic of war-related sexual violence in Guatemala, see for example, Duggan, Bailey, and Guillerot (2008); Kravetz (2016); Leiby (2009); Pa (2008).
98   On the topic of indigenous rights in Guatemala, see for example Crosby (2011); Sieder (2011a, 2011b); Viaene (2010).

criminal proceedings, and non-repetition measures. The final report placed particular emphasis on addressing sexual violence against women, as well as on judicial independence and education of the police force.

Over 90 per cent of the 166 recommendations (encompassing 196 actionable items) were focused on systemic change. We have classified more than half (93) as institutional, 31 as legal, 26 as guarantees of non-repetition, and 3 as constitutional. The CNVJ also called for criminal prosecutions. However, despite being the first item mentioned, reparations to victims seems to have not been a priority. A meagre 12 items were aimed at either material or symbolic reparations. We may, in part, attribute this neglect to weak Haitian civil society and the absence of strong victims' organizations that could put pressure on the commissioners during the drafting of the recommendations. On the positive side, though, the CNVJ recommended several follow-up measures to ensure the implementation of the various recommendations. The big question, of course, is whether these follow-up mechanisms actually secured the implementation of the recommendations.

In the more than 20 years that have passed since the Haitian truth commission handed over its final report to the government, implementation, while patchy and dominated by half-measures, has been far from negligible. A third of the recommendations aimed at institutional reform and half of the legal reform measures have been either fully or partially implemented. Measures of non-repetition have also been taken seriously by the Haiti government: almost two-thirds have been fully implemented. By contrast, no action has been taken on the three recommendations tied to constitutional reform. Likewise, only a third of the recommended reparation measures have been highly or partially implemented. Criminal prosecutions have been limited to a single case, the Raboteau trial, in which 22 individuals were charged with and convicted of massacring civilians. Given Haiti's weak legal system, any attempt at holding alleged human rights perpetrators to account is encouraging.

In sum, although few of the CNVJ recommendations have been highly implemented, the implementation rate looks better when we consider those that have been partially implemented. In total, more than half of all recommendations made by the CNVJ have seen some action toward implementation.[99] Taking into account that Haiti is one of the weakest states in the world and has suffered a series of calamities like earthquakes and cholera pandemics, this is no mean feat. We attribute this relatively high success to the near-constant presence of the United Nations since 1994. The UN, along with bilateral donors and other international

---

[99]   Although 36 per cent of recommendations are recorded as not implemented, there is a chance that some of the recommendations for which the data collectors have not found information (22 per cent of the total) have, in fact, been implemented.

organizations, have both pushed for and financed many of the institutional and legal reforms. For instance, the UN's heavy focus on sexual violence against women has resulted in changes in the Haitian criminal code related to rape. It has also resulted in a big societal focus on rape and sexual violence against women and children.[100] However, many of the issues highlighted by the CNVJ still need attention more than 20 years later. These issues are still salient, and the measures the CNVJ recommended remain highly relevant.

Twelve years ago, Quinn (2009) concluded that Haiti's CNVJ was a failed truth commission. The case study carried out of Haiti for this project shows that perhaps this should be modified to "partly failed". In fact, the truth commission was very ambitious in its long list of recommendations to the Haitian government. Though many of these measures have not been implemented and "the CNVJ and its report are today largely forgotten, … the demand for truth and justice in Haiti still stands" (Selvik 2022).

3.4. PANAMA (2002)

> To reopen those cases of human rights violations which occurred during the period under investigation, where the investigations of the Truth Commission have contributed new evidence to support conviction.

Criminal prosecution is the focus of the first recommendation of Panama's truth commission report. Yet, according to one source "Twenty-three years after the fall of the military dictatorship, not a single conviction has occurred for the crimes committed by the military regime" (Ross and Lucio 2015, 253). Impunity for human rights violations has a long history in Panama.

In another small, under-studied Latin American country, the Panamanian Truth Commission (PTC) was created in 2001

> to contribute to the "clarification of the truth about the violations of the human rights fundamental to life, including enforced disappearance, carried out during the military regime" that governed Panama between 1968 and 1989. The PTC also was tasked with making "recommendations for legal and administrative measures that in their judgement can be adopted to hinder or prevent the [reoccurrence of similar] events." (Rudling 2022).

Unlike many other countries in the Latin American region, the truth commission in Panama was established as the only transitional justice mechanism in the country. Its mandate specified that the Commission could not assume judicial functions typical of the courts, nor interfere with proceedings pending before them.

---

[100] See, for example, Davis (2010); Faedi (2008); Lankenau (2012); Reiz and O'Lear (2016).

Therefore, the investigations would not result in prosecutorial actions. The truth commission could not rule on criminal acts of alleged perpetrators while investigating the facts (Ross and Lucio 2015, 249). Its principal aim, then, was to physically uncover evidence of human rights violations. Supported by several North American and Panamanian anthropologists, the truth commission conducted excavations of over 30 sites spread across several provinces of Panama and identified at least 110 persons who had been assassinated and disappeared (Ross and Lucio 2015, 249–250).

In its 2002 final report, the PTC issued a total of 11 recommendations (which we have coded as 18 actionable measures), most of which had to do with legal and administrative measures that had non-repetition as their explicit goal. These included suggestions to reopen cases where the truth commission had gathered new evidence; moral and material reparation for victims; the creation of a Prosecutor in charge of investigating the crimes of the military regime; reform legislation governing the National Police to ensure civilian control; strengthen human rights education in schools and for law enforcement; publicize the truth commission report; establish a National Day of the Disappeared; carry out excavations where human remains were presumed to be located; use saliva of relatives and remains for their identification; and establish a follow-up body to give continuity to the work of the truth commission.

According to Rudling (2022),

> The main preoccupation of the Panamanian commissioners was to safeguard the work of the PTC in light of its clashes with the General Prosecutor ... and the upcoming presidential elections ... Thus, the repeated disputes ... stimulated concerns about the future of the judicial investigations, so that several recommendations refer directly to this, the archives of the PTC, and the location and identification of the human remains ... Furthermore, the final recommendation directly refers to the establishment of an office that would monitor the development and implementation of the recommendations.

The PTC specifically recommended criminal investigations into human rights cases.

There has been progress in implementing all 11 recommendations. This is definitely encouraging. However, a notable feature of the Panama case is that most of the progress on implementation has been only partial. For instance, there has been limited progress in criminal investigations and prosecutions. The government set up a special prosecutor to investigate human rights violations and crimes against humanity, but progress in these types of cases has been limited. Out of 81 potential criminal court cases, 47 were closed due to statutes of limitations or dismissed because of lack of evidence or witnesses. The remainder may be technically open, but no activity has been observed in years. Pardons and judicial inefficiency are other obstacles (Rudling 2022). Moral and material compensation for victims also has been partial. Interestingly, success has been the result of the intervention by the Inter-American human rights system. There have also been partially successful attempts at reforming the national police. Even a very concrete suggestion "To send saliva samples of the relatives of the forcibly disappeared persons and of the remains recovered, for their subsequent analysis using mitochondrial DNA and analysis" ended up being only partially implemented. While the DNA samples were "provided by the Follow-Up Office … the lists of relatives attached to it do not match, some DNA profiles are missing, and they lack samples for new analyses" (Rudling 2022). Moreover, although the government acted upon a recommendation to establish a follow-up body, it is poorly organized and has carried out limited investigations. In sum, although not unique to Panama, the case reminds us that even though a government may take measures to implement the recommendations made by a truth commission, we should remain critical of how much change is actually achieved.

4. CONCLUSION

The 11 case studies presented in this chapter represent the first attempt at comprehensively and qualitatively documenting the implementation record of all recommendations made by all formal truth commissions in Latin America. Covering a period of almost four decades, we have shown how important it is to apply a long-term perspective when trying to gauge implementation. Note also that we have made a distinction between 'partial' and 'high' implementation to capture the fact that implementation is often not a matter of either/or, but rather a process that may consist of several steps or actions.

Our main finding is that the degree of implementation varies tremendously across Latin American truth commissions, from a low of 40 per cent in Guatemala to full implementation in the case of Argentina's CONADEP and Uruguay's first parliamentary commission. However, we strongly warn against comparing the percentages across cases per se for at least three reasons. First, there is tremendous variation in the number of implementable action items in the recommendations (from two for Uruguay's first commission to Paraguay's 202). It may seem obvious that it takes more time and resources to implement 100 or more recommendations than it does to implement a handful. An implementation rate of 60 per cent for a truth commission with many recommendations is thus more impressive (and presumably has greater societal impact) than an implementation rate of 100 per cent for a truth commission with few recommendations.

It is unclear whether more recommendations are better from a normative point of view. Take the example of reparations measures. Some action has been taken on 22 of 23 actionable items in Peru, nine of 16 in Paraguay, and one-third of reparations measures recommended in Guatemala and Haiti. On the one hand, this represents clear progress in addressing victims' needs.

At the same time, we need to know more about the half-measures, i.e., where partial implementation has occurred, and the items for which no action has been taken. Patterns of implementation may be creating or reinforcing hierarchies of victimhood.[101]

A second important factor to consider is the time-frame for implementation. Across the cases, this varies by 30 years from Argentina's CONADEP report issued in 1984 to Brazil's truth commission final report issued in 2014. Although there is a tendency for implementation to take place immediately or soon after the government has received the truth commission report while the public eye is still on the investigation, this is not true for all countries. The political context in which a report is launched can also be detrimental to implementation. In El Salvador, for example, the CVE report's recommendations, issued by a group of UN-appointed foreigners, was not only ignored, but openly rejected by the government as well as by the armed forces. Consequently, little action on implementation happened over the next two decades, as the same political party (ARENA) that was in power during the war remained in power and continued to protect its own ranks against allegations of human rights abuses. In Argentina, most progress occurred under administrations that ruled more than two decades *after* the publication of CONADEP's report. Furthermore, although the comparatively weak implementation record for the most recent cases suggests that building momentum takes time; these also are post-transitional truth commissions. It may be that marshalling attention is more difficult as memories of the past fade, as research on truth commissions in settler-colonial contexts has found (Wiebelhaus-Brahm 2019).

Third, this brief survey of the cases suggests that implementation may be driven by context-specific factors. For example, implementation appears to have fared better in the wealthier countries in the region. Moreover, certain types of recommendations may be more likely to be implemented in particular contexts. For instance, backward-looking measures that seek to further address past violations like criminal prosecutions, vetting, and reparations are more controversial and are recommended, and implemented, at lower rates than forward-looking measures.

As a general rule, governments must demonstrate a minimum of political will and muster some resources to have recommendations implemented. The fact that implementation of complex recommendations may take place over many years and span several governments further suggests that there needs to be a persistent focus among politicians – but also pressure from civil society – not to forget about truth commission recommendations. In some cases, once an issue is placed on the table, it takes on a life on its own. Although a truth commission may have been the first to recommend something, the issue may

---

[101]   On hierarchies of victimhood, see Jankowitz (2018).

be taken up more broadly by society and/or the international community. In the end, the issue is present, but people may have forgotten that it was (first) raised by the truth commission. The focus on sexual violence against women and children in Haiti serves as an example of this phenomenon.

Finally, a comment on the "firsts". What do truth commissions prioritize in their reports? The first recommendation of each truth commission report jointly tells an interesting story of a variety of foci these bodies have adopted. Victims' rights were foregrounded in many of the reports. Guatemala spoke of the dignity of victims. Chile Valech and Haiti recommended reparations to victims. Four commissions (Chile Rettig, Brazil, Ecuador, Guatemala) urged the state to take institutional responsibility for past human rights abuses through acknowledgement. In the two latter cases, the armed forces were also urged to offer a public apology. Only one commission (Peru) prioritized institutional reform in its first recommendation. One recommended lustration (El Salvador), one a national human rights plan of action (Paraguay), and one simply recommended the establishment of a follow-up body (Uruguay 2003). Three commissions (Argentina, Uruguay 1985 and Panama) directly or indirectly highlighted the need for criminal accountability. This is somewhat surprising because truth commissions do not have prosecutorial power, and the overall number of recommendations mentioning criminal prosecutions across all commissions is actually quite small.

A pertinent question is thus: Does it matter what comes first when it comes to implementation? For the sake of curiosity, we checked the implementation rate for the 13 "firsts" discussed in this chapter. In total, nine out of 13 were highly implemented, two partially implemented and only two remained unimplemented. Interestingly, the two that remain unimplemented both demanded public apologies from the armed forces (Guatemala and Brazil) and one of the partially implemented recommended a purge of the armed forces (El Salvador). These findings strongly suggest that *the first recommendations of truth commission reports tend to be given priority in terms of implementation – except if the recommendation threatens the power or integrity of the armed forces.* Although we cannot assume that commissioners have always made a conscious decision as to what comes first in the order of recommendations, our conclusion is that it does actually matter.

The short case studies of implementation sketched in this chapter provide only a snapshot of the complex politics surrounding the formulation and implementation of truth commission recommendations. More details on each of these cases can be found in the second *Beyond Words* volume (Skaar, Wiebelhaus-Brahm, and García-Godos (eds.) 2022). In the next chapter, we more systematically examine the patterns of implementation in a cross-country analysis.

CHAPTER 6

A CROSS-NATIONAL ANALYSIS
OF IMPLEMENTATION

Promote decisively the dissemination of the final report of the TRC, so that all Peruvians can approach the fuller knowledge of our recent past, preserve the historical and ethical memory of the nation, and draw lessons to prevent the repetition of moments so painful as those experienced.

– First recommendation of Peru's truth commission report

In 2011, truth commission expert Priscilla Hayner noted "the weak record of implementation of the often very strong recommendations of truth commissions" (Hayner 2011, 6). Her conclusion is impressionistic, based upon a selection of 25 – strong as well as weak – truth commissions that had been established around the world over the previous four decades. In this chapter, however, we find that Hayner's conclusions are oversimplified, at least with respect to Latin America. A decade after Hayner published her book, we show that truth commission recommendations are, in fact, often implemented. By taking a systematic, fine-grained approach to studying implementation, we find much greater success, at least in Latin America, than has been commonly acknowledged in the transitional justice field.

Implementation of truth commission recommendations matters for several reasons. If we truly care about what impact truth commissions have on the (re)construction of peace and democracy after periods of authoritarianism and/or armed conflict, we cannot avoid taking into consideration the recommendations that such commissions make in their final reports. As we will argue in this chapter, it is hard to gauge a truth commission's potential short-term or long-term impact without taking its recommendations into consideration. Moreover, as our analysis shows, the recommendations made by truth commissions may potentially have importance for democratization and post-conflict reconstruction way beyond the mandates of the truth commissions themselves.

This chapter analyses the implementation record of nearly 1000 recommendations made by 13 Latin American truth commissions. We draw on an extensive database and 11 rich country studies (Skaar, Wiebelhaus-Brahm, and García-Godos (eds.) 2022), supplemented with secondary sources. As Chapter 3 demonstrated, in their final reports, most Latin American truth commissions have made recommendations in a wide range of areas, spanning institutional and legal reform, reparations, non-repetition measures and many more – in addition to measures to promote truth and justice. In addition to providing an empirical analysis of the kinds of recommendations that have been implemented in the Latin American context, we go beyond the purely descriptive to offer explanations for why we find different degrees of implementation across the different truth commissions and across different types of recommendations. Regardless of when the truth commission was established, in general, after its final report is handed over to the government, there is a loss of momentum. Governments are free to choose to implement the recommendations made by the truth commissions if they want, when they want, in different ways, through different actors and agencies.

The main argument put forth in this chapter is that *implementation rates are higher where special follow-up bodies are established to oversee the implementation of recommendations, where the dissemination of the truth commission's final report is seen as a priority by the government, and where the government has sufficient resources to put into the implementation of recommendations.*

We further argue that *non-systemic recommendations are more likely to have a lower implementation rate than systemic recommendations because of resistance from powerful perpetrators and less interest from the international community.*

This chapter is divided into six further parts. Following this introduction, the first part examines two specific measures that often *are* implemented upon the submission of a truth commission report, namely the dissemination of the report and the setting up of follow-up institutions to secure the implementation of the recommendations. We then take a closer look at the different categories of recommendations. Picking up on the substantive categories developed in Chapter 3, we broadly distinguish between so-called non-systemic recommendations aimed at individuals or collectives (i.e., victims) on the one hand, and systemic recommendations (aimed at state structures and legal and constitutional frameworks) on the other. Next, we dig further into the details of the recommendations that are typically most important to victims: the state's acknowledgement of past wrongs and public apologies; memorialization; dealing with the trauma of detained-disappeared; and criminal prosecution of perpetrators of human rights violations. In the following section, we look at recommendations aimed at securing democratic institutions and protecting human rights. Specifically, we look at different kinds of institutional, legal and constitutional reform, and recommendations aimed at non-repetition of human rights abuses. In our analysis, we identify both general trends and country-specific issues. Afterwards, we provide a brief overview of new themes that have been introduced into the recommendations of more recent truth commissions, such as sexual violations, gender, and indigenous rights. In the next section, we turn to cross-national analysis, providing descriptive statistics and identifying important trends in the data. From there, we focus on the recommendations that have not been implemented and offer some tentative explanation for why certain kinds of recommendations tend to be ignored by governments. The concluding section of this chapter provides some reflections on the importance of truth commission recommendations.

1. FOLLOWING UP ON TRUTH COMMISSION REPORTS

In this chapter, we flesh out some of the substantive issues that the 13 truth commissions have been concerned with in their recommendations. We distinguish between those types of recommendations that many truth commissions have made across time and across countries, and those recommendations that are particular to one or only a few truth commissions. Earlier in this book, we developed an eight-fold typology of recommendations (see Chapter 3 for further details) that we have used to categorize all of the actionable items recommended by the truth commissions in our study. By doing so, we both highlight important trends with respect to implementation and draw attention to some of the more context-specific issues. Before exploring these categories in greater detail, there are two kinds of recommendations that many truth commissions make that in principle weigh heavily on implementation. First, commissions frequently ask governments to make sure that their reports are widely disseminated to reach a broad audience. Second, they typically call for the establishment of a special body or (temporary) institution to oversee the implementation of all the other recommendations made in the report.

1.1. DISSEMINATION

One of the things that commissioners are concerned with is that their final report is disseminated to the public. Dissemination is important for at least three reasons. The first is educational, namely that truth commission findings should be made known to the masses so that the history of repression is no longer part of an obscure, hidden past. Rather, through the dissemination of the report, they become part of a common history. A second goal is prevention. Commissions hope that knowledge about human rights violations will prevent such atrocities from being repeated in the future. A third goal is to maximize the commission's broader long-term impact. In particular, if its recommendations are more widely known to the public as well as to state officials, it may generate more pressure for action, thereby improving the chances for implementation of the recommendations. In other words, our thesis is that, in various ways, dissemination may increase the impact of truth commissions.

Table 6.1 provides a brief overview of what happened to the truth commission reports analyzed in this book after they were finalized. Several truth commissions, like those in Peru and Ecuador, explicitly stated that they wanted their reports to be disseminated or made publicly available. In fact, some commissions went to great lengths in describing how they wanted the reports to be disseminated and whom they wanted to reach. The first Parliamentary Commission in Uruguay simply wanted its report to be handed over to the Executive and to the Supreme Courts. It did not mention public dissemination. By contrast, Chile Valech recommended that its report be disseminated widely, "including its distribution and that of its Summary to schools, universities, public libraries, consulates abroad and other entities, and the development of a website [with the Report's contents]". It also specified that every victim of illegal imprisonment or torture who is recognized in the report should receive a copy. Along the same lines, Panama's Truth Commission urged

> [t]hat the National Government guarantee the adequate dissemination of the contents of the Final Report ... so that it is made available to all Panamanians and contribute to a better and deeper understanding of the pain suffered by the victims and their relatives.

As we saw at the beginning of this chapter, Peru's commission offered a similar recommendation. In short, accessibility of final reports is an abiding concern for truth commissions.

Table 6.1. Dissemination of final truth commissions' reports

Truth commission report	Report disseminated and made available?
Argentina 1984	Yes. Handed over to President. Widely and easily accessible to the general public. Still available in bookstores in Argentina and electronically in Spanish and English translation of full report online.
Uruguay 1985	Partly. Report made available only to executive and the Supreme Court. No public dissemination. The original report not publicly available. However, there is a modern reproduction made by the Uruguayan government, online available, edited in four volumes by Presidency in 2007.
Chile Rettig 1991	Yes. Report widely available, full printed version in Spanish (Vols I–III) plus printed executive summary report in English. Both Spanish and English versions are electronically available online.
El Salvador 1993	Yes. Spanish and English versions of full report electronically available online.

(continued)

Table 6.1 *continued*

Truth commission report	Report disseminated and made available?
Haiti 1996	Yes. French original version of report available online. No English translation.
Guatemala 1999	Yes. Full report in Spanish and short version in English translation available online.
Panama 2002	Partly. Scanned version available online, but readability very poor. No English translation.[102]
Uruguay 2003	Yes. Truth commission handed over to President, who disseminated report. Full report in Spanish available online. No English translation.
Peru 2003	Yes. Full report in Spanish available online. No hardcopy (too many volumes). Abbreviated hardcopy version in Spanish (entitled "Hatun Willakuy"). English version of the Conclusions available on the CVR's webpage.
Chile Valech 2004	Yes. Spanish version of the first report and the additional/supplementary report electronically available. No English translation.
Paraguay 2008	Yes. Spanish version of report available electronically in several separate files. Problem with access to website. No English translation.
Ecuador 2010	Yes. User-friendly version of full report in Spanish available electronically but cannot be downloaded. No English translation.
Brazil 2014	Yes. Full report available in Portuguese, hardcopy and electronically. Conclusions and recommendations contained in the final report available on official website in Portuguese, Spanish and English.

Source: Information based on all 13 truth commission reports and country chapters in Skaar, Wiebelhaus-Brahm, and García-Godos (eds.) (2022).

Some reports were concerned with reaching minorities, or indigenous majority populations. For instance, the Guatemala report stated:

> the Government, in coordination with the organizations of Guatemalan civil society, particularly with indigenous and human rights organizations, to promote a massive campaign of dissemination of the report in accordance with the social, cultural and linguistic diversity of Guatemala.

---

[102] According to Adriana Rudling (2022), "There are, to date, two full printed versions of the PTC report. Both of these versions were published in 2002. The first of these was published with the help of the Office of the Ombudsman in 450 copies, and the second – by the PTC itself in 2000 copies". Apparently, these printed copies somehow disappeared and were never made available to the people in Panama. The Truth Commission had a website where the report could be found in PDF format, but, once the Follow-up Office of the Truth Commission was closed in 2004, the Office of the Human Rights Ombudsman arranged for the report to be placed on its site, where it can still be found today.

The report further urged

> That, respecting the multilingual character of Guatemala, the Guatemalan Academy of Mayan Languages carry out the translation of the Report, with public funding, into the following languages: [A] the complete report should be translated and disseminated to at least five Mayan languages: [A.1] k'iche, [A.2] kaqchikel, [A.3] mam, [A.4] Q'eqchi and [A.5] ixil; and [B] the conclusions and recommendations of the report should be translated into the twenty-one Mayan languages, in both written and oral.

Furthermore, it urged "That the Government provide for and finance the translation of the report's findings and recommendations into the Garifuna language [A] and [B] xinca". It seems that, particularly in multicultural societies, it was important to commissioners that the content of the reports reach the most vulnerable parts of the population.

Given the common focus on accessibility, it is a paradox that accessibility has not been a higher priority for governments. Most strikingly, no report in any country has been made available in local languages in its entirety. Also, given the world-time contexts of the various commissions and development status of their countries, making reports available only electronically – as in the case of Peru – excluded large parts of the population from gaining access to the findings as well as the recommendations. In Haiti, the report is available only in French, the colonial language, rather than Creole, which is the dominant language in the country. In sum, having dissemination as an explicit call in the final report may be an important, but certainly not a sufficient step, for the report to actually reach the majority of the population. How, then, to ensure that the recommendations be widely known, taken seriously and acted upon by the government?

1.2. FOLLOW-UP INSTITUTIONS

Except for the first three truth commissions in Latin America (Argentina's CONADEP, Uruguay's 1985 Parliamentary Commission, and Chile's Rettig Commission) and two later commissions (Chile Valech and Ecuador) that were in post-transitional contexts, the commissions in our study specifically recommended the establishment of a follow-up body to oversee the implementation of the rest of the recommendations made in their final reports. El Salvador's truth commission was the first of these remaining seven commissions to make this kind of suggestion. In its last recommendation,

> The Commission requests the Independent Expert for El Salvador of the United Nations Commission on Human Rights, in the report he is to submit to the

Commission on Human Rights pursuant to his mandate and to the extent allowed by that mandate, *to make corresponding evaluation of the implementation of the recommendations of the Commission on the Truth* (emphasis added).[103]

This was a special case since the truth commission had been set up by the UN.[104] Subsequent truth commissions used this as a model. Rather than request a neutral international entity to monitor implementation, subsequent truth commissions typically recommended a domestic (semi)-permanent institutional structure. For example, in its third-to last recommendation, the Haiti commission urged

> that a committee be set up as soon as possible in order to follow up the recommendations and in general the follow-up of the report of the Commission regarding its publication and dissemination for the education and information for citizens (male and female).

Panama's commission recommended that the government "create a follow-up body to lend continuity to all the material investigated, the declassified documents, the DNA evidence, as well as the remains recovered, which were produced by the investigations of the Panamanian Truth Commission". Though these follow-up bodies vary substantially in form, structure, mandate and permanence, they all share the common goal of making sure that the recommendations of the truth commission are implemented. Some of them, including that of Panama, not only oversaw implementation, but also were actively involved in the implementation of recommendations (i.e., what we call the implementing actor).

Table 6.2. Follow-up institutions

Truth commission report	Was a follow-up institution recommended?	Was a follow-up institution implemented (as of 2017)?
Argentina 1984	No	No
Uruguay 1985	No	No
Chile Rettig 1991	No	Yes (despite not being recommended)
El Salvador 1993	Yes	Yes. The UN followed up. Pedro Nikken (Independent Expert for El Salvador in the United Nations' Commission for Human Rights) was appointed in January 1995.

(continued)

---

103 Translation from the original report into English by the El Salvador data-collection team.
104 The fact that the UN monitored the follow-up meant that information on implementation has been more readily available than for some of the other commissions. See country study in *Beyond Words* (Vol. II) on El Salvador (Martínez-Barahona et al. 2022).

Table 6.2 *continued*

Truth commission report	Was a follow-up institution recommended?	Was a follow-up institution implemented (as of 2017)?
Haiti 1996	Yes.	Partially. No new government organization was established, but an existing Haitian institution did the job.
Guatemala 1999	Yes.	No.
Panama 2002	Yes.	Partially. The Follow-up Office of the TC was officially acknowledged by President Mireya Moscoso in October 2003.[105] According to the Decree, the Follow-up Office aimed to "carry on the effort deployed by the Truth Commission and assist in the achievement of justice and moral reparation for the families of the victims of the military regime". At the time that it was formally recognized, it was meant to function until the end of 2004.
Uruguay 2003	Yes.	Yes. President created *Secretaría de Seguimiento* through Resolution 492 of April 2003. Replaced by *Secretaría de Seguimiento de la Comisión para la Paz* in December 2007. Replaced by *Secretaría de Derechos Humanos para el Pasado Reciente* in 2011.
Peru 2003	Yes.	Only partially implemented. An inter-ministerial working group was established to develop/outline a follow-up institution and monitoring mechanisms. However, we found no evidence the working group fulfilled its mandate.
Chile Valech 2004	No.	
Paraguay 2008	Yes.	Yes. Vice-President Francisco Franco established the National Human Rights Secretary, attached to the Presidency of the Republic (*Dirección General de Verdad, Justicia y Reparación* (DGVJ) through Resolución N° 179/09, in January 2009.
Ecuador 2010	No.	No.
Brazil 2014	Yes.	Partially implemented.[106]

Source: All truth commission reports and country chapters in Skaar, Wiebelhaus-Brahm, and García-Godos (eds.) (2022).

As can be seen in Table 6.2, most states that were advised to set up follow-up bodies actually did so. In fact, follow-up is perceived as so important that the Chilean government set up a follow-up body after the Rettig Commission

---

[105] The Truth Commission reconstituted itself of its own accord into a Follow-Up Office immediately after it handed over its report to President Moscoso (Rudling 2022).

[106] See also Torelly (2018) for more details on the follow-up on the recommendations of the Brazil commission.

without an explicit call from the truth commission to do so. While we have documented whether or not such follow-up institutions were actually set up, we have not gone into the details of the workings of each individual institution and, hence, cannot comment specifically on the efficacy or impact of each institution. Nevertheless, there is a positive relationship between the existence of such follow-up institutions and the implementation record of the recommendations. We are confident in this assertion for at least two reasons. First, the fact that a government spends the time and resources necessary to set up such an institution indicates at least a minimum of political commitment to following up on recommendations. Second, once in place, and particularly if staffed with dedicated people, a follow-up institution makes it more likely that recommendations will actually be implemented by ensuring at least some part of the state is focused on implementation.

In addition to general follow-up institutions, some truth commissions also recommended the establishment of specific institutions to ensure the implementation of particular kinds of recommendations. Haiti, for instance, recommended the creation of a special commission on reparations of damage caused to victims in order to meet the legal, moral and material obligations described in the report. Where international actors were involved in the truth commission itself, specialized transnational bodies could be tasked with following up on certain types of recommendations. For instance, in the case of Guatemala, "CIDH (the Inter-American Commission on Human Rights), through its Task Force against Enforced Disappearance, made significant efforts to implement recommendations connected to enforced disappearance" (Centeno-Martín 2022).

Some truth commissions also recommended the establishment of permanent institutions to protect human rights in general.[107] Chile's Valech Commission, for example, asked for the support of the President of the Republic to create a National Institute of Human Rights. In Brazil, a federal state, the truth commission recommended that

> [i]n the state and municipal arenas, creation and support for the functioning of human rights secretariats must be fostered, such that when acting in the public administrative decision-making sphere, they can develop and coordinate actions of protection and promotion.

Further, the truth commission in Ecuador recommended the creation, within the Human Rights Department of the Ministry of Justice and Human Rights, of a National Observatory of Human Rights Violations that would involve victims'

---

[107] Note that we have classified this as institutional reform when we have coded the data. The purpose of these institutions, though, is to help the implementation of truth commission recommendations and secure the protection of human rights more broadly.

organizations and NGOs and serve both to monitor the human rights situation in the country and to formulate public policies on the matter. For its part, the Brazilian truth commission recommended the establishment of an institution meant to protect and promote human rights.

Most elaborately, the Peruvian CVR recommended three follow-up institutions/mechanisms. The first was a body to follow-up on the CVR's work, similar to most other truth commissions. Second, it urged the establishment of an inter-institutional working group to coordinate the follow-up on recommendations. This was implemented by the Peruvian government. Over the years, the CMAN[108] has strayed a bit from its mandate and has taken the lead on collective reparations in particular. Finally, CVR called for the creation of a National Council for Reparations, which has been implemented, with the main task of setting up the Unified Victims Registry.[109]

The lone exception to the norm of follow-up bodies is Guatemala. There, the CEH's last recommendation urged the National Congress to establish an entity, the *Fundación por la Paz y la Concordia* (Foundation for Peace and Harmony), to support, drive, and monitor compliance with the CEH's recommendations (CEH 1999, 82). However, successive governments have made no effort to create such a body. To fill the void, civil society organizations and human rights activists established the *Instancia Multiinstitucional para la Paz y la Concordia* (Multi-Institutional Authority for Peace and Harmony) to fulfil the recommendation's objectives (Centeno-Martín 2022).

In the next section, we shift the focus to a group of particularly victim-centered recommendations. These jointly comprise what we call non-systemic recommendations in this book (see Chapter 3 for details).

2. IMPLEMENTING NON-SYSTEMIC RECOMMENDATIONS

In this project, we have found it useful to draw a distinction between two groups of recommendation: (1) so-called *systemic recommendations*, i.e., those that aim to change state institutions (e.g., security services, laws, constitutions); and (2) those that do not, i.e., *non-systemic recommendations*. In this section, we are concerned with *non-systemic recommendations*. In particular, we focus on recommendations that are more directly victim-focused. Victims' demands after the end of periods of repression or internal armed conflict often boil down to

---

[108] The High Level Multisectoral Commission (CMAN) is charged with following up on public policies regarding peace, collective reparations, and national reconciliation (Reátegui and Uchuypoma 2022b).

[109] See section of report at: http://www.cverdad.org.pe/ifinal/pdf/TOMO%20IX/2.4 SEGUIMIENTO% 20RECOMENDACIONES%20CVR.pdf.

three things: truth, justice and repair. In this section, we focus on two of these demands, namely claims for reparations and for criminal prosecutions (i.e., justice narrowly defined). Given the centrality of enforced disappearances to the repressive repertoire of most states in this book, we place particular emphasis on the measures put forward to address this crime. Whereas truth, in some form or another, is a product of the truth commission investigation itself, as we show, truth commissions frequently seek to prompt action on reparations and criminal accountability through their recommendations.

2.1. REPARATIONS

Reparations constitute a very diverse group of recommendations. They are directed towards victims of human rights violations and their families. They include compensation, restitution, rehabilitation, and satisfaction. Reparations may be material and/or symbolic measures. Their intended beneficiaries may be individuals, groups, and/or communities (see Chapter 3 for more details). This group of recommendations is mainly geared towards victims and is in that sense backward-looking in nature. Although in theory victims have the right to reparations (United Nations General Assembly 2005), in practice many governments have been reluctant to fulfil this obligation. In his analysis of the potential political impact due to the recommendations made by 15 truth commissions from around the globe, Onur Bakiner (2016, 98–99) notes that

> *The least favored policy by the governments was reparations*: 12 truth commissions demanded compensation for victims, and only the Chilean government initiated a reparations program without delay. Governments in El Salvador, Haiti, Nigeria and Liberia ignored the recommendation for reparations completely (emphasis added).

Although reparations do not make up the largest category of truth commission recommendations in Latin America, we nevertheless find that offering *material or symbolic reparations* to victims seems to be a general government priority after periods of repression and civil war in many countries in the region. This is quite likely because victims' organizations, and civil society more generally, are well-organized in most countries and have placed considerable pressure on their governments to address victims' needs. However, offering material reparations is only possible where there are sufficient resources, and where there is a minimum of political agreement on whom the beneficiaries of reparations should be. Countries like Argentina, Chile, Brazil, Peru, and Guatemala have prioritized material reparations to victims. Aside from direct monetary compensation through pensions, in the region reparations also have taken the form of medical and psychosocial healthcare, housing, and education benefits. Some countries, such as Chile, Peru, Paraguay, and, at least partly, Ecuador have established extensive *national reparations plans* in direct response to recommendations from the truth commissions. In other countries, governments after a transition to democracy and/or peace set in motion separate reparations programs parallel to establishing truth commissions. In yet other countries, such as Brazil, the reparations program was set in motion long before the truth commission started its work (Mezarobba 2016; Torelly 2018). The last two scenarios would obviate the need for commissioners to recommend reparations, unless what has already been developed is incomplete, inoperative, or flawed. In other contexts, reparations have come in the wake of truth commissions.

Research using our data reveals important trends in reparations recommendations (Wiebelhaus-Brahm and Wright 2021). For example, commissions have devoted a greater proportion of their recommendations to reparations since UN General Assembly's 2005 adoption of Basic Principles and Guidelines on the Right to a Remedy and Reparation. In addition, while Latin American commissions recommend individual reparations with greater frequency, collective reparations measures are more likely to be implemented. Finally, while reparations make up a greater proportion of recommendations from post-transitional commissions, they are less likely to be implemented than similar recommendations issued by transitional commissions. Here we want to highlight some important cross-cutting issues that most Latin American truth commissions have emphasized in their recommendations for repair, and about which many victims feel strongly: (1) public recognition of past violations and public apology; (2) memory; (3) detained-disappearance, including investigation, exhumation, and access to information; and (4) truth finding (more generally). Each of these four issues will be discussed in some detail.

2.2. PUBLIC RECOGNITION AND PUBLIC APOLOGY

Frequently considered part of symbolic reparations, public apologies are a practice that has grown in popularity over the years. According to Wohl et al. (2011, 70), "The world has entered into an "age of apology", in which governments, armies, and corporations have increasingly begun apologizing for their role in committing historical and contemporary harms". This term encompasses public statements of contrition made to victims by government officials. Although the effects of public apologies are contested (Blatz, Day, and Schryer 2014; MacLachlan 2015), they are considered important because "it is through acknowledgment that the importance of apologies to victims, and their power as a step toward reconciliation, can be explained" (Govier and Verwoerd 2002, 67).

About half of the 13 reports that we have examined here asked for the public recognition of past violations, explicitly issued recommendations calling for public apologies, or, in the case of Paraguay, did both. Some commissions called for the state to offer an apology; other commissions specifically urged the armed forces or the national police to express contrition. The level of specificity depends on the structure of repression and which state agents were the chief protagonists. Of all the truth commissions, the Paraguayan Truth and Justice Commission (*Comisión Verdad y Justicia*, CVJ) was the most specific in its prescription of public apologies, outlined in no less than seven different recommendations. First, the report recommended

> that the State officially declare their responsibility for human rights violations that occurred during the dictatorship and to apologize to the victims and Paraguayan society therefore pledging not to repeat such aberrant situations, implementing for that all kinds of the resources needed to do it. Dispose that this statement be done by the presidents of the Executive, Legislative and Judicial branches, as well as the Commanders of the Armed Forces and the Police, with a recognition of the responsibility that corresponds to each one following the conclusions of the investigation of the CVJ.

It then went on to recommend that apologies be made to each group of indigenous people; to the victims of sexual violence, especially women and girls, as well as other people of different sexual orientations; and to other sectors that were victims, specifically children and adolescents, political parties, students, farmers, union workers, journalists, church members, and members of the army, among others. The commissioners further called upon the parties and political groups, or other organizations and institutions that supported or collaborated directly and indirectly with the regime of Alfredo Stroessner – in particular the Colorado Party – to accept responsibility for past human rights violations and to offer apologies to the victims. Further, it recommended that the state "Exhort the governments of other States, that supported the Stroessner regime, to offer apologies to the Paraguayan people and accept their responsibility for human rights violations contained in this report" and, given the transnational nature of repression in South America, "Offer apologies from the Paraguayan State to the societies of foreign countries who suffered human rights violations perpetrated in Paraguay or outside the country with support from the Stroessner regime". Finally, the state should "Insist that the alleged individual perpetrators of human rights violations who are alive accept their responsibility for the acts committed and offer apologies to the victims". Unfortunately, apart from a state apology issued in 2008, we do not find evidence that any other of these recommendations regarding public apologies have been implemented in Paraguay.

Ecuador, too, was quite specific in its report. It asked for the perpetrators of human rights violations to apologize to the victims and also that the General Prosecutor, the President of the Supreme Court of Justice, and the President of the Judiciary publicly apologize. Most importantly, its very first recommendation was to

> Offer victims and Ecuadorian society a declaration in the name of the State, made by the President of the Republic accompanied by the Minister of Defense and

Government, and by the Commanders of the Armed Forces and the Police; that recognizes the facts and accepts the responsibility of the State in the violation of human rights established in the Final Report of the Truth Commission, *ask forgiveness for what happened* and commit to preventing such regrettable events from happening again, as well as to promoting their clarification and inquest when necessary (emphasis added).

Recognition and apologies by the state were not sufficient: the commissioners demanded that the culprits ask forgiveness too. This is considered by some scholars to be an important element in reconciliation (Crocker 2003; Worthington Jr 2006).

As summarized in Table 6.3, some governments have complied with recommendations for recognition and apology; others have not. Often, recommendations call for the president to apologize, acting in their capacity as head of state. Of the instances in which they have been recommended, public apologies have been made by the presidents of Chile, Argentina, Uruguay, Paraguay, and Ecuador, but not by their Salvadoran and Guatemalan counterparts. More rarely, commissions have called on other officials to apologize, such as members of the armed forces or the national police. In particular, militaries have responded differently when called upon to express contrition for the past. Whereas the Guatemalan military, for example, has apologized for its involvement in extensive human rights violations, the Brazilian armed forces have not. Furthermore, we find several instances in which state apologies have been offered, even though the truth commission has not specifically advocated this in its report. Panama is a particularly interesting case. Though the truth commission did not specifically recommend a public apology, there was a perception that a public apology would be part of symbolic reparations to victims (Rudling 2022). In response to various cases before the Inter-American Court of Human Rights, no less than four public apologies were offered by four different state officials – including former dictator Omar Torrijos – over a period of eight years.

Table 6.3. Acts of recognition and public apologies

Truth commission report	Acts of recognition or public apology explicitly recommended?	Acts of recognition or public apology offered?
Argentina 1984	No.	Yes. Army Commander in Chief Martin Balza on April 25, 1995 publicly took responsibility for the "mistakes" made by the army.
Uruguay 1985	No.	Yes.*
Chile Rettig 1991	No.	Yes. President Patricio Aylwin apologized on behalf of state when sworn into office in 1991.

(continued)

---

[110] For details, see Barahona (2016).

Table 6.3 *continued*

Truth commission report	Acts of recognition or public apology explicitly recommended?	Acts of recognition or public apology offered?
El Salvador 1993	No.	Yes. Public apology for violations and to family of assassinated Bishop Óscar Romero made by state agents in 2010.[110]
Haiti 1996	No.	NA
Guatemala 1999	Yes. Demanded three different kinds of apology: (1) that the state ask victims and their families for forgiveness; (2) that Congress honour the victims; and (3) that the armed forces ask for forgiveness and assume responsibility for violations.	Partly implemented. (1) Presidents Álvaro Arzú (1996–2000), Alfonso Portillo (2000–2004), Álvaro Colom (2008–2012) all publicly acknowledged that genocide had taken place, but made apologies that were considered insufficient. Current president Jimmy Morales denies genocide took place; (2) Congress has not complied; (3) Military offered apology in 1999.
Panama 2002	No.	Yes. At least four acts of public apology have been made by three sitting presidents and one cabinet minister in connection with interventions by the Inter-American System of Human Rights. The acts took place in 2009, 2010, 2014 and 2017.[111]
Uruguay 2003	No.	Yes.*
Peru 2003	No/Yes.	Yes. President Alejandro Toledo offered a public apology to victims of the internal armed conflict on November 22, 2003, on behalf of the Peruvian state. This was long before the establishment of any follow-up institution or reparations program.
Chile Valech 2004	No/Yes.	NA
Paraguay 2008	Yes (public apology). Yes (public recognition).	Yes. The head of state, President Fernando Lugo, publicly apologized for past wrongs in August 2008.[112]
Ecuador 2010	Yes.	Yes. President Rafael Correa, upon receiving the truth commission report on June 6, 2010, gave a public speech where he, on behalf of the state, acknowledged past wrongs and asked victims for forgiveness.
Brazil 2014	No (public apology). Yes (public recognition).	No.

Source: All truth commission reports and country chapters in Skaar, Wiebelhaus-Brahm, and García-Godos (eds.) (2022).

* Note, however, that Uruguayan President Mujica's 2012 public apology – 30 years after the violations took place – was made in compliance with the *Gelman* ruling of the Inter-American Court of Human Rights, not in compliance with the truth commission report.

---

[111]   Personal communication with Panama expert and country chapter author in *Beyond Words* (Vol. II), Adriana Rudling.

[112]   An official apology was made by the head of state in 2008 in Paraguay (Bobowik et al. 2017, 580).

As Table 6.3 shows, some truth commissions called for so-called "acts of recognition" rather than for public apologies. For example, the Peruvian truth commission did not recommend a public apology directly, but rather "Acts of recognition" from the armed forces and the national police. Along the same lines, Chile Valech did not recommend public apologies directly. Rather, it recommended

> Public recognition by State institutions, as well as those that committed their responsibility or identify with the events described in this Report, with what happened; based on their commitment to not repeat [the occurrences] and promote respect for the rights of all people.

Paraguay's truth commission both recommended a public apology and also to "Make a public recognition, through the State, to the people, the foreign States and national and international organizations that defended and welcomed the victims of the dictatorship" and, further, "Make a public recognition, through the State, to the fighters and victims of the dictatorship in memory of the resistance of state terror and defense of human rights". Finally, Brazil's truth commission did not recommend a public apology directly. Instead, it called for "Acknowledgement by the Armed Forces of their institutional responsibility for gross human rights violations during the period of military dictatorship (1964–1985)".

In fact, since it was a post-transitional commission, debates about a public apology in Brazil had been raging long before the truth commission. Historian Nina Schneider has questioned whether past statements amounted to a "meaningful apology". The fact that "numerous post-1995 public statements (law decrees, legal appeals, Supreme Court verdicts, and official statements) effectively deny the Brazilian state's responsibility for human rights crimes" suggests that the truth commission's recommendation was still sorely needed (Schneider 2014, 69). Moreover, the fact that the truth commission explicitly called for a public apology, and the army refused to give it suggests that Brazilians are still waiting for something they can recognize as "A meaningful state apology – an act that publicly recognizes the state's wrongdoings and expresses regret – changes the social relations between the state and groups of victims and introduces new human rights values" (Schneider 2014, 69).

2.3. MEMORIALIZATION

One of the most important symbolic forms of reparations is what is often called memorialization.[113] Memorialization concerns the construction of human rights

---

[113] For two classic scholarly works on collective memory, see Halbwachs (2004) and Pollak (1992). The study of memorialization is turning into its own sub-field within the transitional

memorials and spaces, and official commemoration of past violations. The main objective of memory activities is to preserve the memory of victims through honouring them. Sometimes listed as a separate cluster of recommendations and at other times as part of reparatory measures, the emphasis on memorialization has increased in truth commission reports over the years. The first reports issued in Argentina, Chile, and Uruguay, for example, did not mention memorialization at all. By contrast, later reports have had a much greater focus on memorialization. Paraguay's truth commission, for instance, devoted six of its recommendations to memorialization. In Peru, there were 35 different recorded memory projects as of the end of 2009, many but not all of which can be traced directly to the recommendations of its truth commission.[114]

Memorialization can take many forms. Typical *memory activities* include the naming of parks and streets after victims, for instance. Detention centers and other sites of violence may be preserved. Chile Valech, for instance, specifically recommended that the main torture centers in the country be declared national monuments and memorials, and the designation of other sites in remembrance of the victims of human rights violations and political violence.

Yet, it was not only the state that was involved in the implementation, but also civil society. For instance, civil society pushed for the conversion of a former concentration camp and torture center on the periphery of Santiago, Chile, into the Villa Grimaldi Peace Park, now open to the public (Baxter 2005). Another clandestine detention and torture center of DINA (the Chilean secret police) called Londres, also in Santiago, has been converted into a memorial site. These are but two of many examples.

Museums may be constructed or established in repurposed buildings that had historical significance in relation to past violations. Others may be built from scratch. The three most well-known in our sample are found in Argentina, Chile and Peru. The ESMA museum is a memorial site built on the former premises of the Naval Academy located in the outskirts of Buenos Aires where around 5,000 people were tortured and died.[115] The second is the *Museo de la Memoria* in Santiago de Chile. This is a new building close to the city center, where the findings of the truth commission reports and all of the victims' testimonies are deposited for the next 100 years.[116] A third museum in Latin

---

justice literature, particularly within Latin America. For recent interesting works, see for example Amilivia (2016); Bakiner (2016); Collins, Hite, and Joignant (2013); Hite (2013); Lessa (2013b).

[114] Informe 2009. "Avances sobre el Cumplimiento de los Acuerdos de Paz" a propósito del 13° Aniversario de la Firma de los Acuerdos de Paz. For discussions of the importance of memoralization in Peru, see for example Ko (2019) and for contestation over history/ memory, see Feldman (2018).

[115] For a detailed account of the importance of ESMA and the contestation around using old sites of repression as memorials, see for example, Andermann (2012).

[116] For an account of the Memory Museum in Chile and its importance, along with another former infamous torture center, see Lazzara (2011).

America is *El Lugar de la Memoria* (memory museum, called Place of Memory, Tolerance, and Social Inclusion – hereafter the Place of Memory) in Lima; a beautiful place overlooking the sea that draws thousands of people – including many students and school children – every year. Brazil's truth commission also recommended the establishment of a Memorial Museum in Brasilia, but, as of 2020, no such museum had been established. Besides museums, which are large undertakings, other kinds of monuments may be erected at significant sites, or in highly visible areas of the country to remember past events and/or the suffering of victims.

Our data reveal significant memorialization efforts across Latin America that were at least partially instigated by truth commission recommendations. Chile, for instance, has had a long series of memorial projects, established by the state as well as by private actors. As a direct follow-up to the recommendations made by the Rettig Commission, in 1994 the state built the Memorial for Disappeared Detainees and Individuals Executed for Political Reasons at Santiago's general cemetery. It is considered a milestone in a series of memorial sites and monuments created for the victims of state terror (Hourcade et al. 2022b). As a direct follow-up to the Peruvian truth commission's recommendations, the project of constructing the Place of Memory began, but only after long discussions on how the country's history should be presented. Work on the museum started in 2009 and was completed in 2015.

Note that memorial projects can be politically controversial, as violent history is often contested by the different parties to the conflict. In Lima, for instance, one of the city's prominent memorial sites, *El Ojo que llora* ("The Eye that Cries"), has not only "become key … in Peru's ongoing 'battles for memory' or 'memory struggles'" (Drinot 2009, 15), but has also suffered vandalism (Milton 2011). Frequently, there are disagreements over how memorials should be designed and, for physical monuments, where they should be located (Naidu 2014). We know little about the effects of memorialization, however (Barsalou and Baxter 2007; Friedman, Sanchez Leon, and Wiebelhaus-Brahm 2019).

Other memorialization efforts are more symbolic in nature. Several truth commissions, such as those of Guatemala, El Salvador, Haiti, Chile Valech, Paraguay, and Panama recommended that a national day of commemoration for victims of human rights abuse be established, though not all have complied (i.e., Panama and El Salvador). They were given names such as a proposed National Day of the Forcibly Disappeared (Panama) and National Day for the Dignity of Victims of Violence (Guatemala). Another typical memory measure is the renaming of public parks or streets, as has happened in Argentina, Chile, Uruguay, and Guatemala. The names of victims of human rights violations also were used to name buildings at educational centers around Guatemala.

Another type of symbolic reparation was to order the dismantling of public monuments and removal of the names from public places of people considered responsible for human rights violations.[117] Several truth commissions called for such action. The Ecuadorian commission explicitly recommended that the government and the Ministry of Defense close and dismantle all of the places that were used as centers for illegal deprivation of liberty and torture, so they can never be used for these purposes again. Instead, the commission urged the state to declare the sites places for memory. Along similar lines, the truth commission in Brazil recommended the prohibition of official events commemorating the military coup of 1964.[118] Perhaps because of the comparatively low cost and ease of establishment, governments have often seem inclined to comply with recommendations for symbolic memorialization.

2.4. ENFORCED DISAPPEARANCES

Enforced disappearance (*desaparición forzada*) has been a common repressive practice among most of the countries included in our analysis. Not surprisingly then, many truth commissions addressed this issue specifically in their recommendations. Some reports, such as the Peruvian CNV's, recommended the creation of a specialized unit to investigate these cases further and sometimes identify new victims the commission was unable to investigate due to time, resources, and/or mandate constraints.[119] Others demanded forensic research into disappearance cases, making sufficient funding an issue. Yet other recommendations demanded the exhumation of mass graves, which often contained people who had "disappeared". A further group of recommendations addressed the follow-up to exhumation, i.e., what to do with the found bodies. Finally, some truth commissions gave recommendations particularly concerning disappeared children.[120]

---

[117] This parallels movements to remove memorials that commemorate colonialism and slavery in North America and Europe.

[118] For details on Brazil and (negative) memorialization, see Ghelfi et al. (2022).

[119] The Peruvian truth commission was particularly detailed in its recommendation: "proposing the creation of a National Commission for missing persons during the internal armed conflict between 1980 and 2000 as an autonomous institution to coordinate and supervise a National Plan for Forensic Anthropological Interventions, comprising the Ministry Public, the Ombudsman, International Red Cross, churches and institutions of civil society. This plan must be implemented by an Office of Missing Persons. It is suggested that the Ombudsman should present to Congress a public bill aimed at work on the criminal procedural aspects relating to the participation of independent experts in forensic anthropological work".

[120] Note that many truth commissions also made recommendations to address the issue of enforced disappearance through law. For example, several commissions urged strengthening of *habeas corpus* laws to inhibit the state's ability to disappear individuals. See more on this in the section on legal reform below.

In our study, commissions vary in the extent to which they focus specifically on enforced disappearances. At least seven commissions in our sample had one or more recommendations pertaining to enforced disappearance. The Guatemala truth commission report issued the most extensive recommendations in this area – no less than six specific recommendations, including a larger number of actionable items (Centeno-Martín 2022). First, the CEH recommended that the government and judiciary investigate cases of the detained-disappeared in order to find the whereabouts of their remains, and, in the cases where remains were located, that they be returned to the families. To date, the government has not taken action on this measure. However, the civil society organization *Fundación de Antropología Forense de Guatemala* (FAFG), with the assistance of the UN Development Program and the Swedish government, have undertaken some forensic investigations in the country. Second, the commission called upon the army and the leftist insurgent-cum-political party the Guatemalan National Revolutionary Unity (*Unidad Revolucionaria Nacional Guatemalteca*; URNG) to provide information regarding the detained-disappeared. To date, only the URNG has provided information.

Three other recommendations dealt specifically with disappeared children in Guatemala. Commissioners urged the government to establish a National Commission on the Search for Disappeared Children to coordinate this effort. Despite significant lobbying by civil society, the government has not supported the effort. In the absence of state action, civil society organizations created the *Comisión Nacional de Búsqueda de Niños Desaparecidos* in 2002 to achieve this end. Other recommendations to pass a law to increase the possibility to obtain information regarding adopted or detained children and to create an official campaign to facilitate the search for disappeared children have been ignored by successive governments (Valle, 2018). None of these recommendations have been implemented.

The issue of disappeared children was not unique to Guatemala. Disappeared children was one of the most contested issues after transitions to democracy in several other countries too, particularly Argentina and Uruguay. It was considered by many one of the most traumatic aspects of the dictatorships (Amilivia 2016). Yet none of the truth commission reports in these two countries addressed the issue. Nevertheless, the search for disappeared children and restoring their identities has continued until this day (Arditti 1999; Gandsman 2009). The crime of abducting and disappearing children has also resulted in a number of court cases, so-called "truth trials" as well as criminal trials (Skaar 2011b) – irrespective of the lack of recommendations by the truth commissions.[121]

---

[121] On the subject of disappeared children, see for example, Corbalán (2019); Crenzel (2020); de Baggis and Pallini (2020).

Closely linked to the issue of searching for the detained-disappeared is the issue of exhumation – another common recommendation made by truth commissions as part of reparations to victims. Exhumation simply means reopening old graves in order to identify bodily remains and to try to establish their identity. This was a very important claim for families of detained-disappeared and the NGOs representing them: they want to identify the remains of disappeared family members and give them a proper burial.[122] Some truth commissions (Guatemala, Panama, Peru, and Ecuador), sensitive to these claims, explicitly ordered exhumations; others did not. Let us use Guatemala as an example. Its truth commission, the CEH, recommended

> That the Government prepare and develop an active policy of exhumation and present to the Congress of the Republic, as a matter of urgency, a draft Law on exhumations that quickly establishes procedures for the same and takes into account the three following recommendations.

These further measures urged included that

> The process of exhumation was carried out with full respect for the cultural values and the dignity of the victims and their families, understanding the exhumation not only as a technical-legal process but, above all, as a measure of individual and collective reparation.

and, moreover, "That the bodies and remains of the victims be handed over to their families to give them a dignified burial in accordance with the culture of each one of them".

Across Latin America, there was significant variation in the frequency with which large-scale disappearances or mass executions were perpetrated. The exhumation of bodies, particularly in mass graves, has taken place in many Latin American countries, including Argentina, Chile, Brazil, Paraguay, Uruguay, Guatemala, El Salvador, Ecuador and Peru (García, Pérez-Sales, and Fernandez-Lina 2010; Navarro-García, Pérez-Sales, and Fernández-Liria 2010), and is still ongoing in several of these countries. These processes have often been assisted by forensic teams. In Peru, for instance, the CVR supervised the collection of forensic evidence at over 2,000 mass graves (Root 2009, 467). Even tiny Uruguay, where fewer than 50 people were recorded as detained-disappeared (and most of these persons disappeared in neighboring Argentina rather than in Uruguay), there were several mass graves identified (Lessa and Skaar 2016). Perhaps the most famous mass grave in Uruguay is nick-named *Caso Zanahoria*, (the carrot case) because the bodies were placed in the grave upright (like carrots) to take up less space.

---

[122]   For the importance of exhumations and memory, see Hite and Jara (2020).

Once mass graves were opened, a number of other problems presented themselves. Many truth commissions, therefore, addressed these through recommendations urging for (1) the identification of victims (through DNA tests of forensic investigation), (2) the issuance of death certificates (which would, for example, allow for the transfer of property and for widows to remarry), (3) proper burial rituals, and (4) the identification of children of the disappeared for the purposes of determining eligibility for scholarships and a range of other reparatory measures that depended on finding the identity of deceased persons. The implementation record for these kinds of post-exhumation recommendations is very uneven across commissions and across countries.

Locating and exhuming bodies from mass graves, and in some instances, restoring the identity of the dead bodies proved that horrendous crimes had indeed taken place in many countries. This knowledge was often what spurred civil society demands for criminal accountability.

2.5. CRIMINAL PROSECUTION

One of the most contentious issues at the time of transition in the countries analyzed in this book was the question of what to do with the perpetrators of human rights violations. Should they be punished or not?[123] Many countries included in our study had amnesty laws in place when the truth commission issued its report. For those that did not, legislatures often passed amnesty laws right after the truth commission report made its findings public, in order to preclude prosecution (Dancy and Wiebelhaus-Brahm 2015). Amnesty laws have different characteristics (partial, blanket, de facto, de jure) (Freeman 2009; Mallinder 2008; Mallinder 2012). In Latin America, some have been subject to legal or constitutional challenge over the years, and some remain operative today (Skaar, Collins, and García-Godos (eds.) 2016). Depending on the level of political tension and the status of amnesty laws in each particular country, truth commission reports have varied as to whether or not they have made calls for criminal prosecution.

If commissioners do urge prosecution, do they issue a blanket demand, or emphasize particular types of crime or professional rank of the alleged perpetrator? Seven of the commissions examined in this book explicitly recommended criminal prosecutions. Two more, Panama and Peru, recommended that investigations into criminal acts take place – with the underlying assumption that investigations, in the next round, would lead to criminal prosecution.

---

[123] For a discussion of this classic dilemma in transitions from authoritarianism to democracy, see for example Malamud-Goti (1991); Nino (1991), and Zalaquett (1989).

Four commissions neither called for criminal prosecutions, nor for investigations (El Salvador, Chile Valech, and the two commissions in Uruguay). Table 6.4 provides a brief overview of the truth commissions that explicitly called for criminal prosecutions or for investigations, and (where available) information on advancement made in this field.

Paraguay's truth commission most explicitly called for prosecutions by urging to the state to

> Start, reopen or continue, by the judicial authorities, the outstanding process to investigate the criminal responsibility of all the people named as alleged perpetrators in the report of the CVJ, given the imprescriptible nature of the crimes against humanity that occurred in Paraguay.

The Panamanian truth commission report is one of the most emphatic, urging further investigation as the foundation for criminal prosecutions. The very first recommendation calls on the state "to reopen those cases of human rights violations which occurred during the period under investigation, where the investigations of the Truth Commission have contributed new evidence of guilt". This is as explicit as it gets. Yet, Panama has not had any progress on trials, though some advances have been made in terms of investigations. Haiti also had a broad approach to criminal prosecution, ordering prosecution for other human rights violations. However, it did particularly highlight the importance of pursuing crimes against humanity and rape. Recognizing that there would be many obstacles to criminal accountability, the commission also asked for foreign assistance in investigating these crimes.

Table 6.4. Criminal prosecution and investigations

Truth commission report	Call for criminal prosecution or further investigations?	Advances in criminal prosecution or investigations
Argentina 1984	Yes. Prosecution.	Yes. Major advances in criminal prosecution.
Uruguay 1985	No.	Yes. Some advances in criminal prosecution.
Chile Rettig 1991	Yes.	Yes. Major advances in criminal prosecution.
El Salvador 1993	No.	Yes. Some advances in criminal prosecution.
Haiti 1996	Yes. Prosecution.	No.
Guatemala 1999	Yes. Prosecution.	Yes. Some advances in criminal prosecution.

(continued)

Table 6.4 *continued*

Truth commission report	Call for criminal prosecution or further investigations?	Advances in criminal prosecution or investigations
Panama 2002	Yes. Investigations.	Yes. Advances in investigations, but no criminal prosecutions.[124]
Uruguay 2003	No.	Yes. Some advances in criminal prosecution.
Peru 2003	Yes. Investigations.	Yes. Some advances in investigations and also in criminal prosecution.
Chile Valech 2004	No.	Yes. Big advances in criminal prosecution.
Paraguay 2008	Yes. Investigation and prosecution.	Yes. Some advances, but limited.
Ecuador 2010	Yes. Prosecution and extradition.	Yes. Some advances, but very limited.[125]
Brazil 2014	Yes. Prosecution	No.

Source: All TC reports and country chapters in Skaar, Wiebelhaus-Brahm, and García-Godos (eds.) (2022).

If we look at the three regions, most of the activity of criminal prosecutions has taken place in the Southern Cone. As can be seen from Table 6.4, there are many different scenarios. Some countries called for criminal prosecutions, and had large-scale trials (Argentina, Chile). Argentina's CONADEP was the first truth commission in Latin America to call for criminal prosecution of perpetrators of human rights abuses. Despite an amnesty law in place at the time of democratic transition, and two more amnesty laws being passed explicitly to hinder prosecution after the military threatened a coup in response to potential trials, ultimately Argentina is the country in the region that has seen the most trials and had the most people (mainly former military and police personnel) convicted for human rights violations.[126] The second-most successful country

---

[124] According to Rudling in the dataset on Panama, "The [truth commission] put forward 110 cases of extrajudicial execution (70) and enforced disappearance (40). The Follow-up Office of the TC formally presented 58 cases before the Public Ministry, in which there was new evidence. According to the report published upon the closing of this body, 41 had been opened, but had not seen any advancement due to statutes of limitations, 3 had been sent to the Supreme Court because the defendants were public servants, and 13 had been reopened and were under investigation".

[125] According to our country experts on Ecuador, "Although the creation of this specific office represented the starting point of a judicial process, as of 2014, the majority of the cases were still at the stage of preliminary investigation. One year later, of 118 cases reported by the Commission, only six had advanced" (Reátegui, with Uchuypoma, and Hurtado 2022).

[126] For accounts of the Argentine trials and the changes in amnesty laws over time, see, for example, Balardini (2016); Skaar (2011b).

in terms of prosecutions is neighboring Chile. Chile Rettig called for criminal prosecutions, despite the 1978 Amnesty Law being in force and former dictator Agosto Pinochet remaining head of the armed forces. When prosecutions finally started after Pinochet's 1998 arrest in London, the number of trials soared in a matter of months.[127]

Truth commissions have had a much more limited impact on criminal prosecution in other countries.[128] Neighbouring Uruguay, for example, had the infamous *Ley de Caducidad* in place at the time of transition, which effectively protected the Uruguayan military from prosecution until the law was declared unconstitutional and in violation of international law in 2011. Advances in criminal justice thus cannot really be attributed to the two truth commissions.[129] The first truth commission ordered that its report be sent to the Supreme Court, signalling that it at least indirectly hoped that this would lead to investigations. Yet, the government never acted on the recommendation.

Further variation in the form of the recommendation and the extent of implementation can be found across the region. Some truth commissions that called for criminal prosecutions have witnessed some advances in the form of limited trial activity in their wake (Guatemala, Peru). Some countries had truth commissions explicitly calling for criminal prosecution, but no follow-up by courts or governments is evident (Haiti, Brazil).[130] Other countries did not explicitly call for trials, but nevertheless have seen some trials occur (Uruguay, El Salvador). In fact, El Salvador is the only truth commission in our sample that did not explicitly call for criminal prosecution. The commission acknowledged that "The question is not whether the guilty should be punished, but whether justice can be done". It concluded that, given the weak state of the justice system at the time, "it is clear that, for now, the only judicial system which the Commission could trust to administer justice in a full and timely manner would be one which had been restructured in the light of the peace agreements".[131] Nonetheless, it identified individuals whom it concluded were responsible for atrocities, and recommended that military officers be removed from office based upon their behaviour during the civil

---

[127] For developments in criminal accountability in Chile, see for example, Collins (2016); Collins (2019); Skaar (2011b).

[128] For a discussion of criminal prosecution over time for nine Latin American cases, see also Skaar, García-Godos, and Collins (eds.) (2016).

[129] For developments in criminal accountability in Uruguay, see for example, Lessa and Skaar (2016).

[130] In Haiti, the truth commission explicitly recommended criminal prosecution in rape cases. However, according to our country expert on Haiti, "No legal action was taken by the government. There was no prosecution of perpetrators of sexual violence, and thereby no punishment. And as a consequence, no reparations to victims either." For more details on Haiti, see Selvik (2022) and the dataset on Haiti at: https://www.cmi.no/data/beyondwords.

[131] El Salvador TC report English official translation, no page numbers in electronic version.

war. Two decades later, there was a window of opportunity opening allowing trials to take place.[132]

Hence, this rather erratic pattern suggests that the causal links between truth commissions calling for criminal prosecutions and these in fact taking place may be quite tenuous. In some countries, we know that there has been an explicit link between truth commissions and trials. For example, evidence collected by CONADEP in Argentina or by the Rettig and Valech Commissions in Chile was explicitly used as evidence in trials. We also know that in other cases, like in Uruguay in the early 1980s, information on human rights violations was sent from the truth commission to the courts, but that no subsequent action was taken on the information. Later trials, therefore, took place for other reasons than in response to truth commission demands. In some cases, it took years for trials to be undertaken, sometimes as a result of chance. For instance, the arrest of former Peruvian dictator Alberto Fujimori in Chile and subsequent extradition to Peru eventually led to trials for genocide. Similarly, a very active and brave prosecutor in Guatemala, Claudia Paz y Paz, succeeded in putting former dictator Efraín Ríos Montt on trial and had him convicted of genocide.[133] These world-famous trials also opened up for criminal prosecutions of lower-level officials. It is difficult to say whether these trials might have still occurred in the absence of truth commission investigations.

Note that there are also countries in which attempts have been made at pursuing the search for the disappeared without tying this effort to criminal prosecution. For example, in Peru, victims' groups, human rights organizations, and international actors for many years demanded that the search for the disappeared be unlinked from criminal prosecutions (Reátegui and Uchuypoma 2022).

3. IMPLEMENTING SYSTEMIC RECOMMENDATIONS

Apart from recommendations aimed at individuals or collectives through addressing issues of truth, justice and reparations, Latin American truth commissions have also put a lot of effort into making recommendations that in

---

[132] A wide-reaching amnesty law was passed in El Salvador within a week of the truth commission report being launched, effectively barring prosecution. According to Martínez-Barahona et al. (2022), "On July 13th 2016, the Constitutional Court declared the Amnesty Law unconstitutional, thus opening a new stage in the fight against impunity and the prosecution cases investigated by the CVES, among others. The case of the El Mozote massacres, involving the killing of approximately 1000 people by military personnel in 1981, was re-opened in March 2017." For a historic account of impunity in El Salvador, see Collins (2010).

[133] See Burt (2009). For a more general discussion of prosecution of former heads of state in Latin America, see Lutz and Reiger (2009); Roht-Arriaza (2009).

one way or another would strengthen democratic institutions which had been weakened or absent during military rule or internal armed conflict. Moreover, re-establishing the rule of law, ensuring respect for human rights, and preventing future violations are a common preoccupation for truth commissions. Indeed, as shown in Chapter 3, three-quarters of all recommendations are what we have called systemic, i.e., aimed at improving the democratic system and respect for human rights. We now turn to a brief summary of the implementation of recommendations in four different categories of systemic measures: institutional change, legal and constitutional reform, and measures of non-repetition. Rather than trying to cover the huge variety of recommendations given by truth commissions in all four categories, in this section we highlight some common patterns.

3.1. INSTITUTIONAL REFORM

The human rights violations examined by truth commissions are the result of the state's failure to protect its citizens from violence and human rights abuses and/or predatory state institutions that actually perpetrated violations on the public. So, to prevent such violence from occurring in the future, truth commissions typically advocate the reform of a wide range of state institutions in ways that are designed to ensure non-repetition. The overall (implicit or explicit) aim of most of these reforms is to strengthen democratic institutions and, thereby, prevent future human rights violations.

Typically, institutional reform has been aimed at the courts, the police, and the military. There are also instances where truth commissions have called for the establishment of new institutions principally to protect human rights and secure democratic institutions. For example, the Peruvian commission recommended the creation of a Military Ombudsman as well as an autonomous body responsible for the protection victims and witnesses.

3.2. LEGAL REFORM

In Chapter 3, we defined legal reform as the "creation of new laws or revision of existing laws; *habeas corpus* laws and other measures designed to curb the state's ability to detain individuals arbitrarily and indefinitely". Truth commissions across Latin America have recommended legal reform in a number of different areas. Broadly speaking, these reforms are of one of three types. First, truth commissions often recommend the abolition of certain laws. The most frequent targets for this type of recommendation are amnesty laws and repressive national security/emergency laws. Second, commissions frequently call upon the state to ratify international human rights treaties.

Finally, usually some attention is paid in recommendations to the codification of certain violent acts (like torture, sexual violence and forced disappearance) as human rights violations in the criminal code.

The sheer diversity of legal reform measures that have been devised by truth commissions defies adequate treatment here.[134] Rather, we focus here on one of the most common, and arguably one of the most important, types of recommendation made by most, though not all, truth commissions in Latin America; namely, to incorporate international human rights treaties and conventions into national legal frameworks. Since the ratification of treaties is a highly ritualized public process, implementation is relatively easy to trace. Thus, we can say with a high degree of certainty that many countries in the region have in fact enacted legislation that accepted new human rights obligations under international law in the aftermath of truth commission investigations. Table 6.5 provides an overview of whether each truth commission made an explicit call for the acceptance of new international human rights treaty obligations. We also note whether the recommendation made a general call for ratification, or if the truth commission flagged specific conventions and treaties to which it wanted the government to accede. Finally, we provide information on the degree of compliance with these recommendations. For instance, if a convention was adopted by the National Assembly, but not ratified, we have characterized implementation as "partial".

Table 6.5. Implementation of international human rights treaties and conventions

Truth commission report	Did the TC call for inclusion of international human rights treaties and laws into national legal framework and/or ratification of international treaties and conventions?	Did the TC specify which treaties to incorporate? (general/specific)	Degree of implementation
Argentina 1984	Yes.	Yes.	High.
Uruguay 1985	No.	No.	
Chile Rettig 1991	Yes.	Yes.	High.
El Salvador 1993	Yes.	Yes. Eight different treaties specified.	High. Seven of eight treaties ratified.[135]
Haiti 1996	Yes.	Yes. Five different treaties specified.	Partial. Three highly implemented, one partially, one not implemented.

(continued)

---

[134] For details on the range of legal reforms recommended by the 13 truth commissions and their implementation status, see Skaar, Wiebelhaus-Brahm, and García-Godos (eds.) (2022).
[135] For details, see Table 3 in Martínez-Barahona et al. (2018).

Table 6.5 *continued*

Truth commission report	Did the TC call for inclusion of international human rights treaties and laws into national legal framework and/or ratification of international treaties and conventions?	Did the TC specify which treaties to incorporate? (general/specific)	Degree of implementation
Guatemala 1999	Yes.	Yes. Six different treaties specified.	High. All implemented.
Panama 2002	Yes.	No.	Four implementing events: highly implemented.
Uruguay 2003	Yes.	No.	High. One convention and one treaty ratified.
Peru 2003	Yes.	No.	Five implementing events: highly implemented.
Chile Valech 2004	Yes.	Yes. Three different treaties or conventions specified.	Partially. Two ratified, one missing info.
Paraguay 2008	Yes.	Yes. Seven implementing events specified.	High. Seven implementing events specified: five highly implemented, two partially implemented.[136]
Ecuador 2010	Yes.	Yes. Eight implementing events specified.	Partial implementation. One treaty ratified.[137]
Brazil 2014	No.		

---

[136] The convention that was ratified is possibly most relevant to our discussion here: International convention for the protection of all the people against enforced disappearance (2006). The status of HR treaty ratifications can be found at https://indicators.ohchr.org/.

[137] Ecuador: in addition to ratifying the International Convention for the Protection of all Persons from Enforced Disappearance (2010), other grave human rights violations have been incorporated into the national organic criminal code: "En el Código Orgánico Integral Penal se ha incluido dentro del capítulo de graves violaciones a los derechos humanos y delitos contra el derecho internacional humanitario, el genocidio (art. 79), la agresió (art. 88), lesa humanidad (art. 89), personas protegida spor el derecho internacional humanitario (art. 111) y bienes protegidos por el derecho internacional humanitario (art. 112)." Note that Ecuador had already ratified several other human rights treaties prior to the publication of the truth commission report in 2010. See Reátegui, with Uchuypoma, and Hurtado (2022) and dataset for Ecuador.

As can be seen from Table 6.5, we can make some important observations. First, and most importantly, all but two truth commissions (Uruguay's 1985 Parliamentary Commission and Brazil) made at least one recommendation regarding the incorporation of international human rights treaties and conventions into national (sometimes also constitutional) legal frameworks.

Second, there is variation in the degree of specificity with which these recommendations were made. Some made very general recommendations, like Chile's Rettig Commission, which advised "that the Chilean government ratify all international agreements that may be adopted or have been adopted in the area of human rights and to which Chile is not yet a signatory", without providing any further guidance. Most truth commissions, however, provide specific lists of treaties and conventions that they want the government to adopt and ratify. El Salvador tops the list with eight concrete conventions/treaties, followed by Paraguay (seven), Guatemala (six), Haiti (five), and Chile Valech (three). The Salvadoran truth commission specifically recommended that:

> Certain decisions should also be taken at the international level to reinforce the country's adherence to global and regional systems for the protection of human rights. To that end, the Commission recommends that El Salvador:
>
> (a) Ratify the following international instruments: Optional Protocol to the International Covenant on Civil and Political Rights, Optional Protocol to the American Convention on Human Rights (Protocol of San Salvador), Conventions Nos. 87 and 98 of the International Labour Organization, Convention on the Non-Applicability of Statutory Limitations to War Crimes and Crimes against Humanity, United Nations Convention against Torture and Other Cruel, Inhuman or Degrading Treatment or Punishment and the Inter-American Convention to Prevent and Punish Torture [7 implementing events], and
>
> (b) Recognize the compulsory jurisdiction of the Inter American Court of Human Rights established by the American Convention on Human Rights, as all the other Central American Republics have done [1 implementing event].

On the other end of the spectrum, Argentina's CONADEP is the only truth commission in our sample that made only one specific recommendation regarding one law: "That laws be passed which: 1. Declare forced abduction a crime against humanity".

Third, there are truth commissions that made very general recommendations (Paraguay, Uruguay 2003 and Peru), and, in response, governments operationalized the recommendations into several implementable events. Fourth, and importantly for our project, *implementation rates overall are high, regardless of the degree of specificity of the recommendation.* Governments in Argentina,

Chile, El Salvador, Guatemala, Panama, and Peru have fully implemented the recommendations made in this area. The governments of Haiti, Chile (after Valech), and Paraguay have partially implemented the recommendations made by the truth commissions. In two cases, we found that a country had signed, but not ratified, a convention (Guatemala and Haiti). Variation in implementation may partially be related to the passage of time; because truth commissions fall at different points in time, governments have obviously had varying amounts of time in which to respond. It also could reflect shifting political alliances and the changing levels of political support for particular governments.

A final comment on the outlier on recommendations related to treaty ratification: Brazil. The Brazilian truth commission made no recommendations regarding international human rights treaties or conventions. In fact, the Brazilian government had already adopted relevant treaties by the time the commission was established. The Brazilian government was one of the signatories to the International Convention for the Protection of all Persons from Enforced Disappearance in 2007 and ratified the convention in 2010 – i.e., four years prior to the truth commission report being launched.

The adoption of the International Convention for the Protection of all Persons from Enforced Disappearance may indeed be considered one of the great advances to protect human rights in the Latin American region, supported by most of the governments we have analyzed here. El Salvador is the only country in our sample that is not a signatory to this convention. Two more countries, Guatemala and Haiti, are signatories but have not ratified the convention (see Appendix VI for details).

3.3. CONSTITUTIONAL REFORM

Eight Latin American truth commissions made recommendations calling for constitutional reform. More than half of them made only one (Haiti, Chile Valech, and Ecuador) or two (El Salvador and Brazil) recommendations in this area. The commissions that ventured into constitutional reform more substantially were Chile Rettig (four recommendations), Peru (six recommendations) and Paraguay (eight recommendations). If we add together the main and sub-recommendations made by all commissions combined, our data counts 30 action items for constitutional reform found in recommendations across the region. This does not seem much, as it constitutes a minute percentage of all the truth commission recommendations we catalogued.

Nevertheless, there are some important observations to be made. First, for the commissions that made few recommendations in this category, they tended to highlight the need to change problematic constitutional provisions that gave rise to abuses or to insert new language that would serve a preventive purpose. Here is the text of the recommendations to illustrate:

Haiti: The Commission encourages the government to continue its efforts to remove the Armed Forces of Haiti as a separate body of law enforcement ... and recommends that the Constitution be amended accordingly.

Chile Valech: Review of the constitutional and legal regulations on the constitutional states of exception, to regulate restrictive practices of administrative non-communication of detainees, always allowing doctors and lawyers to visit detainees, and the proceedings of judicial recourse (amparo), in order to verify that the conditions of detention ordered under such conditions are consistent with the requirements of respect for the right to physical and mental integrity of the individual.

Ecuador: The Ecuador commission made only one recommendation, namely that Article 80 of the Constitution of the Republic be expanded to include punishment not only for the crimes of genocide, war crimes against humanity, enforced disappearance and aggression but for all serious human rights violations and breaches of humanitarian law.

El Salvador: One of the most glaring deficiencies which must be overcome in the Salvadorian judicial system is the tremendous concentration of functions in the Supreme Court of Justice, and in its President in particular, as the body which heads the judiciary. This concentration of functions seriously undermines the independence of lower court judges and lawyers, to the detriment of the system as a whole. The formal origin of this problem is constitutional, with the result that solving it requires analysing whether the relevant provisions should be amended, through the procedure provided for in the Constitution itself, so that the Court, without losing its status as the country's highest court, is not also the administrative head of the judiciary.

El Salvador: The constitutional force of human rights provisions should be reaffirmed, including those not set forth expressly in the Constitution but in other instruments such as human rights conventions binding on El Salvador.

Brazil: Constitutional legal changes must therefore be promoted to ensure the disassociation of state military police from the Armed Forces and that entails the full demilitarization of the police corps, with a view toward unification of forces in each state.

Brazil: Demilitarization of state polices should include the complete elimination of Military Justice state institutions that might still remain. Constitutional changes must be adopted to achieve this goal, therefore remaining a unique Military Justice at the federal level.

The implementation record of these recommendations is dismal. We lack information on implementation for most of these measures. Where information does exist, the implementation record is quite poor.

By contrast, for the three commissions that invested more energy in constitutional reform proposals, there has been greater success on implementation. The first truth commission in Latin America to address constitutional reform was Chile Rettig. It issued four recommendations, all of which have been enacted:

> The issuance of a binding interpretative regulation of constitutional rank declaring both that every juridical norm should be understood in the way that best protects human rights.

> Setting in motion the constitutional reforms necessary to make it possible to replace the present system in which the president appoints Supreme Court judges.

> It is recommended ... to consider the possibility of extending the scope of protected rights by the protection mechanism to all or a few of the constitutional rights that do not yet have this protection. It is proposed, in any case, to establish protection measures adjusted to the country's situation for those rights that, for practical reasons, would be advisable to exclude from the protection mechanism.

> Repeal of the constitutional provision (Article 41, No. 3, part one). Repeal of the constitutional provision (Article 41, No. 3, part two).

Paraguay's truth commission has had more limited success in implementing its eight constitutional reform proposals. Nationality was one concern identified by commissioners. The truth commission wanted constitutional guarantees for national citizenship for *sons and grandsons* of Paraguayans born abroad as a consequence of exile and a constitutional reform that would allow the descendants of the Paraguayans who live abroad to acquire Paraguayan nationality (i.e., dual nationality). Further, it wanted Paraguayans living abroad to have the constitutional right to vote. Only this latter provision has been enacted.

The Paraguayan commission further called for constitutional reforms that would strengthen various democratic institutions. In particular, it wanted constitutional changes that would guarantee an independent and efficient administration of justice, introduce recall referenda for elected officials, ensure a more independent Ombudsman, and give constitutional status to international humanitarian and criminal law to which Paraguay is a state-party. Commissioners offered a final general recommendation to include in all constitutional and legal reforms a gender perspective that ensures the rights of women and of other sexual identities. We find evidence of progress on implementation only for administration of justice.

Peru's truth commission also invested more effort in constitutional reform. Like Paraguay's commission, it urged the incorporation of international law into its constitution, in particular giving constitutional status to treaties on human rights. This has been fully implemented. The other recommendations to constitutionally strengthen various democratic institutions. In particular, commissioners called for changes that would: constitutionally distinguish between defense, on the one hand, and internal order and public security, on the other; constitutionally and legally define the National Police as a non-militarized civil institution and modernize the police profession; strengthen the role of Interior Minister for the purposes of guaranteeing public order, crime prevention and application of the law; bring military justice under the jurisdiction of the Supreme Court; and constitutionally guarantee that the purpose of the prison system should be the re-education, rehabilitation and reintegration of the prisoner into society. We find that, with the exception of reining in the military justice system, progress has been achieved on all of these measures.

In sum, Latin American truth commissions have made relatively few recommendations for constitutional reform. Most suggestions have to do with strengthening democratic institutions and human rights – and, in the case of Paraguay, rights of nationals in exile. Interestingly, for the commissions that invested more in recommendations pertaining to constitutional reform, there has been more success with implementation. This suggests that commissioners were pragmatic in their recommendations. Where the prospect of constitutional reform seemed remote, they may have concluded that significant effort in this area might be wasted. In addition, implementation seems to be more successful for legal changes that require constitutional reform compared to institutional reform that requires constitutional amendment.

3.4. GUARANTEES OF NON-REPETITION AND DEVELOPMENTS IN HUMAN RIGHTS

According to Naomi Roht-Ariazza (2016, 9), guarantees of non-repetition serve an explicitly preventative purpose. Unlike reparations or criminal prosecution, they are forward-looking measures. Nonetheless, the meaning and content of non-repetition measures have changed across time. They typically include demobilization and dissolution of armed groups, vetting, and security and justice sector reform. According to Onur Bakiner, (almost) all truth commissions recommend something along these lines, but the vague nature of these recommendations makes assessment very difficult. Guarantees of non-repetition frequently intersect or overlap with other categories, such as institutional, legal or constitutional reform, which also are forward-looking in nature. Guarantees of non-repetition include legislation (see above); education (see below); the creation of new institutions (like an Ombudsman's office) or the reform or elimination of existing institutions (especially repressive institutions); rule-of-law reform; security-sector reform; and cultivation of a culture of human rights/tolerance/social justice. Most of these reforms are recommended by other domestic and international actors too. Therefore, attributing these changes to truth commissions may be more difficult than with other types of recommendations.

In this section, we highlight one important, broad substantive issue that many Latin American truth commissions have been concerned with; namely, some form of education regarding human rights, with the purpose of strengthening democratic culture and practices. This is a cross-cutting issue that often includes elements of legal or institutional reform – as well as having non-repetition as an overall objective. We here highlight some of the different ways in which truth commissions in the Latin American region have addressed human rights education and analyze whether we can see any trends in terms of implementation.[138]

All but one of the truth commissions – predictably, the outlier Uruguayan Parliamentary Commission – have issued recommendations regarding education. These recommendations fall roughly into three different categories: (i) the right to education (reparatory measures); (ii) amending/changing laws to reform educational policies (legal change to reform public policies); and (iii) providing human rights education to different groups with the aim to strengthen democratic values and respect for human rights (non-repetition measures). It is the latter group of recommendations, numbering close to 80 implementable actions, that forms the focus for the rest of this section.

The number of recommendations made on education as a measure of non-repetition varies from a single measure, in each of the cases of Argentina's CONADEP and Panama's truth commission, to almost 30 recommendations on education as a measure of non-repetition for the truth commissions of Ecuador and Paraguay respectively. The other commissions fall somewhere in between these two extremes in terms of how many recommendations they have devoted to education with non-repetition as an explicit aim.[139]

We should not let numbers alone blind us, though. CONADEP's fourth recommendation that laws be passed which "Make the teaching of the defence and diffusion of human rights obligatory in state educational establishments, whether they be *civilian, military or police*" (emphasis added)[140] encompasses three entirely different sectors (the civilian population, the military and the police). Other truth commissions in our sample have treated each of these

---

[138]   Little research addresses the subject of truth commissions and recommendations regarding education. Paulson and Bellino (2017) in their analysis of 25 truth commissions globally cover a wide range of issues regarding education (not only non-repetition measures), but are much more superficial in their analysis and provide only selective anecdotal evidence on implementation.

[139]   It is not always unproblematic to decipher the exact meaning of the recommendations, as the borders between education, dissemination, and truth-finding may be blurred.

[140]   Implementation: Ley 24195 "Ley de educación federal" (implemented April 14, 1993).

different sectors independently in a number of separate recommendations, validating our focus on actionable items rather than the recommendations as delineated in the report.

If we look across all truth commissions, recommendations for human rights education are made for most actors at most levels: primary school, secondary school, higher education, the military, the police, the judiciary, the public ministry, etc. Recommendations are made for formal as well as informal channels. Most of the education recommendations are aimed at the educational sector and the security apparatus (military and police). There are some interesting exceptions, though. The Rettig Commission, for example, states that,

> In non-formal education we suggest that occasions for training be developed so as to allow other professional people (doctors, police and military, lawyers, midwives, social workers, psychologists, civil engineers, and so forth) as well as other social actors (parents, leaders of organizations, businesspeople, and so forth) to make the exercise of their profession or their work an occasion for human rights education. Formal education is thus not the only avenue for this kind of work.

As suggested by the above, recommendations on education are made at very different levels of specificity. Some recommendations are very general, such as Panama's sole education-focused recommendation "To strengthen human rights education at all levels of education and in the law enforcement sector". Other recommendations are very specific. This one by Chile's Rettig Commission features among the most comprehensive recommendations on education in our data:

> We suggest that in preschool and elementary school, human rights be brought into the whole curriculum and the whole activity of the school, on the basis of the Declaration of the Rights of the Child. Emphasis should be given to bringing the child to internalize values like respect, tolerance, cooperation, proper use of language, being able to express ideas independently, and so forth. From middle school to the end of high school, human rights should be integrated into all subjects and should be expressed in the problems that arise in the subject matter, as well as in the psychological and social development of young people, and in their confrontation with the historic and social reality in which they find themselves. In this regard education must go beyond Chile's recent experience to incorporate all those elements of learning that shape the individual for civic life and to assure that the rights enshrined in the United Nations Charter are fully in effect. In higher education, all training for professional careers should create appropriate spaces in which students can be imbued with the duties and rights proper to all persons. To that end we suggest that there be a chair or that there be seminars, workshops, or other forms of academic activity devoted to this area. On the graduate level, we think it is essential to create a body of knowledge around human rights by encouraging dissertations, papers, and so forth, on the issue.

As exemplified above, some truth commissions cram a lot of detailed instructions into one recommendation. Other truth commissions prefer to portion out recommendations in many smaller parts. The three commissions that stand out in terms of a broad and systematic focus on human rights education in general are the commissions of Chile Rettig, Paraguay, and Ecuador. All three commissions direct their education measures at the general public in addition to specifically mentioned sectors of society. Although the Rettig Commission made fewer recommendations than the more recent commissions of Paraguay and Ecuador, all three cover a wide range of actors and institutions. The Paraguay and Ecuador commissions should be commended for stressing education in matters of gender and multiculturalism with an aim to promote respect for human rights and democracy. We would also like to highlight the use of the truth commission reports for education purposes. In Ecuador "One clear achievement of the Ombudsman's Office was the dissemination of the final report in the public education system in order to show how this past period affected the present context" (Reátegui, with Uchuypoma, and Hurtado 2022).

Whereas some commissions adopted a broad and comprehensive approach to the importance of human rights education, other commissions took a much narrower approach. El Salvador's commission, for instance, issued only three recommendations on education: all of them were specifically aimed at the armed forces and all stressed training courses in human rights and democracy. Brazil, too, issued only three recommendations on education, two of which were aimed at the armed forces and police forces (the third was for human rights education more broadly). By contrast, the Guatemalan commission, in one of its five recommendations on education, urged

> That the State co-financing with the national human rights NGOs and developing an education campaign on a culture of mutual respect and peace, addressed to the various political and social sectors. The campaign must be based on principles such as respect for human rights, democracy, tolerance, and dialog as an instrument for the peaceful settlement of disputes, as well as the promotion of development and the free flow of information, with particular emphasis on the content of the Universal Declaration of Human Rights and on the fundamental principle of peace.

In terms of the implementation, we make three observations. First, recommendations on education seem, in general, to have been taken quite seriously by governments across Latin America. For the recommendations on which we have information, most are either recorded as highly implemented or partially implemented. Indeed, very few recommendations are recorded as not implemented. In particular, recommendations aimed at human rights education for the military and/or police seem to generally be highly implemented (as in the cases of Chile, El Salvador, Peru, Paraguay, Ecuador), and in one case (Haiti) partially implemented. This suggests that many countries in the region have been concerned with reforming the state security apparatus after transitions to democratic rule, and that installing democratic values and respect for human rights in the military and the police was considered an important part of the transition.

Second, and perhaps surprisingly, recommendations aimed at the education sector in general (from primary school up to the university sector) have a more uneven implementation record. Many reform efforts are recorded as partially implemented. This may simply be because reform of education is much broader in scope (encompassing primary, secondary and university education) than, for instance, the armed forces, requires a lot of resources, is harder to implement, and possibly also harder to "measure".

Third, there does not seem to be any particular relationship between the implementation rates for specific versus more general recommendations. A discernible pattern, though, is that recommendations that list a lot of details on who should be involved and who the recommendation should benefit have a tendency to be recorded as partially implemented rather than fully implemented. This is logical, as the more elements there are to implement, the more likely it is that some elements are not achieved and, thus, all items in the box cannot be checked. In sum, human rights education is considered a priority within measures of non-repetition. It is one of the areas dealt with in the recommendations of Latin American truth commissions where we can safely say that substantial progress has been made in terms of implementation.

4. INCORPORATING NEW RIGHTS CONCERNS INTO TRUTH COMMISSIONS

As argued in this book, most truth commissions have made relatively similar recommendations with respect to many of the categories that we have analyzed. Perhaps this is not so surprising, as most countries have been concerned with the same kind of issues after emerging from authoritarian rule or civil war: building democratic institutions, putting in place better laws, providing reparations to victims, and pursuing criminal accountability. In our data, though, we also see new types of concerns that have been gradually seeping into the work and recommendations of truth commissions. These issues have become more salient in newer commissions and reflect changing international norms and procedures in the human rights field, what we call "world-time". In fact, research using our data finds that mentions of specific identity groups often closely follow global and regional initiatives to address the rights of groups (Wiebelhaus-Brahm and Wright 2021). However, in general, this growing attention does not seem to compel governments to implement these recommendations. In this section, we briefly discuss three such topics: indigenous rights, sexual violence, and gender/LGBT rights. Although only a handful of truth commissions have dealt with these issues, they might be setting trends for future truth commissions in the region and beyond as they seek to fulfil their own mandates.

4.1. INDIGENOUS RIGHTS

Only four commissions in our study provided recommendations with respect to indigenous rights: Guatemala, Peru, Paraguay, and Ecuador. Not surprisingly, these are the four countries that have the largest indigenous populations of the 11 countries that we have analyzed. Nonetheless, truth commissions in other countries with significant indigenous populations failed to highlight the unique experiences and needs of this demographic.

Guatemala's CEH was the first to make indigenous rights a focus. It made a number of recommendations on the subject. Some were aimed at memorialization and judicial integration; some concerned the army, and the security sector. One important recommendation regarding collective symbolic reparations was that the commemorations and ceremonies for the victims of the civil war should take into consideration the multicultural nature of the Guatemalan nation. Commissioners recommended that this should be done by raising monuments and creating communal cemeteries in accordance with the forms of Mayan collective memory, and by respecting places that Mayans consider sacred. All these recommendations were implemented by the state (Martínez-Barahona et al. 2018).

Another set of recommendations sought to promote the political participation and civic engagement of indigenous peoples. Specifically, they called for the inclusion of qualified and experienced indigenous professionals in state institutions and for the establishment and financing of a program of scholarships for the training and specialization of indigenous professionals (CEH 1999, 81). Some progress has been made in the years since, though indigenous peoples continue to be underrepresented in a variety of areas, including the fields of public administration and politics (IWGIA 2018).

A third area was full compliance with the Agreement on the Identity and Rights of Indigenous Peoples, a deal forged between the Guatemalan government and the URNG as part of the peace process (CEH 1999, 81). Furthermore, tax reform was proposed to benefit the poorer segments of society – mainly indigenous people (CEH 1999, 82), but we found no evidence that the state has followed up on this.[141] Overall, despite the implementation of several measures, today, indigenous people continue to experience severe discrimination in Guatemala (Saquec 2016).

In Peru, the truth commission came up with two important recommendations: the recognition and integration of the rights of indigenous peoples and of their

---

[141]   For more details on recommendations on indigenous issues and their implementation in Guatemala, see Centeno-Martín (2022).

communities in the national juridical framework, and the creation of a state body dedicated to Indigenous policies and matters. Both recommendations were implemented within seven years of the report's launch, suggesting that indigenous rights were relatively high on the agenda of the governments of both Alejandro Toledo (2001–2006) and Ollanta Humala (2011–2016).

Paraguay and Ecuador also issued a number of recommendations in this area. As we have noted in other contexts, the recommendations are quite similar in character. Paraguay's truth commission offered the following recommendations specifically targeted at indigenous people:

> Instruct the National Secretariat of Human Rights and the National Indigenous Institute to undertake research about the cases of killings and other human rights violations against indigenous people during the dictatorship, with the purpose of clarify the dates, locations, offenders and victims, and proposing options for repair, including the situation of the rights of indigenous children that were sold as servants.

> Increase by an appropriate amount through the National Congress the budget for the National Institute of Indigenous People (INDI), so that indigenous peoples may access, according to their culture, decent conditions of health, education, as well as other basic services, following the principles and rights contained in the United Nations Declaration on the Rights of Indigenous Peoples.

> Entrust the Ministry of Education and Culture and the National Institute of Indigenous People (INDI) with the design and realization of specialized training programs in indigenous peoples' rights for public functionaries and civil society organizations.

> Carry out programs of human rights promotion for groups in situations of particular vulnerability and risk, such as women, children, indigenous people, elderly persons, people with alternative sexual identities, AIDS sufferers, exiles, displaced people and refugees, people deprived of liberty, migrant labourers, among others.

> Restore their rights as people to the indigenous peoples victims of the violations, through legal reforms that provide them with lands, health and education centers, as well as basic services, and by so doing recognizing their autonomy and forms of governance.

> Reincorporate the indigenous labour rights that were abolished in the last legislative reform of the Labour Code.

> Guarantee the fulfilment by the State of the provisions expressed by the National Constitution of 1992, in Chapter V, articles 62 to 67, so that attacks against indigenous peoples' life, physical integrity and the right over their habitat, do not continue.

While the specialized training program has been created and some progress has been made in reducing attacks against indigenous peoples, the implementation record is weak.

We find a similar story in Ecuador. The truth commission's recommendations mentioning indigenous populations called for the following:

Undertake programs to promote human rights of indigenous peoples, Afro-Ecuadorians and montubios, by the Council for Ethnic Equality in coordination with the National Directorate of Intercultural Bilingual Education of the Ministry Education, the Ministry of Culture and the Ministry of Justice and Human Rights.

Fulfil the right of consent and prior consultation of indigenous and tribal peoples on projects and policies that affect them, in accordance with Convention 169 of the International Labour Organization and the Declaration of the United Nations on the rights of indigenous peoples.

To urge the Public Defender's Office to elaborate:

a)   annually, a report on the situation of human rights in Ecuador in which specific recommendations to overcome the problems and identified obstacles are made;

b)   periodically, reports on the situation of human rights of different peoples and nationalities in Ecuador as indigenous peoples, Afro-Ecuadorians and *montubios*, including an analysis of the human rights violations perpetrated in the past;

c)   current and periodic reports on the situation of human rights of persons deprived of liberty, including recommendations and a work plan to improve respect and guarantee their rights.

Implement, based on the constitutional framework and international law, the content of the Declaration on the Rights of Indigenous Peoples of 2007, in order to strengthen the protection of the rights of indigenous peoples. Regulate, with the participation of different nationalities and indigenous peoples, rights to free, prior and informed consent, and consultation and cooperation. Promote reforms aimed at protecting indigenous self-government, land, water and environmental resources of these peoples, food sovereignty, political participation, among others.

Push a bill to establish indigenous justice in accordance with the principles established in the Constitution, and the Organic Code of the Judiciary, with the participation and decisions of different peoples.

To date, however, we find, if anything, less progress on these recommendations. Our data reveals only limited progress on enshrining indigenous justice in Ecuador's legal system and in raising the visibility of indigenous rights through the Public Defender's Office. We found no evidence of other implementation activity on these recommendations, but we keep the possibility open that we simply failed to find such evidence of implementation.

Thus, although recognition of the relevance of truth commissions in the pursuit of transitional justice for indigenous populations has increased in recent years (Wiebelhaus-Brahm 2019), as we have shown, with the exception of Peru, follow-through has been an issue in the Latin American cases. In our research, we see evidence that indigenous communities' political and economic marginalization has hampered their ability to mobilize for implementation.

4.2. SEXUAL VIOLENCE

Sexual violence formed part of the repression in many countries. More generally, sexual violence, especially against women, had been rampant throughout the region. Yet, only three commissions, Haiti, Paraguay, and Ecuador, explicitly addressed this issue in their recommendations. What makes this particularly surprising is that several Latin American commissions documented sexual violence in their investigations. Yet, they did not address this issue in their recommendations.[142] For instance, the Guatemala truth commission documented widespread rape and sexual violence (especially against Mayan women and girls) in its report, but it was conspicuously silent on these issues in its recommendations.[143]

We have to understand this against the general lack of international focus on women's rights at the time of some of the earliest Latin American truth commissions. The Convention on the Elimination of All Forms of Discrimination against Women was adopted in December 1979,[144] and had started to gain international traction (Bareiro 2018; Hellum and Aasen 2013; Zwingel 2005). Nonetheless, the 1995 World Conference on Women in Beijing, widely hailed as a landmark event promoting gender equity globally, took place shortly before the Haitian truth commission released its report. Thus, women's rights were turning into a global concern. Yet, at least as late as the mid-2000s, Rosser (2007, 391) argued that,

> Amidst calls for gender mainstreaming and "women's rights as human rights," truth commissions and human rights bodies must work harder at the conceptual level to interrogate how gender, "race," class, nation and other intersecting oppressions are at work, both during a genocide and afterwards, in the construction of truths and the reconstruction of societies.

Of the truth commissions that do explicitly address sexual violence in their recommendations, Haiti stands out. The commissioners focused their

---

[142] On war-related sexual violence in Latin American countries, see for example, Leiby (2009); Kravetz (2016).

[143] See, for example, Rothenberg (2016); Rosser (2007).

[144] See CEDAW Convention at https://www.ohchr.org/en/professionalinterest/pages/cedaw.aspx.

recommendations on rape specifically and on sexual violence more generally. With its report issued in 1996, the Haiti commission was the very first in Latin America and the Caribbean to flag sexual violence as a problem to be dealt with by the government. More than a half dozen of the actionable items mentioned in the Commission's recommendations dealt with the issue. Specifically, it called for:

> The classification of rape in the Haitian Penal Code among indecency offences tends to draw more attention to the status and honour of the victim than to the interference with her physical integrity and well-being. This is how one attributes less importance to the rape of a woman who is not a virgin, by the pretext that her honour is no longer involved. The commission recommends that this classification of rape that carries prejudice to the victim be modified.

> The commission recommends regulations concerning rape certificates to be modified in the sense of extending the competence of doctors/physicians to certain health workers in this domain. This extension will facilitate the examination and ascertainment of rape in rural areas where there are no doctors.

> The commission recommends the creation of programs designed to improve the behaviour and working methods for all staff engaged in services to victims of rape. One of the objectives of these programs is to develop a climate that encourages the reporting of the crimes by women who are victims.

> The commission recommends the creation of education programs and internships for all those working in the administration of justice, police officers and judges, in order to better understand the phenomenon of rape. The goal is to have in every police station an officer especially trained to receive complaints of rape.

> The commission recommends the creation of specialized services for abused women, including counselling and care to victims and their families, especially children.

> The commission recommends the creation of programs and internships that provide female victims of sexual violence opportunities to rehabilitate and fully reintegrate into private, public and social life.

> The commission recommends the promotion of educational programs in the private and public sector in order to arouse the Haitian public's attention on the problems and solutions related sexual violence against women.

> The commission recommends that judicial proceedings be commenced against the alleged perpetrator of rape … Moreover, in all of the cases where the Commission has determined that there was rape, without the perpetrator's name being mentioned, investigations must also be conducted, and if the perpetrator is identified, he should be tried and punished according to law.

> All rape victims identified by the Commission's criteria should receive compensation.

We found that the government has neglected demands for justice, whether retributive or reparative, for instances of sexual violence that were identified by the commission. Furthermore, no evidence was found for the development of programs to provide specialized services for victims of sexual violence or to raise awareness about sexual violence. At least some progress has been achieved in implementing the remaining recommendations.

The other two truth commissions that specifically addressed sexual violence in their recommendations did so in very different ways. Paraguay recommended only that the National Secretariat of Human Rights undertake research on the cases of sexual violence, particularly the ones that were against children and adolescents, including sexual slavery. It advocated that the research must be accompanied by an awareness campaign about the topic. Our research found no evidence of implementation. In Ecuador, by contrast, the commission issued eight different recommendations dealing with various aspects of sexual violence. The recommendations read:

> Establish networks and routes of healthcare. Create a network (in coordination with the existing ones linked to issues of sexual violence or childhood) of professionals, especially in the cities of Quito, Guayaquil, Cuenca and Lago Agrio, where more cases have been identified by the Truth Commission, with displacement capacity that offers comprehensive care in mental health and the psychological impacts on the victims of human rights violations.

> Specific attention in cases of sexual violence. The prevention of sexual violence, psychosocial care and interdisciplinary, immediate and specialized healthcare for victims of sexual violence must be strengthened. The standards of comprehensive care for gender-based violence that already exist must be socialized with the institutions that are handling this in populations such as children and adolescents, with forensic experts involved in court cases, etc.

> It is recommended to assign unique compensation amounts for victims of illegal or arbitrary detention, torture and sexual violence, and other injuries not resulting from torture, extrajudicial executions and enforced disappearances. Such compensation should be granted to victims recognized as such by the report of the Truth Commission, and to the new ones that may be recognized by the reparations program through administrative channels that are recommended to be created. The consultation process which the Truth Commission carried out with victims suggests the adoption of compensation as single sums of money, instead of pensions. It is also recommended to grant additional compensation to victims who, in the context of illegal deprivation of freedom, torture, sexual violence, extrajudicial execution or enforced disappearance, could have suffered great destruction or loss of property and housing, as reflected in the report of the Truth Commission.

> Forming a body of specialized professionals enrolled in the Judicial Council for conducting medical and psychological assessments that have specialized protocols, specifically in line with the Istanbul Protocol, for the determination of torture and sexual violence.

Redesigning a research protocol on sexual violence in accordance with international standards such as the Istanbul Protocol, which would allow the State General Attorney's Office to evaluate the hypothesis of occurrence of sexual violence prior to murder, in which the psychological expert report is taken into account as evidence of sexual violence.

Promote penal reform in which an adequate and complete definition of crimes of sexual violence and other gender-based crimes is made, incorporating rape, other abusive sexual acts, sexual slavery and forced prostitution, forced pregnancy, forced sterilizations, forced nudity, sexual mutilation, forced marriage or cohabitation, servitude or domestic slavery, persecution based on gender, sexual harassment, trafficking for sexual exploitation and other behaviours of comparable gravity.

Incorporate into criminal legislation the possibility for psychological expertise to be accepted as evidence of sexual violence, and other evidentiary standards stated in the Istanbul Protocol in reference to torture.

Decriminalize abortion in cases where the pregnancy is the result of sexual violence, when the life or health of the woman is in danger or when there is severe fatal malformation incompatible with life outside the womb.

Ecuador's implementation record is comparatively strong. Although we found no evidence that the government has incorporated the Istanbul Protocol into its domestic legal system, at least some steps have been taken to implement the other recommendations. Unlike elsewhere, Ecuador's government gets high marks for developing programs to treat victims of sexual violence (Reátegui, with Uchuypoma, and Hurtado 2022).

In short, sexual violence has suffered from relative neglect by truth commissions. Where it has been a focus of the commissions in their recommendations, the implementation record is relatively poor. The provision of programs intended to promote prevention or treatment of future victims seem to fare better than measures to address the needs of past victims. One explanation for this finding could be that forward-looking programs gel with the foreign aid priorities of donor governments, a theme that Selvik (2022) emphasizes in Haiti in particular.

4.3. GENDER/LGBTQ RIGHTS/SEXUAL AND REPRODUCTIVE RIGHTS

Aside from sexual violence, a few Latin American truth commissions have identified other rights related to sexuality and gender identity that need attention in their recommendations. Gender was placed on the truth commission agenda only a little over a decade ago with the truth commissions of Paraguay, Ecuador, and Brazil. Paraguay, for instance, recommended that the state incorporate a gendered perspective, by which it specified how the rights of women and of other sexual identities, would be incorporated into all constitutional and legal reforms. We found no evidence of action implementing this reform. In Brazil, the truth commission called for the removal of "discriminatory language against homosexuals in legislation, particularly with respect to homosexuals in the Armed Forces." In contrast to Paraguay, new legislation was adopted a year after the Brazilian truth commission report was released.

Again, Ecuador stands out as the commission making the longest and most detailed list of all recommendations. In its recommendations, the commission identified 10 action items specifically concerning gender and LGBT rights. Specifically, the commission advocated for:

> Integrating the gender equity approach in institutional practices and promoting it to be a cross-cutting issue in all levels of education, as mandated by law for Educational Democracy.

> Requesting the Ministry of Education, in coordination with the Equality Council, to periodically train teachers in human rights issues with an age, gender and multicultural perspective.

> Urge the Ministry of Education and the Public Defender to conduct training in non-formal education to community leaders about the human rights approach with an age, gender and multiculturalism perspective.

> Include in the various programs of human rights education with a gender perspective, the issue of sexual and reproductive rights from a preventive and restorative perspective.

> Urge the Ministry of Justice and Human Rights to permanently train the suppliers, conciliators and mediators in human rights issues with an age, multicultural and gender perspective.

> Incorporate into education programs and training of the Armed Forces, National Police and Security, content on the prevention of sexual and gender-based violence [SGBV], and its action in cases involving children, and adolescents. Its fulfilment must be evaluated.

> Ensure that same-sex couples are beneficiaries of all legal remedies under the same conditions as heterosexual couples.

> Incorporate public policies that favour non-discrimination based on sexual orientation and gender identity, involving the active participation of civil society organizations in their formulation.

> Promote a penal reform in which an adequate and complete definition of crimes of sexual violence and other gender-based crimes is made, incorporating rape, other abusive sexual acts, sexual slavery and forced prostitution, forced pregnancy, forced sterilizations, forced nudity, sexual mutilation, forced marriage or cohabitation, servitude or domestic slavery, persecution based on gender, sexual harassment, trafficking for sexual exploitation and other behaviours of comparable gravity.

> Incorporate into criminal legislation the possibility for psychological expertise to be accepted as evidence of sexual violence, and other evidentiary standards stated in the Istanbul Protocol in reference to torture.

While the Ecuadorian commission may have set a standard for recognizing gender and sexual minorities in its recommendations, implementation patterns has not fared so well. Only a handful of these recommendations were ever followed up by the government. SGBV training programs have been set up for the military and police. Furthermore, there has been some progress on penal reform and adopting a gender equity approach in education. We found no evidence of action on any of the other seven recommendations, however.

In sum, we find that Paraguay (2008) and Ecuador (2010) have provided the most and the most detailed recommendations in the emerging areas of indigenous rights, rights based on gender and sexuality, sexual violence, and sexual and reproductive rights. Several reasons may explain this. First, of the 13 cases in our study, these two commissions provided the most recommendations and the most detailed recommendations overall. By sheer numbers, the subject matter is likely to be most wide-ranging. Second, this may reflect changing global norms. Both commissions used the UN Basic Principles when they drafted and structured their recommendations, though there is no specific mention of gender or reproductive rights in the UN document.[145] Nonetheless, as two "late" commissions (plus Brazil), they followed the Indigenous and Tribal Peoples Convention of 1989 (No. 169) and the emergence of the Women, Peace and Security agenda in the twenty-first century. More generally, women's rights, sexual violence and LGBT rights have become important issues flagged by the international community. The fact that a recommendation on the rights of LGBT persons was highlighted in the Brazilian commission's relatively short list of recommendations, despite the fact that violence against gender and sexual minorities was not considered a central form of human rights violations by the report itself, shows that these truth commissions were operating in a different international arena from that of the early commissions in the 1980s and 1990s. Nonetheless, although Wiebelhaus-Brahm and Wright (2021) find evidence that global and regional promotion of the rights of these individuals is associated with an increase in recommendations addressing these individuals, such recommendations are often unimplemented.

5. ANALYSING IMPLEMENTATION ACROSS LATIN AMERICA

We shift our attention in this section to examine general patterns in the implementation rates across the 13 truth commissions we analyze in the study.

---

145 See https://digitallibrary.un.org/record/559224/?.

We hypothesized in Chapter 2 that variation in implementation rates is determined by at least four factors: (i) the number of recommendations, (ii) time, (iii) contextual factors, and (iv) the types of recommendations.

5.1. THE NUMBER OF RECOMMENDATIONS

Hypothesis 1: *Truth commission reports that make few recommendations are likely to have a better implementation record than those that make many recommendations.*

This hypothesis is perhaps obvious. It is intuitive that a government is more likely to act upon a relatively small set of recommendations, particularly if they are comparatively modest measures that are less politically contentious. Obviously, when the Ecuadorean and Paraguayan commissions issue hundreds of recommendations, they are asking much more of a government compared to cases like Argentina and Uruguay where there are only a handful of recommendations to be implemented. As Figure 6.1 illustrates, there appears to be a negative relationship between the number of recommendations and implementation rates. In other words, commissions that have made fewer recommendations have better implementation rates than commissions that make many recommendations.

Figure 6.1. The number of recommendations and implementation rates

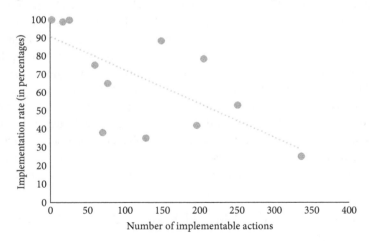

Note: Here we have collapsed the data for "high implementation" and "partial implementation". We thus distinguish recommendations with any action from those without.

As documented in Chapter 3, there has been a general increase in the number of recommendations issued by Latin American truth commissions over time. However, there is no clear linear trend. The early truth commissions of the 1980s issued comparatively few recommendations: the number of recommendations never topped 50. In the 1990s, commissions roughly presented twice as many recommendations as in the previous decade. By the end of the 1990s up to the present, there has been a divergence. Transitional truth commissions, and those that were the first truth commissions to be established in the country, tended to have higher numbers of recommendations. By contrast, post-transitional commissions, especially if they were a follow-up to a previous truth commission or other transitional justice mechanism, issued few recommendations on average.

These patterns suggest that commissioners are not actively studying previous truth commissions and concluding that more is better. This conforms to commissioners and staff reflections on the formulation process that were discussed in Chapter 4. Perhaps only the global fame of the South African Truth and Reconciliation Commission (TRC), with its voluminous recommendations issued in 2000, impacted recommendation norms in Latin America in the 2000s; though, aside from Peru's decision to hold public hearings like South Africa when this had not been the norm in earlier Latin American commissions, our interviews do not highlight the South African TRC as a model. The only two commissions that followed a similar blueprint were those of Ecuador and Paraguay. They both structured their recommendations according to the UN Basic Guidelines and are thus quite similar in structure – partly also in content – and both have a high number of recommendations.

Rather, much more context-specific factors seem to be at play in explaining the number of recommendations commissioners formulate. Two truth commissions with 150-200 implementable actions recommended stand out with rates of implementation activity exceeding 80 per cent. Some variables that appear important in influencing implementation rates include the nature of past abuses, their frequency, and the length of time across which they occurred. Also, although we have no evidence that commissioners were concerned with the likelihood of implementation when they drafted their recommendations, this may have shaped their decisions as to how many recommendations to include in the report. Certainly, examples like Haiti's focus on sexual violence and Brazil's mention of LGBT rights suggests commissioners were strategic and opportunistic in using the platform of recommendations to draw attention to important human rights issues for the country.

5.2. TIME

Hypothesis 2a: *Implementation of truth commission recommendations is likely to increase over time because governments have more time to implement, and political tensions may have lessened since the commission.*

Hypothesis 2b: *Implementation of truth commission recommendations is less likely with time because the truth commission fades from memory and is overshadowed by other issues.*

To test these hypotheses, we begin by distinguishing those recommendations in which any activity has occurred from those in which we find no discernible evidence of government action. Figure 6.2 depicts implementation rates for recommendations. In doing so, we collapse "high implementation" and "partial implementation" into one category, and "no implementation" and "no information" into another. The "no information" category represents those recommendations about which we could not obtain definitive information on implementation status. We code recommendations in this way because, given the attention recommended reforms typically attract from former commissioners and staff, civil society, and/or their transnational allies, it is unlikely that implementation activity would have been missed. Thus, we provide a conservative estimate of implementation rates.

Figure 6.2. Action vs. inaction on implementation

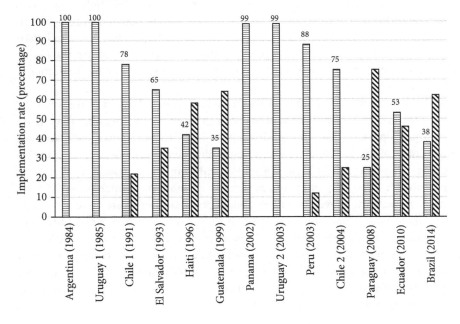

Truth commission reports

⊟ High + partial implementation (horizontal)

◩ No implementation + no information (diagonal)

The data in Figure 6.2 supports the hypothesis that implementation takes time. The four truth commissions in which some action has been taken on 100 per cent of recommendations are Argentina, Panama, and both of Uruguay's commissions. For each, more than a decade has passed since the recommendations were published. Another five truth commissions: both of Chile's commissions plus Ecuador, El Salvador, and Peru, have strong implementation records, by which we mean that some action toward implementation has occurred for more than half of the recommendations. Only four truth commissions have seen implementation activity on less than half of their recommendations. In fact, the most recent truth commissions, Paraguay and Brazil in particular, have some of the weakest implementation records. Overall, fully nine of the 13 truth commissions have more than half of their recommendations either fully or partially implemented.[146]

In Figure 6.3, we provide further nuance to implementation. Specifically, we distinguish "high implementation", in which the government has fully complied with the recommendation, from "partial implementation", in which the government has taken some steps to implement, but action has fallen short of what the commission recommended. Note that recommendations for which we do not have information on implementation are excluded from Figure 6.3.[147]

If it is true that the passage of time works in favour of truth commission recommendation implementation, we would expect the following trends: (i) the proportion of "high implementation" to be higher for early commissions than late commissions (because they have had more time to implement their recommendations); (ii) the proportion of "partial implementation" to decrease over time (as it is gradually replaced by "high implementation"; and (iii) the proportion of "not implemented" recommendations to be higher for later commissions than for early commissions. How do these expectations square with our data?

---

[146] It also is the case that many of the truth commissions that offered the most recommendations have the worst track record on implementation activity, suggesting that too many recommendations may leave governments overwhelmed and unable to prioritize.

[147] This means that summing up the data on implementation recorded in series 1, 2 and 3 adds up to 100% only in the cases where there is full information. Where there is missing information, the sum will be less than 100%.

Figure 6.3. High, partial, or no implementation

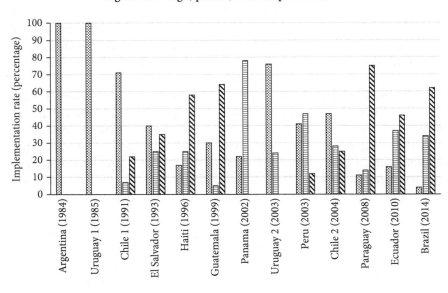

Truth Commission Report

⊞ High implementation (polka dots)
⊟ Partial implementation (horizontal)
◩ No implementation (diagonal)

Source: Based on data from all tables in foregoing section. The unit of analysis is (implementable) recommendations.

When we recognize commissions are in chronological order in Figure 6.3, there appear to be two distinct waves of implementation success, rather than a linear pattern. Panama's truth commission (case no. 7) stands out, as most of its 10 recommendations were recorded as "partially implemented". More generally, "partial implementation" is a more common characteristic of twenty-first-century truth commissions.

Furthermore, the data on "no implementation" reveals that cases from the 1990s have the highest proportion of recommendations in this category. The truth commissions in El Salvador, Haiti, and Guatemala have a higher percentage of non-implemented recommendations than most of the truth commissions that published their reports and made their recommendations much more recently. A few things distinguish these three cases from others in the study. First, they are comparatively weak states. Second, foreigners played disproportionate roles in these commissions. In El Salvador and Guatemala, commissioners were foreign diplomats and academics selected by the UN. The Haitian diaspora figured prominently in the commission in their home country. Finally, as we explore further below, they are among the poorest countries in the region to have established truth commissions. A further explanation for this pattern may be that countries in which more recent truth commissions have occurred face more pressure to implement, given the expansion of transitional justice norms and transnational human rights activism.

On the whole, only four truth commissions (Haiti, Guatemala, Paraguay, and Brazil) have non-implementation rates of 50 per cent or more. That means that seven of the 13 Latin American commissions examined here have at least partially implemented more than half of their recommendations. Moreover, two of the commissions (Paraguay 2008 and Brazil 2014) with the highest non-implementation rates are also among the two most recent commissions (which means a short time for implementation to have taken place). Additionally, Paraguay has the highest number of recommendations among all commissions, which means that the task of implementation is much larger for this country than for the cases with far fewer recommendations.

5.3. CONTEXTUAL FACTORS

Undoubtedly, a variety of social, political, and economic factors shape the likelihood of truth commission recommendations being implemented. Although the implementation rates for the post-conflict Central American states are mediocre, they do not clearly stand out from their post-authoritarian counterparts. Similarly, there is not an obvious pattern in implementation rates between transitional and post-transitional commissions.

However, the state's level of economic development is one variable that seems likely to influence implementation. Recommendations are often costly in terms of resources. This may be most obvious in the provision of material reparations, but other types of measures like institutional reform and prosecutions cost money too. There may be a perceived trade-off between budgeting for implementing truth commission recommendations and other economic development priorities. Even when the recommendation requires little funding, governments still may be wary of it distracting from more pressing economic concerns. In comparatively wealthy countries, by contrast, these perceived trade-offs may not be felt as acutely. Thus, we offer the following:

Hypothesis 3: *Countries with more developed economies are more likely to implement truth commission recommendations than poorer countries.*

Our data support this hypothesis. As Table 6.6 illustrates, there is not a clear relationship between national wealth and high implementation of recommendations. However, if we consider partial implementation as well, in almost every instance richer countries in the Southern Cone have higher rates of implementation than their poorer counterparts. As outlined in Chapter 1, Table 1.2, we identified each country's World Bank income group status at the time the report was released. In general, countries in the upper middle-income category had stronger implementation rates than their poorer counterparts. The most recent truth commissions, namely the Ecuadorian and Brazilian truth commissions, fared less well. It may be that their governments have had less time to respond to the truth commission recommendations rather than being due to a lack of resources. Moreover, these countries have been mired in corruption scandals and economic crisis since the final reports were released. Overall, implementation rates are much higher in the Southern Cone countries than for the rest of the continent. Part of the explanation also has to do with the nature of the recommendations themselves (see section 5.4 below).

Table 6.6. Overall implementation rates by level of economic development

Upper-Middle Income*	% Recommendations Highly Implemented	Low and Lower-Middle Income*	% Recommendations Highly Implemented
Argentina 1984	100	Chile 1991	71
Uruguay 1985	100	El Salvador 1993	40
Panama 2002	22	Haiti 1996	17
Uruguay 2003	77	Guatemala 1999	31
Chile 2004	47	Panama 2002	22
Ecuador 2010	16	Peru 2003	41
Brazil 2014	4	Paraguay 2008	11

Source: Based on implementation data collected for each truth commission. See Appendix IV for details.

* World Bank income group status at the time the report was released. For more on the World Bank's categorization, see: https://datahelpdesk.worldbank.org/knowledgebase/articles/378834-how-does-the-world-bank-classify-countries.

5.4. THE TYPES OF RECOMMENDATIONS

Chapter 3 shows that three quarters (76 per cent) of the over 900 truth commission recommendations are aimed at reform of state institutions, laws, or constitutions (i.e., systemic measures) – and thereby contribute to non-repetition of human rights violations. The remaining quarter (24 per cent) concern reparations, criminal prosecutions, and the establishment of follow-up organs (i.e., non-systemic). One might hypothesize that systemic recommendations would have a lower implementation rate than non-systemic recommendations. Changes to political, social, and economic institutions often require more steps and the acquiescence of more actors in order to complete. In general, then, the more "veto players" and the greater the number of bureaucratic or legislative hurdles that must be overcome to enact a recommendation, the lower the likelihood that implementation will be accomplished.

At the same time, systemic reforms may be less threatening, benefit a broader constituency, and better meld with foreign donors' agendas than non-systemic recommendations. Perpetrators will do what they can to avoid accountability for their actions. Past cross-national research also finds that reparations have a poor implementation record (Bakiner 2016). Not only might such programs be expensive, but beneficiaries may be less likely to effectively mobilize to pressure the state to act. Finally, judicial and security sector reform fit nicely with donors' good governance agenda. Thus, countries are likely to face more external pressure to enact systemic recommendations.

Thus, we test contrary hypotheses:

Hypothesis 4a: *Systemic recommendations are more likely to have a lower implementation rate than non-systemic recommendations because implementation is more complex.*

Hypothesis 4b: *Non-systemic recommendations are more likely to have a lower implementation rate than systemic recommendations because of resistance from powerful perpetrators and less interest from the international community.*

Our data provides stronger support for Hypothesis 4b. As shown in Table 6.7, a somewhat higher percentage of non-systemic recommendations has seen no action on implementation. More consistently with Hypothesis 4a, however, where governments have taken some action toward implementation, a higher percentage of systemic recommendations has been seen through to completion.

Table 6.7. Implementation rates across recommendation type*

Recommendation type	Total number of recommendations	Implementation rate		
		High	Partial	None or no info
Institutional	389	31%	22%	45%
Legal	250	35%	21%	43%
Constitutional	30	40%	10%	50%
Criminal	51	22%	25%	53%
Reparations	223	22%	26%	52%
Non-repetition	501	32%	23%	45%
Follow-up	64	21%	33%	46%
Other	30	32%	25%	43%

*Sometimes totalling less than 100% due to rounding.

Source: Summaries of implementation data collected for each truth commission. See Appendix IV for details.

The implementation rates across different types of recommendations vary less than expected. Constitutional reforms unexpectedly emerged as the type of recommendation with the largest proportion of being highly implemented (40 per cent). Commissioners seemed to be prescient in anticipating whether and on what topics constitutional amendment would prove viable. In line with Hypothesis 4b, criminal justice, reparations, and follow-up measures, by contrast, are at the bottom (20–21 per cent).

This relationship is inverse when it comes to partial implementation rates, which vary from a low of 10 per cent for constitutional reform to 26 per cent for reparations and 33 per cent for follow-up measures. Constitutional reform seems to be an all-or-nothing proposition. Criminal prosecution stands out as the type of recommendation that is most often not implemented (53 per cent).[148] Progress has frequently been blocked by the continued political and military power of perpetrators and by the presence of amnesty laws.

5.5. SUMMARY COMMENTS ON IMPLEMENTATION BY RECOMMENDATION TYPE

Our analysis of the implementation data across the 13 truth commissions reveals several important patterns. First, countries in different sub-regions, having different levels of wealth and different levels of international involvement in the truth commission, have similar implementation rates for recommendations coded as *Institutional* and *Legal*. That is, in most countries, at least some action has been taken on a majority of recommendations related to institutional and legal reform.

Second, *constitutional reform* seems to be much more of an all-or-nothing proposition. These types of recommendations are typically either fully implemented or completely ignored. Part of the explanation for this may be that there are relatively few recommendations in this category. Because changing constitutions is often difficult, it might be appealing to bundle all of the proposed changes into one constitutional reform package. The low number of recommendations dealing with constitutional change also may reflect the slim odds commissioners place on real reform happening. In Latin America, truth commissions have typically followed negotiated transitions in which armies return to their barracks. A common concession in such negotiations is that existing constitutions, which frequently ensconce military immunity and autonomy, are preserved. In fact, given the difficulty of achieving constitutional

---

[148] Although 53% covers both no implementation + no information, criminal prosecution is a very visible kind of activity. Therefore, the chances are that 53% is quite close to the real number for "no implementation".

reform, the implementation rates are actually quite high. It is remarkable, then, that truth commissions appear to have been relatively successful in prompting later change. Commissioners seem to be relatively effective at "reading the tea leaves" as to the prospects for constitutional reform.

Third, when it comes to *criminal prosecutions*, one of the things that jumps out is the number of truth commissions that did not make recommendations in this category. For the many truth commissions that followed a negotiated transition, they faced a situation in which perpetrators remained powerful, and often remained popular among a significant portion of the population. In such contexts, commissioners may have concluded that calling for prosecution risked jeopardizing the rest of their reform agenda, if not the political transition itself. Critics have long warned of a "peace vs justice" trade-off, in which putting perpetrators on trial, particularly when perpetrators remain powerful and political institutions, weak, in fragile transitional contexts (Snyder and Vinjamuri 2003–04).

Where truth commissions have called for prosecutions however, it is somewhat surprising that most such recommendations have seen at least some action. With the exception of Haiti, there has been some progress on most recommendations in this category across the region. With the exception of Haiti, however, the most recent truth commissions have the lowest rates of implementation of recommendations dealing with criminal accountability. One might expect higher rates of implementation in more recent times as a result of the spread of the so-called anti-impunity norm (Engle 2014; Engle, Miller, and Davis 2016; Pensky 2008). The most recent commissions (Paraguay, Ecuador, and Brazil) are all examples of post-transitional justice. With a greater number of perpetrators dead, retired, or in other ways politically side-lined in such contexts, one might expect that the obstacles to trials would be comparatively low. Yet, this also might make prosecution appear less urgent, as perpetrators may be less of a threat. Furthermore, the short time-frame for implementation also may help explain why relatively little has happened to hold alleged human rights abusers accountable in these countries. For Brazil, the Amnesty Law, which was passed by the military regime in 1979 and upheld by Brazil's Supreme Court in 2010, continued to shield perpetrators from prosecution for kidnappings, disappearances, and torture (Mezarobba 2016) until finally declared unconstitutional in 2019.

Action on implementing recommendations related to *reparations* does seem to be closely connected to economic performance. Rates of implementation are much higher for more developed countries than for poorer ones. For richer countries, it is easier to afford reparations programs. Brazil is the one exception, but it has been mired in economic crisis since the final report was issued in 2014.

Measures of non-repetition form a broad category that encompasses a range of measures. As such, it is a bit challenging to identify patterns of implementation among such a diverse set of recommendations. Nonetheless, three inferences can be drawn from the data on implementation rates. First, implementation rates are higher in wealthier countries, which, with the exception of Argentina, also tend to be countries in which the number of past violations was comparatively small. To be sure, there are some exceptions. El Salvador's rate of non-implementation is not too different from that of Chile's Rettig Commission. This may reflect the influence of international actors in El Salvador. At the same time, international pressure does not appear to have had the same affect in Guatemala. Second, economics may influence implementation in another way. Rates of non-implementation are high in situations in which truth commissions have produced their recommendations within the last decade. While this may simply mean that there has been less time for action, truth commissions in Paraguay, Ecuador, and Brazil also issued their recommendations in the wake of the so-called Great Recession which commenced in late 2007. As governments struggled with the economic ramifications of what was the most serious global economic slowdown since the Great Depression, implementing truth commission recommendations may have been an unwelcome distraction.

Finally, truth commission recommendations related to the establishment of *follow-up bodies* fared well overall. Commissioners generally viewed it as essential that some new entity be charged with carrying forward their mission of addressing the past. Governments often seemed to agree. In fact, governments established such institutions following the Rettig Commission in Chile and Uruguay's first commission, despite the fact that neither commission had called for their creation. Overall, implementation rates indicate that governments generally accept the value of such bodies and set them up regularly. Again, we see that rates of non-implementation are highest in some of Latin America's poorest countries.

5.6. ACTORS AND FACTORS THAT FACILITATE IMPLEMENTATION

Implementation of truth commission recommendations is likely to be influenced by a number of factors, including: public awareness of the truth commission report and its recommendations; the legitimacy of the commission; the relative power of pro- and anti-truth commission sentiments; political will to implement the recommendations; sufficient resources; other reform trends in the Latin American region; and international factors. The balance of forces between the "drivers of justice" and "the spoilers of justice" has rightly been stressed in the literature on transitional justice mechanisms in general and is highly relevant as a contextual explanation of implementation – or lack thereof (Skaar and Wiebelhaus-Brahm 2013a, b; Sriram 2013).

As we have noted already, a key issue is *who* will be affected by the recommendations and what power do they have to promote or obstruct implementation. To illustrate this point, the Supreme Court in El Salvador, which was heavily criticized in the truth commission report for having done little to hinder or combat the rampant human rights violations that took place during the 12-year civil war, was totally opposed to implementing any of the several reforms targeting the judiciary in general and the Supreme Court in particular (Martínez-Barahona et al. 2018).

Furthermore, the international community may play a role in pushing for implementation (Hayner 2011). In our study, we see this most clearly in the case of Haiti. Being a country in economic and institutional shambles, struck by one catastrophe after the other (massive earthquake, cholera epidemic, etc.), Haiti has been almost completely reliant on the UN and international donors for funding. This has created opportunities for external actors to press for implementing the truth commission recommendations that fit their own agendas for the country (Selvik 2022). We also see this in the case of Panama, where action on implementation, however partial, has often been driven by rulings of the Inter-American Court of Human Rights and the Inter-American Commission on Human Rights (Rudling 2022).

However, it is important to highlight that the presence of international actors is no guarantee for implementation. Ultimately, it is up to the national government to prioritize (and normally fund) the implementation of various reforms and activities. For instance, the UN was involved in the peace processes and the set-up of truth commissions in both El Salvador and Guatemala. Yet, the implementation record of truth commission recommendations was initially much poorer in El Salvador than in Guatemala – principally due to the active reluctance of successive Salvadoran governments to comply with the truth commission recommendations. Especially where the "spoilers" would be affected by the recommendations, implementation will be a challenge.

6. CONCLUSION

This chapter has taken stock of the implementation record of close to 1000 recommendations made by 13 truth commissions in 11 Latin American countries over a period of almost 35 years. We have used a combination of primary sources collected by this project and secondary sources. Using the eight categories developed in Chapter 3, we systematically examined the implementation rate for different kinds of recommendations. The first half of the chapter dealt in-depth with some of the main types of recommendations made by these commissions, while the second half of the chapter tried to dig into patterns of implementation across various types of recommendations.

Our first finding was that *truth commission reports that make few recommendations are likely to have a better implementation record than those that make many recommendations.* There are at least two reasons for this finding. The first, perhaps more obvious, explanation is that there are simply fewer recommendations to implement. The second, more subtle reason is that, with fewer recommendations, the government might feel less overwhelmed. Simultaneously, fewer recommendations make it more difficult for cynical, reluctant politicians to feign concern and compliance by identifying some relatively costless token measures to implement. The number of recommendations has generally increased over time, but there is no linear relationship. There also seems to be no particular learning effect between successive commissions in terms of how many recommendations to make or how to structure them.

Further, we found support for our hypothesis that *implementation takes time.* Earlier commissions have higher implementation rates than later commissions. Yet, interestingly, we found that three cases from the 1990s (the truth commissions in El Salvador, Haiti, and Guatemala) have a higher percentage of non-implemented recommendations than most of the truth commissions that published their reports and made their recommendations much more recently. We attribute this to a combination of these countries having weak state institutions, poor economies, and foreigners playing outsized roles in these commissions.

Nonetheless, we found that what often happens in the (relatively) immediate aftermath of the launching of a truth commission report matters a lot for the prospects for implementation. Dissemination of the truth commission report not only provides information to the public. It also makes it easier to hold state officials accountable where the findings and recommendations are known to the public as well as to state officials. Where follow-up institutions are established to oversee implementation, whether recommended by the truth commission or not, implementation rates also are higher. The production of reports, press releases, and the like on implementation keeps continued pressure on the state to act.

In addition, we explored how characteristics of the recommendations themselves shaped their prospects for implementation. On a basic level, we have made a distinction between recommendations aimed at democratizing and strengthening institutions and laws (so-called systemic recommendations) and recommendations aimed at more directly addressing the past by focusing on the needs and rights of individuals and collectives (so-called non-systemic factors). We have also tried to find out whether it matters if recommendations are aimed at state and structures or at individuals and collectives. We found support for our hypothesis that *non-systemic recommendations are more likely to have a lower implementation rate than systemic recommendations because of resistance from powerful perpetrators and less interest from the international community.*

Interestingly, and unexpectedly, constitutional reforms emerged as the type of recommendation with the highest proportion being highly implemented. In particular, the more attention commissioners pay to constitutional reform in their recommendations, the greater the likelihood of implementation appears. Quantity seems to signal importance, at least with this type of recommendation.

This chapter has further shown that most governments have been willing to carry out institutional and legal reforms after transitions to democratic rule. Non-repetition has been high on the agenda. Many truth commissions have specifically advised increasing human rights protection through ratification of international conventions. This turns out to be one of the more "implementable" recommendations. The result is that international human rights norms have gained traction in Latin America through incorporation into national legal frameworks. We have also shown that human rights education has been given substantial attention by truth commissions, and subsequently followed up by governments, albeit unevenly. Newer commissions have also incorporated themes like gender issues, sexual and reproductive rights, and indigenous rights. Though the implementation record is not great in these new areas, we argue that these commissions may be setting an important new agenda for truth commissions internationally.

What about measures to further address past crimes, which matter most to many victims? Within the larger category of reparation to victims, we have found that governments are often willing to enact symbolic measures. States often follow recommendations to acknowledge past wrongs and make public apologies. In the case of Chile, Anita Ferrara (Ferrara 2014, 66) has argued that President Aylwin's public apology, made to the nation at the same time as he received the report from the Rettig Commission, "was probably the most important symbolic reparation victims' relatives had received". Most truth commissions have made recommendations along these lines, and most states have responded positively, although some countries (like Ecuador) delayed making an official apology for years after the transition to democracy. We also find that states have taken recommendations regarding memorialization quite seriously.

Material reparations and measures that come closer to holding individual perpetrators accountable are more rarely implemented. Enforced disappearances has been a politically thorny and legally complicated issue due to the presence of amnesty laws in many countries at the time when truth commission reports were launched, for example. At the same time, several more governments have proved willing to investigate cases of enforced disappearance – including those of disappeared children. Nonetheless, few Latin American truth commissions explicitly ordered criminal prosecutions, and trials have been rare outside Argentina and Chile.

Most importantly, this chapter has documented that the recommendations made by Latin American truth commissions have in fact, by and large, been acted upon, even if only partially. This is a promising finding given the pessimism that has surrounded the importance and impact of recommendations made by truth commissions. Our analysis shows that recommendations matter.

What can the international community do to improve the implementation record further? First, it needs to invest in countries that are confronting their pasts. We found that *countries with more developed economies are more likely to implement truth commission recommendations than poorer countries.* In general, countries in the upper middle-income category had stronger implementation rates than their poorer counterparts. Legal and institutional reform, in particular, is more likely to be implemented the more involved outside actors are. Non-systemic recommendations like reparations and criminal prosecutions, by contrast, are less likely to be implemented. Thus, a second conclusion is that the international community needs to more concretely support criminal accountability and transformative justice. Although donor governments and the Sustainable Development Goals tout the importance of accountability and the promotion of the rights of marginalized groups as being critical for promoting long-term peace and prosperity, the relatively poor implementation record for recommendations dealing with criminal prosecution, reparations, and the needs of indigenous people, women, and LGBT persons suggests that this support is largely rhetorical.

CHAPTER 7

CONCLUSIONS

Words are the only things that last forever; they are more durable than the eternal hills.

– William Hazlitt, essayist (1778–1830)

The 13 Latin American truth commission reports analyzed in detail in this book have proven to be durable testimonies to the work undertaken by the commissions that wrote them. Written over a period of almost 30 years (1983–2014), these reports still exist in physical and/or digital form. The reports are easily accessible and widely known in some countries, like Chile, Argentina, and Peru. By contrast, to get hold of a hard copy of the truth commission report in Uruguay, Panama, or Haiti requires a bit of determination and detective work. Whether easily accessible or not, the recommendations made in all these reports jointly form an important legacy of the truth-finding efforts of 11 Latin American countries. In many countries, they remain important to political discourse.

In this project, we advance understanding of truth commissions and their impact in important ways. Although we have not been principally concerned with the *impact* of truth commissions, we do argue that that implementation of their recommendations conditions some of the short-term as well as long-term impact of truth commissions. Conceptually, then, we differentiate the "implementation" of specific recommendations from the "impact" of the truth commission that issued them. In this project we understand implementation both as a process (the implementation process) and as specific events (implementing events) that result in some policy, legal, or procedural change. To demonstrate this, we systematically examined the kinds of recommendations Latin American truth commissions have produced. Further, we explored the circumstances in which those recommendations were formulated. Finally, we determined how, when, and by whom the recommendations have been implemented. Through a comparative approach, we have sought to uncover the factors that shape the recommendations produced by truth commissions, and to examine patterns of implementation across time and space. We defined recommendations not as commissions themselves do, which is often messy and complex, but by distinguishing individual implementing events. This enabled a more accurate assessment of the extent to which governments have acted upon commissions' counsel. To examine patterns in formulation and implementation across the region, we developed a system for classifying recommendations according to their different characteristics. Further, we identified contextual factors that we hypothesize shape the likelihood of implementation. Overall, we concluded that the recommendations made by truth commissions really do matter, in ways that were anticipated *and* unanticipated.

In this concluding chapter, we reflect upon the theoretical and policy implications of our study of truth commission recommendations. Following a brief summary and discussion of the book's central findings, we propose a model for further exploring the formulation and implementation of truth commission recommendations. Beyond the conceptual value of the model, such a tool has the potential to advance debates about the impact of truth commissions. From there, we outline the policy implications of our research, highlighting common pitfalls to avoid when crafting recommendations, and provide some suggestions for what commissioners and staff can do to increase the likelihood of implementation.

1. WHAT HAVE WE LEARNED ABOUT TRUTH COMMISSION RECOMMENDATIONS?

The empirical foundation for this book is a database containing all recommendations issued by 13 Latin American truth commissions issued over three decades (1984–2014). While we focused on the recommendations sections of the respective final reports, because commissioners sometimes lump together distinct policy proposals we did not adopt the numbering schemes of the commissions themselves. Rather, we delineated each proposal that was individually actionable. Thus, with a scope encompassing all recommendations issued by all truth commissions in an entire region across time, this database represents the most exhaustive effort to date to study truth commission recommendations. With this inductive approach, we link the concerns that truth commission reports themselves flag as their most important contributions to changing society with a close reading of what they actually recommend that governments do.

Having coded for several characteristics of recommendations, our research reveals several important findings about Latin America's three decades of truth commission experimentation. The 13 reports themselves vary tremendously. On a basic level, their lengths differ a great deal. With respect to recommendations in particular, there are vastly different amounts of ink spilled on them, and there is significant variation in the themes addressed in the recommendations. With the exception of the Ecuadorian and Paraguayan truth commissions, which structured their reports according to the UN Basic Principles, the other 11 commissions developed their own unique ways of presenting their recommendations. The eclectic nature of this collection of truth commission reports provides a unique laboratory in which to examine the formulation and implementation of truth commission recommendations.

On a basic level, our data provide a survey of the subject matter with which recommendations dealt. When we started this project, we expected truth commissions to principally be concerned with addressing victims' needs. This is primarily because truth commissions have been touted as victim-centered and victims' organizations in many countries were at the forefront in making claims for truth and justice. Our database, however, shows that more than three-quarters of all recommendations seek systemic change. In other words, the vast majority of recommendations promote reform of state institutions, constitutions, and legal frameworks. The chief concern of truth commissions, then, is to make recommendations that will strengthen political institutions, encourage democratic practices, and, hence, prevent the recurrence of human rights violations in the future. The fact that recommendations are predominantly forward-looking is one of our most important findings. Unfortunately, this reinforces the transitional justice literature's common refrain that victims' rights and needs are given short shrift.

In Chapter 3, we explored patterns in the recommendations themselves. In general, more recent commissions have issued more recommendations. Commissions created by poorer countries and in the aftermath of civil war also tend to have more lengthy recommendations sections than more recent commissions.

Overall, most commissions have issued recommendations in a wide variety of areas. Institutional and legal reform was the most common category, indicative of a concern with non-repetition. These measures are less prevalent in post-transitional contexts, however. In contrast to transitional contexts where the fluidity of the time suggests a window of opportunity for reform, commissioners may conclude that the odds of dramatic systemic change are lower during periods of "routine" politics. Victim reparation was another common subject of recommendations. Recognizing the importance of continued pressure, most truth commissions also recommended that follow-up bodies be established to continue investigations and/or focus on implementation. By contrast, criminal prosecution and constitutional reform were less common.

Concerning the formulation of truth commission recommendations, Chapter 4 highlights that, except for Argentina's CONADEP, all Latin American truth commissions were explicitly mandated to deliver recommendations. We found that resource constraints and a desire to have recommendations that are informed by the investigation often leads commissions to devote little time and attention to recommendations until the proverbial last minute. On a fundamental level, recommendations are shaped by dynamics internal to the commission, such as how it is organized and the characteristics of commissioners and staff. Recommendations also are shaped by contextual factors domestically, regionally, and globally. More recent truth commissions are more likely to consult with civil society on the drafting of recommendations. In fact, we find evidence that recommendations also reflect the world time in which they are formulated, as international human rights standards as well as multilateral institutions and transnational activists shape the subject matter, and even the language used in recommendations.

Although our interviews did not reveal clear evidence of this, we hypothesized in Chapter 3 that, in circumstances in which commissioners have little confidence that governments will follow through on their recommendations, they may adopt one of two contrasting strategies on the number of recommendations. On the one hand, they may keep the recommendations section brief, thinking that their efforts are more productively spent elsewhere. On the other hand, they may view their report as a once-in-a-generation opportunity to get issues on the political agenda. Future research should explore this topic further.

Chapter 5 provided a comprehensive account of the implementation record of all recommendations made by 13 formal truth commissions in Latin America. Covering a period of almost four decades, we have shown how important it is to apply a long-term perspective when trying to gauge implementation. Overall, our study shows that the recommendations made by Latin American truth commissions have, in fact, by and large, been implemented. This is a promising finding given the pessimism that has surrounded the importance and impact of recommendations made by truth commissions. Our analysis ultimately shows that recommendations matter. Nonetheless, the degree of implementation ranges from 40 per cent for Guatemala's truth commission to full implementation for Argentina and for Uruguay's first parliamentary commission.

Our country cases show that the implementation of truth commission recommendations requires political will and resources by the respective governments. The fact that implementation of complex recommendations may take place over many years and span several governments further suggests that there needs to be a persistent will among politicians – but also pressure from civil society – not to forget about truth commission recommendations. In some cases, once an issue is placed on the national agenda, it takes on a life of its own.

Although there are some exceptions, our study finds that implementation is more likely to begin immediately or soon after the government has received the truth commission report. In other words, the salience of recommendations is likely to decline over time as other issues supplant the investigation in the political agenda. This means that the political context in which the report is launched is critical for the fate of recommendations. Conditions that are inhospitable to implementation, like the open rejection of the commission's findings by the Salvadoran government, might impede long-term implementation. As Chapter 6 shows, the aftermath of a truth commission report's release matters a lot for the prospect of recommendations being implemented. Public dissemination of the report not only provides information to national and international audiences, but also makes it easier to hold state officials accountable for the findings and for follow-up of the recommendations. Nonetheless, implementation often takes time. Where follow-up institutions are established to oversee implementation,

implementation rates are notably higher. The production of reports, press releases and the like on implementation, whether by official follow-up bodies or by civil society, keeps continued pressure on the state to act. This finding is consistent with comparative research that includes cases outside Latin America (Bakiner 2016).

The most general qualitative distinction we made between recommendations was what commissions sought to affect. In other words, we examined differences between recommendations aimed at state and structures and those targeting specific individuals or groups. Some recommendations aimed to transform society writ large. This category encompasses measures that democratize and strengthen institutions and laws. Other recommendations focus on the needs and rights of a specific subset of society. What we call non-systemic recommendations target particular identity groups, such as women or indigenous persons, or, based upon the commission's investigation, identify some other set of individuals for which some measures should be enacted. We found a lower implementation rate among non-systemic recommendations compared to systemic recommendations. Indeed, in Latin America, constitutional reform is the type of recommendation with the best chance of being highly implemented. Amongst the most common forms of non-systemic recommendations are victims' reparation measures. Within the larger category of reparation to victims, state acknowledgment of past wrongs and the issuance of public apologies are salient in terms of implementation.

We argue that the relative cost of these recommendations explains implementation patterns. Systemic recommendations promote non-repetition or in other ways seek to change the future. These measures may face less resistance from powerful perpetrators because they do not directly lead to accountability. At the same time, these measures are often compatible with the international donor community's rule of law and good governance agenda. Non-systemic recommendations, by contrast, are more likely to be backward-looking, which could be more threatening to perpetrators and require the mobilization of beneficiaries – who are often politically marginalized – to be implemented.

Beyond this, what other factors matter for implementation? The first is a simple numerical observation; namely that truth commissions that focus on a few recommendations tend to have better implementation records than those that produce extensive lists. On one level, this finding is intuitive. Theoretically, a handful of measures can be more quickly acted upon and society can move on. A longer list of recommendations, by contrast, may touch on more elements of the state and society, require capacity in a more diverse set of dimensions, and encounter a more diverse set of "veto points" that obstruct implementation. Governments might feel overwhelmed; paralyzed by an inability to prioritize. Even where capacity exists, reluctant governments might feign paralysis to justify inaction. Over time, the number of recommendations has tended to increase, though not in a linear fashion. Aside from Ecuador and Paraguay drawing upon the UN Principles, we also find no evidence of commissions studying the number and nature of recommendations issued by their predecessors in the region. Future research should examine more carefully whether the number of recommendations itself matters, or if certain circumstances and/or truth commission characteristics might influence the number of recommendations or their nature.

A second overarching conclusion is that antecedent conditions shape the number and nature of recommendations, as well as the prospects for implementation. On a basic level, implementation often takes time. Latin America's earliest truth commissions have higher implementation rates than their later counterparts. Nonetheless, it is not a linear relationship. The truth commissions in El Salvador, Haiti, and Guatemala from the 1990s have lower rates of implementation than most commissions that came after. Characteristics of these three countries suggest further factors shaping implementation. They are among the poorest countries in the Americas. As a result, they may lack the resources and bureaucratic capacity to enact recommendations that their more developed peers have. Furthermore, each of these three commissions was largely run by foreigners or members of the diaspora. This left the recommendations with fewer visible domestic champions in the report's aftermath.

2. A MODEL OF TCRs' FORMULATION AND IMPLEMENTATION

Having inductively built our model of the factors that shape the formulation and implementation of truth commission recommendations, we briefly present it here. Our intention in presenting the framework summarized in Table 7.1 is to provide a model that can travel beyond the Latin American context to systematically explore formulation and implementation of recommendations for any truth commission case.

Table 7.1. A model of TCRs' formulation and implementation

FORMULATION		IMPLEMENTATION	
Temporal	Time between violations and truth commission report World time	*Temporal*	Time between violations and truth commission report World time
Characteristics of the truth commission	Mandate Findings Organizational aspects Composition of the commission	*Characteristics of the recommendation*	Subject matter Style

(continued)

Table 7.1 *continued*

FORMULATION		IMPLEMENTATION	
Domestic factors	Civil society	*Domestic factors*	Follow-up body
	Power of perpetrators		Civil society
			Power of perpetrators
			Political will
			Resources
International factors	Regional diffusion of norms	*International factors*	International actors
	Pressure from external actors		External funding

3. EXPLAINING THE FORMULATION OF RECOMMENDATIONS

The formulation of truth commission recommendations is difficult to reconstruct, particularly long after the fact. Unless it is broadly inclusive, the process through which commissions devise a set of recommendations often lacks transparency. Our knowledge as researchers depends on the recollections of participants. Carefully tracing the development of recommendations by ongoing truth commissions, such as the one in Colombia (2018–2021), would provide valuable insights. Here, we outline the factors observers should look for.

Studies of formulation may be concerned with at least two distinct issues. First, one may seek to explain the inclusion of certain recommendations (and not others) in a truth commission's final report. What topics were considered? What was the process through which topics were raised for consideration? How did the commission decide what topics to include, and what to leave out? Second, once the topics have been determined, the text of the recommendations is drafted. Here, stylistic decisions are made about how to order the recommendations, and authors engage in wordsmithing to produce the desired effect. These questions need not be considered sequentially, as is implied here, but every truth commission confronts these issues one way or another.

The passage of time makes it difficult for us to fully reconstruct the formulation process for each of our 13 cases. Nonetheless, our findings suggest several factors that should be considered. We may group these into four sets.

A first set of factors are *temporal* in nature. Time matters in reference to both domestic and global developments. Domestically, the length of time that has passed between the occurrence of the human rights violations under investigation and the issuance of the report with recommendations may influence the selection of recommendations. Here, we have made a distinction between transitional truth commissions and post-transitional truth commissions. In transitional contexts, politics is more fluid, which can create possibilities for more significant change. Governments also may be more anxious to curry favor with the international community. By contrast, the further in the past violations recede to, the less immediacy there may be to address them. Other issues may overtake addressing the past. Eventually, perpetrators and victims age and die.

The point at which the truth commission operates in world history also may influence the recommendations, as exemplified by different emphases on human rights between the Cold War and post-Cold War worlds. The development of international best practices also may be influential, as we saw with the UN Principles being reflected in the Ecuadorian and Paraguayan recommendations. Further, the evolution of global norms may lead truth commissions to highlight particular human rights issues. For example, no recommendation makes mention of gender until the mid-1990s. Mentions of LGBTQ+ persons do not appear until the late 2000s. Thus, international context may lead commissioners to focus on particular issues in their recommendations. Research using our data finds that commissioners are often attune to global and regional human rights developments as they formulate recommendations, though this does not necessarily make governments more likely to implement such measures (Wiebelhaus-Brahm and Wright 2021).

Second, *characteristics of the truth commission* itself may influence the formulation of recommendations. At the beginning, the mandate of a truth commission defines the focus of its work. Mandates delineate the time-period to be investigated as well as the kinds of violations the commission will document. The recommendations should, at least in part, answer the mandate. The truth commission's findings, which usually reflect the mandate, typically inform the recommendations. The background of the commissioners also may shape their recommendations. Each individual brings their unique preferences, experience, ideology, personality, and even more mundane attributes such as writing style to the table, all of which may be significant for the selection and formulation of recommendations. In addition, the way the commission has internally organized itself may help shape the form and substance of recommendations. Furthermore, the process that commissioners devise to identify potential measures will influence the pool of possible recommendations. Open processes involve extensive consultation with civil society organizations and other stakeholders. At the other extreme, closed processes involve more cloistered reflection by commission personnel. Finally, the time allotted throughout the truth-finding process to prepare recommendations matters. Are they kept in mind throughout, or do commissioners franticly draw up recommendations at the last minute as they draft the report? The importance which commissioners attach to recommendations relative to other tasks will shape their selection and formulation.

Third, *domestic actors* seek to shape the recommendations to be produced by the commission. Politicians have constituents with particular policy preferences on dealing with the past. As such, presidents and legislators will likely use what power they have to align recommendations with their own interests. Victims' groups, human rights activists, and other civil society organizations often have their own strong preferences about further measures that are needed to achieve justice for past abuses and about how to best ensure non-repetition. For their part, perpetrators, too, seek to rally domestic supporters, engage in sabre-rattling, and in other ways use their power to influence the content of recommendations. Commissioners and staff are rarely unaware of this jockeying happening in broader society.

Lastly, *external actors* may try to influence the process. Where truth commissions are established or supported by international bodies (such as by the UN in Guatemala and El Salvador), commissions may consist of a mix of national and international commissioners and staff. Besides their potential external institutional and/or political ties, international commissioners will directly bring in outside experiences to the truth-finding process and to the formulation of recommendations. If a commission is supported by transnational experts like the ICTJ, they will have ideas that may serve as guidelines for setting up the truth commission and for framing recommendations. Recommendations may further be influenced by international human rights norms and models through regional diffusion (Greenhill 2010; Zimmermann 2016). In the Latin American context, we know that rulings from the Inter-American Commission and Court have influenced transitional justice policies in many countries (Engstrom and Low 2019; Skaar, García-Godos, and Collins 2016). Therefore, international norms and specific court rulings may influence how commissioners think and strategize around particular recommendations. Where international donors are involved in (co-)financing a truth commission, they could have an interest in shaping the formulation of recommendations – for example in line with international human rights norms. Finally, there may also be situations in which donors have been involved/complicit (through financing, training of the military, etc.) in committing human rights abuses in a country. As a result, they may have an interest in preventing recommendations that facilitate the disclosure of their complicity, or the criminal prosecution of such abuses. In Haiti, for example, the United States government "seized records and documents that would have been of significant value to the truth commission" (Quinn 2010, 99). Where the formulation of recommendations is hastily done at the last minute just before the report is released, and the process is non-transparent, there is a risk that pressure from external actors may be particularly high.

4. EXPLAINING THE IMPLEMENTATION OF RECOMMENDATIONS

Studying the implementation of recommendations has its own challenges too. We have argued in this book that the type of recommendation (i.e., content and style) matters for implementation, along with several other factors. Similarly to the approach suggested for studying the formulation of recommendations, we divide these factors into four sets: temporal factors, characteristics of the recommendation, domestic factors and international factors.

Starting with the *temporal dimension*, three types of time matter: (i) the time that has passed between the violations and the truth commission report; (ii) world time; and (iii) the time it takes to implement the recommendation. Firstly, depending on the time that has passed between the human rights violations and the recommendation, some types of recommendations will be easier to implement than others. For instance, criminal prosecution for human rights violations may seem impossible if a truth commission recommends this at the time of transition when political tension is high and perpetrators still strongly influential. A few years or decades down the line, the political and legal context may allow such prosecutions to take place. By contrast, reparations to victims may be easier for the state to follow up on right after a truth commission report is issued, especially if there is pressure for reparations from victims' organizations.

Secondly, the international climate (which we refer to as "world time") in which a truth commission issues its report also may influence the likelihood of implementation. The post-Cold War 1990s was a decade in which human rights, rule of law, and good governance were prominent themes. After 9/11, by contrast, security and counterterrorism dominated global discourse. Recommendations may be more likely to be implemented when they feature contemporary development buzzwords.

The third, and understudied, important temporal dimension is the time it takes to implement the recommendation. Some recommendations can be implemented in a short time-span (for example, the passage of a specific law); others may take decades to implement (for example, providing human rights education for diverse sectors of society, which may entail changing laws, institutions, textbooks and other teaching materials, and pedagogy). Emerging research suggests that backward-looking recommendations are implemented more slowly than forward-looking ones, suggesting perpetrators and their supporters obstruct measures that would further implicate them.[149] The same study finds that implementation happens more quickly in wealthier countries, when the commission was created by executive order and quickly follows a political transition that was not negotiated. In short, an analysis of implementation should bear in mind that different temporal dimensions could work differently for different kinds of recommendations.

Moving to a second set of factors, the *characteristics of the recommendation* matter for implementation. One dimension is the subject matter that they address. In the broadest sense, one can use dichotomies to capture different topics addressed, such as distinguishing systemic vs. non-systemic and forward-

---

[149]   Centeno-Martín, Héctor, Eric Wiebelhaus-Brahm, Ana Belén Nieto-Librero, and Dylan Wright. forthcoming. "Explaining the Timeliness of Implementation of Truth Commission Recommendations." *Journal of Peace Research.*

looking vs. backward-looking recommendations. In the case of reparations, it may be useful to distinguish individual from collective and symbolic from material reparations proposals. We have found that recommendations that have diffuse benefits and do not even implicitly cast blame for past abuses are more likely to be implemented. The style of recommendations also may influence the probability of implementation. Qualities that might be important include the level of specificity in the recommendation and the complexity of the language used. More generally, the number of recommendations also matters. Implementing a handful of recommendations is likely to be easier and less costly than implementing a large number of recommendations. There may be a danger that a government will feel paralyzed if there are too many tasks to tackle at once.

With respect to *domestic factors*, there are at least five things that may matter for implementation of recommendations. Perhaps most importantly, the establishment of a follow-up body or secretariat (often recommended by the truth commission itself), tasked with monitoring the implementation of recommendations, increases the likelihood of implementation, though it poses no guarantee for implementation. Civil society pressure can be of utmost importance for "keeping the flame alive" by exercising pressure on the government after the commission completes its work and delivers its report. This is particularly true for recommendations of reparations or other justice measures. Perpetrators, on the other hand, will invariably push for impunity and resist the implementation of measures that involve accountability of any kind, from the disclosure of names of alleged perpetrators to prosecution through criminal procedures. Because truth commissions are temporary bodies, they cannot shepherd recommendations through to implementation. Follow-up bodies and civil society may prompt government action, but, for most recommendations, the decision whether to implement ultimately lies with politicians. Politicians, and the political parties to which they belong, are more likely to enact recommendations if they feel it will help them gain or retain power. Governments will consider whether the necessary resources (manpower and financial) can be made available for implementation, or if doing so will jeopardize other policy priorities. Where political tensions are high, and where the military is still strong, some politicians may obstruct implementation of certain (types of) recommendations. Ultimately, politicians will act if they believe that doing so will help them gain the votes of important electoral blocs. Implementing recommendations requires not only political support, but also sufficient resources. The resources allocated to the implementation of recommendations are likely a product of both political will to dedicate sufficient resources and the availability of such resources in a country. The poorer the country, the fewer resources are likely to be available for implementation.

Fourth and finally, the implementation of recommendations may also be influenced by *international factors*. International actors can press for reforms or implementation. Human rights bodies within the UN and Inter-American system can put diplomatic pressure on governments to act. Transnational activists can try to name and shame governments (and the foreign governments that support them) to enact measures. Donors can also supply additional resources for implementation of recommendations or condition their aid upon the introduction of particular measures, likely those that conform to the donor's interests and ideology.

5. CHALLENGES AND SOLUTIONS TO IMPLEMENTATION

The implementation of truth commission recommendations seems to be strongly dependent on the will and resources of the government that receives a truth commission report. As our analysis clearly shows, governments are not necessarily favorably disposed toward truth commissions and may even be actively opposed to implementing certain recommendations – especially those that have to do with criminal accountability. This is particularly true in countries where the military hangs on to power after a transition to (formal) democracy and where political tensions are high, as in the cases of El Salvador and Guatemala. It is also true where political leaders are sympathetic to past military regimes, as in Brazil. Furthermore, implementation is difficult in resource-poor countries, or where post-conflict demands in different sectors are so great that the government is overburdened, as in the case of Haiti.

Our findings are quite consistent with the tendencies that can be identified in relation to the implementation of recommendations issued by transnational institutions. The general conclusion from recent research in this area is that, like truth commission recommendations, some types of recommendations are more likely to be implemented than others. Scholars studying the Inter-American Commission on Human Rights, for instance, show that there is moderate state compliance with measures to reform laws, policies, and practices. The measures that states are the least willing to comply with are recommendations that concern justice and accountability (Abi-Mershed 2020, 172). States also generally seem reluctant to implement reparations ordered by multilateral institutions, but this depends on the type of reparation. The reparation measures ordered by the Inter-American Commission on Human Rights that are most often complied with relate to monetary compensation (Abi-Mershed 2020, 172). Outside the Latin American context, scholars have found that implementation rates are low for reparations and measures of non-repetition ordered by decisions and judgments adopted by human rights supranational treaty bodies (Murray and Sandoval 2020, 101–102).

Should these rather discouraging findings dissuade truth commissions from making recommendations that seem less likely to be implemented? Or are there ways of formulating recommendations that may make governments more inclined to implement them? Furthermore, is there anything victims, domestic activists and pro-justice politicians, or transnational activists, donor governments, and multilateral institutions can do to increase the odds of implementation? In the section below we examine what lessons, if any, may be drawn from the practice of the Inter-American Commission on Human Rights and other transnational institutions that make recommendations addressing human rights violations. We distinguish between two main issues: (i) improving implementation, and (ii) improving the measurement of implementation.

5.1. WHAT CAN BE DONE TO IMPROVE THE IMPLEMENTATION OF RECOMMENDATIONS?

As summarized in Table 7.1 above, there are numerous factors that may enhance (or hinder) implementation. Three things that commissioners have at least some control over are (i) how many recommendations are produced, (ii) what kinds of recommendations they choose to include in the final truth commission report, and (iii) how they formulate the recommendations. In the following discussion, we focus on the third point. Specifically, we first look at the nature of recommendations, and reflect upon the relative merits of setting deadlines and identifying implementing agents in recommendations. Then, we shift our focus to other explanatory factors that may influence implementation. Once a recommendation is published in a truth commission's final report, its fate is largely out of the hands of the commissioners. We focus mainly on the challenge of state compliance and explore how follow-up bodies and victims' mobilization can encourage implementation.

5.2. THE CHARACTERISTICS OF RECOMMENDATIONS

We have argued in this book that the characteristics (i.e., subject matter and style) of a recommendation matter. This is worth reflecting upon further. What we call characteristics, other scholars have referred to as "specificities".[150] When it comes to the implementation of international orders or recommendations, the conventional wisdom is that *greater specificity of the measures helps compliance* (Murray and Sandoval 2020, 102). How is this relevant to the recommendations made by truth commissions? A useful suggestion made by Murray and Sandoval (2020, 102) in their study of reparations is to "unpack" specificity "in terms of the content of the reparation, deadlines imposed, who is responsible [for implementation] and who is a victim, and how the decision is reasoned".

---

[150] See the 2020 Special Issue of the *Journal of Policy Implementation*, for example, which focuses on specificity.

Whereas the victim is particularly relevant to reparations, the other dimensions are relevant for any truth commission recommendation. Content deals with the substance of the recommendation. Truth commissions also provide justification for their recommendations, though it is not always explicit or laid out in the recommendations section of the report. In the following, we focus on two elements that we have not discussed in detail already: deadlines and who is responsible for implementation.

5.3.   DEADLINES IMPOSED

Our research has shown that implementation can be a matter of time. In general, the more time that has passed, the higher the likelihood of implementation. Sometimes, the passage of time can open up possibilities for implementation of politically contentious recommendations, as in the case of El Salvador. Yet, implementation efforts also can lose momentum with time. Recommendations are simply "put on the backburner" by states, even forgotten. This is a tendency observed also for recommendations made by international institutions to states. As a result, the Inter-American Court has introduced a six-month time-frame during which it expects states to act on its ruling and recommendations. This time-frame may be too short for implementation, though. As noted by (Abi-Mershed 2020, 174), "Initially requests for extensions were infrequent. Over time, however, it has become common for states to request multiple extensions. This *sometimes produces substantive steps towards compliance, and sometimes produces only delay*" (emphasis added). Other scholars are more positive toward the introduction of deadlines for implementation. Murray and Sandoval (2020, 107), for instance, argue that,

> Specificity does not just relate to the content or type of reparation but also the time frame relevant to its implementation. The supranational bodies use deadlines in a number of ways, the majority of them to indicate when the state should report back on the actual implementation of the measures. The African Commission on Human and Peoples' Rights and the UN Human Rights Committee routinely ask that the state report back within a 180-day deadline … As a general rule, the Inter-American Court of Human Rights gives the state a year to report on actual implementation of measures and this is counted from the moment of notification of the judgment.[151]

---

[151]   Note that many of the cases studied in Murray and Sandoval's project "included individual forms of reparation, but fewer included guarantees of non-repetition, with the exception of the Inter-American Court and Inter-American Commission on Human Rights, which often order and recommend them. Guarantees of non-repetition are those measures aimed at preventing the recurrence of similar violations in the future by trying to address the root and structural causes of human rights violations" (Murray and Sandoval 2020, 103).

In contrast to these two regional courts, truth commissions have not imposed deadlines for the implementation of recommendations. At best, governments may make vague commitments to implement when creating the commission or upon receiving the final report. Although national truth commissions do not have the same leverage over state compliance as regional bodies do, a case could nevertheless be made for the inclusion of such deadlines. When they formulate recommendations, commissioners could seek to estimate time-to-implementation as part of their consultation process. Thus, commissions could generate expectations for state action to which governments could be held accountable. At the same time, deadlines must be realistic. Otherwise, it provides the state with another excuse not to act.

5.4. WHO IS RESPONSIBLE FOR IMPLEMENTATION?

As argued by Murray and Sandoval (2020, 108), "Naming institutions might be important, particularly in states that do not have a system yet in place to implement orders or recommendations given by supranational bodies, as this would pre-empt the lack [of] implementation." In our book, we have examined whether truth commissions in their recommendations have specified who the implementing actor will be. Most recommendations made by Latin American truth commissions are directed toward the state in a generic sense. The exceptions tend to be recommendations that target reforms of the military, judiciary, and police. Those recommendations often specifically call upon the institution to change, sometimes even specifying particular departments that should act. Only a few other types of recommendations frequently identify the implementing actor. For example, ministries of education are often called upon to enact recommendations that deal with (human rights) education. Commissioners address this in a general sense, given the frequent calls for follow-up bodies, and the positive implementation record of these recommendations suggests that governments value them. It is possible that more targeted direction may boost implementation of at least some types of recommendations. Thus, paying more attention to who should be responsible for implementation may be worth thinking about for commissioners when they formulate recommendations. Doing so, though, requires knowledge of bureaucratic structures and standard operating procedures, information which already overburdened truth commissions would likely have to strain to acquire.

A word of caution, though, about making recommendations too specific: In a comparative analysis of the implementation of a number of decisions adopted by some UN treaty bodies and regional human rights commissions and courts in Africa, the Americas and Europe, Murray and Sandoval (2020, 101) find that "specificity must also be considered vis-à-vis the degree of discretion that is given (or not) to states to act on orders or recommendations given by supranational bodies in individual cases". If a recommendation is too specific, the authors argue, states will have less leeway in deciding how to carry out implementation. At the extreme, governments may genuinely be unable to act as directed. Therefore, very specific recommendations may make it harder for the state to fully implement.

There seems to be a potential trade-off, then, between principle and pragmatism. Giving states clear direction may make recommendations more "implementable" by giving states a ready blueprint on how enact the measure. At the same time, instructions must not be so detailed that they become impossible to implement. Commissioners may miscalculate and produce recommendations that are too ambitious for present political and economic circumstances. If the measure is too ambitious or gives the government little leeway in implementation, it may result in zero rather than incremental progress.

5.5.   STATE WILLINGNESS TO COMPLY

Regarding a state's willingness to comply with a truth commission's recommendations, our research has concluded that what we have called "political will", which could be rephrased as a commitment to human rights, is of central importance. A government committed to truth finding is more likely to also implement the recommendations made by a truth commission than a state that has been opposed to documenting human rights violations committed by past governments.[152] State compliance is also a central question in studies of international court rulings and recommendations issued by multilateral treaty bodies. Research on the political commitment of states to implement recommendations from the Inter-American Commission on Human Rights demonstrates that states that are parties to the American Convention on Human Rights are more likely to implement recommendations made by the Commission compared to non-states-parties:

> Of the 27 countries with cases included in follow up reporting as of the close of 2018, seven have yet to ratify the Convention. *All the reported cases with full compliance (the vast majority resolved through friendly settlement) concern parties to the Convention*, along with one instance of full compliance by a non-party to the Convention (Abi-Mershed 2020, 173) (emphasis added).

To be party to the Convention signals the importance of commitment and expectations for implementation. In short, it demonstrates at least a minimum of political commitment.

---

[152]   Note that it is not always the government that establishes a truth commission that implements its recommendations.

This finding suggests that pushing states to ratify human rights treaties, which is something truth commissions often recommend, can pay off. Getting states to publicly commit to implement, whether in the commission's mandate, at the unveiling of the final report, or some other visible opportunity to pledge action, could promote implementation. Further, in the case of compliance with international rulings, Abi-Mershed (2020, 176) argues that, "For the implementing state, having a serious process is a reflection of institutional commitment." In the case of truth commission recommendations, governments might demonstrate this commitment through establishing follow-up bodies, inter-ministerial working groups, or even dedicated ministries of transitional justice (Lamont, Quinn, and Wiebelhaus-Brahm 2019).

Overall, broad consultation on the formulation of recommendations will likely pay dividends when it comes to implementation. Research on the European Court of Human Rights, for instance, finds that "interventions by [civil society organizations] or national human rights institutions at an early stage … can help identify appropriate remedial measures and even define the specific scope of the follow-up process" (Donald, Long, and Speck 2020, 131). If truth commissions proactively engage state institutions and civil society organizations, they are more likely to get "buy-in" from stakeholders and produce recommendations that are feasible. This, in turn, should improve the prospects of implementation.

5.6. MONITORING IMPLEMENTATION

Research on the implementation of human rights recommendations given to states by multilateral treaty bodies finds that it is not only important to establish a detailed understanding of what exactly the recommendation entails, but also to develop monitoring procedures that help states comply (Principi 2020). There are several factors that better ensure the effectiveness of monitoring in boosting implementation rates. First, dedicated follow-up bodies provide a focal point for implementation. In the absence of a body specifically designated for follow-up, the establishment of good reporting procedures is a viable substitute. Second, these mechanisms are only effective if they are publicly accessible. Follow-up bodies and procedures need to provide sufficient information, and to do so in a transparent fashion, in order to accurately gauge progress on implementation. Third, this data is critical for victims' groups and other civil society organizations to serve as watchdogs. These issues are directly relevant to the implementation of truth commission recommendations as well. The rest of this section focuses on different ways in which implementation can be effectively monitored to enhance truth commission impact.

One of our findings is that countries that have opted for the establishment of a follow-up body to oversee the implementation of truth commission recommendations have higher implementation rates than those that lack such a body. This, too, is consistent with findings of implementation in other contexts. If we look towards the practice of international bodies that give recommendations in the field of human rights more broadly, we see variation as to the presence or absence of specific follow-up bodies. For instance Murray and Sandoval (2020, 108) find that the Inter-American Court sometimes orders the establishment of a new body to implement a ruling, but at other times defers to existing domestic institutions.

Existing research also demonstrates that the existence of a follow-up body is not enough. Among other things, the body must have procedures to facilitate the monitoring of implementation. Without them, it would be difficult for policymakers, activists, and researchers to know whether a recommendation has in fact been implemented. As it turns out, collecting information on implementation is not only challenging for truth commission observers, but also for those charged with monitoring recommendations issued by international human rights bodies. Practice varies among different bodies. As argued by Donald, Long, and Speck (2020, 125),

> Assessing the extent to which states have implemented the decisions of supranational human rights bodies is a challenging task. It requires supranational bodies – be they judicial, quasi-judicial or political – *to create an evidence-based public record of the status quo of implementation at any point in time and determine whether the measures taken do, in fact, satisfy the requirements of the decision.* This, in turn, relies upon states engaging in good faith, victims having a voice, and civil society organizations seizing the opportunity to influence the follow-up process (emphasis added).

Using empirical data from interviews with officials in selected states in the regions with the most well-developed human rights institutions (Europe, the Americas, and Africa), as well as within regional and United Nations bodies, they argue that "in no human rights 'system' are all these expectations met, in part because follow-up work is inadequately resourced" (Donald, Long, and Speck 2020, 125). What appear to be most important are formal assessments of implementation that make public information about activity in a timely manner. A scorecard that routinely reports on the status of implementation can enable domestic and international actors to monitor compliance and provide the basis for naming and shaming if necessary. The follow-up body to the 2011 Bahrain Independent Commission of Inquiry created something like this, though there were disputes about the accuracy of its assessments (Wiebelhaus-Brahm 2019). Thus, when it comes to delineating the structure and powers of a follow-up body, here may be instances where greater specificity in recommendations is beneficial.

In fact, measuring compliance is easier said than done. Based upon a detailed analysis of the implementation and monitoring procedures used by regional human rights bodies in Europe and the Americas, Hillebrecht (2009, 362) argues that "the means by which these human rights instruments measure compliance with their rulings suffers from ambiguity and inconsistency". She notes three main problems with current approaches to measuring compliance:

> First, the current measurement approaches obscure important differences among the discrete obligations states face when the tribunals hand down an adverse judgment … Second, the extant approaches to measuring compliance with the tribunals' rulings do not provide a way to compare compliance across cases, states or tribunals without first doing a massive amount of background work … Third, the current approaches to measuring compliance do not allow for the easy aggregation of cases, thus thwarting any attempt at creating a "bigger picture" about compliance with human rights tribunals (Hillebrecht 2009, 370).

Measuring compliance is a critical challenge. Among other things, a proper coding scheme is essential.

There are many potential coding schemes, though. One study lauds the approach taken by the Inter-American Commission on Human Rights. In its annual reports, it codes compliance with its judgments,

> according to whether it is "full" (or "total"), "partial" or "pending" … These categories mean, respectively, that the state has fully complied with all of the friendly settlement clauses or recommendations; that it has complied with some, but not all, of them or has taken some, but not all, required steps for each of them; or that it has taken no steps, or has taken steps that have yielded no concrete results, or has expressly indicated that it will not comply with the friendly settlement clauses or recommendations, or has not reported to the Commission and there is no information from other sources to suggest otherwise (Donald, Long, and Speck 2020, 140).

Establishing good criteria for implementation is, as we have experienced, no simple task. Many of the challenges Donald et al. (2020) highlight, are relevant to truth commissions. First, how does one give content to vaguely formulated recommendations. For instance, how to you establish indicators to measure the implementation of anti-discrimination measures? Or, in the case of many truth commissions concerned with non-repetition measures, how does one determine whether "a human rights culture" has been successfully or partially established?

A second question flagged by these authors is when and how to determine when the information collected is sufficient. When should follow-up end? This is a very important point because implementation can take place over several years, sometimes decades. Whereas the international human rights bodies that have been studied typically respond to individual complaints and usually issue recommendations regarding reparations (or sometimes, but less frequently, measures for non-repetition), truth commissions issue recommendations of an extremely broad nature. Some of the more complex recommendations may involve multiple actors that make them complicated and time consuming to implement. It is, therefore, important that commissioners think consciously about formulating recommendations in a way that is "implementable". Thirdly, Donald, Long, and Speck (2020, 133) argue that gleaning information from diverse sources about the actions – or omissions – of states is a prerequisite for effective follow-up. Thus, follow-up bodies, governments and stakeholders should take care to consult different sources when assessing implementation.

In this book, we coded implementation at three levels: no implementation, partial implementation and full implementation. This is not a perfect way of doing things. In particular, it is difficult to know what goes into the "partially implemented" category.[153] Another challenge when measuring implementation is that the focus is on the degree of implementation rather than on the substance or the importance of the recommendations. Implementing a rather simple recommendation, like establishing a memorial site, gets a higher score if the site is established (=fully implemented) compared to establishing a national program for human rights education that targets various sectors like school children, teachers, judges, the police, the military, etc. In such a case, it will be more difficult to reach "full implementation" regardless of how hard the state tries and how many resources are allocated to implementation (so it would be hypothetically coded partially implemented). To resolve this problem, some institutions, like the Inter-American Commission on Human Rights, have recently introduced the use of percentages to record how much of a given recommendation is implemented (Donald, Long, and Speck 2020, 140–141). However, some scholars have noted the weakness of this system by pointing out that while "the Commission estimates the percentage of compliance based on the measures effectively implemented and those that remain pending, … this has the peculiarity of treating recommendations with very different significance as being of equal weight" (Abi-Mershed 2020, 172). While introducing percentages or weighting systems does not appear desirable for assessing the implementation of truth commission recommendations, it may be useful for those charged with implementation to think very concretely about how to document implementation.

For many, the ultimate gauge of truth commission success, or any transitional justice measure for that matter, is whether victims' needs and demands are met. Research on implementation of recommendations made by multinational bodies suggests that an effective way of monitoring implementation could be to involve

---

[153]   This problem is echoed by scholars trying to assess implementation in other contexts. Drawing heavily on Hillebrecht (2009), Donald, Long, and Speck (2020, 133) argue that "the 'broad and ambiguous' category of partial compliance does not explain either the various forms or degrees that partial compliance takes or its causes. Insufficient differentiation may have the perverse effect of increasing states' existing tendency to take minimalistic steps in response to a judgment … by creating an incentive for them to earn the status of partial compliance by picking 'the lowest-hanging fruit', such as payment of reparations or symbolic reparations, rather than implementing more 'durable' and politically challenging measures, like the prosecution of perpetrators".

victims and victims' organizations more in the process. This is particularly true of recommendations that have to do with reparations. Some of these lessons may be relevant also for truth commissions. Abi-Mershed (2020, 176), for example, finds that, in the case of the Inter-American Commission, "the participation of the victims and their representatives is highly relevant to successful implementation". As Donald, Long and Speck (2020) argue, "elicit[ing] victims' views on the adequacy of reparation measures" is particularly important.

> There are certain reparation measures that victims are uniquely well placed to assess, among them symbolic measures such as memorials or public acts of acknowledgement of responsibility. These are arguably meaningless, if not counterproductive, if victims are not satisfied with them (Donald, Long, and Speck 2020, 129–130).

This fits quite nicely with the common refrain to have victims more deeply involved in transitional justice processes.

At the same time, there are limits to how much burden can and should be placed on victims. Furthermore, Abi-Mershed (2020, 176) cautions that victims' marginalization may impede them from playing this role. As such, victims may need support, such as access to legal aid, to be effective monitors of implementation. For its part, the European Court of Human Rights created a website to facilitate civil society involvement (Donald, Long, and Speck 2020, 131). It is unclear whether that support would be more effective if it were state- or civil society-driven. Either way, a potential risk would be that it would disempower more radical voices among victims. Furthermore, victims also may not be well positioned to be arbiters of some types of recommendations. Measures for non-repetition may be one of those areas. Donald, Long, and Speck (2020, 129–130), for instance, argue that victims groups cannot "be expected to report on the need for, and impact of, broader reforms of a legislative, administrative, judicial or other nature".

5.7. SUMMARY POINTS AND POLICY RECOMMENDATIONS

Combining the findings from our research on truth commission recommendations with scholarly assessments of the implementation records of recommendations made by regional and UN treaty bodies, we may extract at least nine concrete policy recommendations for future truth commissions:

(i) Truth commissions should identify particular state authorities to implement particular recommendations in order clarify the lines of responsibility and promote accountability.
(ii) Truth commissions should suggest a suitable timeline for the implementation of the recommendations.

(iii) When making recommendations for reparations, truth commissions should identify who is a victim and, thus, to whom reparation is owed.[154]

(iv) To encourage a higher implementation rate for recommendations addressing victims' needs, victims should be actively involved in the process of implementation. This also would heighten victims' satisfaction, which is essential for positive impact.

(v) Truth commissions should recommend the establishment of a follow-up body to ensure the implementation of recommendations.

(vi) The follow-up body should develop a system for measuring implementation.

(vii) The follow-up body should proactively seek out diverse sources of information and adopt transparent and responsive working methods to enable "real time" participation by all interested parties.[155]

(viii) Follow-up work must be adequately resourced.

(ix) As they often do, truth commissions should recommend that states sign international human rights treaties. Treaties' monitoring bodies can provide another layer of support for implementation of recommendations that are related to treaty obligations.

For all of these measures, crafting recommendations through broad consultation with stakeholders, state and non-state alike, should make them more realistic and increase the odds of implementation.

6. CONCLUSIONS AND A FUTURE RESEARCH AGENDA

Our research shows that many of the recommendations made by Latin American truth commissions have been implemented, though there is significant variation among different countries and based upon the subject matter of the recommendation. Our findings also raise several important questions that future research can fruitfully address. Here, we highlight a few lacunae.

Starting with the recommendation itself, more research is needed on the importance of how recommendations are formulated and to what effect. Regarding the style, what kind of language is used? Is the text short and to the point? Long-winded? Convoluted or straightforward? Are the actions that are needed made explicit or implied? Qualitative characteristics are highly subjective, but we encourage researchers to empirically measure qualities like these. Further, it would be valuable to explore the conditions under which truth commission recommendations take different rhetorical forms and how these

---

[154] Here we draw upon the research of Murray and Sandoval (2020, 110).

[155] We here draw on the advice of Donald, Long, and Speck (2020, 125) for supranational bodies.

differences influence the likelihood of implementation. Focusing on the text itself may be important.

It also would be useful to apply our model to truth commissions in other regions of the world. Depending on content and context, some of the categories of recommendations we have used in our coding scheme may or may not be applicable. Other regional contexts may warrant inclusion of categories such as vetting or lustration measures, which few Latin American truth commissions have recommended. In sum, the categories of recommendations included in a truth commission report may be different from report to report and from region to region, but the factors likely to shape formulation and implementation should be similar.

Causal connections are notoriously hard to pin down in qualitative research. In our individual case studies, we analyze the factors that have facilitated or hampered implementation of different kinds of recommendations (Skaar, Wiebelhaus-Brahm, and García-Godos (eds.) 2022). However, we have not systematically controlled for other factors that may matter for implementation, either directly or indirectly. Thus, more work is needed on how to address this with qualitative methodology. We encourage further comparative research related to the formulation and implementation of recommendations. One path would be more in-depth case studies that carefully reconstruct the processes through which particular (sets of) recommendations are formulated and implemented in specific national contexts. Advances in process-tracing methodology are promising in this regard (Beach and Pedersen 2019; Bennett and Checkel 2015). Relatedly, exploring conditions of necessity and sufficiency would be valuable. For example, judicial reform may have come about with or without truth commission recommendations, which in turn may have improved the odds of criminal accountability.[156] A second avenue would be cross-regional research, comparing one or more Latin American truth commissions with counterparts from other parts of the world. This would help illuminate the role of history and culture in shaping truth commission processes. Finally, one could compare the implementation of recommendations made by national truth commissions to those made by regional and global treaty bodies like the Inter-American Commission on Human Rights and the Inter-American Court. Among other things, this could address the question of whether governments are more or less likely to react favorably to external demands, expectations, and pressure for (particular types of) reform.

The use of statistical techniques to examine our data also would be welcome.[157] Quantitative methods are an effective means of examining patterns

---

[156]   For an up-to date discussion on the connections between judicial reform and justice in Guatemala, see Maldonado Urbina (2020).

[157]   For an early example, see Centeno-Martín et al. (forthcoming).

in large quantities of data. More importantly, statistical techniques enable us to determine with a high degree of certainty whether the patterns we observe are due to random chance or a systematic relationship between two variables. In part, this comes through controlling for other variables that also might theoretically have an effect on our outcome of interest. Applied to our data, quantitative methods can help determine the independent effect of temporal dimensions, recommendation characteristics as well as domestic and international factors on the likelihood of implementation. Further, it would be possible to explore whether certain factors shape the recommendations themselves. Early statistical evidence indicates that implementation is driven much more by contextual factors than by characteristics of the recommendations themselves (Centeno-Martín, et al. forthcoming).

We conclude with an astute observation from Donald, Long, and Speck (2020, 125). As they note,

> Assessing the extent to which states have implemented the decisions of supranational human rights bodies is a challenging task. It requires supranational bodies – be they judicial, quasi-judicial or political – to create an evidence-based public record of the status quo of implementation at any point in time and determine whether the measures taken do, in fact, satisfy the requirements of the decision. This, in turn, relies upon states engaging in good faith, victims having a voice, and civil society organizations seizing the opportunity to influence the follow-up process.

In the case of truth commissions, there are no supranational bodies to create these records of implementation. Nevertheless, there is a lot that states and other actors can do to ensure that the recommendations made by truth commissions in response to gross human rights violations are taken seriously, acted upon, and hence contribute to improving the country's future. Governments may be unwilling or unable to do so. Whether or not they do, civil society and researchers have and will continue to play a critical watchdog role.

APPENDIX I

Latin American Truth Commission Reports

ARGENTINA, 1984
National Commission on the Disappeared
Comisión Nacional sobre la Desaparición de Personas (CONADEP)

TC report: *Informe de la Comisión Nacional Sobre la Desaparición de Personas*

Spanish version available at
http://www.desaparecidos.org/arg/conadep/nuncamas/

English version available at
http://web.archive.org/web/20031004074316/nuncamas.org/english/library/
nevagain/nevagain_001.htm

English version available at https://www.amazon.com/Nunca-Mas-Never-Again-
Report/dp/0571138497/ref=sr_1_1?ie=UTF8&qid=1489094735&sr=8-1&keyw
ords=nunca+mas+argentina (official English translation, for sale)

URUGUAY, 1985
Investigative Commission on the Situation of Disappeared People and its Causes
Comisión Investigadora Parlamentaria Sobre la Situación de Personas Desaparecidas y Hechos que la Motivaron

TC report: *Informe Final de la Comisión Investigadora Parlamentaria Sobre Situación de Personas Desaparecidas y Hechos que la Motivaron*

Spanish version available at (see only pp. 1–25):
http://archivo.presidencia.gub.uy/_web/noticias/2007/06/tomo4.pdf

Note that the original report is not publicly available. However, there is a modern reproduction made by the Uruguayan government, online available, edited in 4 volumes by Presidency in 2007. This 2007 publication by the Uruguayan government of the TC reports was reproduced as part of implementing a recommendation from the ComiPaz. The five-volume publication is titled *Investigación Histórica sobre Detenidos Desaparecidos*, and the TC reports are re-produced in Vol. IV. See:
http://archivo.presidencia.gub.uy/_web/noticias/2007/06/2007060509.htm

The entire 2007 volume is available in Spanish here:

Volume 1:
http://archivo.presidencia.gub.uy/_web/noticias/2007/06/tomo1.pdf

Volume 2:
http://archivo.presidencia.gub.uy/_web/noticias/2007/06/tomo2.pdf

Volume 3:
http://archivo.presidencia.gub.uy/_web/noticias/2007/06/tomo3.pdf

Volume 4:
http://archivo.presidencia.gub.uy/_web/noticias/2007/06/tomo4.pdf

Volume 5:
http://archivo.presidencia.gub.uy/_web/noticias/2007/06/tomo5.pdf

The re-production is also available through this site:
http://www.desaparecidos.org/uru/

English version not available.

CHILE RETTIG, 1991
National Commission for Truth and Reconciliation "The Rettig Commission"
Comisión Rettig

TC report: *Informe de la Comisión Nacional de Verdad y Reconciliación* ("Informe Rettig") Vol. 1–3

Spanish version available at:
http://www.ddhh.gov.cl/wp-content/uploads/2015/12/tomo1.pdf (Volume 1),

http://www.ddhh.gov.cl/wp-content/uploads/2015/12/tomo2.pdf (Volume 2) and

http://www.ddhh.gov.cl/wp-content/uploads/2015/12/tomo3.pdf (Volume 3)

English version (Report of the Chilean National Commission on Truth and Reconciliation) available at:
http://www.usip.org/sites/default/files/resources/collections/truth_commissions/Chile90-Report/Chile90-Report.pdf

EL SALVADOR, 1993
Commission on the Truth for El Salvador
Comisión de la Verdad para El Salvador (CVES)

TC report: *De la locura a la esperanza. La guerra de 12 años en El Salvador*

Spanish version available at
http://www.derechoshumanos.net/lesahumanidad/informes/elsalvador/informe-de-la-locura-a-la-esperanza.htm and

https://www.scribd.com/document/137504386/De-la-locura-a-la-esperanza-La-guerra-de-12-anos-en-El-Salvador

English version available at
http://www.usip.org/sites/default/files/file/ElSalvador-Report.pdf

HAITI, 1996
National Truth and Justice Commission
Commission Nationale de Vérité et de Justice (CNVJ)

TC report: *Si m pa rele: 29 September 1991–14 Octobre 1994*

French version available at
http://ufdcweb1.uflib.ufl.edu/UF00085926/00001
Annex I and II available at http://ufdc.ufl.edu/UF00085926/00002 and Annex III available at http://ufdc.ufl.edu/UF00085926/00003, or both available at https://kuscholarworks.ku.edu/handle/1808/10910.

English version not available, but a very rough translation of the recommendations are listed in USAID's report:
http://pdf.usaid.gov/pdf_docs/PNABZ701.pdf, Appendix B, 18 pages.

GUATEMALA, 1999
Commission for Historical Clarification of Guatemala
Comisión para el Esclarecimiento Histórico de Guatemala (CEH)

TC report: *Guatemala: Memoria del Silencio*

Spanish versions available at
http://www.undp.org/content/dam/guatemala/docs/publications/UNDP_gt_PrevyRecu_MemoriadelSilencio.pdf (short, 96 pages) and http://www.centro dememoriahistorica.gov.co/descargas/guatemala-memoria-silencio/guatemala-memoria-del-silencio.pdf (long, 4383 pages).

English version (short, 82 pages) available at
https://www.aaas.org/sites/default/files/migrate/uploads/mos_en.pdf.

PANAMA, 2002
Panama Truth Commission
Comisión de la Verdad de Panamá

TC report: *Informe Final de la Comisión de la Verdad. "La verdad os hará libres"*

Spanish version available at
http://www.defensoriadelpueblo.gob.pa/index.php?option=com_flippingbo
ok&view=book&id=6:informe-final-de-la-comision-de-la-verdad&catid=6:
informes

English version not available.

URUGUAY, 2003
Commission for Peace
Comisión para la Paz (COMIPAZ/ComiPaz)

TC report: *Informe Final de la Comisión para la Paz*

Spanish version available at
https://www.usip.org/sites/default/files/file/resources/collections/commissions/
Uruguay-Report_Informal.pdf

English version not available.

PERU, 2003
Truth and Reconciliation Commission
Comisión de la Verdad y Reconciliación (CVR)

TC report: *Informe Final de la Comisión de la Verdad y Reconciliación*
(Abbreviated version: *Hatun Willakuy*)

Full Spanish 2003 version available, in several separate files, at: http://www.
cverdad.org.pe/ifinal/index.php and http://www.usip.org/publications/truth-
commission-peru-01.

Abbreviated Spanish 2004 version available at
http://idehpucp.pucp.edu.pe/wp-content/uploads/2012/11/hatun-willakuy-cvr-
espanol.pdf.

English version of the Conclusions, available at the CVR's webpage: http://www.
cverdad.org.pe/ingles/ifinal/conclusiones.php

CHILE VALECH, 2004
National Commission on Political Imprisonment and Torture
Comisión Nacional sobre Prisión Politica y Tortura ("Comisión Valech")

TC report: *Informe de la Comisión Nacional sobre Prisión Politica y Tortura*
(Informe Valech)

Spanish version of the first report and the complimentary report available at
http://www.comisiontortura.cl/
and http://www.archivochile.com/Derechos_humanos/com_valech/

PARAGUAY, 2008
Truth and Justice Commission
Comisión de Verdad y Justicia (CVJ)

TC report: *Informe Final. Anive haguâ oiko*

Spanish version, in several separate files, available at http://www.cipae.org.py/V2/informe-final-anive-agua-oiko/

English version not available.

ECUADOR, 2010
Truth Commission to Impede Impunity
Comisión de la Verdad para Impedir la Impunidad

TC report: *Informe de la Comisión de la Verdad Ecuador 2010: Sin verdad no hay justicia*

Spanish version available at
https://issuu.com/triguero/docs/ecuador._sin_verdad_no_hay_justicia

English version not available.

BRAZIL, 2014
National Truth Commission
Comissão Nacional da Verdade (CNV)

TC report: *Relatório da Comissão Nacional da Verdade, volume I, II & III*

Portuguese version available at
http://www.cnv.gov.br/index.php?option=com_content&view=article&id=571

Read the conclusions and recommendations contained in the final report of the National Truth Commission in Portuguese

http://www.cnv.gov.br/images/pdf/relatorio/Capitulo%2018.pdf (official site)

English version not available.

APPENDIX II

Information on 13 Latin American Truth Commission Reports and their Recommendations

13 LATIN AMERICAN TRUTH COMMISSION REPORTS: DESCRIPTIVE INFORMATION

Truth commission (TC)	Total pages TC report/ pages recommendations	Main categories/themes of recommendations as listed in Table of Contents of TC report
Argentina TC (CONADEP) 1984	Report: 420 pages Recommendations: 1 page	3 concrete recommendations plus 1 main category i) Present evidence from TC to executive; (ii) present evidence to courts to enable criminal prosecution; (iii) reparations; (iv) law/legal reform. Only the last category (*law/legal reform*) includes more than one recommendation.
Uruguay TC 1985	Report: 4 pages Recommendations: 1 page	No categories. 2 concrete recommendations
Chile TC (Rettig) 1991	Report: 1303 pages Recommendations: 48 pages (pp. 1253–1301)	3 main categories (i) "*Propuestas*" and reparations; (ii) prevention of future violations; (iii) other recommendations. Each of the 3 main categories broken down into a total of 8 sub-groups of measures, which again are subdivided into several themes, before listing the concrete TCRs.
El Salvador TC (CVES) 1993	Report: 198 pages Recommendations: 13 pages (pp. 185–198)	4 main categories (i) Recommendations directly related to findings of report; (ii) eradication of structural causes directly linked to the acts examined; (iii) institutional reform to prevent future violations; (iv) measures aimed at national reconciliation. Each of the 4 main categories contains 3 or more thematic areas – around 16 sub-groups of measures in total.

(continued)

continued

Truth commission (TC)	Total pages TC report/ pages recommendations	Main categories/themes of recommendations as listed in Table of Contents of TC report
Haiti TC (CNVJ) 1996	Report: 242 pages **Recommendations: 46 pages** (pp. 196–242)	5 main categories (i) Reparations; (ii) sexual violence against women; (iii) judicial reform; (iv) follow-up commission; (v) other recommendation. One of the 5 main categories is divided into three sub-categories of measures. For instance, *(v) other reforms* is divided into five main sub-categories A–E.
Guatemala TC (CEH) 1999	Report: 4383 pages (Vols. I–V) **Recommendations: 26 pages** (pp. 59–85)	6 main categories (i) Preservation of memory; (ii) reparations; (iii) human rights observation; (iv) institutional reform (to strengthen democratic process); (v) peace promotion; (vi) mechanisms for follow-up of TC recommendations. Each of the 6 main categories contains one or more specific recommendations – around 13 sub-groups of measures in total.
Panama TC 2002	Report: 633 pages **Recommendations: 1 page**	*No categories.* 12 concrete recommendations.
Uruguay TC (COMIPAZ) 2003	Report: 85 pages **Recommendations: 7 pages** (pp. 28–34 and pp. 40–43)	2 categories: (i) Specific recommendations, (ii) general recommendations. These two categories contain 7 concrete TCRs, some of which may be broken down into sub-recommendations.
Peru TC (CVR) 2003	Report: 3371 + 492 pages **Recommendations: 189 pages** (pp. 109–298)	4 main categories: i) Institutional reform; (ii) reparations; (iii) national plan for forensic anthropological investigations; (iv) mechanisms for follow-up of CVR recommendations. Each of the 4 main categories contains a number of sub-groups of measures, organized at 6 different levels. Most importantly, there is a very detailed programme for reparations.

(continued)

continued

Truth commission (TC)	Total pages TC report/ pages recommendations	Main categories/themes of recommendations as listed in Table of Contents of TC report
Chile TC (Valech) 2004	Report: 635 pages **Recommendations: 18 pages** (pp. 615–635)	1 main category: Reparations (detailed at three distinct sub-groups (i.e. individual; symbolic/ collective; institutional), which again are divided into a number of themes containing concrete recommendations.
Paraguay TC (CVJ) 2008	Report: 113 pages **Recommendations: 21 pages** (pp. 92–113)	5 main categories: (i) Satisfaction, (ii) restitution, (iii) compensation, (iv) rehabilitation, (v) non-repetition. Each of the 5 main categories contains one or more specific recommendations – around 25 sub-groups of measures total.
Ecuador TC 2010	Report: 462 pages **Recommendations: 23 pages** (pp. 439–462)	6 main categories: (i) Satisfaction, (ii) restitution, (iii) rehabilitation, (iv) compensation (*indemnización*), (v) guarantees of non-repetition, (vi) administrative reparations. Each of the 6 main categories contains one or more specific recommendations – around 15 sub-groups of measures total.
Brazil TC (CNV) 2014	Report: 3388 pages (Vols. I–III) Vol I (with TCRs): 976 pages **Recommendations: 11 pages** (pp. 964–975)	3 main categories: (i) Institutional measures; (ii) legal and constitutional reforms; (iii) follow-up measures to ensure implementation of recommendations. Each of the 3 main categories contains one or more specific recommendations – in all 29 concrete TCRs. Several of these TCRs may be further divided into sub-recommendations.

Sources: Table of contents for all original truth commission reports.

APPENDIX III

Excerpts from the Truth Commission Recommendations Data Code Book[159]

Each truth commission has a separate Excel file. Each file contains three sheets, comprising in total four main parts (A–D):

1. A) General information about the truth commission recommendations (TCRs), and B) Categorizing truth commission recommendations (TCR) by type.
2. C) Formulation of TCRs.
3. D) Events surrounding TCR implementation (or lack thereof).

Parts A and B deal with the characteristics of **individual truth commission recommendations** (sheet one).

Part C deals with the **circumstances in which the TRCs were created** (sheet two).

Part D deals with the **implementation of the TCRs** (sheet three).

Each TCR is given an identification number so that we can easily trace the formulation and implementation of a particular TCR.

Sheet One: Truth Commission Recommendations (TCRs) [Country Name]

The goal of this sheet is to (A) record all of the recommendations listed in the TC's report, and (B) to categorize TCRs into various types that we hypothesize may influence the likelihood of the TCR being implemented. In the Type area of the sheet, for each TCR, please check the boxes (by typing an "X") that best describe the TCR. NOTE: Each TCR may fall within more than one type. Descriptions of each type can be found below.

OVERVIEW OF TRUTH COMMISSION RECOMMENDATIONS

Column A: truth commission short name: Already provided. Repeat if you add new lines.

---

[159] Excerpts from the Data Code Book relevant to this book are on file with the authors. The whole Code Book used for data collection and registration for the Beyond Words project will be made publicly available with the database through the Chr. Michelsen Institute website https://www.cmi.no/data/beyondwords.

Column B: Rec ID: Each recommendation in the dataset will have its own unique identification number. The first recommendation for TC 1 (Argentina) will have a Rec ID = ARG 1.1, the third recommendation listed in Brazil's report will have a Rec ID = BRA 2.3, etc. Recommendations may be long and complex; multiple recommendations may be listed under what the commission has labelled one recommendation. If the recommendation actually contains several recommendations, record the entire text of the recommendation in the row. We will deal with the complexity of implementing different parts of a complex recommendation in sheet three (more details below).

If you add more lines for additional recommendations, number them consecutively. Again, each recommendation should be listed in this sheet in the same order in which they are presented in the TC report.

Column C: Volume and chapter: Record where in the TC report the recommendation is listed.

Column D: Pages: Provide the exact page(s) where the TCR appears in the TC report.

Column E: Recommendation (original language): List the recommendation word-for-word as it appears in the original text of the TC report.

Column F: Recommendation (English): Provide an English translation of the recommendation.

Column G: Description of recommendation (language of report): If the main recommendation is explicitly divided into several parts, enter a new row for each item, but keep the original ID. The point of listing them separately line-by-line is so that we can distinguish between the implementation (or lack thereof) of different parts of the TCR. To enable us to track each row separately, please use small letters, as in ARG 1.3a, 1.3b, 1.3c, etc.

Column H: Description of recommendation (English) Provide an English translation of the sub-category/sub-recommendation in Column G.

Column I: Notes: Here you may record any information that you find important, confusing, problematic, etc. related to the text of the TCR.

Column J: Number of implementing events: Enter the number of specific events related to the implementation of that specific recommendation. The number indicated here should be the same as the number of implementing events listed/discussed in sheet three. For example, if in sheet three the last implementing event for TCR ARG 2.2 has an implementation ID of 2.2.6, you should enter 6 in this column.

TYPES OF RECOMMENDATION

Column L: Institutional reform: Does the TCR address institutional reform (such as reform of the courts, the police, the military, etc.)?

Column M: Legal: Does the TCR relate to legal or administrative reform? Does it recommend that new laws be created, or existing ones be revised?

Column N: Constitutional: Does the TCR call for the constitution to be amended?

Column O: Criminal: Does the TCR call for the prosecution of individuals for past crimes?

Column P: Reparations: Does the TCR call for the provision of reparations for victims?

Column Q: Non-repetition: Is the TCR intended to reduce in the future the types of human rights violations that occurred in the past?

Column R: Follow-up: Does the TCR urge the government to create a body to monitor/coordinate the implementation of TCRs and/or further address past human rights violations?

Column S: Other: Please provide comments (or suggest new categories) if you feel the TCR provides some means of addressing past human rights abuses that is not covered by the other categories.

Column T: Notes: Here you may record any information that you find important, confusing, problematic, etc. related to coding the TCR type.

APPENDIX IV

Implementation of the Recommendations
Made by 13 Latin American Truth Commissions

ARGENTINA 1984: *Informe de la Comisión Nacional Sobre la Desaparición de Personas*

Year	Country	No. of main recs	No. of sub-recs	Total no. of recs.	Implementation status				
					High	Partial	None	No info.	Total
1984	Argentina 1984	4	7	9					
	Institutional	1	6	7	7	0	0	0	7
	Legal	1	7	8	8	0	0	0	8
	Constitutional	0	0	0	0	0	0	0	0
	Criminal	1	2	3	3	0	0	0	3
	Reparations	1	1	2	2	0	0	0	2
	Non-repetition	0	5	5	5	0	0	0	5
	Follow-up	1	0	1	1	0	0	0	1
	Other	0	0	0	0	0	0	0	0
	TOTAL TCRs			26	26	0	0	0	26
	IMPLEMENTED				100%	0	0	0	100%

URUGUAY 1985: *Informe Final de la Comisión Investigadora Parlamentaria Sobre la Situación de Personas Desaparecidas y Hechos que la Motivaron*

Year	Country	No. of main recs.	No. of sub-recs.	Total no. of recs.	Implementation status				
					High	Partial	None	No info.	Total
1985	Uruguay 1985	2	0	2					
	Institutional	0	0	0	0	0	0	0	0
	Legal	0	0	0	0	0	0	0	0
	Constitutional	0	0	0	0	0	0	0	0
	Criminal	0	0	0	0	0	0	0	0
	Reparations	0	0	0	0	0	0	0	0
	Non-repetition	0	0	0	0	0	0	0	0
	Follow-up	0	0	0	0	0	0	0	0
	Other	2	0	2	2	0	0	0	2
	TOTAL TCRs			2	2	0	0	0	2
	IMPLEMENTED				100%	0	0	0	100%

CHILE RETTIG 1991: *Informe de la Comisión Nacional de Verdad y Reconciliación*

Year	Country	No. of main recs.	No. of sub-recs.	Total no. of recs.	Implementation status				
					High	Partial	None	No info.	Total
1991	Chile Rettig 1991	48	62	110					
	Institutional	25	26	51	35	0	0	16	51
	Legal	13	26	39	32	4	0	3	39
	Constitutional	4	3	7	7	0	0	0	7
	Criminal	0	2	2	2	0	0	0	2
	Reparations	11	7	18	10	5	0	3	18
	Non-repetition	36	54	90	60	5	0	24	89
	Follow-up	0	0	0	0	0	0	0	0
	Other	0	0	0	0	0	0	0	0
	TOTAL TCRs			207	146	14	0	46	206
	IMPLEMENTED				71%	7%	0	22%	100%

EL SALVADOR 1993: *De la locura a la esperanza. La guerra de 12 años en El Salvador*

Year	Country	No. of main recs.	No. of sub-recs.	Total no. of recs.	Implementation status				
					High	Partial	None	No info.	Total
1993	El Salvador 1993	43	0	43					
	Institutional	23	0	23	9	5	9	0	23
	Legal	12	0	12	6	2	4	0	12
	Constitutional	2	0	2	0	0	2	0	2
	Criminal	0	0	0	0	0	0	0	0
	Reparations	5	0	5	2	1	2	0	5
	Non-repetition	26	0	26	12	6	8	0	26
	Follow-up	7	0	7	2	4	1	0	7
	Other	2	0	2	0	1	0	1	2
	TOTAL TCRs			77	31	19	26	1	77
	IMPLEMENTED				40%	25%	34%	1%	100%

HAITI 1996: *Si m pa rele: 29 September 1991–14 Octobre 1994*

Year	Country	No. of main recs.	No. of sub-recs.	Total no. of recs.	Implementation status				
					High	Partial	None	No info.	Total
1996	Haiti 1996	75	91	166					
	Institutional	39	54	93	11	27	25	28	91
	Legal	11	20	31	9	5	13	3	30
	Constitutional	1	2	3	0	0	2	1	3
	Criminal	4	7	11	1	2	8	0	11
	Reparations	8	4	12	1	3	7	1	12
	Non-repetition	12	14	26	8	6	11	1	26
	Follow-up	3	13	16	2	5	1	8	16
	Other	1	3	4	1	0	3	0	4
	TOTAL TCRs			196	33	48	70	42	193
	IMPLEMENTED				17%	25%	36%	22%	100%

GUATEMALA 1999: *Guatemala: Memoria del Silencio*

Year	Country	No. of main recs.	No. of sub-recs.	Total no. of recs.	Implementation status				
					High	Partial	None	No info.	Total
1999	Guatemala 1999	84	0	84					
	Institutional	27	0	27	9	2	16	0	27
	Legal	22	0	22	5	1	16	0	22
	Constitutional	0	0	0	0	0	0	0	0
	Criminal	2	0	2	0	2	0	0	2
	Reparations	8	4	38	13	1	24	0	38
	Non-repetition	36	0	36	12	1	23	0	36
	Follow-up	3	0	3	0	0	3	0	3
	Other	0	0	0	0	0	0	0	0
	TOTAL TCRs			128	39	7	82	0	128
	IMPLEMENTED				30%	5%	64%	0	99%

PANAMA 2002: *Informe Final de la Comisión de la Verdad. "La verdad os hará libres"*

Year	Country	No. of main recs.	No. of sub-recs.	Total no. of recs.	Implementation status				
					High	Partial	None	No info.	Total
2002	Panama 2002	11	0	11					
	Institutional	2	0	2	0	2	0	0	2
	Legal	2	0	2	0	2	0	0	2
	Constitutional	0	0	0	0	0	0	0	0
	Criminal	2	0	2	1	1	0	0	2
	Reparations	3	0	3	2	1	0	0	3
	Non-repetition	5	0	5	1	4	0	0	5
	Follow-up	2	0	2	0	2	0	0	2
	Other	2	0	2	0	2	0	0	2
	TOTAL TCRs			18	4	14	0	0	18
	IMPLEMENTED				22%	78%	0	0	100%

URUGUAY COMIPAZ 2003: *Informe Final de la Comisión para la Paz*

Year	Country	No. of main recs.	No. of sub-recs.	Total no. of recs.	Implementation status				
					High	Partial	None	No info.	Total
2003	Uruguay 2003	8	2	10					
	Institutional	2	0	2	2	0	0	0	2
	Legal	3	1	4	3	1	0	0	4
	Constitutional	0	0	0	0	0	0	0	0
	Criminal	0	0	0	0	0	0	0	0
	Reparations	0	1	1	1	0	0	0	1
	Non-repetition	5	1	6	3	3	0	0	6
	Follow-up	2	0	2	2	0	0	0	2
	Other	1	1	2	2	0	0	0	2
	TOTAL TCRs			17	13	4	0	0	17
	IMPLEMENTED				76%	24%	0	0	100%

PERU 2003: *Informe Final de la Comisión de la Verdad y Reconciliación*

Year	Country	No. of main recs.	No. of sub-recs.	Total no. of recs.	Implementation status				
					High	Partial	None	No info.	Total
2003	Peru 2003	82	0	82					
	Institutional	53	0	53	24	21	7	1	53
	Legal	13	0	13	6	6	1	0	13
	Constitutional	6	0	6	4	2	0	0	6
	Criminal	4	0	4	2	1	1	0	4
	Reparations	23	0	23	3	19	1	0	23
	Non-repetition	40	0	40	21	13	5	1	40
	Follow-up	6	0	6	0	5	1	0	6
	Other	4	0	4	1	3	0	0	4
	TOTAL TCRs			149	61	70	16	2	149
	IMPLEMENTED				41%	47%	11%	1%	100%

CHILE VALECH 2004: *Informe de la Comisión Nacional sobre Prisión Politica y Tortura*

Year	Country	No. of main recs.	No. of sub-recs.	Total no. of recs.	Implementation status				
					High	Partial	None	No info.	Total
2004	Chile Valech 04	28	14	42					
	Institutional	7	1	8	3	4	0	1	8
	Legal	7	0	7	3	0	0	4	7
	Constitutional	1	0	1	0	0	0	1	1
	Criminal	0	0	0	0	0	0	0	0
	Reparations	13	3	16	9	4	0	3	16
	Non-repetition	17	5	22	9	7	0	6	22
	Follow-up	3	2	5	3	2	0	0	5
	Other	0	1	1	1	0	0	0	1
	TOTAL TCRs			60	28	17	0	15	60
	IMPLEMENTED				47%	28%	0	25%	100%

PARAGUAY 2008: *Informe Final. Anive haguâ oiko*

Year	Country	No. of main recs.	No. of sub-rec.	Total no. of recs.	Implementation status				
					High	Partial	None	No info.	Total
2008	Paraguay 2008	177	25	202					
	Institutional	47	11	58	9	7	1	40	57
	Legal	51	11	62	8	9	2	43	62
	Constitutional	8	0	8	1	1	1	5	8
	Criminal	15	0	15	0	3	1	11	15
	Reparations	57	5	62	4	5	6	47	62
	Non-repetition	100	6	106	13	21	0	72	106
	Follow-up	6	10	16	1	0	0	15	16
	Other	9	0	9	1	0	0	8	9
	TOTAL TCRs			336	37	46	11	241	335
	IMPLEMENTED				11%	14%	3%	72%	100%

ECUADOR 2010: *Informe de la Comisión de la Verdad Ecuador 2010: Sin verdad no hay justicia*

Year	Country	No. of main recs.	No. of sub-recs.	Total no. of recs.	Implementation status				
					High	Partial	None	No info.	Total
2010	Ecuador 2010	155	1	156					
	Institutional	47	0	47	9	14	9	15	47
	Legal	39	0	39	8	17	6	8	39
	Constitutional	1	0	1	0	0	0	1	1
	Criminal	9	0	9	1	3	2	3	9
	Reparations	33	0	33	3	14	4	12	33
	Non-repetition	114	0	114	16	41	17	40	114
	Follow-up	4	0	4	0	3	1	0	4
	Other	4	0	4	3	1	0	0	4
	TOTAL TCRs			251	40	94	39	79	251
	IMPLEMENTED				16%	37%	15%	31%	99%

BRAZIL 2014: *Relatório da Comissão Nacional da Verdade*

Year	Country	No. of main recs.	No. of sub-recs.	Total no. of recs.	Implementation status				
					High	Partial	None	No info.	Total
2014	Brazil 2014	29	14	43					
	Institutional	15	6	18	1	4	1	12	18
	Legal	9	3	11	0	6	1	4	11
	Constitutional	2	0	2	0	0	0	2	2
	Criminal	2	0	2	0	1	0	1	2
	Reparations	7	6	10	0	4	1	5	10
	Non-repetition	17	11	25	1	8	1	15	25
	Follow-up	1	1	2	1	1	0	0	2
	Other	0	0	0	0	0	0	0	0
	TOTAL TCRs			70	3	24	4	39	70
	IMPLEMENTED				4%	34%	6%	56%	100%

APPENDIX V

Implementation Rates for Recommendations Made by 13 Latin American Truth Commissions, by Category

Type of Recommendation	Total number of recommendations	Highly implemented	Partially implemented	Not implemented	No information	Total
Total recs. institutional reform	389	119	87	68	113	387
Implemented		31%	22%	17%	29%	99%
Total recs. legal reform	250	88	53	43	65	249
Implemented		35%	21%	17%	26%	99%
Total recs. constitutional reform	30	12	3	5	10	30
Implemented		40%	10%	17%	33%	100%
Total recs. criminal prosecution	51	11	13	12	15	51
Implemented		22%	25%	24%	29%	100%
Total recs. reparations	223	50	57	45	71	223
Implemented		22%	26%	20%	32%	100%
Total recs. non-repetition	501	161	115	65	159	500
Implemented		32%	23%	13%	32%	100%
Total recs. follow-up	66	14	22	7	23	66
Implemented		21%	33%	11%	35%	100%
Total recs. other	28	9	7	3	9	28
Implemented		32%	25%	11%	32%	100%

APPENDIX VI

Overview of Commissioners of
12 Formal Latin American Truth Commissions[160]

ARGENTINA

Composition of the National Commission on the Disappeared
(CONADEP)

Function	Name	Background
National commission member and President of the Commission	Ernesto Sábato (M)	Writer.
National commission member	Ricardo Colombres (M)	Former Judge at National Supreme Court of Justice.
National commission member	René Favaloro (M)	Medical surgeon. He resigned in June of 1984, before the CONADEP completed its work.
National commission member	Hilario Fernández Long (M)	Civil engineer, former Chancellor of the University of Buenos Aires.
National commission member	Carlos Gattinoni (M)	Protestant Pastor. Founder of the Ecumenical Movement for Human Rights (*Movimiento Ecuménico por los Derechos Humanos*, MEDH) and the Permanent Assembly for Human Rights (*Asamblea Permanente por los Derechos Humanos*, APDH).
National commission member	Gregorio Klimovsky (M)	Epistemologist. Dean of the School of Social and Natural Sciences of the University of Buenos Aires.
National commission member	Marshall Meyer (M)	Rabbi. Doctor in Philosophy. Member of the APDH and Co-President of the Jewish Movement for Human Rights. Commissioner until June 1984.

(continued)

---

[160] The tables in this Appendix contain the names of the commissioners, indicating gender in parenthesis. M=male; F=female.

Note that the information contained in the tables draws heavily upon the 11 country chapters in Volume II of this two-volume series, *Beyond Words* Vol. II (Skaar, Wiebelhaus-Brahm, and García-Godos (eds.) 2022). Here we do not provide the full references but mention only the country name of each chapter. Where additional sources are included, these are referred to in the footnotes section or under "sources". The truth commissions are presented in the same order as the country mini studies of implementation in Chapter 5 of this volume.

Note that the first truth commission in Uruguay is not addressed here, as we did not find any information on who the commissioners were.

continued

Function	Name	Background
National commission member	Jaime De Nevares (M)	Bishop of the province of Neuquén. Attorney and Co-founder of APDH.
National commission member	Eduardo Rabossi	Attorney specializing in Philosophy of Law.
National commission member	Magdalena Ruiz Guiñazú (F)	Journalist.
National commission member	Santiago López (M)	Unión Cívica Radical (UCR) congress representative (*diputado*).
National commission member	Hugo Piucill (M)	UCR congress representative.
National commission member	Horacio Huarte (M)	UCR congress representative.
National commission member	NONE	Three designated Senators (planned, not appointed).

To manage their work, the commissioners established five subcommittees. Those in charge of these sub-committees, summarized in the table below, were awarded a category equivalent to the position of National Judge.

CONADEP Subcommittees

Subcommittee	Secretary
Reports	Graciela Fernández Meijide (F)
Procedures	Raúl Aragón (M)
Documentation and Data Processing	Daniel Salvador (M)
Administration	Leopoldo Silgueira (M)
Legal Matters/Affairs	Alberto Mansur (M)

Sources: "Argentina's CONADEP: A Lasting Human Rights Agenda", *Beyond Words*, Vol. II; (Crenzel 2008).

CHILE

Composition of the National Commission for Truth and Reconciliation ("Rettig Commission")

Function	Name	Background
National commission member and Chairman of the Commission	Raúl Rettig Guissen (M)	Professor, attorney, and politician. Member of the Radical Party. Presided over the party in 1950. Senator between 1949 and 1957. Undersecretary of the Ministry of the Interior and Ministry of Foreign Relations during the government of Pedro Aguirre Cerda (1938–1941).[161]

(continued)

---

[161] http://historiapolitica.bcn.cl/resenas_parlamentarias/wiki/Mauricio_Ra%C3%BAl_Rettig_Guissen.

continued

Function	Name	Background
National commission member	Jaime Castillo Velasco (M)	Attorney, professor, politician. Founder of the Christian Democratic Party. After the coup, he founded and directed the *Secretariado Latinoamericano de Derechos Humanos* (Latin American Secretariat of Human Rights) (SELADEH). Founded the National Commission of Human Rights in 1978.[162]
National commission member	José Luis Cea Egaña (M)	Attorney. Professor of Political Law, Constitutional Law and Political Science at the *Pontificia Universidad Católica de Chile* (Pontifical Catholic University of Chile), University of Chile and Diego Portales University. Docent at the Academy of Police Sciences of the Chilean Carabineers (Chilean National Police Force).[163]
National commission member	Mónica Jiménez de la Jara (F)	Social worker. Former Director of the School of Social Work at the *Universidad Católica* (Catholic University). Linked to the Christian Democratic Party.[164]
National commission member	Ricardo Martín Díaz (M)	Attorney. Former Supreme Court judge (1964–1971) and designated Senator (1990–1998).[165]
National commission member	Laura Novoa Vásquez (F)	Prominent jurist.[166] Later academic at *Universidad de Chile* (University of Chile).
National commission member	Gonzalo Vial Correa (M)	Attorney, journalist, and historian. Conservative and nationalist intellectual, Minister of Education during Pinochet's de facto government (1978).[167]
National commission member	José Zalaquett Daher (M)	Attorney. As of 1973, directed the Legal Department of the *Comité de Cooperación para la Paz* (Cooperation Committee for Peace) in Chile, after directing the *Vicaría de la Solidaridad* (Vicariate for Solidarity). Following his expulsion from Chile in 1976, he became a member of Amnesty International, acting as Deputy Secretary General and President.[168]

---

[162] https://www.camara.cl/prensa/noticias_detalle.aspx?prmid=122285.
[163] http://www.institutodechile.cl/instituto/cea.pdf.
[164] http://www.archivochile.com/Gobiernos/gob_paylwin/de/GOBdeaylwin0004.pdf.
[165] http://historiapolitica.bcn.cl/resenas_parlamentarias/wiki/Ricardo_Martin_D%C3%ADaz.
[166] https://es.wikipedia.org/wiki/Comisi%C3%B3n_Nacional_de_Verdad_y_Reconciliaci%C3%B3n.
[167] http://www.memoriachilena.cl/602/w3-article-100642.html.
[168] http://www.uchile.cl/portal/presentacion/consejo-de-evaluacion/presentacion/50053/prof-jose-zalaquett-daher.

Secretariat of the Rettig Commission

Secretary of the Commission	Political and/or social background
Jorge Correa Sutil (M)	**Attorney.** Christian Democratic attorney. Dean of the School of Law of the Diego Portales University.[169]

Source: "Chile's Rettig and Valech Commissions: Truth and Reparation under the Sign of Reconciliation", *Beyond Words*, Vol. II.

CHILE

Composition of the National Commission on Political Imprisonment and Torture (Valech Commission)

Function	Name	Background
National commission member and President	Sergio Valech Aldunate (M)	Monsignor, human rights advocate, former member of the *Vicaría de la Solidaridad*.[170]
National commission member and Executive Vice President	María Luisa Sepúlveda Edwards (F)	Social worker, member of the Committee of Cooperation for Peace (*Comité de Cooperación para la Paz – Comité Pro Paz*) and former member of *Vicaría de la Solidaridad* (Vicariate of Solidarity). Advised Ricardo Lagos regarding the outcome of *Mesa de Diálogo*.[171]
National commission member	Luciano Fouillioux Fernández (M)	Attorney, former executive secretary of the Ministry of Interior's Human Rights Program. Participated in the *Mesa de Diálogo*.[172]
National commission member	José Antonio Gómez Urrutia (M)	Attorney, militant in the Chilean Social Democratic Radical Party.[173]
National commission member	Elizabeth Lira Kornfeld (F)	Psychologist recognized for her work treating victims of repression during the military dictatorship. Member of the Christian Church Social Assistance Foundation (*Fundación de Ayuda Social de las Iglesias Cristianas –* FASIC). Participated in the *Mesa de Diálogo*.[174]
National commission member	Lucas Sierra Iribarren (M)	Attorney and academic. Constitutional Law and political institution specialist.[175]
National commission member	Álvaro Varela Walker (M)	Attorney, human rights advocate. Served on the Committee of Cooperation for Peace (*Comité de Cooperación para la Paz*) in Chile and member of the *Vicaría de la Solidaridad*.[176]

Source: "Chile's Rettig and Valech Commissions: Truth and Reparation under the Sign of Reconciliation", *Beyond Words*, Vol. II.

---

[169] http://www.archivochile.com/Gobiernos/gob_paylwin/de/GOBdeaylwin0004.pdf.
[170] http://defensoresydefensoras.indh.cl/defensores-as-en-la-historia/dictadura/sergio-valech/.
[171] http://www.indh.cl/resena-institucional/consejo-indh/maria-luisa-sepulveda-edwards.
[172] https://cl.linkedin.com/in/luciano-fouillioux-21472764.
[173] http://www.defensa.cl/biografia-ministro-gomez-urrutia/.
[174] http://derecho.uahurtado.cl/academicos/elizabeth-lira-kornfeld/.
[175] https://www.cepchile.cl/lucas-sierra-i/cep/2016-03-23/122003.html.
[176] http://www.freedomcollection.org/interviews/alvaro_varela_walker/.

URUGUAY

Composition of the Commission for Peace

Function	Name	Background
National commission member and President of the Commission	Monsignor Nicolás Cotugno (M)	Archbishop of Montevideo.
National commission member	José D'Elía (M)	Long-standing union representative, Honorary President of the *Plenario Intersindical de Trabajadores* (Inter-Union Worker Plenary Meeting) National Worker Convention, PIT-CNT.
National commission member	Luis Pérez Aguirre (M)	Catholic priest, human rights activist. He was the founder of SERPAJ of Uruguay. He was included in the Commission in his capacity as spokesperson of the group *Asociación de Madres y Familiares de Uruguayos Detenidos Desaparecidos* (FAMIDESA). Died in January 2001 while serving on the commission.
National commission member	Jorge Osorio (M)	Catholic priest. Replaced Pérez Aguirre following his death in January 2001.
National commission member	José Claudio Williman Ramírez (M)	Prominent *Partido Nacional* politician and a close personal friend of President Batlle.
National commission member	Gonzalo Fernández (M)	Attorney. Legal expert and advisor to Tabaré Vasques of *Partido Encuentro-Progresista – Frente Amplio* (Batlle's principal opponent in the presidential campaign)
National commission member	Carlos Ramela Regules (M)	*Partido Colorado*. Advisor to President Batlle.

Source: "Uruguay's Commission for Peace: An Unfulfilled Experience?", *Beyond Words*, Vol. II.

PARAGUAY

Composition of the Truth and Justice Commission (CVJ)

Function	Name	Background
National commission member and President of the Commission	Mons. Mario Melanio Medina Salinas (M)	Theologist and Philosopher. Director of the magazine *Nuestro Tiempo*, first diocesan bishop of Benjamín Aceval. Residential Bishop of San Juan Bautista de las Misiones. Founder of several organizations.
National commission member	Miguel Ángel Aquino Britos (M)	Lawyer, member of numerous legal organizations. Exiled 1971–1989. He was congressman in the period 1989–1993.

(continued)

continued

Function	Name	Background
National commission member	Luis Casablanca Rodríguez (M)	Lawyer. Participated in the founding of the National Commission of Human Rights and Never Again to State Terrorism. Leader of the Paraguayan Communist Party and member of its Central Committee.
National commission member	Yudith Rolón Jacquet (F)	Specialist in Accounting and Administrative Sciences. A founding member of the Human Rights and Victims Commission of the Stronist dictatorship of the Misiones department. Also supported the establishment of the Victims' House in 2002. Has been a delegate of the San Ignacio Guazú Office of the Ombudsman since March 2002 to date. Member of the National Commission of Victims of the Dictatorship.
National commission member	Margarita Durán Estragó (F)	Historian. Belonged to the Congregation of Dominican sisters from where she began her work with the peasantry, worked with the agrarian leagues, especially from 1969 to 1974. Professor at the Catholic University. Author of numerous investigations. Member of the Paraguayan Academy of History.
National commission member	Jorge Rolón Luna (M)	Lawyer, Doctor in Law. Electoral judge from 1996 to 2002, worked for the new penal legislation, professor of the Catholic University.
National commission member	Juan Enrique Díaz Bordenave (M)	Educator and communicator. Consultant at UNESCO, UNICEF; UNFPA, World Bank, Inter-American Development Bank, USAID; IICA. Sunday columnist for the newspaper *Noticias*.

Source: "Paraguay's Truth and Justice Commission: Recommending Justice without Political Change", *Beyond Words*, Vol. II.

BRAZIL

Composition of the National Truth Commission (CNV)

Function	Name	Background
National commission member	Gilson Dipp (M)	Vice-president of the Superior Tribunal of Justice. First coordinator of the CNV (May–September 2012).
National commission member	Claudio Fonteles (M)	Former head of the Federal Public Prosecutor's Office. Second coordinator of the CNV (September 2012–February 2013). Member until June 2013 and substituted by Pedro Dallari.

(continued)

continued

Function	Name	Background
National commission member	Paulo Sergio Pinheiro (M)	Political scientist. Professor of Political Science and Associate Researcher at the Unit for Studies on Violence at the University of Sao Paulo. Former Secretary of State on Human Rights during the government of Fernando Henrique Cardoso. Member of the working group appointed by former president Luis Inácio Lula da Silva to prepare the law proposal for the National Truth Commission. Several roles and appointments at the United Nations. Third coordinator of the CNV (February–May 2013).
National commission member	Rosa Maria Cardoso da Cunha (F)	Attorney, human rights defender. Professor at the State University of Rio de Janeiro. Fourth coordinator of the CNV (May–August 2013).
National commission member	José Carlos Dias (M)	Attorney, specialist in criminal law. Advisor and former president of the Commission for Justice and Peace of Sao Paulo. Fifth coordinator of the CNV (August–November 2013).
National commission member	Pedro Dallari	Attorney. Professor, director of the Institute of International Relations and coordinator of the Ibero-American Center at the University of Sao Paulo. Last coordinator of the CNV, from November 2013.
National commission member	José Paulo Cavalcanti (M)	Attorney. Specialist in criminal law. Secretary General of the Ministry of Justice and Minister of Justice (interim) during the José Sarney government.
National commission member	María Rita Kehl (F)	Psychoanalyst, writer, journalist. Former editor of *Jornal Movimento*.

Source: Official website of the Comissaão Nacional da Verdade http://cnv.memoriasreveladas.gov.br/institucional-acesso-informacao/membros.html.

See also "Brazil's National Truth Commission: Recommendations for a Pending Democratic Agenda", *Beyond Words*, Vol. II.

ECUADOR

Composition of the Truth and Justice Commission

Function	Name	Background
National commission member and Chair	Sister Elsie Monge Yoder (F)	Teacher, nun, and human rights activist. Executive Director of the Ecumenical Human Rights Commission in Ecuador (CEDHU) since 1981.[177]

(continued)

---

[177] https://www.fidh.org/IMG/pdf/bio-elsie_monge-en.pdf.

continued

Function	Name	Background
National commission member	Julio César Trujillo Vásquez (M)	Ecuadorian lawyer and politician. Participated in the Constitutional Assembly of 1998, which recognized the collective rights of indigenous people and afro descendants.[178]
National commission member	Monseñor Luis Alberto Luna Tobar (M)	Catholic priest. Archbishop of Quito in 1977 and Archbishop of Cuenca in 1981. In 2007 led the Special Commission to Investigate the Foreign debt.[179]
National commission member	Pedro José Restrepo Bermúdez (M)	Colombian engineer. His two sons, Carlos Santiago and Pedro Andrésdisappeared during the Febres-Cordero administration.[180]

Ecuador TC Support Committee

Function	Name	Background
Executive Secretary	Romel Jurado (M) (2008) Cristhian Bahamonde Galarza (M) (2009)	Director General on Public Policy at the Ombudsman Office[181]
General Counsellor	Alejandro Valencia Villa (M)	Colombian lawyer. Advisor for the Office of the High Commissioner for Human Rights (OHCHR) and expert witness at IACtHR. Participated in the truth commissions of Peru, Paraguay, and Guatemala[182]
Counsellor	Francisco Terán Hidalgo (M)	–

Sources: References in footnotes and "Ecuador's Truth Commission: Official Support, Weak Compliance", *Beyond Words*, Vol. II.

PERU

Composition of the Truth and Reconciliation Commission (CVR)

Function	Name	Background
National commission member and President of the Commission	Salomón Lerner Febres (M)	Philosopher. Rector of *Pontificia Universidad Católica del Perú*.
National commission member	Sofía Macher Batanero (F)	Sociologist. Human rights activist. Former executive secretary of *Coordinadora Nacional de Derechos Humanos*.

(continued)

---

[178] http://www.expectativa.ec/julio-cesar-trujillo-50-anos-de-trayectoria-en-el-ambito-juridico/.
[179] http://www.elcomercio.com/tendencias/fallecimiento-monsenor-lunatobar-iglesiacatolica-cuenca.html.
[180] https://www.planv.com.ec/historias/perfiles/pedro-restrepo-una-lucha-inquebrantable-que-desnudo-un-pais.
[181] https://www.mininterior.gov.ar/prensa/prensa.php?i=11416.
[182] http://www.icdhcolombia.org/cursointernacional/index.php/es/ponentes-curso?showall=&start=6.

continued

Function	Name	Background
National commission member	Carlos Iván Degregori (M)	Anthropologist. Former director of *Instituto de Estudios Peruanos*.
National commission member	Carlos Tapia García (M)	Agronomist engineer. Former congressman from *Izquierda Unida*.
National commission member	Rolando Ames Cobián (M)	Political scientist. Professor at *Pontificia Universidad Católica del Perú*. Former senator from *Izquierda Unida*.
National commission member	Enrique Bernales Ballesteros (M)	Constitutionalist. Former senator from *Izquierda Unida*. Former Special Rapporteur to the United Nations Human Rights Commission.
National commission member	Beatriz Alva Hart (F)	Lawyer. Former deputy minister of Labour during the Fujimori administration and congresswoman from the Fujimori organization.
National commission member	Monseñor José Antúnez de Mayolo (M)	Former apostolic administrator of the Archdiocese of Ayacucho during the period 1959–1961. Member of the Salesian community.
National commission member	Inspector General (retired) Luis Arias Graziani (M)	Former Inspector General of the Air Force; chief of the Major Estate; general of the FAP and president of the Joint Command of the Armed Forces and Minister of the Air Force.
National commission member	Padre Gastón Garatea Yori (M)	Member of *Congregación de los Sagrados Corazones*. Former prelate of Ayaviri (Puno). Former *Padre Provincial de los Sagrados Corazones*.
National commission member	Pastor Humberto Lay Sun (M)	Architect. Member of *Grupo de Iniciativa Nacional Anticorrupción*; and of *Junta Nacional de la Alianza Cristiana y Misionera*.
National commission member	Alberto Morote Sánchez (M)	Chemical engineer. Former dean of *Filial Departamental de Ayacucho del Colegio de Ingenieros del Perú* and technical advisor to *Instituto Nacional de Desarrollo de Comunidades Campesinas y Nativas*. Professor, deputy administrative rector, and former Rector of the *Universidad Nacional de San Cristóbal de Huamanga*.
Observer	Monseñor Luis Bambarén Gastelumendi S.J. (M)	Jesuit Priest. Former Prefect of *Colegio Inmaculada* in Lima and Rector of *Colegio San Ignacio de Piura*. Former Auxiliary Bishop of Lima, vice-president of *Caritas Internationalis* and vice-president of the United Nations Convention of the Child. Former bishop of Chimbote, secretary general of *Conferencia Episcopal Peruana* and former President of *Conferencia Episcopal Peruana*.

Source: Truth and Reconciliation Commission of Peru website: http://www.cverdad.org.pe/lacomision/nlabor/comisionado.php. See also "Peru's Truth and Reconciliation Commission: Recommending a Piecemeal Approach to Transitional Justice", *Beyond Words*, Vol. II.

EL SALVADOR

Composition of the Truth Commission (CVES)

Function	Name (Gender)	Background
International commission member, Chairman	Belisario Betancur (M)	Former President of Colombia.
International commission member	Reinaldo Figueredo Planchart (M)	Former Minister of Foreign Affairs in Venezuela, member of the Venezuelan National Congress.
International commission member	Thomas Buergenthal (M)	Professor of International and Comparative Law, George Washington University Law School, and Director of the George Washington University National Law Center. Served as Judge (1979–1991), Vice-President (1983–1985) and President (1985–1987) of the Inter American Court of Human Rights. Vice-President of the Administrative Tribunal of the Inter-American Development Bank.

El Salvador TC Support Committee

Function	Name (Gender)	Background
Executive Director	Patricia Tappatá de Valdez (F)	Argentinian lawyer. Human rights defender.

Sources: CVES report accessed at https://www.usip.org/sites/default/files/file/ElSalvador-Report.pdf. See also "El Salvador's Truth Commission: Recommending Peace in Exchange for Justice", *Beyond Words*, Vol. II.

GUATEMALA

Composition of the Commission for Historical Clarification (CEH)

Function	Name (Gender)	Background
International commission member and President of the Commission	Christian Tomuschat (M)	Professor of international law. Independent expert for Guatemala for the UN Human Rights Commission (1990–1993).
National commission member	Otilia Lux de Cotí (F)	Kiché, indigenous leader. Secretary of Culture and Sports of Guatemala (2000–2004)
National commission member	Edgar Alfredo Balsells Tojo (M)	Attorney. Newspaper columnist. Former Constitutional Court judge. Former president of the College of Lawyers of Guatemala.

Sources: "Guatemala's Commission of Historical Clarification: The Memory of Silence or the Silence of Memory?", *Beyond Words*, Vol. II; Ross (1999), 197.

HAITI

Composition of the National Truth and Justice Commission (CNVJ)

Function	Name	Background
National Commission member and Chair	Françoise Boucard (F)	Exiled Haitian who spent considerable time in Montreal. Sociologist.
National commission member	Ertha Elysée (F)	Exiled, living in Montreal. Jurist.
National commission member	Freud Jean (M)	Selected from the Haitian NGO community. Social scientist.
National commission member	René Magloire (M)	Exiled, living in Montreal. Left mid-way to become Minister of Justice. Jurist.
International commission member	Bacre Waly Ndiaye (M)	From Senegal. Jurist. UN Special Rapporteur on extrajudicial, summary or arbitrary executions (1992–1998).
International commission member	Oliver Jackman (M)	From Barbados. Jurist. Judge on the Inter-American Court of Human Rights (1995–2001).
International commission member	Patrick Robinson (M)	From Jamaica. Jurist. Commissioner of the OAS (1988–1995), and UN Special Rapporteur on the Rights of Indigenous Peoples (1991–1995).

Sources: "Haiti's Truth and Justice Commission: Forgotten Recommendations, Living Demands", *Beyond Words*, Vol. II.

PANAMA

Composition of the Truth Commission

Function	Name (Gender)	Background
National commission member and President of the Commission	Alberto Almanza (M)	Lawyer. Once the PTC submitted its report Almanza became the unofficial chief of the Follow-up Office later endorsed by President Mireya Moscoso.
National commission member	Juan Antonio Tejada Mora (M)	Lawyer. Member until April 18, 2002.
National commission member	Osvaldo Velasquez (M)	Lawyer. Member until April 18, 2002.
National commission member	Julio E. Murray (M)	Anglican Bishop. Member until April 18, 2002.
National commission member	Fernando Berguido (M)	Lawyer. Member until October 2001.
National commission member	Otilia Tejeira (F)	Public figure, human rights activist. Member until May 2001.
National commission member	Rosa Maria de Britton (F)	Medical doctor, writer. Member until April 2001.

Source: "Panama's Truth Commission Recommendations: Out of Sight, Out of Mind?", *Beyond Words*, Vol. II.

APPENDIX VII

Latin American Countries Signatories to and Ratification of the International Convention for the Protection of All Persons from Enforced Disappearance (2006)[183]

Participant	Signature	Accession(a), Ratification
Argentina	February 6, 2007	December 14, 2007
Brazil	February 6, 2007	November 29, 2010
Chile	February 6, 2007	December 8, 2009
Ecuador	May 24, 2007	October 20, 2009
Guatemala	February 6, 2007	
Haiti	February 6, 2007	
Panama	September 25, 2007	June 24, 2011
Paraguay	February 6, 2007	August 3, 2010
Peru		September 26, 2012 a
Uruguay	February 6, 2007	March 4, 2009

---

[183] See United Nations Treaty Collection at: https://treaties.un.org/pages/ViewDetails.aspx?src=IND&mtdsg_no=IV-16&chapter=4&clang=_en. The Convention entered into force on December 23, 2010, No. 48088.

BIBLIOGRAPHY

Abi-Mershed, Elizabeth. 2020. "The Inter-American Commission on Human Rights and Implementation of Recommendations in Individual Cases." *Journal of Human Rights Practice* no. 12 (1):171–177.

Acosta, Ingrid Marisol Ortiz. 2017. "Seeking Truth in Colombia: Perspectives on a Truth Commission." *Razón Crítica* no. 2:21–50.

Amstutz, Mark R. 2005. *The Healing of Nations: The Promise and Limits of Political Forgiveness*. Lanham, MD: Rowman & Littlefield Publishers.

Andermann, Jens. 2012. "Returning to the site of horror: On the reclaiming of clandestine concentration camps in Argentina." *Theory, Culture & Society* no. 29 (1):76–98.

Arditti, Rita. 1999. *Searching for life: The grandmothers of the Plaza de Mayo and the disappeared children of Argentina*. London: University of California Press.

Arellano, Diana. 2012. "Reparar lo irreparable: Las víctimas de exilio frente a las políticas de reparación social en Paraguay." Paper presented at *Jornadas de Trabajo sobre Exilios Políticos del Cono Sur en el siglo XX. Agendas, problemas y perspectivas conceptuales*. 26, 27 y 28 de septiembre at La Plata, Argentina.

———. 2014. *Proceso de Transición a la Democracia y Políticas de Reparación Social: La Comisión de Verdad y Justicia del Paraguay*. Maestría en Antropología Social, Universidad Nacional de Misiones. Facultad de Humanidades y Ciencias.

Arthur, Paige. 2016. "Notes from the Field: Global Indicators for Transitional Justice and Challenges in Measurement for Policy Actors." *Transitional Justice Review* no. 1 (4): 283–308.

Atencio, Rebecca. 2014. *Memory's Turn: Reckoning with Dictatorship in Brazil*. Madison, Wisconsin: The University of Wisconsin Press.

Backer, David. 2010. "Watching a Bargain Unravel? A Panel Study of Victims' Attitudes about Transitional Justice in Cape Town, South Africa." *International Journal of Transitional Justice* no. 4 (3):443–456.

Bakiner, Onur. 2014. "Truth commission impact: An assessment of how commissions influence politics and society." *International Journal of Transitional Justice* no. 8 (1):6–30.

———. 2016. *Truth Commissions: Memory, Power, and Legitimacy*. Philadelphia, PA: University of Pennsylvania Press.

Balardini, Lorena. 2016. "Argentina: regional protagonist of transitional justice." In *Transitional Justice in Latin America: The Uneven Road from Impunity towards Accountability*, edited by Elin Skaar, Jemima García-Godos, and Cath Collins, 50–76. London and New York: Routledge.

Baloyra-Herp, Enrique A. 1995. "Elections, Civil War, and Transition in El Salvador, 1982–1994." In *Elections and Democracy in Central America, Revisited*, edited by Mitchell A. Seligson and John A. Booth. Chapel Hill NC: The University of North Carolina Press.

Barahona de Brito, Alexandra. 1992. *A Comparative Study of Truth Telling in the Southern Cone: The "Never Again" Reports of Brazil, Argentina and Uruguay and the Informe Rettig of Chile in the Transition from Military Rule to Democratic Rule.* Unpublished Ph.D. thesis, Political Science, Oxford University.

———. 1997. *Human Rights and Democratization in Latin America: Uruguay and Chile.* Oxford: Oxford University Press.

Barahona de Brito, Alexandra, Carmen González-Enríquez, and Paloma Aguilar (eds.). 2001. *The Politics of Memory. Transitional Justice in Democratizing Societies.* Oxford: Oxford University Press.

Bareiro, Line. 2018. *Between legal equality and de facto discrimination: Recommendations of the Committee on the Elimination of Discrimination against Women (CEDAW) for the States of Latin America and the Caribbean.* Santiago: United Nations.

Barsalou, Judy, and Victoria Baxter. 2007. "The Urge to Remember: The Role of Memorials in Social Reconstruction and Transitional Justice." In *Stabilization and Reconstruction Series No. 5.* Washington DC: United States Institute of Peace. https://www.usip.org/sites/default/files/srs5.pdf.

Basch, Fernando, Leonardo Filippini, Ana Laya, Mariano Nino, Felicitas Rossi, and Bárbara Schreiber. 2010. "The Effectiveness of the Inter-American System of Human Rights Protection: A Quantitative Approach to its Functioning and Compliance With its Decisions." *SUR – International Journal of Human Rights* no. 7 (12 (June)):9–35.

Bates, Genevieve, Ipek Cinar, and Monika Nalepa. 2020. "Accountability by Numbers: A New Global Transitional Justice Dataset (1946–2016)." *Perspectives on Politics* no. 18 (1):161–184.

Baxter, Victoria. 2005. "Civil society promotion of truth, justice, and reconciliation in Chile: Villa Grimaldi." *Peace & Change* no. 30 (1):120–136.

Beach, Derek, and Rasmus Brun Pedersen. 2019. *Process-tracing methods: Foundations and guidelines.* Ann Arbor MI: University of Michigan Press.

Bennett, Andrew, and Jeffrey T. Checkel (eds.). 2015. *Process tracing.* Cambridge: Cambridge University Press.

Bickford, Louis N. 2000. "Human Rights Archives and Research on Historical Memory: Argentina, Chile, and Uruguay." *Latin American Research Review* no. 35 (2):160–182.

Biebesheimer, Christina, and Francisco Mejía (eds.). 2000. *Justice Beyond Our Borders: Judicial Reforms for Latin America and the Caribbean.* Washington, D.C.:Inter-American Development Bank (through Johns Hopkins University Press).

Blatz, Craig W, Martin V Day, and Emily Schryer. 2014. "Official public apology effects on victim group members' evaluations of the perpetrator group." *Canadian Journal of Behavioural Science/Revue canadienne des sciences du comportement* no. 46 (3):337.

Bobowik, Magdalena, Darío Páez, Maitane Arnoso, Manuel Cárdenas, Bernard Rimé, Elena Zubieta, and Marcela Muratori. 2017. "Institutional apologies and socio-emotional climate in the South American context." *British Journal of Social Psychology* no. 56 (3):578–598.

Borer, Tristan Anne. 2006. "Truth Telling as a Peace-Building Activity: A Theoretical Overview." In *Telling the Truths: Truth Telling and Peace Building in Post-Conflict Societies*, edited by Tristan Anne Borer, 1–57. South Bend, IN: University of Notre Dame Press.

Brahm, Eric. 2007. "Uncovering the Truth: Examining Truth Commission Success and Impact." *International Studies Perspectives* no. 8 (1):16–35.

——. 2009. "What Is a Truth Commission and Why Does It Matter?" *Peace and Conflict Review* no. 3 (2):1–14.

Brody, Reed, and Felipe Gonzáles. 1997. "Nunca Mas: An Analysis of International Instruments on 'Disappearances'." *Human Rights Quarterly* no. 19 (2):365–405.

Buergenthal, Thomas. 1994. "The United Nations Truth Commission for El Salvador." *Vanderbilt Journal of Transnational Law* no. 27:497.

Bunselmeyer, Elisabeth. 2020. *Truth, Reparations and Social Cohesion: Transitional Justice Lessons from Peru.* Abingdon and New York: Routledge.

Burt, Jo-Marie. 2009. "Guilty as charged: The trial of former Peruvian president Alberto Fujimori for human rights violations." *International Journal of Transitional Justice* no. 3 (3):384–405.

Buscaglia, Edgardo Jr., Maria Dakolias, and William Ratliff. 1995. *Judicial Reform in Latin America: A Framework for National Development.* Stanford, CA: Stanford University Press.

Cassel, Douglass. 2007. "The Inter-American Court of Human Rights." In *Victims Unsilenced: The Inter-American Human Rights System and Transitional Justice in Latin America*, edited by Katya Salazar and Thomas Antkowiak. Washington D.C.: Due Process of Law Foundation (DPLF).

Centeno-Martín, Héctor. 2022. "Guatemala's Commission of Historical Clarification: The Memory of silence or the silence of memory?" In *Latin American Experiences with Truth Commission Recommendations: Beyond Words, Vol. II*, edited by Elin Skaar, Eric Wiebelhaus-Brahm, and Jemima García-Godos. Cambridge: Intersentia.

Centeno-Martín, Héctor, Eric Wiebelhaus-Brahm, Ana Belén Nieto-Librero, and Dylan Wright (forthcoming). "Explaining the Timeliness of Implementation of Truth Commission Recommendations." *Journal of Peace Research.*

Cerna, Christina M, and Tom J Farer. 1992. "Review of *The Battle of Human Rights. Gross, Systematic Violations and the Inter-American System.* By Cecilia Medina Quiroga. Dordrecht, Boston, London: Martinus Nijhoff Publishers, 1988." *American Journal of International Law* no. 86 (4):853–854.

Chapman, Audrey R. 2009. "Truth Finding in the Transitional Justice Process." In *Assessing the Impact of Transitional Justice: Challenges for Empirical Research*, edited by Hugo Van der Merwe, Victoria Baxter and Audrey R. Chapman, 91–113. Washington, DC: USIP Press.

Chapman, Audrey R, and Patrick Ball. 2001. "The truth of truth commissions: Comparative lessons from Haiti, South Africa, and Guatemala." *Human Rights Quarterly* no. 23 (1): 1–43.

Collier, Paul. 2000. "Ethnicity, politics and economic performance." *Economics & Politics* no. 12 (3):225–245.

Collins, Cath. 2010. *Post-Transitional Justice: Human Rights Trials in Chile and El Salvador.* University Park, PA: Pennsylvania State University Press.

——. 2016a. "Chile: incremental truth, late justice." In *Transitional Justice in Latin America: The Uneven Road from Impunity towards Accountability*, edited by Elin Skaar, Jemima García-Godos, and Cath Collins, 126–150. London and New York: Routledge.

——. 2016b. "Paraguay: accountability in the shadow of Stroessner." In *Transitional Justice in Latin America: The Uneven Road from Impunity towards Accountability*, edited by Elin Skaar, Jemima García-Godos and Cath Collins, 151–177. London and New York: Routledge.

——. 2017. "Truth-Justice-Reparations Interaction Effects in Transitional Justice Practice: The Case of the Valech Commission' in Chile." *Journal of Latin American Studies* no. 49 (1):55–82.

——. 2019. "Chilean Human Rights Prosecutions: Jurisprudence and Case Analysis 1990–2019." Available at SSRN 3405158.

——. 2020a. "Lustration" In *Memory of Nations: Democratic Transition Guide: The Chilean Experience*, 24–27. CEVRO and National Endowment for Democracy.

——. 2020b. "Investigation and Prosecution of the Crimes of the Regime." In *Memory of Nations: Democratic Transition Guide: The Chilean Experience*, 28–30. CEVRO and National Endowment for Democracy.

Collins, Cath, with Boris Hau. 2016. "Chile: incremental truth, late justice." In *Transitional Justice in Latin America: The Uneven Road from Impunity towards Accountability*, edited by Elin Skaar, Jemima García-Godos, and Cath Collins, 126–150. London and New York: Routledge.

Collins, Cath, Katherine Hite, and Alfredo Joignant. 2013. *The Politics of Memory in Chile: From Pinochet to Bachelet*. Boulder: Lynne Rienner Publishers, Incorporated.

Comisión de la Verdad para Impedir la Impunidad, Ecuador. 2010. *Informe de la Comisión de la Verdad Ecuador 2010: Sin verdad no hay justicia*.

Comisión de Verdad y Justicia, Paraguay. 2008. *Informe Final. Anive haguâ oiko*.

CONADEP. 1984. Nunca Mas: Informe de la Comisión Nacional Sobre la Desaparición de Personas. Buenos Aires: EUDEBA. Republished in English as Nunca Más. The Report of the Argentine National Commission on the Disappeared. New York: Farrar, Straus, Giroux, 1986.

Corbalán, Ana. 2019. "Ethical Questions about Human Trafficking during Times of Dictatorship: Kidnapped Children in Spain and Argentina." *Transatlantic Studies: Latin America, Iberia, and Africa* no. 21:218.

Cornejo Chavez, Leiry, Juan-Pablo Pérez-León-Acevedo, and Jemima García-Godos. 2019. "The Presidential Pardon of Fujimori: Political Struggles in Peru and the Subsidiary Role of the Inter-American Court of Human Rights." *International Journal of Transitional Justice* no. 13 (2):328–348.

Corntassel, Jeff, and Cindy Holder. 2008. "Who's sorry now? Government apologies, truth commissions, and Indigenous self-determination in Australia, Canada, Guatemala, and Peru." *Human Rights Review* no. 9 (4):465–489.

Correa, Cristián. 2013. *Reparations in Peru: From Recommendations to Implementation*. New York: International Center for Transitional Justice, (ICTJ) (available at http://ictj. org/sites/default/files/ICTJ_Report_Peru_Reparations_2013.pdf).

Crenzel, Emilio. 2008. "Argentina's National Commission on the Disappearance of Persons: Contributions to Transitional Justice." *International Journal of Transitional Justice* no. 2 (2):173–191.

——. 2012. *The Memory of the Argentina Disappearances: The Political History of Nunca Más*. Vol 1. London and New York: Routledge.

——. 2020. "The ghostly presence of the disappeared in Argentina." *Memory Studies* no. 13 (3):253–266.

Crocker, David A. 2003. "Reckoning with Past Wrongs: A Normative Framework." In *Dilemmas of Reconciliation: Cases and Concepts*, edited by Carol A.L. Prager and Trudy Govier, 39–63. Waterloo, Ontario, Canada: Wilfrid Laurier University Press.

Crosby, Alison, and M. Brinton Lykes. 2011. "Mayan Women Survivors Speak: The Gendered Relations of Truth Telling in Postwar Guatemala." *International Journal of Transitional Justice* no. 5 (3):456–476.

Cueva, Eduardo Gonzalez. 2004. "The contribution of the Peruvian Truth and Reconciliation Commission to prosecutions." *Criminal Law Forum* 15, 55–66.

Dakolias, Maria. 1996. *The Judicial Sector in Latin America and the Caribbean. Elements of Reform.* Washington, D.C.: The World Bank.

Daly, Erin. 2008. "Truth Scepticism: An Inquiry into the Value of Truth in Times of Transition." *International Journal of Transitional Justice* no. 2 (1) 23–41.

Dancy, Geoff, Hunjoon Kim, and Eric Wiebelhaus-Brahm. 2010. The Turn to Truth: Trends in Truth Commission Experimentation." *Journal of Human Rights* no. 9 (1) (January):45–64.

Dancy, Geoff, and Eric Wiebelhaus-Brahm. 2015. "Timing, Sequencing, and Transitional Justice Impact: A Qualitative Comparative Analysis of Latin America." *Human Rights Review* no. 16 (4):321–342.

Davis, Lisa. 2010. "Still trembling: State obligation under international law to end post-earthquake rape in Haiti." *University of Miami Law Review* no. 3 (65):867–892.

de Baggis, Cecilia, and Susanna Pallini. 2021. "Traumatic Experiences of the Living Disappeared in Argentina: A Review." *Child Psychiatry & Human Development* no. 52 (1): 114–128.

De Feyter, Koen, Stephan Parmentier, Marc Bossuyt, and Paul Lemmens (eds.). 2005. *Out of the Ashes. Reparation for Victims of Gross and Systematic Human Rights Violations.* Antwerpen and Cambridge: Intersentia.

de Greiff, Pablo 2006a (ed.). *The Handbook of Reparations.* Oxford: Oxford University Press.

———. 2006b. "Repairing the Past: Compensation for Victims of Human Rights Violations." In *The Handbook of Reparations*, edited by Pablo de Greiff, 1–18. Oxford: Oxford University Press.

———. 2006c. "Justice and Reparation." In *The Handbook of Reparations*, edited by Pablo de Greiff, 451–477. Oxford: Oxford University Press.

———. 2008. "The Role of Apologies in National Reconciliation Processes: On Making Trustworthy Institutions Trusted." In *The Age of Apology: Facing up to the Past*, edited by Mark Gibney, 120–134. Philadelphia PA: University of Pennsylvania Press.

Diamond, Larry. 2020. "Breaking Out of the Democratic Slump." *Journal of Democracy* no. 31 (1):36–50.

Domingo, Pilar. 1999. "Judicial Independence and Judicial Reform in Latin America." In *The Self Restraining State: Power and Accountability in New Democracies*, edited by Andreas Schedler, Larry Diamond, and Marc F. Plattner, 151–175. Boulder, CO: Lynne Rienner Publishers, Inc.

Domingo, Pilar, and Rachel Sieder. 2001. *Rule of law in Latin America: The international promotion of judicial reform.* Washington D.C.: Brookings Institution Press.

Donald, Alice, Debra Long, and Anne-Katrin Speck. 2020. "Identifying and assessing the implementation of human rights decisions." *Journal of Human Rights Practice* no. 12 (1):125–148.

Drinot, Paulo. 2009. "For whom the eye cries: Memory, monumentality, and the ontologies of violence in Peru." *Journal of Latin American Cultural Studies* no. 18 (1):15–32.

Duggan, Colleen, Claudia Paz y Paz Bailey, and Julie Guillerot. 2008. "Reparations for sexual and reproductive violence: Prospects for achieving gender justice in Guatemala and Peru." *The International Journal of Transitional Justice* no. 2 (2):192–213.

Dulitzky, Ariel E. 2007. "The Inter-American Commission on Human Rights." In *Victims Unsilenced: The Inter-American Human Rights System and Transitional Justice in Latin America*, edited by Katya Salazar, and Thomas Antkowiak, 129–150. Washington D.C.: Due Process of Law Foundation (DPLF).

Edelstein, J. 1994. "Rights, Reparations and Reconciliation: Some comparative notes." Seminar No. 6, 27 July. Unpublished paper. Centre for the Study of Violence and Reconciliation, Johannesburg, South Africa: CSVR.

Engle, Karen, Zinaida Miller, and Denys Mathias Davis (eds.). 2016. *Anti-impunity and the human rights agenda*. Cambridge University Press.

Engle, Karen. 2014. "Anti-impunity and the turn to criminal law in human rights." *Cornell L. Rev.* no. 100:1069.

Engstrom, Par. 2018. *The Inter-American human rights system: Impact beyond compliance.* Springer.

Ensalaco, Mark. 1994a. "In with the New, Out with the Old? The Democratizing Impact of Constitutional Reforms in Chile." *Journal of Latin American Studies* no. 26 (2):656–675.

——. 1994b. "Truth commissions for Chile and El Salvador: A report and assessment." *Human Rights Quarterly* no. 16 (4):656–675.

Fabra-Zamora, Jorge Luis, Molina-Ochoa, Andrés, and Doubleday, Nancy C. 2021. *The Colombian Peace Agreement: A Multidisciplinary Assessment*, Routledge.

Faedi, Benedetta. 2008. "The double weakness of girls: Discrimination and sexual violence in Haiti." *Stanford Journal of International Law* no. 44:147.

Falcón, Julissa Mantilla. 2005. "The Peruvian Truth and Reconciliation Commission's treatment of sexual violence against women." *Human Rights Brief* no. 12 (2):1–5.

Feldman, Joseph P. 2018. "Yuyanapaq no entra: Ritual dimensions of post-transitional justice in Peru." *Journal of the Royal Anthropological Institute* no. 24 (3):589–606.

Ferrara, Anita. 2014. *Assessing the Long-Term Impact of Truth Commissions: The Chilean Truth and Reconciliation Commission in Historical Perspective, Transitional Justice Series.* London: Routledge.

Finkel, Jodi S. 2008. *Judicial Reform as Political Insurance: Argentina, Peru, and Mexico in the 1990s.* Notre Dame, IN: University of Notre Dame Press.

Freeman, Mark 2006. *Truth Commissions and Procedural Fairness.* New York: Cambridge University Press.

——. 2009. *Necessary Evils. Amnesties and the Search for Justice.* New York: Cambridge University Press.

Freeman, Mark, and Priscilla B. Hayner. 2003. "Truth-Telling." In *Reconciliation after Violent Conflict: A Handbook*, edited by David Bloomfield, Teresa Barnes, and Luc Huyse. Halmstad, Sweden: International Institute for Democracy and Electoral Assistance (IDEA).

Fried Amilivia, Gabriela. 2016. *State Terrorism and the Politics of Memory in Latin America: Transmissions Across the Generations of Post-dictatorship Uruguay, 1984–2004.* Cambria Press.

Friedman, Rebekka, Nelson Camilo Sanchez Leon, and Eric Wiebelhaus-Brahm. 2019. "Securing the Peace and Promoting Human Rights in Post-Accord Colombia." In *As War Ends: What Colombia Can Tell Us about the Sustainability of Peace and Transitional Justice*, edited by James Meernik, Jacqueline HR DeMeritt, and Mauricio Uribe-López, 305–324. New York: Cambridge University Press.

Frühling, Hugo. 1998. "Judicial Reform and Democratization in Latin America." In *Fault Lines of Democracy in Post-Transitional Latin America*, edited by Felipe Agüero and Jeffrey Stark. Miami: North-South Center Press of the University of Miami.

Gamarra, Ronald. 2009. "A Leader Takes Flight: The Indictment of Alberto Fujimori." In *Prosecuting Heads of State*, edited by Ellen Lutz and Caitlin Reiger, 95–110. New York: Cambridge University Press.

Gandsman, Ari. 2009. "'Do You Know Who You Are?' Radical Existential Doubt and Scientific Certainty in the Search for the Kidnapped Children of the Disappeared in Argentina." *Ethos* no. 37 (4):441–465.

García, Susana Navarro, Pau Pérez-Sales, and Alberto Fernandez-Lina. 2010. "Exhumation processes in fourteen countries in Latin America." *Journal for Social Action in Counselling & Psychology* no. 2 (2):48–83.

García-Godos, Jemima, and Félix Reátegui. 2016. "Peru: beyond paradigmatic cases." In *Transitional Justice in Latin America: The Uneven Road from Impunity towards Accountability*, edited by Elin Skaar, Jemima García-Godos, and Cath Collins, 227–251. London and New York: Routledge.

García-Godos, Jemima, and Luis Raúl Salvadó. 2016. "Guatemala: Truth and memory on trial." In *Transitional Justice in Latin America: The Uneven Road from Impunity towards Accountability*, edited by Elin Skaar, Jemima García-Godos, and Cath Collins, 203–226. London and New York: Routledge.

Garcia-Godos, Jemima. 2008. "Victim Reparations in the Peruvian Truth Commission and the Challenge of Historical Interpretation." *International Journal of Transitional Justice* no. 2 (1):63–82.

——. 2013. "Victims' Rights and Distributive Justice: In Search of Actors." *Human Rights Review* no. 14 (3):241–255.

——. 2016. "Victims in Focus." *International Journal of Transitional Justice* no. 10 (2): 350–358.

——. 2018. "Victims and Victimhood in Reparation Programs: Lessons from Latin America." In *The Politics of Victimhood in Post-conflict Societies*, edited bv Vincent Druliolle and Roddy Brett, 25–51. Springer.

Garretón, Manuel Antonio. 1999. "Chile 1997–1998: The Revenge of Incomplete Democratization." *International Affairs* no. 75 (2):259–267.

Garro, Alejandro M. 1993. "Nine Years of Transition to Democracy in Argentina: Partial Failure or Qualified Success?" *Colombia Journal of Transnational Law* no. 31 (1):1–102.

Ghelfi, Federico, Sol Hourcade, Luz Palmás Zaldua, and Marcela Perelman. 2022. "Brazil's National Truth Commission: Recommendations for a Pending Democratic Agenda." In *Latin American Experiences with Truth Commission Recommendations: Beyond Words*, Vol. II, edited by Elin Skaar, Eric Wiebelhaus-Brahm, and Jemima García-Godos. Cambridge: Intersentia. 197–230.

Gianella Malca, Camila. 2015. "Peru: changing contexts for transitional justice." In *After Violence: Transitional Justice, Peace, and Democracy*, by Elin Skaar, Camila Gianella Malca, and Trine Eide. London and New York: Routledge.

Gibson, James L. 2005. "The truth about truth and reconciliation in South Africa." *International Political Science Review* no. 26 (4):341–361.

González Vera, Myriam. 2002. "Los Archivos del Terror del Paraguay. La historia oculta de la represión." In *Los archivos de la represión: Documentos, memória y verdad*, edited by Elizabeth Jelin and Ludmila Silva Catela, 85–114. Madrid: Siglo XXI.

Government of Canada. 2020. *Delivering on Truth and Reconciliation Commission Calls to Action*. Government of Canada 2019 [cited 11 July 2020]. Available from https://www.rcaanc-cirnac.gc.ca/eng/1524494530110/1557511412801.

Govier, Trudy, and Wilhelm Verwoerd. 2002. "The promise and pitfalls of apology." *Journal of social philosophy* no. 33 (1):67–82.

Grandin, Greg. 2005. "The instruction of great catastrophe: Truth commissions, national history, and state formation in Argentina, Chile, and Guatemala." *The American Historical Review* no. 110 (1):46–67.

Gready, Paul, and Simon Robins. 2017. "Rethinking civil society and transitional justice: lessons from social movements and 'new' civil society." *The International Journal of Human Rights* no. 21 (7):956–975.

Greenhill, Brian. 2010. "The company you keep: International socialization and the diffusion of human rights norms." *International Studies Quarterly* no. 54 (1):127–145.

Grodsky, Brian. 2008. "Justice without transition: Truth commissions in the context of repressive rule." *Human Rights Review* no. 9 (3):281–297.

Halbwachs, Maurice. 2004. *La memoria colectiva*. Vol. 6: Prensas de la Universidad de Zaragoza.

Harris, Leila M, and María Cecilia Roa-García. 2013. "Recent waves of water governance: Constitutional reform and resistance to neoliberalization in Latin America (1990–2012)." *Geoforum* no. 50:20–30.

Hayner, Priscilla B. 1994. "Fifteen Truth Commissions – 1974 to 1994: A Comparative Study." *Human Rights Quarterly* no. 16 (4):597–655.

———. 2001. *Unspeakable truths: Confronting state terror and atrocity*. New York: Routledge.

———. 2011. *Unspeakable Truths: Transitional Justice and the Challenge of Truth Commissions*. London and New York: Routledge (2nd edition).

Hellum, Anne, and Henriette Sinding Aasen. 2013. *Women's human rights: CEDAW in international, regional and national law*. Vol. 3: Cambridge: Cambridge University Press.

Hillebrecht, Courtney. 2009. "Rethinking compliance: The challenges and prospects of measuring compliance with International Human Rights Tribunals." *Journal of Human Rights Practice* no. 1 (3):362–379.

Hirsch, Michal Ben-Josef. 2007. "Agents of Truth and Justice: Truth Commissions and the Transitional Justice Epistemic Community." In *Rethinking Ethical Foreign Policy: Pitfalls, Possibilities and Paradoxes*, edited by David Chandler and Volker Heins, 184–205. New York: Routledge.

———. 2014. "Ideational change and the emergence of the international norm of truth and reconciliation commissions." *European Journal of International Relations* no. 20 (3): 810–833.

Hite, Katherine, and Daniela Jara. 2020. "Special Issue: Ghosts, Exhumations and Unwieldy Pasts." *Memory Studies* no. 13 (3).

Hite, Katherine. 2013. *Politics and the Art of Commemoration*. London and New York: Routledge.

Holá, Barbora, Róisín Mulgrew, and Joris van Wijk. 2019. "Introduction: National Prosecutions of International Crimes: Sentencing Practices and (Negotiated) Punishments." *International Criminal Law Review* no. 19 (1):1–14.

Hourcade, Sol, Federico Ghelfi, Luz Palmás Zaldua, and Marcela Perelman. 2022a. "Argentina's Pioneering CONADEP: A Lasting Human Rights Agenda." In *Latin American Experiences with Truth Commission Recommendations: Beyond Words, Vol. II*, edited by Elin Skaar, Eric Wiebelhaus-Brahm, and Jemima García-Godos, 27–62. Cambridge: Intersentia.

——. 2022b. "Chile's Rettig and Valech Commissions: Truth and Reparation under the Sign of Reconciliation." In *Latin American Experiences with Truth Commission Recommendations: Beyond Words, Vol. II*, edited by Elin Skaar, Eric Wiebelhaus-Brahm, and Jemima García-Godos, 63–110. Cambridge: Intersentia.

Hunter, Wendy, and Timothy J Power. 2019. "Bolsonaro and Brazil's illiberal backlash." *Journal of Democracy* no. 30 (1):68–82.

Huntington, Samuel P. 1991. *The Third Wave: Democratization in the Late Twentieth Century*. New York and London: Cambridge University Press.

Huyse, Luc. 1995. "Justice after Transition: On the Choices Successor Elites Make in Dealing with the Past." *Law & Social Inquiry* no. 20 (1):51–78.

Ignatieff, Michael. 1996. "Articles of faith." *Index on Censorship* no. 25 (5):110–122.

Inter-American Court of Human Rights. 2001. *Velásquez Rodríguez Case, order of the Court of September 10, 1996* Inter-American Court of Human Rights [http://www1.umn.edu/humanrts/iachr/rodr9-10.htm] 10 September 1996.

——. 2011. "Case *Gelman v. Uruguay*. Judgment of February 24, 2011 (Merits and Reparations)."

International Center for Transitional Justice (ICTJ). 2013. *Drafting a Truth Commission Mandate: A Practical Tool*, edited by Eduardo González. New York: ICTJ.

Jankowitz, Sarah. 2018. "The 'hierarchy of victims' in Northern Ireland: A framework for critical analysis." *International Journal of Transitional Justice* no. 12 (2):216–236.

Jelin, Elizabeth. 2007. "Public Memorialization in Perspective: Truth, Justice and Memory of Past Repression in the Southern Cone of South America." *International Journal of Transitional Justice* no. 1 (1):138–156.

——. 2010. "Silences, visibility, and agency: Ethnicity, class, and gender in public memorialization." In *Identities in Transition: The Challenge of Transitional Justice in Divided Societies*, edited by Paige Arthur, 187–213. New York: Cambridge University Press.

Kaiser, Susana. 2002. "Escraches: Demonstrations, communication and political memory in post-dictatorial Argentina." *Media, Culture & Society* no. 24 (4):499–516.

Kamstra, Jelmer, Ben Pelzer, Willem Elbers, and Ruerd Ruben. 2016. "Constraining Is Enabling? Exploring the Influence of National Context on Civil Society Strength." *VOLUNTAS: International Journal of Voluntary and Nonprofit Organizations* no. 27 (3): 1023–1044.

Karl, Terry Lynn. 1991. "El Salvador's negotiated revolution." *Foreign Affairs*. no. 71:147.

Kaye, Mike. 1997. "The role of truth commissions in the search for justice, reconciliation and democratisation: The Salvadorean and Honduran cases." *Journal of Latin American Studies* no. 29 (3):693–716.

Ko, Ñusta Carranza. 2019. "Repairing and Reconciling with the Past." In *Monument Culture: International Perspectives on the Future of Monuments in a Changing World*, edited by Laura A. Macaluso, 71–84. Lanham, MD: Rowman & Littlefield.

Kravetz, Daniela. 2016. "Promoting domestic accountability for conflict-related sexual violence: The cases of Guatemala, Peru, and Colombia." *American University International Law Review* no. 32 (3):707.

Kritz, Neil J. 2009. "Policy Implications of Empirical Research on Transitional Justice." In *Assessing the Impact of Transitional Justice: Challenges for Empirical Research*, edited by Hugo van der Merwe, Victoria Baxter, and Audrey R. Chapman, 13–21. Washington, DC: USIP Press.

Lamont, Christopher K., Joanna R Quinn, and Eric Wiebelhaus-Brahm. 2019. "The ministerialization of transitional justice." *Human Rights Review* no. 20 (1):103–122.

Lanegran, Kimberly. 2015. "The Kenyan Truth, Justice and Reconciliation Commission: The Importance of Commissioners and Their Appointment Process." *Transitional Justice Review* no. 1 (3):41–71.

Lankenau, Shannon D. 2012. "Toward Effective Access to Justice in Haiti: Eliminating the Medical Certificate Requirement in Rape Prosecutions." *Hastings Law Journal* no. 64:1759.

Laplante, Lisa J., and Kimberly Susan Theidon. 2007. "Truth with Consequences: Justice and Reparations in Post-Truth Commission Peru." *Human Rights Quarterly* no. 29 (1): 228–250.

——. 2010. "Commissioning Truth, Constructing Silences. The Peruvian Truth Commission and the Other Truths of 'Terrorists'." In *Mirrors of Justice. Law and Power in the Post-Cold War Era*, edited by Kamari Maxine Clarke and Mark Goodale, 291–315. New York: Cambridge University Press.

Lazzara, Michael. 2011. "Dos propuestas de conmemoración pública: Londres 38 y el Museo de la Memoria y los Derechos Humanos (Santiago de Chile)." *A Contracorriente: una revista de estudios latinoamericanos* no. 8 (3):55–90.

Leebaw, Bronwyn Anne 2008. "The Irreconcilable Goals of Transitional Justice." *Human Rights Quarterly* no. 30 (1):95–118.

Leiby, Michele L. 2009. "Wartime sexual violence in Guatemala and Peru." *International Studies Quarterly* no. 53 (2):445–468.

Lessa, Francesca. 2013a. "Parliamentary Investigative Commission on the Situation of Disappeared Persons and Its Causes / Comision Investigadora Parlamentaria sobre Situacion de Personas Desaparecidas y Hechos que la Motivaron (Uruguay)." In *Encyclopedia of Transitional Justice*, edited by Lavinia Stan and Nadya Nedelsky. New York: Cambridge University Press.

——. 2013b. *Memory and Transitional Justice in Argentina and Uruguay: Against Impunity*. New York: Palgrave Macmillan.

——. 2019. "Operation Condor on Trial: Justice for Transnational Human Rights Crimes in South America." *Journal of Latin American Studies* no. 51 (2):409–439.

Lessa, Francesca, and Vincent Druliolle. 2011. *The Memory of State Terrorism in the Southern Cone: Argentina, Chile, and Uruguay*. New York: Palgrave Macmillan.

Lessa, Francesca, and Gabriela Fried. 2011. "Las múltiples máscaras de la impunidad: la Ley de Caducidad, desde el Sí Rosado hasta los desarrollos recientes." In *Luchas contra la impunidad. Uruguay 1985–2011*, edited by Gabriela Fried, Francesca Lessa, with Brenda Falero, 31–44. Montevideo: Trilce.

Lessa, Francesca, and Elin Skaar. 2016. "Uruguay: Halfway towards accountability." In *Transitional justice in Latin America: The Uneven Road from Impunity towards Accountability*, edited by Elin Skaar, Jemima García-Godos, and Cath Collins, 77–102. Abingdon: Routledge.

Lessa, Francesca, Tricia D. Olsen, Leigh A. Payne, Gabriel Pereira, and Andrew G. Reiter. 2014. "Overcoming Impunity: Pathways to Accountability in Latin America." *International Journal of Transitional Justice* 8(1): 75–98.

Lira, Elizabeth, and Brian Loveman. 2005. *Políticas de reparación: Chile 1990–2004*: Santiago de Chile: Lom Ediciones.

Lora, Eduardo. 1997. "A Decade of Structural Adjustment: All Pain No Gain?" In *Latin America after a Decade of Reforms. Economic and Social Progress in Latin America, 1997 Report*, edited by Inter-American Development Bank, 31–96. Washington D.C.: Inter-American Development Bank.

Lutz, Ellen, and Caitlin Reiger. 2009. *Prosecuting Heads of State*. New York: Cambridge University Press.

MacLachlan, Alice. 2015. "'Trust Me, I'm Sorry': The Paradox of Public Apology." *The Monist* no. 98 (4):441–456.

Malamud-Goti, Jaime. 1991. "Punishment in a Rights-Based Democracy." *Criminal Justice Ethics* no. 10 (2):3–13.

Maldonado Urbina, Wendy Johara. 2020. "The Justice Spring of the Judicial System in Guatemala and the Implementation of the Judgments Issued by the Inter-American Court of Human Rights." *Journal of Human Rights Practice* no. 12 (1) (Practice Note): 211–216.

Mallinder, Louise. 2008. *Amnesty, Human Rights and Political Transitions: Bridging the Peace and Justice Divide*. Oxford and Portland, OR: Hart Publishing.

——. 2012. "Amnesties' Challenge to the Global Accountability Norm? Interpreting Regional and International Trends in Amnesty Enactment." In *Amnesty in the Age of Human Rights Accountability: Comparative and International Perspectives*, edited by Francesca Lessa and Leigh A. Payne, 69–96. New York: Cambridge University Press.

Mamdani, Mahmood. 2002. "Amnesty or impunity? A preliminary critique of the report of the Truth and Reconciliation Commission of South Africa (TRC)." *Diacritics* no. 32 (3/4):33–59.

Martínez-Barahona, Elena, and Martha Liliana Gutiérrez Salazar. 2016. "El Salvador: the difficult fight against impunity." In *Transitional Justice in Latin America: The Uneven Road from Impunity towards Accountability*, edited by Elin Skaar, Jemima García-Godos, and Cath Collins, 178–202. London and New York: Routledge.

Martínez-Barahona, Elena, Sonia Rubio-Padilla, Héctor Centeno-Martín, and Martha Gutiérrez-Salazar. 2018. "La Comisión de la Verdad para El Salvador. Manteniendo la paz, a Cambio de la Justicia." In *CMI Report Series (No.12)*. Bergen: Chr. Michelsen Institute.

——. 2022. "El Salvador's Truth Commission: Recommending Peace in Exchange for Justice." In *Latin American Experiences with Truth Commission Recommendations: Beyond Words, Vol. II*, edited by Elin Skaar, Eric Wiebelhaus-Brahm, and Jemima García-Godos, 317–371. Cambridge: Intersentia.

Mayer-Rieckh, Alexander, and Howard Varney. 2019. Recommending Change. Truth Commission Recommendations on Institutional Reforms: An Overview. Geneva: DCAF (Geneva Centre for Security Sector Governance).

McEvoy, Kieran, and Kirsten McConnachie. 2012. "Victimology in transitional justice: Victimhood, innocence and hierarchy." *European Journal of Criminology* no. 9 (5):527–538.

McSherry, J. Patrice. 2012. *Predatory states: Operation Condor and covert war in Latin America*. Lanham MD: Rowman & Littlefield Publishers.

Mendeloff, David. 2004. "Truth-Seeking, Truth-Telling and Post-Conflict Peacebuilding: Curb the Enthusiasm?" *International Studies Review* no. 6 (3):355–380.

———. 2009. "Trauma and Vengeance: Assessing the Psychological and Emotional Effects of Post-Conflict Justice." *Human Rights Quarterly* no. 31 (3):592–623.

Méndez, Juan E. 1997. "Accountability for Past Abuses." *Human Rights Quarterly* no. 19 (2): 255–282.

Mezarobba, Glenda, and Roberto M Cesar Jr. 2016. "Notes from the Field: The Role of Datasets in Transitional Justice Research: The Case of Brazilian Truth Commission." *Transitional Justice Review* no. 1 (4):8.

Mezarobba, Glenda. 2016. "Brazil: the tortuous path to truth and justice." In *Transitional Justice in Latin America: The Uneven Road from Impunity towards Accountability*, edited by Elin Skaar, Jemima García-Godos and Cath Collins, 103–125. London and New York: Routledge.

Michel, Verónica, and Kathryn Sikkink. 2013. "Human Rights Prosecutions and the Participation Rights of Victims in Latin America." *Law & Society Review* no. 47 (4): 873–907.

Milton, Cynthia E. 2011. "Defacing memory: (Un)tying Peru's memory knots." *Memory Studies* no. 4 (2):190–205.

Minow, Martha. 1998. *Between Vengeance and Forgiveness: Facing History After Genocide and Mass Violence*. Boston, MA: Beacon Press.

Montes, J. Esteban, and Tomás Vial. 2005. *The Role of Constitution-Building Processes in Democratization: Case Study Chile*. Stockholm: IDEA.

Murray, Rachel, and Clara Sandoval. 2020. "Balancing Specificity of Reparation Measures and States' Discretion to Enhance Implementation." *Journal of Human Rights Practice* no. 12 (1):101–124.

Naidu, Ereshnee. 2014. "Memorialisation in Post-Conflict Societies in Africa: Potentials and Challenges." In *Memorials in Times of Transition*, edited by Susanne Buckley-Zistel and Stefanie Schäfer, 27–46. Cambridge: Intersentia.

Navarro-García, Susana, Pau Pérez-Sales, and Alberto Fernández-Liria. 2010. "Exhumations in Latin America: Current status and pending challenges. A psychosocial view." *Peace & Conflict Review* no. 4 (2):1–18.

Nino, Carlos Santiago. 1989. "Transition to Democracy, Corporatism and Constitutional Reform in Latin America." *University of Miami Law Review* no. 44:129.

———. 1991. "The Duty to Punish Past Abuses of Human Rights Put into Context: The Case of Argentina." *Yale Law Journal* no. 100:2619–2640.

———. 1992. "The Debate Over Constitutional Reform in Latin America." *Fordham International Law Journal* no. 16 (3):635–651.

———. 1996. *Radical Evil on Trial*. New Haven CT: Yale University Press.

Office of the UN High Commissioner for Human Rights. "Basic Principles and Guidelines on the Right to a Remedy and Reparation for Victims of Gross Violations of International Human Rights Law and Serious Violations of International Humanitarian Law", adopted and proclaimed by the UN General Assembly resolution 60/147 of 16 December 2005. Available from: http://www.ohchr.org/EN/ProfessionalInterest/Pages/RemedyAndReparation.aspx.

Olsen, Tricia D., Leigh A. Payne, and Andrew G. Reiter. 2010. *Transitional Justice in Balance: Comparing Processes, Weighing Efficacy.* Washington DC: United States Institute of Peace Press.

Olsen, Tricia D., Leigh A. Payne, Andrew G. Reiter, and Eric Wiebelhaus-Brahm. 2010. "When Truth Commissions Improve Human Rights." *International Journal of Transitional Justice* no. 4 (3):457–476.

Pa, Alfredo Boccia. 2008. "Los 'archivos del horror' de Paraguay: los papeles que resignificaron la memoria del stronismo." In *Ditadura e Democracia na América Latina: Balanco Histórico e Perspectivas*, edited by Carlos Fico, Marieta de Moraes Ferreira, Maria Paula Araujo, and Samantha Viz Quadrat, 28–49. Rio de Janeiro: FGV Editora.

Parada Galarza, Katya. 2020. *La importancia de la judicialización de los casos de graves violaciones a Derechos Humanos documentados en la Comisión de la Verdad del Ecuador del 2010, dentro de la justicia transicional.* Trabajo de titulación para la elaboración de la Tesis de grado como requisito para la obtención del título de Abogada, Escuela de Derecho, Universidad Internacional Sek, Quito.

Pasqualucci, Jo M. 2013. *The Practice and Procedure of the Inter-American Court of Human Rights.* Cambridge, UK: Cambridge University Press, 2nd. Edition.

Paulson, Julia, and Michelle J Bellino. 2017. Truth commissions, education, and positive peace: An analysis of truth commission final reports (1980–2015)." *Comparative Education* no. 53 (3):351–378.

Pelli, Aldo. 2003. "Oportunidad para la democracia del Paraguay: Implementación y funcionamiento de la Comisión de Verdad y Justicia." *Derechos Humanos en Paraguay 2003.* 435–446.CLACSO.

Pelsinger, Shawn. 2010. "Liberia's long tail: How web 2.0 is changing and challenging truth commissions." *Human Rights Law Review* no. 10 (4):730–748.

Pena, Mariana, and Gaelle Carayon. 2013. "Is the ICC Making the Most of Victim Participation?" *International Journal of Transitional Justice* no. 7 (3):518–535.

Pensky, Max. 2008. "Amnesty on trial: impunity, accountability, and the norms of international law." *Ethics & Global Politics* no. 1 (1–2):1–40.

Peterson, Anna L, and Brandt G Peterson. 2008. "Martyrdom, sacrifice, and political memory in El Salvador." *Social Research: An International Quarterly* no. 75 (2):511–542.

Pion-Berlin, David. 1994. "To Prosecute or to Pardon? Human Rights Decision in the Latin American Southern Cone." *Human Rights Quarterly* no. 16 (1):105–130.

Pollak, Michael. 1992. "Memória e identidade social." *Revista Estudos Históricos* no. 5 (10): 200–215.

Popkin, Margaret L. 2000. *Peace without Justice: Obstacles to Building the Rule of Law in El Salvador.* University Park, PA: Pennsylvania State University Press.

Popkin, Margaret L., and Naomi Roht-Arriaza. 1995. "Truth as Justice: Investigatory Commissions in Latin America." *Law & Social Inquiry* no. 20 (1) 79–116.

Principi, Kate Fox. 2020. "Implementation of UN Treaty Body Decisions: A Brief Insight for Practitioners." *Journal of Human Rights Practice* no. 12 (1):185–192.

Quinn, Joanna R. 2004. "Constraints: The Un-Doing of the Ugandan Truth Commission." *Human Rights Quarterly* no. 26 (2):401–427.

———. 2009. "Haiti's Failed Truth Commission: Lessons in Transitional Justice." *Journal of Human Rights* no. 8 (3):265–281.

———. 2010. *The politics of acknowledgement: Truth commissions in Uganda and Haiti.* Vancouver BC: UBC Press.

———. 2019. "Diaspora influence on the thin sympathetic response in transitional justice." *Ethnic and Racial Studies* no. 42 (11):1830–1849.

Quinn, Joanna R. and Mark Freeman. 2003. "Lessons Learned: Practical Lessons Gleaned from Inside the Truth Commissions of Guatemala and South Africa." *Human Rights Quarterly* no. 25 (4):1117–1149.

Reátegui, Félix, Tania Gómez, and Eduardo Hurtado. 2022. "Paraguay's Truth and Justice Commission: Recommending Justice without Political Change." In *Latin American Experiences with Truth Commission Recommendations: Beyond Words, Vol. II*, edited by Elin Skaar, Eric Wiebelhaus-Brahm, and Jemima García-Godos, 139–195. Cambridge: Intersentia.

Reátegui, Félix and Diego Uchuypoma. 2022. "Peru's Truth and Reconciliation Commission: Recommending a Piecemeal Approach to Transitional Justice." In *Latin American Experiences with Truth Commission Recommendations: Beyond Words, Vol. II*, edited by Elin Skaar, Eric Wiebelhaus-Brahm, and Jemima García-Godos, 277–314. Cambridge: Intersentia.

Reátegui, Félix, with Diego Uchuypoma, and Eduardo Hurtado. 2022. "Ecuador's Truth Commission: Official Support, Weak Compliance." In *Latin American Experiences with Truth Commission Recommendations: Beyond Words, Vol. II*, edited by Elin Skaar, Eric Wiebelhaus-Brahm, and Jemima García-Godos, 233–276. Cambridge: Intersentia.

Reiz, Nicole, and Shannon O'Lear. 2016. "Spaces of violence and (in) justice in Haiti: a critical legal geography perspective on rape, UN peacekeeping, and the United Nations status of forces agreement." *Territory, Politics, Governance* no. 4 (4):453–471.

Reyes, Carlos, Gino Grondona-Opazo, Marcelo Rodríguez, and Darío Páez. 2018. "Posttraumatic growth of victims informed by the Truth Commission of Ecuador." *Revista Interamericana de Psicologia/Interamerican Journal of Psychology* no. 52 (3): 379–388.

Roehrig, Terence. 2009. "Executive leadership and the continuing quest for justice in Argentina." *Human Rights Quarterly* no. 31:721.

Roht-Arriaza, Naomi. 2005. *The Pinochet Effect: Transnational Justice in the Age of Human Rights.* Philadelphia PA: University of Pennsylvania Press.

———. "The Multiple Prosecutions of Augusto Pinochet." In *Prosecuting Heads of State*, edited by Ellen Lutz and Caitlin Reiger, 77–94. New York: Cambridge University Press.

———. 2016. "Measures of Non-Repetition in Transitional Justice: The Missing Link?" *Legal Studies Research Paper Series* (Research Paper No. 160): 1–41.

Rombouts, Heidy. 2002. "Importance and difficulties of victim-based research in post-conflict societies." *European Journal of Crime Criminal Law and Criminal Justice* no. 10 (2):216–232.

Roniger, Luis, and Mario Sznajder. 1999. *The Legacy of Human Rights Violations in the Southern Cone. Argentina, Chile, and Uruguay.* New York: Oxford University Press.

Roniger, Luis, Leonardo Senkman, and María Antonia Sánchez. 2016. "The Legacy of Authoritarianism and the Construction of Historical Memory in Post-Stroessner Paraguay." In *The Struggle for Memory in Latin America*, edited by Eugenia Allier-Montaño and Emilio Crenzel, 91–108. Springer.

Root, Rebekka K. 2009. "Through the Window of Opportunity: The Transitional Justice Network in Peru." *Human Rights Quarterly* no. 31 (2):452–473.

Ross, Amy J. 1999. *The Body of the Truth: Truth Commissions in Guatemala and South Africa.* PhD Thesis: Dept. of Geography, University of California, Berkeley.

Ross, Ann H, and José Vicente Pachar Lucio. 2015. "Forensic scientific practice in Panama." In *Forensic Archaeology: A Global Perspective* edited by W.J. Mike Groen, Nicholas Márquez-Grant and Robert C. Janaway, 247–254. John Wiley & Sons.

Rosser, Emily. 2007. "Depoliticised speech and sexed visibility: Women, gender and sexual violence in the 1999 Guatemalan Comisión para el Esclarecimiento Histórico Report." *The International Journal of Transitional Justice* no. 1 (3):391–410.

Rothenberg, Daniel. 2016. *Memory of silence: The Guatemalan truth commission report*: Springer.

Rowat, Malcom, Waleed H Malik, and Maria Dakolias. 1995. *Judicial reform in Latin America and the Caribbean: proceedings of a World Bank conference.* Washington D.C.: The World Bank.

Rubio-Marín, Ruth. 2008. *What Happened to the Women? Gender and Reparations for Human Rights Violations.* New York: Social Science Research Council.

Rudling, Adriana. 2022. "Panama's Truth Commission Recommendations: Out of Sight, Out of Mind?" *Latin American Experiences with Truth Commission Recommendations: Beyond Words, Vol. II*, edited by Elin Skaar, Eric Wiebelhaus-Brahm, and Jemima García-Godos, 451–483. Cambridge: Intersentia.

Sabsay, Daniel A., and José M. Onaindia. 1998. *La Constitución de los Argentinos. Análisis y comentario de su texto luego de la reforma de 1994.* 4th ed. Buenos Aires: ERREPAR S.A.

Salazar, Katya, and Thomas Antkowiak. 2007. *Victims Unsilenced: The Inter-American Human Rights System and Transitional Justice in Latin America.* Washington DC: Due Process of Law Foundation (DPLF).

Salmón, Elizabeth. 2006. "Reflections on international humanitarian law and transitional justice: Lessons to be learnt from the Latin American experience." *International Review of the Red Cross* no. 88 (862):327–353.

Sandoval, Clara. 2008. "The Challenge of Impunity in Peru: The Significance of the Inter-American Court of Human Rights." *Essex Human Rights Review* no. 5 (1):1–20.

Sandoval-Villalba, Clara. 2009. "The Concepts of 'Injured Party' and 'Victim' of Gross Human Rights Violations in the Jurisprudence of the Inter-American Court of Human Rights: A Commentary on their Implications for Reparations." In *Reparations for victims of genocide, war crimes and crimes against humanity: systems in place and systems in the making*, edited by Carla Ferstman, Mariana Goetz, and Alan Stephens, 243–282. The Netherlands: Brill.

Saona, Margarita. 2014. *Memory matters in transitional Peru*. London: Palgrave Macmillan.

Saquec, Daniel (ed). Acuerdo sobre Identidad y Derechos de los Pueblos Indígenas. Avances y desafíos a 20 años de la firma de los Acuerdos de Paz, Programa Maya – PNUD http://onu.org.gt/wp-content/uploads/2017/03/AIDPI-Informe-final-PDF.pdf.

Sarkin, Jeremy, ed. 2019. *The Global Impact and Legacy of Truth Commissions*. Cambridge: Intersentia.

Schneider, Nina. 2011. "Breaking the 'silence' of the military regime: New politics of memory in Brazil." *Bulletin of Latin American Research* no. 30 (2):198–212.

——. 2013. "'Too little too late' or 'Premature'? The Brazilian Truth Commission and the Question of 'Best Timing." *Journal of Iberian and Latin American Research* no. 19 (1): 149–162.

——. 2014. "Waiting for a Meaningful State Apology: Has Brazil Apologized for Authoritarian Repression?" *Journal of Human Rights* no. 13 (1):69–84.

——. 2020. "Bolsonaro in Power: Failed Memory Politics in Post-Authoritarian Brazil?" *Modern Languages Open* (1): 25.

Selvik, Lisa-Marie Måseidvåg. 2022. "Haiti's Truth and Justice Commission: Forgotten Recommendations, Living Demands". In *Latin American Experiences with Truth Commission Recommendations: Beyond Words, Vol. II*, edited by Elin Skaar, Eric Wiebelhaus-Brahm, and Jemima García-Godos, 409–449. Cambridge: Intersentia.

Shihata, Ibrahim F.I. 1995. "Legal framework for development: The World Bank's role in legal and judicial reform." *Judicial Reform in Latin America and the Caribbean: proceedings of a World Bank conference*: The World Bank, 13–18.

Sieder, Rachel. 2011a. "'Emancipation' or 'regulation'? Law, globalization and indigenous peoples' rights in post-war Guatemala." *Economy and Society* no. 40 (2):239–265.

——. 2011b. "Legal Cultures in the (Un)Rule of Law: Indigenous Rights and Juridification in Guatemala." In *Law in Many Societies. A Reader*, edited by Rogelio Pérez-Perdomo Lawrence M. Friedman, and Manuel A. Gómez, 152–158. Stanford, CA: Stanford University Press.

Sikkink, Kathryn, and Carrie Booth Walling. 2007. "The Impact of Human Rights Trials in Latin America." *Journal of Peace Research* no. 44 (4):427.

Sikkink, Kathryn. 1993. "Human rights, principled issue-networks, and sovereignty in Latin America." *International Organization* no. 47 (3):411–441.

——. 2011. *The Justice Cascade: How Human Rights Prosecutions are Changing World Politics*. New York: W.W. Norton & Co.

Skaar, Elin, and Eric Wiebelhaus-Brahm. 2013a. "Drivers of Justice after Violent Conflict: An Introduction." *Nordic Journal of Human Rights* no. 31 (2):119–126.

——. 2013b. "The drivers of transitional justice: An analytical framework for assessing the role of actors." *Nordic Journal of Human Rights* no. 31 (2):127–148.

Skaar, Elin, Camila Gianella Malca, and Trine Eide. 2015. *After Violence: Transitional Justice, Peace and Democracy*. London and New York: Routledge.

Skaar, Elin, Cath Collins, and Jemima García-Godos. 2016. "Conclusions: The uneven road towards accountability in Latin America." In *Transitional Justice in Latin America: The Uneven Road from Impunity towards Accountability*, edited by Elin Skaar, Jemima García-Godos and Cath Collins, 275–298. London: Routledge.

Skaar, Elin, Eric Wiebelhaus-Brahm, and Jemima García-Godos (eds.). 2022. *Latin American Experiences with Truth Commission Recommendations: Beyond Words, Vol. II*. Cambridge: Intersentia.

Skaar, Elin, Jemima García-Godos, and Cath Collins (eds.). 2016. *Transitional justice in Latin America: The Uneven Road from Impunity towards Accountability*. London: Routledge.

Skaar, Elin. 1994. *Human Rights Violations and the Paradox of Democratic Transition: A Study of Chile and Argentina*. Bergen: Chr. Michelsen Institute.

——. 1999. "Truth commissions, trials – or nothing? Policy options in democratic transitions." *Third World Quarterly* no. 20 (6):1109–1128.

——. 2011a. "Impunidad versus Responsabilidad Jurídica en el Uruguay: El Rol de la Ley de Caducidad." In *Luchas contra la impunidad. Uruguay 1985–2011*, edited by Francesca Lessa and Gabriela Fried, with Brenda Falero, 135–154. Montevideo: Trilce.

——. 2011b. *Judicial Independence and Human Rights in Latin-America: Violations, Politics and Prosecution*. New York: Palgrave Macmillan.

——. 2018. "Transitional Justice for Human Rights: The Legacy and Future of Truth and Reconciliation Commissions." In *International Human Rights Institutions, Tribunals, and Courts*, edited by Gerd Oberleitner, 1–21. Singapore: Springer.

Smulovitz, Catalina. 2012. "The past is never dead: Accountability and justice for past human rights violations in Argentina." In After Oppression: Transitional Justice in Latin America and Eastern Europe, edited by Vesselin Popovski. 64–85. United Nations University Press.

Snyder, Jack, and Leslie Vinjamuri. 2003/4. "Trials and Errors: Principle and Pragmatism in Strategies of International Justice." *International Security* no. 28 (3):5–44.

Sobrino, Jon. 2016. *Archbishop Romero: Memories and Reflections*: Orbis Books.

Solís Chiribog, María Cristina. 2019. "La judicialización de los casos documentados por la Comisión de la verdad." *Revista de la Facultad de Derecho de México* no. 69 (274–1): 27–62.

Sondrol, Paul C. 1992. "1984 Revisited? A Re-Examination of Uruguay's Military Dictatorship." *Bulletin of Latin America Research* no. 11 (2):187–203.

South African Truth and Reconciliation Commission and Desmond Tutu. 1998. *Truth and Reconciliation Commission of South Africa Report*. Cape Town: The Commission.

Sriram, Chandra Lekha. 2013. "Spoilers of Justice." *Nordic Journal of Human Rights* no. 31 (2):248–61.

Stahn, Carsten. 2001. "Accommodating individual criminal responsibility and national reconciliation: the UN Truth Commission for East Timor." *American Journal of International Law* no. 95 (4):952–966.

Steunenberg, Bernard, and Mark Rhinard. 2010. "The transposition of European law in EU member states: between process and politics." *European Political Science Review* no. 2 (3):495–520.

Stewart, Brandon, and Eric Wiebelhaus-Brahm. 2017. "The Quantitative Turn in Transitional Justice Research: What Have We Learned About Impact?" *Transitional Justice Review* no. 1 (5):97–133.

Sveaass, Nora. 2013. "Gross human rights violations and reparation under international law: approaching rehabilitation as a form of reparation." *European Journal of Psychotraumatology* no. 4.

Talavera, Fabián Novak, and Elizabeth Salmón Gárate. 2002. "Entrevista al Doctor Salomón Lerner Febres." *Agenda Internacional* no. 8 (16):11–17.

Thoms, Oskar N.T., James Ron, and Roland Paris. 2010. "State-Level Effects of Transitional Justice: What Do We Know?" *International Journal of Transitional Justice* no. 4 (3):329–354.

Thorp, Rosemary, Corinne Caumartin, and George Gray Molina. 2006. "Inequality, ethnicity, political mobilisation and political violence in Latin America: The cases of Bolivia, Guatemala and Peru." *Bulletin of Latin American Research* no. 25 (4):453–480.

Torelly, Marcelo. 2018. "Assessing a late truth commission: Challenges and achievements of the Brazilian National Truth Commission." *International Journal of Transitional Justice* no. 12 (2):194–215.

Torné, Carlos Fernandez. 2015. "Truth Commissions and the Accountability Relationships They Generate: A New Framework to Evaluate Their Impact." *Asian Journal of Peacebuilding* no. 3 (2):233–251.

Torné, Carlos Fernández. 2017. *How Truth Commissions Promote Accountability: An Evaluation of Impact of the Commissions Established in Nepal and Sri Lanka.* Departament de Dret Públic i Ciències Historicojurídiques, Universitat Autònoma de Barcelona.

United Nations. 2010. "United Nations Approach to Transitional Justice: Guidance Note of the Secretary-General".

United Nations General Assembly. 2005. "Basic Principles and Guidelines on the Right to a Remedy and Reparation for Victims of Gross Violations of International Human Rights Law and Serious Violations of International Humanitarian Law", Arts. 19–23, See www.un.org/ga/search/view_doc.asp?symbol=A/RES/60/147. United Nations.

——. 2013. Report of the Special Rapporteur on the Promotion of Truth, Justice, Reparation and Guarantees of Non-Recurrence A/HRC/24/42 edited by Pablo de Greiff: United Nations, Human Rights Council (Twenty-fourth session).

United Nations Office for the High Commissioner of Human Rights. 2006. "Rule-of-Law Tools for Post-conflict States: Truth Commissions", at www.ohchr.org/Documents/Publications/RuleoflawTruthCommissionsen.pdf.

——. 2013. "Truth commissions become victims of their own success, cautions UN expert on transitional justice". https://newsarchive.ohchr.org/EN/NewsEvents/Pages/DisplayNews.aspx?NewsID=13722&LangID=E.

Van Cott, Donna Lee. 2002. "Constitutional reform in the Andes: Redefining indigenous-state relations." In *Multiculturalism in Latin America: Indigenous rights, diversity and democracy*, edited by Rachel Sieder. 45–73. Springer.

Van de Poel, Ibo. 2011. "The relation between forward-looking and backward-looking responsibility." In *Moral Responsibility*, edited by Nicole A. Vincent, Ibo van de Poel, and Jeroen van den Hoven. 37–52. Springer.

Viaene, Lieselotte. 2010. "Life is Priceless: Maya Q'eqchi' Voices on the Guatemalan National Reparations Program." *International Journal of Transitional Justice* no. 4 (2): 4–25.

Walter, Knut, and Philip J. Williams. 1993. "The Military and Democratization in El Salvador." *Journal of Interamerican Studies and World Affairs* no. 35 (1 (Spring)):39–87.

Wiebelhaus-Brahm, Eric. 2010a. "Truth Commissions and Other Investigative Bodies." In *The Pursuit of International Criminal Justice: A World Study on Conflicts, Victimization, and Post-conflict Justice*, edited by M. Cherif Bassiouni. Intersentia Uitgevers N V.

——. 2010b. *Truth Commissions and Transitional Societies: The Impact on Human Rights and Democracy.* New York: Routledge.

——. 2011. "Truth Commissions." In *Routledge Handbook of International Criminal Law*, edited by William A. Schabas and Nadia Bernaz. New York: Routledge.

——. 2013. "Truth-Seeking at a Distance: Engaging Diaspora Populations in Transitional Justice Processes." In *Human Rights and Information Communication Technologies: Trends and Consequences of Use*, edited by John Lannon and Edward F. Halpin, 72–85. IGI Global.

——. 2019. "Truth Commissions in Non-Transitional Contexts: Implications for Their Impact and Legacy." In *The Legacies of Truth and Reconciliation Commissions*, edited by Jeremy Sarkin. Cambridge, UK: Intersentia.

——. 2021a. "Competition for Control of the State and the Transitional Justice Agenda Among Tunisian Civil Society Organisations." *Peacebuilding* no. 9 (2):160–174.

——. 2021b. "Global Transitional Justice Norms and the Framing of Truth Commissions in the Absence of Transition." *Negotiation and Conflict Management Research* no. 14 (3): 170–186.

Wiebelhaus-Brahm, Eric, and Dylan Wright. 2021. "Temporal Patterns in Latin American Truth Commission Recommendation Formulation and Implementation." International Criminal Law Review 21: 990–1023.

Wilson, Richard A. 2001. *The Politics of Truth and Reconciliation in South Africa: Legitimizing the Post-Apartheid State.* Cambridge: Cambridge University Press.

Winston, Carla. 2021. "Truth commissions as tactical concessions: The curious case of Idi Amin." *The International Journal of Human Rights* no. 25 (2):251–273.

Wohl, Michael J.A., Matthew J. Hornsey, and Catherine R. Philpot. 2011. "A critical review of official public apologies: Aims, pitfalls, and a staircase model of effectiveness." *Social Issues and Policy Review* no. 5 (1):70–100.

Worthington Jr., Everett L. 2006. *Forgiveness and reconciliation: Theory and application.* London: Routledge.

Zalaquett, José. 1989. "Confronting Human Rights Violations Committed by Former Governments: Principles Applicable and Political Constraints." In *State Crimes: Punishment or Pardon*, edited by Justice and Society Program of The Aspen Institute, 23–70. Queenstown MD: The Aspen Institute.

——. 1992. "Balancing Ethical Imperatives and Political Constraints: The Dilemma of New Democracies Confronting Past Human Rights Violations." *Hastings Law Journal* no. 42 (6):1425–1438.

Zimmermann, Lisbeth. 2016. "Same same or different? Norm diffusion between resistance, compliance, and localization in post-conflict states." *International Studies Perspectives* no. 17 (1):98–115.

Zwingel, Susanne. 2005. "From intergovernmental negotiations to (sub) national change: A transnational perspective on the impact of CEDAW." *International Feminist Journal of Politics* no. 7 (3):400–424.

INDEX*

---

*   Some entries and page references are in bold to indicate that they are core entries.

ABOUT THE AUTHORS

ELIN SKAAR (Research Professor, Chr. Michelsen Institute (CMI), Bergen, Norway) works in the intersection between law and politics and has published widely on transitional justice, human rights, and courts.

ERIC WIEBELHAUS-BRAHM (Associate Professor, School of Public Affairs, University of Arkansas at Little Rock) is the author of three books and over two dozen articles and book chapters on transitional justice, human rights, and peacebuilding.

JEMIMA GARCÍA-GODOS (Professor, Dept. Sociology and Human Geography, University of Oslo) is a human geographer working and publishing in the fields of transitional justice, human rights, victims' rights and state-society relations.

Ingram Content Group UK Ltd.
Milton Keynes UK
UKHW030140220323
418962UK00007B/416